Pro Spring Boot 4

An Authoritative Guide with Best Practices

Fourth Edition

Felipe Gutierrez
DaShaun Carter

Apress®

Pro Spring Boot 4: An Authoritative Guide with Best Practices, Fourth Edition

Felipe Gutierrez
Fuquay Varina, NC, USA

DaShaun Carter
Grain Valley, MO, USA

ISBN-13 (pbk): 979-8-8688-2639-9
ISBN-13 (electronic): 979-8-8688-2640-5
https://doi.org/10.1007/979-8-8688-2640-5

Managing Director, Apress Media LLC: Welmoed Spahr
Acquisitions Editor: Melissa Duffy
Editorial Assistant: Gryffin Winkler

Cover designed by eStudioCalamar

Cover image designed by masaaki-komori on unsplash

Distributed to the book trade worldwide by Springer Science+Business Media New York, 1 New York Plaza, New York, NY 10004. Phone 1-800-SPRINGER, fax (201) 348-4505, e-mail orders-ny@springer-sbm.com, or visit www.springeronline.com. Apress Media, LLC is a Delaware LLC and the sole member (owner) is Springer Science + Business Media Finance Inc (SSBM Finance Inc). SSBM Finance Inc is a **Delaware** corporation.

For information on translations, please e-mail booktranslations@springernature.com; for reprint, paperback, or audio rights, please e-mail bookpermissions@springernature.com.

Apress titles may be purchased in bulk for academic, corporate, or promotional use. eBook versions and licenses are also available for most titles. For more information, reference our Print and eBook Bulk Sales web page at http://www.apress.com/bulk-sales.

Any source code or other supplementary material referenced by the author in this book is available to readers on GitHub. For more detailed information, please visit https://www.apress.com/gp/services/source-code.

If disposing of this product, please recycle the paper

Dedicated to my family—Norma, Laura, Nayely, Ximena, Rocio, and Felipe—for their endless patience and support.

Table of Contents

About the Authors

Felipe Gutierrez is a solutions software architect with bachelor's and master's degrees in computer science from Instituto Tecnologico y de Estudios Superiores de Monterrey Campus Ciudad de Mexico. Felipe has over 30 years of IT experience and has developed programs for companies in multiple vertical industries, such as government, retail, healthcare, education, and banking. He is currently working as Staff Engineer for Cockroach Labs, specializing in content development for Cockroach University and the new learning site `https://learn.cockroachlabs.com/`, Distributed SQL, Multiregion with CockroachDB, Distributed Transactions, and more. Felipe has been working with Spring Framework, Spring Cloud Native Applications, Kotlin, Groovy, and RabbitMQ, among other technologies for more than 20 years. He has also worked as a Solutions Architect for big companies like VMware, Broadcom, EMC, Dell, Nokia, Apple, Redbox, IBM, and Qualcomm. He is the author of *Spring Boot Messaging* (Apress, 2017) and *Spring Cloud Data Flow* (Apress, 2020).

DaShaun Carter is a Spring Developer Advocate at Broadcom and a seasoned software engineer with over 25 years of experience. He is a recognized expert in Redis, Cloud Foundry, and Spring, passionate about building high-performance, scalable software. His career spans diverse sectors including fintech, healthcare, and cybersecurity, featuring leadership roles such as VP of Engineering and Senior Partner Solution Architect. DaShaun is also a keynote speaker, Testcontainer Champion, Agentic AI Foundation Ambassador, Raspberry Pi enthusiast, and former professional cheerleader. DaShaun is deliberately practicing to build, run, and manage, better software, faster. When he's not coding, he's also a mediocre triathlete.

About the Technical Reviewer

Manuel Jordan is an autodidactic developer and researcher who enjoys learning new technologies for his own experiments about creating new integrations among them.

Manuel won the 2010 Springy Award—Community Champion and Spring Champion 2013. In his little free time, he reads the Bible and composes music on his bass and guitar.

Manuel considers that constant education and training is very valuable for any developer, same thought about code refactoring and testing. Manuel can offer these professional services, among others, in Java and Spring for your company.

You can reach him through his LinkedIn account.

Acknowledgments

This book would not exist without the continuous support of my family: Norma, Laura, Nayely, Ximena, and my beloved parents, Rocio and Felipe. Thank you for your patience during the countless hours spent researching and writing. Additionally, a special acknowledgment goes to the Spring team. Thank you for building and maintaining an outstanding framework that continues to define modern enterprise development and provides the core foundation for this book.

—Felipe

CHAPTER 1

Spring Boot Quick Start

Welcome to the first chapter of *Pro Spring Boot 4*! This chapter will quickly immerse you in Spring Boot and demonstrate how easy it is to use by walking you through a simple project that exposes a list of customers through a REST API. If you are new to Spring Boot, this chapter will help you to rapidly familiarize yourself with the framework. If you are an experienced developer, feel free to quickly review the setup of the project and move on to the next chapter.

Project: Customer CRM

The project that we are going to build, named Customer CRM, will expose a simple read-only API over the Web. To keep things simple, we won't use a database in this chapter. Instead, we'll start with a hardcoded list of customers.

These are the requirements for the project:

- A customer must have an ID, a name, an email address, and a phone number.
- A hardcoded list is used to hold the customer information.
- It exposes a REST API to retrieve the list of customers.

Initial Setup

To start with Spring Boot, you need to have the following installed:

- **Java 21 or Later**: You can install this from various sources, such as OpenJDK.

F. Gutierrez and D. Carter, *Pro Spring Boot 4*, https://doi.org/10.1007/979-8-8688-2640-5_1

- **An IDE**: As a suggestion, you can use Microsoft Visual Studio Code, the Community edition of IntelliJ IDEA from JetBrains, or Spring Tools.
- **A Command-Line HTTP Client**: Tools like `curl` or `httpie` are useful for testing web APIs. This chapter will use `curl`.

Start @ `https://start.spring.io`

The easiest way to start a new Spring Boot project is by using the Spring Initializr at `https://start.spring.io`. It's a web-based tool that generates a basic project structure for you, eliminating the need to manually configure the project structure and dependencies.

Key features and benefits:

- **Streamlined Project Creation**: Generates a complete, ready-to-run project structure.
- **Curated Dependencies**: Offers a selection of common libraries and frameworks (called "starters") to easily add to your project.
- **Customization**: Allows you to choose the build tool (Maven or Gradle), language (Java, Kotlin, Groovy), and Spring Boot version.

For our customer management application, configure the project as follows:

- **Project**: Maven
- **Language**: Java
- **Spring Boot**: The latest stable version of Spring Boot 4.
- **Project Metadata**: **Group**: `com.apress.crm` **Artifact**: `customer` **Name**: `customer` **Description**: A simple customer CRM application. **Package Name**: `com.apress.crm.customer`
- **Packaging**: Jar
- **Java**: 21

Next, add the necessary dependency:

- **Spring Web**: This starter includes everything you need to build a web application, including an embedded Tomcat server and libraries for creating REST APIs.

Unzip it and open it in your folder.

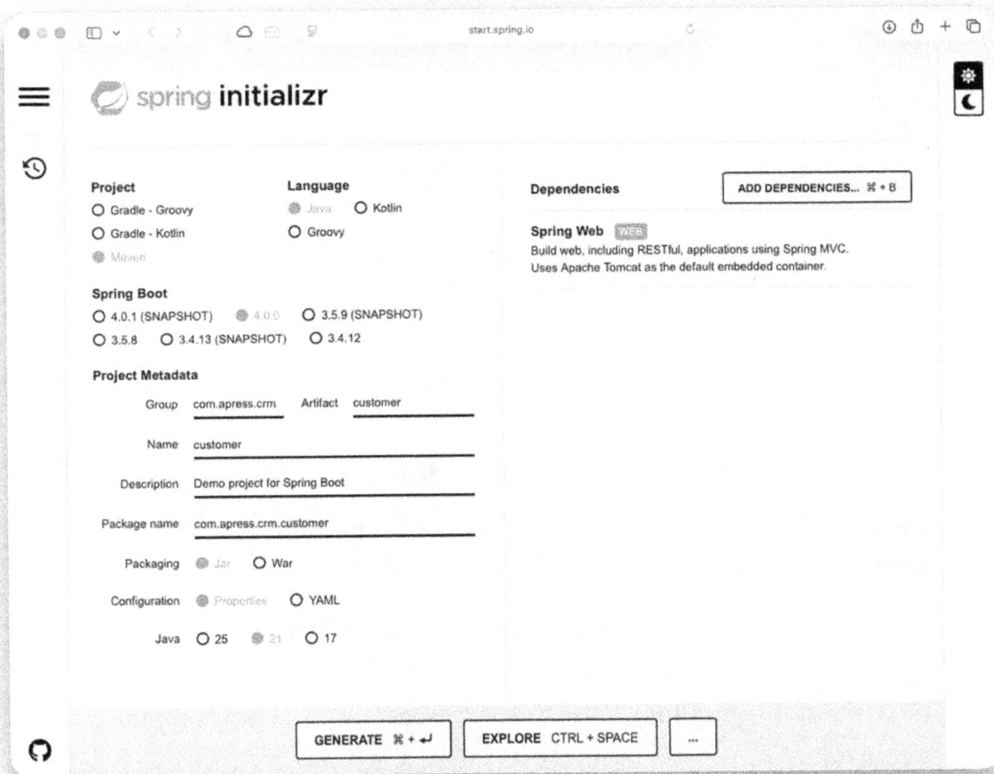

Figure 1-1. Spring Initializr Configuration for the Customer CRM

Understanding the Project Structure

When you open the project in your IDE, you should see the following structure:

```
customer/
├── .mvn/
├── src/
│   ├── main/
│   │   ├── java/
│   │   │   └── com/apress/crm/customer/
│   │   │       └── CustomerApplication.java
│   │   └── resources/
│   │       └── application.properties
│   └── test/
│       └── java/
│           └── com/apress/crm/customer/
│               └── CustomerApplicationTests.java
├── .gitignore
├── mvnw
├── mvnw.cmd
└── pom.xml
```

Figure 1-2. *Customer CRM Project Structure in an IDE*

Here is a breakdown of the key files and directories:

- **`pom.xml`**: This is the Project Object Model file for Maven. It defines the project's dependencies, build process, and other configuration.
- **`src/main/java`**: This folder contains all your application's source code. The Spring Initializr creates a main application class (`CustomerApplication.java`) that serves as the entry point for the application.
- **`src/main/resources`**: This folder is for configuration files and static assets. The `application.properties` file is used for configuring your Spring Boot application.
- **`src/test/java`**: This folder contains all your test source code. The Initializr generates a basic test class (`CustomerApplicationTests.java`) to get you started.

A Look at the pom.xml

The pom.xml file is the heart of a Maven project, managing its dependencies and build configuration. Let's examine the key parts of the file generated by the Spring Initializr.

Listing 1-1. pom.xml

```
<?xml version="1.0" encoding="UTF-8"?>
<project xmlns="http://maven.apache.org/POM/4.0.0"
xmlns:xsi="http://www.w3.org/2001/XMLSchema-instance"
    xsi:schemaLocation="http://maven.apache.org/POM/4.0.0
    https://maven.apache.org/xsd/maven-4.0.0.xsd">
    <modelVersion>4.0.0</modelVersion>
    <parent>
        <groupId>org.springframework.boot</groupId>
        <artifactId>spring-boot-starter-parent</artifactId>
        <version>4.0.0</version>
        <relativePath/> <!-- lookup parent from repository -->
    </parent>
    <groupId>com.apress.crm</groupId>
    <artifactId>customer</artifactId>
    <version>0.0.1-SNAPSHOT</version>
    <name>customer</name>
    <description>A simple customer CRM application.</description>
    <properties>
        <java.version>21</java.version>
    </properties>
    <dependencies>
        <dependency>
            <groupId>org.springframework.boot</groupId>
            <artifactId>spring-boot-starter-webmvc</artifactId>
        </dependency>
        <dependency>
            <groupId>org.springframework.boot</groupId>
            <artifactId>spring-boot-starter-webmvc-test</artifactId>
            <scope>test</scope>
        </dependency>
```

```
    </dependencies>
    <build>
        <plugins>
            <plugin>
                <groupId>org.springframework.boot</groupId>
                <artifactId>spring-boot-maven-plugin</artifactId>
            </plugin>
        </plugins>
    </build>
</project>
```

Key elements of this file include:

- **<parent>**: The `spring-boot-starter-parent` provides useful Maven defaults. It manages dependency versions for common libraries and provides a default configuration for the build plugins.
- **<properties>**: Here we declare the Java version our project will use, which is 21.
- **<dependencies>**: This section lists the project's dependencies.
- **spring-boot-starter-webmvc**: As mentioned, this starter brings in all the necessary dependencies for building a servlet-based web application (Spring MVC).

  spring-boot-starter-webmvc-test: This starter includes libraries for testing Spring Boot web applications, such as JUnit 5, Spring Test, and AssertJ. The `<scope>test</scope>` tag means this dependency is only available for the test build and is not included in the final application package.

Creating the Customer Domain Model

With the project set up, our first coding task is to create a model for our customers. In modern Java, the best way to model immutable data is by using a `record`. Records are a concise way to create classes that are primarily used to hold data.

Create a new Java record named Customer inside the com.apress.crm.customer package. This record will have fields for the customer's ID, name, email, and phone number.

Listing 1-2. src/main/java/com/apress/crm/customer/Customer.java

```
package com.apress.crm.customer;

import java.util.UUID;

public record Customer(UUID id, String name, String email, String phone) {

    public Customer(String name, String email, String phone) {
        this(UUID.randomUUID(), name, email, phone);
    }

}
```

This declaration gives us a Customer type with id, name, email, and phone attributes. We also added a compact constructor to automatically generate a UUID for the id field when creating a new customer. The Java compiler automatically generates a constructor, equals(), hashCode(), and toString() methods, saving us from writing boilerplate code.

Creating the Repository

To keep our application architecture clean, we should separate the data access logic from the web layer. We'll define a generic repository interface and a specific implementation for our customers.

First, create a generic repository interface:

Listing 1-3. src/main/java/com/apress/crm/customer/Repository.java

```
package com.apress.crm.customer;

public interface Repository <T, ID> {

    T save(T entity);

    T findById(ID id);
```

```
    Iterable<T> findAll();

    void deleteById(ID id);

}
```

Next, create the CustomerRepository implementation. For this chapter, we will use a ConcurrentHashMap to simulate an in-memory database.

Listing 1-4. src/main/java/com/apress/crm/customer/CustomerRepository.java

```
package com.apress.crm.customer;

import org.springframework.stereotype.Component;
import java.util.Map;
import java.util.UUID;
import java.util.concurrent.ConcurrentHashMap;

@Component
public class CustomerRepository implements Repository<Customer, UUID> {

    Map<UUID, Customer> customers = new ConcurrentHashMap<>();

    @Override
    public Customer save(Customer entity) {
        if (entity.id() == null) {
            entity = new Customer(entity.name(), entity.email(), entity.
            phone());
        }
        customers.put(entity.id(), entity);
        return entity;
    }

    @Override
    public Customer findById(UUID id) {
        return customers.get(id);
    }
```

```
    @Override
    public Iterable<Customer> findAll() {
        return customers.values();
    }

    @Override
    public void deleteById(UUID id) {
        customers.remove(id);
    }

}
```

The @Component annotation is crucial here. It tells Spring to manage this class as a bean, allowing us to inject it into other parts of our application, such as the controller.

Building the REST Controller

Now that we have our Customer model and a repository to manage it, we can create the REST controller. This controller will expose endpoints to perform CRUD (Create, Read, Update, Delete) operations.

Create a new class named CustomerController and replace its content with the following:

Listing 1-5. src/main/java/com/apress/crm/customer/CustomerController.java

```
package com.apress.crm.customer;

import org.springframework.web.bind.annotation.*;
import java.util.UUID;

@RestController
@RequestMapping("/api/v1/customers")
public class CustomerController {

    private final Repository<Customer, UUID> repository;

    public CustomerController(Repository<Customer, UUID> repository) {
        this.repository = repository;
    }
```

```
    @GetMapping
    Iterable<Customer> findAll() {
        return repository.findAll();
    }

    @GetMapping("/{id}")
    Customer findById(@PathVariable UUID id) {
        return repository.findById(id);
    }

    @PostMapping
    Customer save(@RequestBody Customer customer) {
        return repository.save(customer);
    }

    @DeleteMapping("/{id}")
    void deleteById(@PathVariable UUID id) {
        repository.deleteById(id);
    }
}
```

Let's break down the changes:

- **@RequestMapping("/api/v1/customers")**: This annotation sets the base path for all endpoints in this controller. Using a versioned API path is a best practice.
- **Dependency Injection**: We defined a constructor that takes a `Repository<Customer, UUID>`. Spring Boot automatically injects the `CustomerRepository` bean we created earlier. This is known as constructor injection.
- **HTTP Methods**:
- **@GetMapping**: Maps GET requests. We have one for listing all customers and one for retrieving a specific customer by ID using `/{id}`.
- **@PostMapping**: Maps POST requests to create or update a customer. The `@RequestBody` annotation tells Spring to deserialize the incoming JSON into a `Customer` object.

- **`@DeleteMapping("/{id}")`**: Maps DELETE requests to remove a customer by ID.
- **`@PathVariable`**: Binds the `{id}` placeholder in the URL to the method parameter.

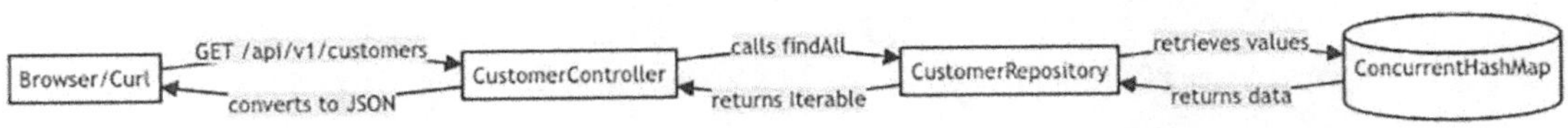

***Figure 1-3.** Request Handling in the Customer CRM*

Populating Initial Data

To make it easier to test our application, we can pre-populate our repository with some sample data when the application starts. We can do this by creating a configuration class that listens for the `ApplicationReadyEvent`.

Create a new class named `CustomerConfiguration` in the `com.apress.crm.customer` package:

Listing 1-6. src/main/java/com/apress/crm/customer/CustomerConfiguration.java

```
package com.apress.crm.customer;

import org.springframework.boot.context.event.ApplicationReadyEvent;
import org.springframework.context.ApplicationListener;
import org.springframework.context.annotation.Bean;
import org.springframework.context.annotation.Configuration;
import java.util.UUID;
import static java.lang.System.out;

@Configuration
public class CustomerConfiguration {

    @Bean
    ApplicationListener<ApplicationReadyEvent> customerAppReady(Repository
    <Customer, UUID> customerRepository) {
        return event -> {
```

```
            customerRepository.save(new Customer("John", "john@example.
            com", "1-800-PHONE"));
            customerRepository.save(new Customer("Jane", "jane@example.
            com", "1-800-PHONE"));
            customerRepository.save(new Customer("Jack", "jack@example.
            com", "1-800-PHONE"));
            customerRepository.findAll().forEach(out::println);
        };
    }
}
```

In this class:

- **@Configuration**: Marks the class as a source of bean definitions.
- **ApplicationListener<ApplicationReadyEvent>**: This bean creates a listener that is triggered once the Spring Boot application has fully started and is ready to service requests.
- **Data Injection**: We inject our `Repository<Customer, UUID>` and use it to save three sample customers.
- **Console Output**: We print the saved customers to the console so we can verify the data was loaded.

Running and Testing the Application

Spring Boot applications are easy to run. The Spring Initializr generates a main application class (`CustomerApplication.java`) with a `main` method, which is the application's entry point.

To start the application, you can simply run this `main` method from your IDE. Alternatively, you can use the Maven wrapper included with the project:

```
./mvnw spring-boot:run
```

Once the application starts, check your console output. You should see the three customers we created in `CustomerConfiguration` being printed, along with the log indicating the server is running on port 8080.

Since we have pre-populated data, we can immediately retrieve the list of customers. Open a terminal and use `curl` to send a GET request:

```
curl http://localhost:8080/api/v1/customers
```

The response should be a JSON array containing the three customers ("John", "Jane", "Jack").

You can also add a new customer using a POST request:

```
curl -X POST -H "Content-Type: application/json" -d '{"name":"New
User","email":"new@example.com","phone":"555-0199"}' http://localhost:8080/
api/v1/customers
```

And verify it was added by running the GET request again.

Automated Testing with @SpringBootTest

While manual testing with `curl` is useful for a quick check, a robust application needs automated tests. Spring Boot 4 provides excellent support for testing with the `RestTestClient`. Let's modify the generated test class `CustomerApplicationTests.java` to create a comprehensive integration test.

Listing 1-7. src/test/java/com/apress/crm/customer/CustomerApplicationTests.java

```java
package com.apress.crm.customer;

import org.junit.jupiter.api.Test;
import org.springframework.beans.factory.annotation.Autowired;
import org.springframework.boot.resttestclient.autoconfigure.AutoConfigureR
estTestClient;
import org.springframework.boot.test.context.SpringBootTest;
import org.springframework.http.MediaType;
import org.springframework.test.annotation.DirtiesContext;
import org.springframework.test.web.servlet.client.RestTestClient;
import static org.assertj.core.api.Assertions.assertThat;

@SpringBootTest(webEnvironment = SpringBootTest.WebEnvironment.RANDOM_PORT)
@AutoConfigureRestTestClient
```

```
@DirtiesContext
class CustomerApplicationTests {

    @Autowired
    private RestTestClient restTestClient;

    @Test
    void shouldRetrieveAndCreateCustomers() {
        // Verify initial data (3 customers from CustomerConfiguration)
        restTestClient.get().uri("/api/v1/customers")
                .exchange()
                .expectStatus().isOk()
                .expectBody(Customer[].class)
                .value(customers -> assertThat(customers).hasSize(3));

        // Create a new customer
        Customer customer = new Customer("New User", "new@example.com",
        "555-0199");
        restTestClient.post().uri("/api/v1/customers")
                .contentType(MediaType.APPLICATION_JSON)
                .body(customer)
                .exchange()
                .expectStatus().isOk()
                .expectBody(Customer.class)
                .value(savedCustomer -> {
                    assertThat(savedCustomer.id()).isNotNull();
                    assertThat(savedCustomer.name()).isEqualTo(customer.
                    name());
                });

        // Verify list now has 4 customers
        restTestClient.get().uri("/api/v1/customers")
                .exchange()
                .expectStatus().isOk()
                .expectBody(Customer[].class)
                .value(customers -> assertThat(customers).hasSize(4));
    }
}
```

Let's break down the key parts of this test:

- **`@SpringBootTest(webEnvironment = …)`**: This annotation loads the full application context and starts the web server on a random port, ensuring a realistic testing environment.
- **`@AutoConfigureRestTestClient`**: This annotation specifically configures the `RestTestClient`, which is a powerful, fluent client designed for testing REST services.
- **`RestTestClient`**: We inject this client to perform HTTP requests against our running application.
- **`shouldRetrieveAndCreateCustomers()`**:
- **Initial Verification**: We send a GET request and verify that the body contains an array of `Customer` objects with a size of 3 (our pre-loaded data). Note the use of `.expectBody(Customer[].class)` to deserialize the JSON array.
- **POST Request**: We create a new `Customer` object and send it via a POST request. We check that the response status is OK and assert that the returned customer has a valid ID and the correct name.
- **Final Verification**: We send another GET request to ensure the new customer was persisted, verifying the total count is now 4.

You can run this test directly from your IDE or by executing `./mvnw test` in your terminal. This automated test ensures that both your initial data loading and your REST API endpoints are working correctly together.

Project: Management CRM (Reactive)

In addition to the Customer CRM, we will also explore a more advanced project: the Management CRM. This application handles a broader set of domains, including customers, companies, addresses, and communications. To showcase the versatility of Spring Boot, this project will be built as a **reactive web application** using **Gradle** as the build tool.

Reactive Setup with Gradle

For this project, we'll use the Spring Initializr with the following settings:

- **Project**: Gradle—Groovy
- **Language**: Java
- **Spring Boot**: 4.0.0
- **Project Metadata: Group**: `com.apress.crm` **Artifact**: `management`
- **Dependencies**: **Spring Reactive Web**: To build reactive web applications with Spring WebFlux and Project Reactor.

Here is the `build.gradle` file for the Management CRM:

Listing 1-8. build.gradle

```
plugins {
    id 'java'
    id 'org.springframework.boot' version '4.0.0'
    id 'io.spring.dependency-management' version '1.1.7'
}
group = 'com.apress.crm'
version = '0.0.1-SNAPSHOT'
java {
    toolchain {
        languageVersion = JavaLanguageVersion.of(21)
    }
}
repositories {
    mavenCentral()
}
dependencies {
    implementation 'org.springframework.boot:spring-boot-starter-webflux'
    testImplementation 'org.springframework.boot:spring-boot-starter-
    webflux-test'
```

```
}
tasks.named('test') {
    useJUnitPlatform()
}
```

Key differences to note:

- **`spring-boot-starter-webflux`**: Instead of the standard `spring-boot-starter-webmvc` (used for Servlet-based apps), we use the WebFlux starter. This enables the reactive stack, based on Project Reactor and Netty.
- **Gradle DSL**: We are using the Groovy DSL for Gradle, which is common in many Spring projects.

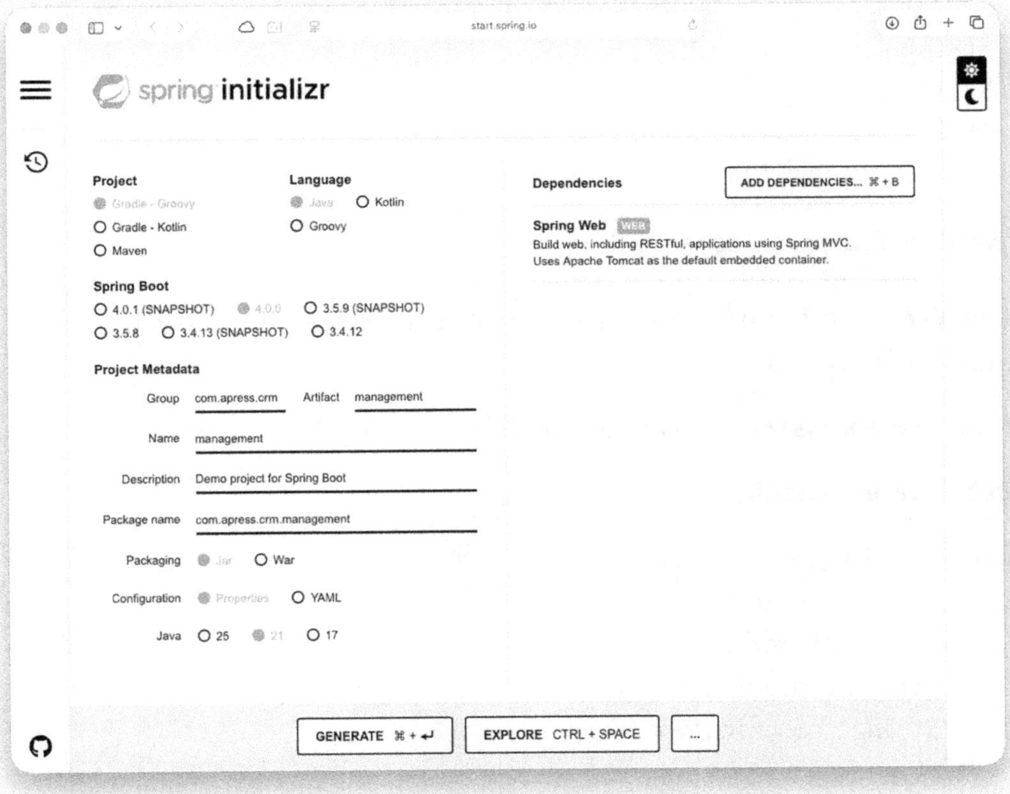

Figure 1-4. *Management CRM (Reactive) Project Setup*

Defining the Reactive Domain Models

In the Management CRM, we have several entities to manage. We'll use Java records to define our domain models.

First, the Address class:

Listing 1-9. src/main/java/com/apress/crm/management/model/Address.java

```
package com.apress.crm.management.model;

import java.util.UUID;

public record Address (

    UUID addressId;
    UUID customerId;
    String street;
    String city;
    String state;
    String zip;
){}
```

Next, the Communication record:

Listing 1-10. src/main/java/com/apress/crm/management/model/Communication.java

```
package com.apress.crm.management.model;

import java.util.UUID;

public record Communication(
        UUID communicationId,
        UUID customerId,
        String communicationType,
        String communicationValue
) {}
```

Then, the Company record:

Listing 1-11. src/main/java/com/apress/crm/management/model/Company.java

```
package com.apress.crm.management.model;

import java.util.UUID;

public record Company(
        UUID companyId,
        String companyName,
        String industry,
        String website
) {}
```

The Customer class:

Listing 1-12. src/main/java/com/apress/crm/management/model/Customer.java

```
package com.apress.crm.management.model;

import java.util.UUID;

public record Customer (

    UUID customerId;
    String firstName;
    String lastName;
    String jobTitle;
    String email;
    String phone;
    UUID companyId;
){}
```

And finally, the CustomerDetailsDTO to aggregate the information:

Listing 1-13. src/main/java/com/apress/crm/management/model/CustomerDetailsDTO.java

```
package com.apress.crm.management.model;

import java.util.List;

public record CustomerDetailsDTO(
        Customer customer,
        Company company,
        List<Address> addresses,
        List<Communication> communications
) {}
```

Creating Reactive Repositories

Just like in the Customer CRM, we need repositories to handle our data. We'll start by defining the generic Repository interface in com.apress.crm.management.repository:

Listing 1-14. src/main/java/com/apress/crm/management/repository/Repository.java

```
package com.apress.crm.management.repository;

public interface Repository <T, ID> {

    T save(T entity);

    T findById(ID id);

    Iterable<T> findAll();

    void deleteById(ID id);

}
```

Now, let's implement the specific repositories using ConcurrentHashMap for our in-memory storage.

AddressRepository.java:

Listing 1-15. src/main/java/com/apress/crm/management/repository/AddressRepository.java

```java
package com.apress.crm.management.repository;

import com.apress.crm.management.model.Address;
import org.springframework.stereotype.Component;
import java.util.Map;
import java.util.UUID;
import java.util.concurrent.ConcurrentHashMap;
import java.util.stream.Collectors;

@Component
public class AddressRepository implements Repository<Address, UUID> {

    private final Map<UUID, Address> addresses = new ConcurrentHashMap<>();

    @Override
    public Address save(Address entity) {
        // Implementation omitted for brevity
        return entity;
    }

    @Override
    public Address findById(UUID uuid) {
        return this.addresses.get(uuid);
    }

    @Override
    public Iterable<Address> findAll() {
        return this.addresses.values();
    }

    @Override
    public void deleteById(UUID uuid) {
        this.addresses.remove(uuid);
    }

    public Iterable<Address> findAllByCustomerId(UUID customerId) {
        return this.addresses.values().stream()
```

```
                .filter(address -> address.customerId().equals(customerId))
                .collect(Collectors.toList());
    }

}
```

CommunicationRepository.java:

Listing 1-16. src/main/java/com/apress/crm/management/repository/CommunicationRepository.java

```
package com.apress.crm.management.repository;

import com.apress.crm.management.model.Communication;
import org.springframework.stereotype.Component;
import java.util.Map;
import java.util.UUID;
import java.util.concurrent.ConcurrentHashMap;
import java.util.stream.Collectors;

@Component
public class CommunicationRepository implements
Repository<Communication, UUID> {

    private final Map<UUID, Communication> communications = new
    ConcurrentHashMap<>();

    @Override
    public Communication save(Communication entity) {
        // Implementation omitted for brevity
        return entity;
    }

    @Override
    public Communication findById(UUID uuid) {
        return this.communications.get(uuid);
    }

    @Override
    public Iterable<Communication> findAll() {
```

```
        return this.communications.values();
    }

    @Override
    public void deleteById(UUID uuid) {
        this.communications.remove(uuid);
    }

    public Iterable<Communication> findAllByCustomerId(UUID customerId) {
        return this.communications.values().stream()
                .filter(communication -> communication.customerId()
                .equals(customerId))
                .collect(Collectors.toList());
    }

}
```

CompanyRepository.java:

Listing 1-17. src/main/java/com/apress/crm/management/repository/CompanyRepository.java

```
package com.apress.crm.management.repository;

import com.apress.crm.management.model.Company;
import org.springframework.stereotype.Component;
import java.util.Map;
import java.util.UUID;
import java.util.concurrent.ConcurrentHashMap;

@Component
public class CompanyRepository implements Repository<Company, UUID> {

    private final Map<UUID, Company> companies = new ConcurrentHashMap<>();

    @Override
    public Company save(Company entity) {
        // Implementation omitted for brevity
        return entity;
    }
```

```
    @Override
    public Company findById(UUID uuid) {
        return this.companies.get(uuid);
    }

    @Override
    public Iterable<Company> findAll() {
        return this.companies.values();
    }

    @Override
    public void deleteById(UUID uuid) {
        this.companies.remove(uuid);
    }
}
```

CustomerRepository.java:

Listing 1-18. src/main/java/com/apress/crm/management/repository/CustomerRepository.java

```
package com.apress.crm.management.repository;

import com.apress.crm.management.model.Customer;
import org.springframework.stereotype.Component;
import java.util.Map;
import java.util.UUID;
import java.util.concurrent.ConcurrentHashMap;

@Component
public class CustomerRepository implements Repository<Customer, UUID> {

    private final Map<UUID, Customer> customers = new
    ConcurrentHashMap<>();

    @Override
    public Customer save(Customer entity) {
```

```
        // Implementation omitted for brevity
        return entity;
    }

    @Override
    public Customer findById(UUID uuid) {
        return this.customers.get(uuid);
    }

    @Override
    public Iterable<Customer> findAll() {
        return this.customers.values();
    }

    @Override
    public void deleteById(UUID uuid) {
        this.customers.remove(uuid);
    }
}
```

Creating the Service Layer

To handle more complex business logic, we introduce a service layer. The service layer acts as an orchestrator, communicating with multiple repositories to fulfill a single business request.

Create the ManagementService.java class:

Listing 1-19. src/main/java/com/apress/crm/management/service/ManagementService.java

```
package com.apress.crm.management.service;

import com.apress.crm.management.model.*;
import com.apress.crm.management.repository.*;
import org.springframework.stereotype.Service;
import java.util.List;
import java.util.UUID;
import java.util.stream.Collectors;
```

```
import java.util.stream.StreamSupport;

@Service
public class ManagementService {

    private final CustomerRepository customerRepository;
    private final AddressRepository addressRepository;
    private final CommunicationRepository communicationRepository;
    private final CompanyRepository companyRepository;

    public ManagementService(CustomerRepository customerRepository,
    AddressRepository addressRepository,
                             CommunicationRepository communicationRepository,
                             CompanyRepository companyRepository) {
        this.customerRepository = customerRepository;
        this.addressRepository = addressRepository;
        this.communicationRepository = communicationRepository;
        this.companyRepository = companyRepository;
    }

    public CustomerDetailsDTO createCustomerWithDetails(Customer customer,
    Company company, Address address, Communication communication) {
        // Implementation omitted for brevity
        return new CustomerDetailsDTO(customer, company, List.of(address),
        List.of(communication));
    }

    public CustomerDetailsDTO getCustomerDetails(UUID customerId) {
        Customer customer = this.customerRepository.findById(customerId);
        if (customer == null) {
            return null;
        }
        Company company = this.companyRepository.findById(customer.
        companyId());
        List<Address> addresses = StreamSupport.stream(this.addressRepository.
        findAllByCustomerId(customerId).spliterator(), false)
```

```
                .collect(Collectors.toList());
        List<Communication> communications = StreamSupport.stream(this.
        communicationRepository.findAllByCustomerId(customerId).
        spliterator(), false)
                .collect(Collectors.toList());
        return new CustomerDetailsDTO(customer, company, addresses,
        communications);
    }
}
```

Implementing Reactive REST Handlers

For the Management CRM, we'll demonstrate the functional style using handlers and routers.

Create the `ManagementHandlers.java` class:

Listing 1-20. src/main/java/com/apress/crm/management/reactive/ManagementHandlers.java

```
package com.apress.crm.management.reactive;

import com.apress.crm.management.model.CustomerDetailsDTO;
import com.apress.crm.management.service.ManagementService;
import org.springframework.stereotype.Component;
import org.springframework.web.reactive.function.server.ServerRequest;
import org.springframework.web.reactive.function.server.ServerResponse;
import reactor.core.publisher.Mono;
import java.util.UUID;

@Component
public class ManagementHandlers {

    private final ManagementService managementService;

    public ManagementHandlers(ManagementService managementService) {
        this.managementService = managementService;
    }
```

```
    public Mono<ServerResponse> getCustomerDetails(ServerRequest request) {
        String id = request.pathVariable("id");
        CustomerDetailsDTO details = managementService.
        getCustomerDetails(UUID.fromString(id));
        if (details != null) {
            return ServerResponse.ok().bodyValue(details);
        } else {
            return ServerResponse.notFound().build();
        }
    }
}
```

Configuring the Reactive Router

In the functional web framework, we use a `RouterFunction` to map incoming requests to handler functions.

Create `ManagementConfiguration.java`:

Listing 1-21. src/main/java/com/apress/crm/management/configuration/ManagementConfiguration.java

```
package com.apress.crm.management.configuration;

import com.apress.crm.management.model.*;
import com.apress.crm.management.reactive.ManagementHandlers;
import com.apress.crm.management.service.ManagementService;
import org.springframework.boot.context.event.ApplicationReadyEvent;
import org.springframework.context.ApplicationListener;
import org.springframework.context.annotation.Bean;
import org.springframework.context.annotation.Configuration;
import org.springframework.web.reactive.function.server.RouterFunction;
import org.springframework.web.reactive.function.server.ServerResponse;
import static org.springframework.web.reactive.function.server.RequestPredi
cates.GET;
```

```
import static org.springframework.web.reactive.function.server.RouterFuncti
ons.route;

@Configuration
public class ManagementConfiguration {

    @Bean
    ApplicationListener<ApplicationReadyEvent> managementReady(ManagementSe
    rvice managementService) {
        return event -> {
            // ... data initialization ...
        };
    }

    @Bean
    RouterFunction<ServerResponse> managementRoutes(ManagementHandlers
    handlers) {
        return route(GET("/api/v1/management/customers/{id}"),
        handlers::getCustomerDetails);
    }

}
```

Testing the Reactive Application

Testing a reactive application requires tools that can handle asynchronous streams.

Create the `ManagementApplicationTests.java` class:

Listing 1-22. src/test/java/com/apress/crm/management/ManagementApplicationTests.java

```
package com.apress.crm.management;

import com.apress.crm.management.model.Customer;
import com.apress.crm.management.model.CustomerDetailsDTO;
import com.apress.crm.management.repository.CustomerRepository;
import org.junit.jupiter.api.Test;
import org.springframework.beans.factory.annotation.Autowired;
```

```
import org.springframework.boot.test.context.SpringBootTest;
import org.springframework.boot.test.autoconfigure.web.reactive.AutoConfigu
reWebTestClient;
import org.springframework.test.web.reactive.server.WebTestClient;
import static org.assertj.core.api.Assertions.assertThat;

@SpringBootTest(webEnvironment = SpringBootTest.WebEnvironment.RANDOM_PORT)
@AutoConfigureWebTestClient
class ManagementApplicationTests {

    @Autowired
    private WebTestClient webTestClient;

    @Autowired
    private CustomerRepository customerRepository;

    @Test
    void shouldRetrieveCustomerDetails() {
        // ... test logic ...
    }
}
```

Why Spring Boot?

Even though we are just getting started, it is important to understand what the Spring Framework is and why Spring Boot is so important. The Spring Framework has the following guiding principles:

- **Provide Choice at Every Level**: Spring lets you defer design decisions as late as possible.
- **Accommodate Diverse Perspectives**: Spring embraces flexibility and is not opinionated about how things should be done.
- **Maintain Strong Backward Compatibility**: Spring's evolution has been carefully managed to force few breaking changes between versions.

- **Care About API Design**: The Spring team puts a lot of thought and time into making APIs that are intuitive and that hold up across many versions and many years.
- **Set High Standards for Code Quality**: The Spring Framework puts a strong emphasis on meaningful, current, and accurate Javadoc.

The biggest advantage of using Spring Boot is that it is based on the Spring Framework, making it enterprise-ready with all the best practices applied. And because Spring Boot is **opinionated**, it will configure everything for you, resulting in (sometimes) zero configuration.

Summary

Congratulations! You've just built and run your first Spring Boot 4 application. In this chapter, we covered the fundamental steps of creating a web application, from project initialization to creating a REST endpoint.

You've learned how to:

- Bootstrap a project with the Spring Initializr.
- Define a data model using a Java record.
- Create a REST controller to handle web requests.
- Run and test your application.
- Understand the basic principles behind Spring and Spring Boot.

While this application is very basic, it forms the foundation for the more complex applications we will build in the upcoming chapters. In the next chapter, we will explore Spring Boot's internals in more detail and learn how to connect our application to a database to persist our customer data.

CHAPTER 2

Spring Boot Internals and Features

In the previous chapter, we built the "Customer CRM" application, a simple REST API backed by an in-memory repository. You saw how quickly you can get a web application running with Spring Boot. Now, it is time to look under the hood.

This chapter goes beyond the "magic" of auto-configuration. We will explore the core features that Spring Boot provides to help you build production-ready applications. We will modify our **Customer CRM** project to demonstrate how to control the startup process, manage configuration externally, handle logging, internationalization, and task scheduling, and even how to leverage aspect-oriented programming (AOP).

How Spring Boot Works (The Magic)

Before we start customizing, it is crucial to understand what is happening behind the scenes. When you run your `CustomerApplication`, Spring Boot does a lot of heavy lifting to get your REST API up and running. This "magic" is primarily driven by **auto-configuration**.

The `@SpringBootApplication` Annotation

It all starts with the `@SpringBootApplication` annotation on your main class. This is a meta-annotation that combines three other important annotations:

1. **`@SpringBootConfiguration`**: Marks the class as a configuration source for bean definitions (essentially an alias for `@Configuration`).

F. Gutierrez and D. Carter, *Pro Spring Boot 4*, https://doi.org/10.1007/979-8-8688-2640-5_2

2. **`@ComponentScan`**: Tells Spring to scan the current package (`com.apress.crm.customer`) and its sub-packages for components, configurations, and services. This is why our `CustomerController` and `CustomerRepository` are automatically found.

3. **`@EnableAutoConfiguration`**: This is where the real magic happens. It tells Spring Boot to "guess" how you want to configure your application based on the jar dependencies that you have added.

Auto-Configuration Internals

In Spring Boot 4, auto-configuration is more modular than ever. Instead of relying on a single massive configuration file, libraries and starters declare their own auto-configurations.

When the application starts, `@EnableAutoConfiguration` triggers a search for files named `META-INF/spring/org.springframework.boot.autoconfigure.AutoConfiguration.imports` inside all the jar files on your classpath. These files contain lists of configuration classes that **might** be applied.

For each candidate configuration class, Spring Boot checks a series of conditions (using `@Conditional` annotations) to decide whether to load it or not.

Tracing the Customer CRM Startup

Let's trace what happens when we start our Customer CRM:

1. **Dependency Detection**: Spring Boot sees `spring-boot-starter-webmvc` on the classpath.

2. **Web Server Configuration**: It finds a configuration candidate (e.g., `ServletWebServerFactoryAutoConfiguration`). It checks: "Is there a Tomcat class on the classpath?" (Yes, brought in by the starter). "Is there already a user-defined server bean?" (No). **Result**: It configures an embedded Tomcat server listening on port 8080.

3. **Spring MVC Configuration**: It finds `WebMvcAutoConfiguration`. It checks: "Is this a web application?" (Yes). **Result**: It configures the `DispatcherServlet`, default error handling, and JSON message converters (Jackson) for our REST API.

4. **Application Logic**: Finally, thanks to `@ComponentScan`, it finds and registers your `CustomerController` and `CustomerRepository` beans, wiring them together.

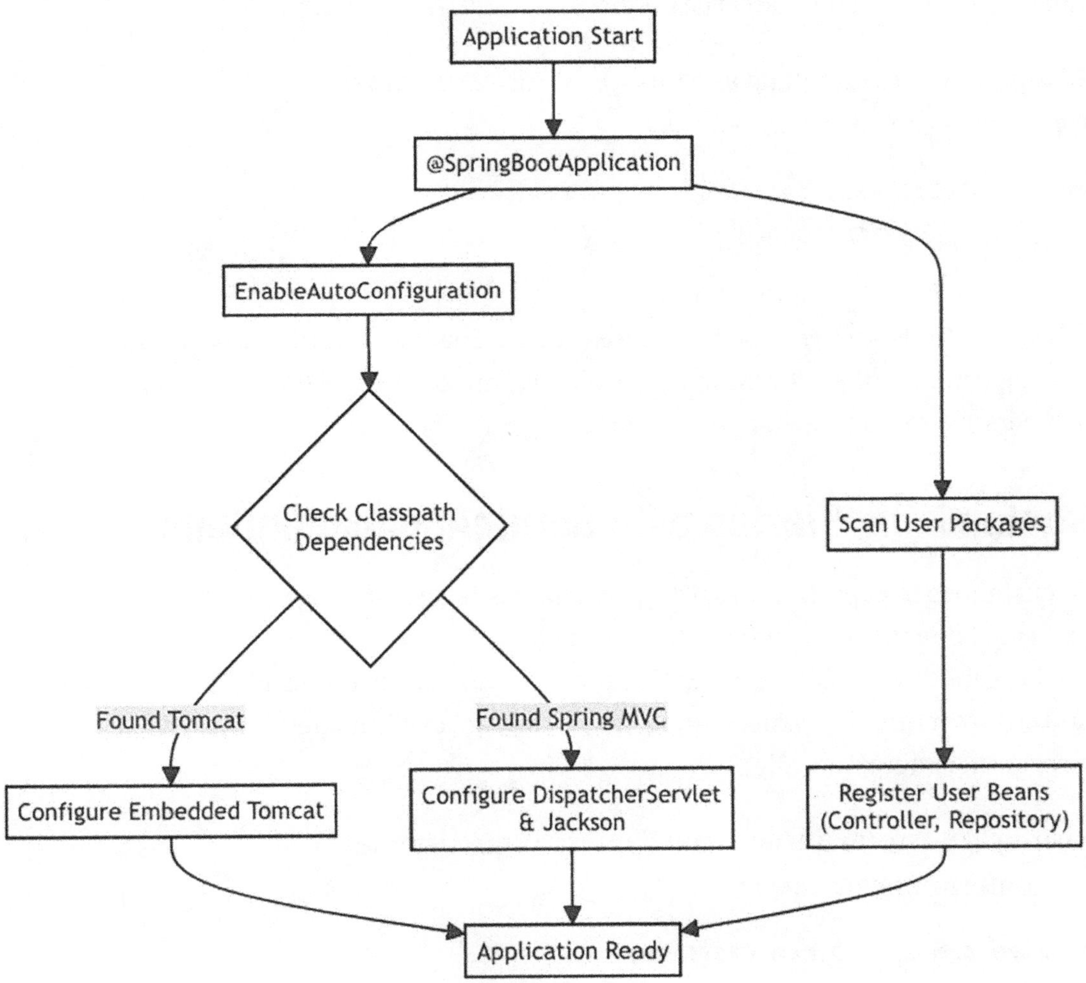

***Figure 2-1.** Spring Boot Startup Process*

This "convention over configuration" approach means Spring Boot makes reasonable defaults for you (like "use Tomcat on port 8080") but backs away immediately if you define your own configuration (like defining your own `ServerFactory` bean).

The SpringApplication Class

The `SpringApplication` class is the entry point for your Spring Boot application. In Chapter 1, we used the static `run` method:

Listing 2-1. src/main/java/com/apress/crm/customer/CustomerApplication.java

```
public static void main(String[] args) {
    SpringApplication.run(CustomerApplication.class, args);
}
```

While this is sufficient for most cases, the `SpringApplication` class offers extensive customization options for the startup process. You can control the application type, add listeners, customize the banner, and more.

Customizing Startup with SpringApplicationBuilder

To customize the application startup, we can create an instance of `SpringApplication` or use the fluent `SpringApplicationBuilder`.

Let's modify our `CustomerApplication` class to disable the banner programmatically and ensure it runs as a generic application (though it will still detect the web environment automatically).

Listing 2-2. src/main/java/com/apress/crm/customer/CustomerApplication.java

```
package com.apress.crm.customer;

import org.springframework.boot.Banner;
import org.springframework.boot.autoconfigure.SpringBootApplication;
import org.springframework.boot.builder.SpringApplicationBuilder;
```

```
@SpringBootApplication
public class CustomerApplication {

    public static void main(String[] args) {
        new SpringApplicationBuilder(CustomerApplication.class)
                .bannerMode(Banner.Mode.OFF)
                .logStartupInfo(true)
                .run(args);
    }

}
```

- We disable the printing of the Spring Boot banner on startup.

Customizing the Banner

If you do want a banner, you can make it unique to your application. By default, Spring Boot looks for a banner.txt file in src/main/resources.

Create a file named banner.txt in src/main/resources with the following content:

Listing 2-3. src/main/resources/banner.txt

```
   ______           __                          __________  __  ___
  / ____/_  _______/ /_____  ____ ___  ___  _____/ ____/ __ \/  |/  /
 / /   / / / / ___/ __/ __ \/ __ `__ \/ _ \/ ___/ /   / /_/ / /|_/ /
/ /___/ /_/ (__  ) /_/ /_/ / / / / / /  __/ /  / /___/ _, _/ /  / /
\____/\__,_/____/\__/\____/_/ /_/ /_/\___/_/   \____/_/ |_/_/  /_/
:: Customer CRM ::  (v1.0.0)
```

Now, if you remove .bannerMode(Banner.Mode.OFF) from your application class, you will see this ASCII art when the application starts. You can even use variables inside this file, such as ${spring-boot.version} to display the current boot version.

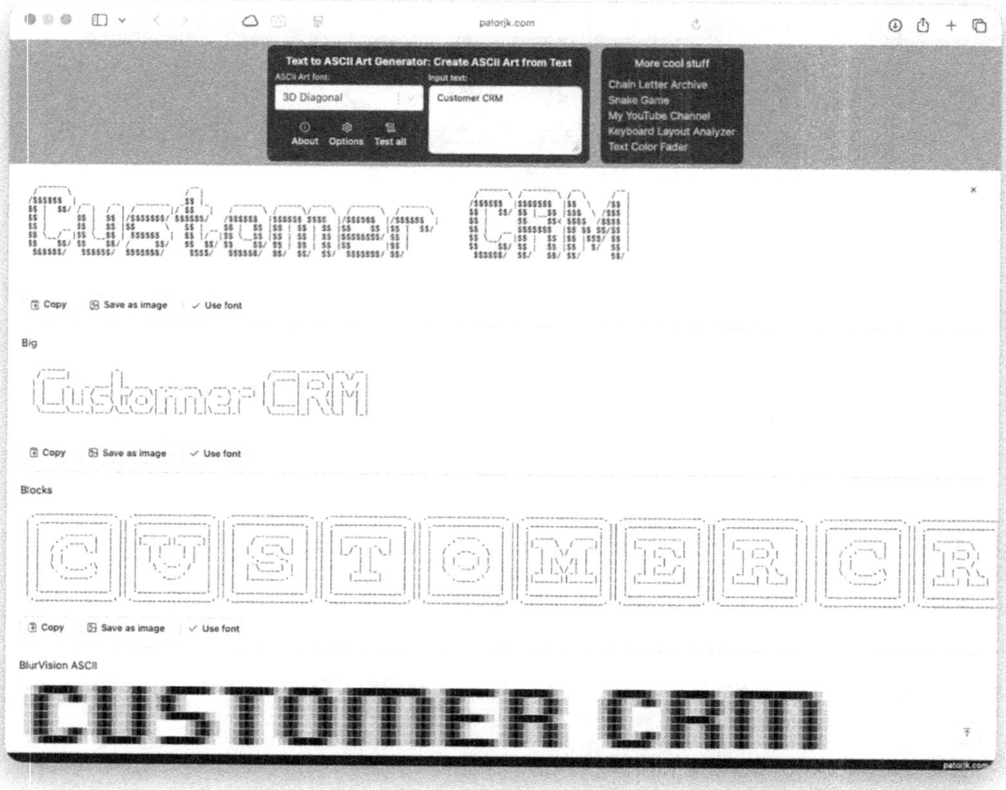

Figure 2-2. *ASCII Art—`https://patorjk.com/software/taag/`*

Externalized Configuration

One of the most powerful features of Spring Boot is its support for externalized configuration. This allows you to run the same application code in different environments (development, testing, production) without modification. You can use properties files, YAML files, environment variables, and command-line arguments to manage your configuration.

Spring Boot uses a very specific order of precedence to resolve properties, but most of the time you will work with `application.properties` or `application.yaml` located in `src/main/resources`.

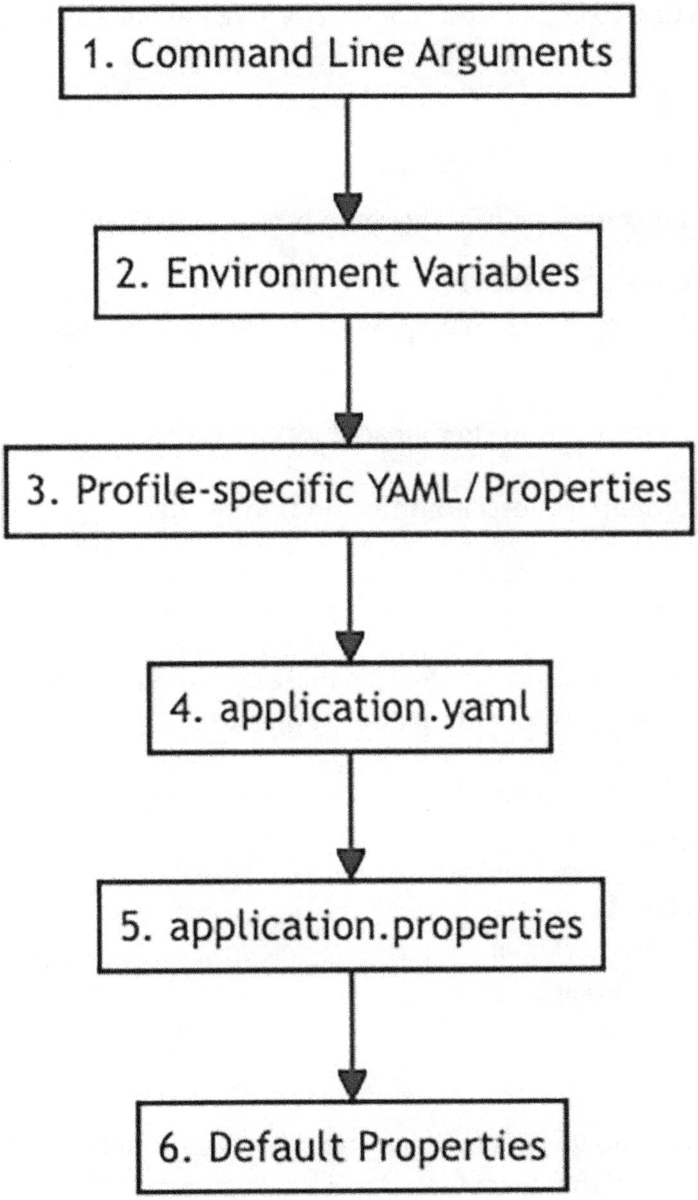

Figure 2-3. *Spring Boot Configuration Precedence*

Type-Safe Configuration Properties

While you can use the `@Value` annotation to inject individual properties, Spring Boot encourages the use of **type-safe configuration properties**. This involves creating a class (or a record) that maps to a specific prefix in your configuration file.

Let's create a CrmProperties record to hold settings for our Customer CRM.

Listing 2-4. src/main/java/com/apress/crm/customer/CrmProperties.java

```
package com.apress.crm.customer;

import org.springframework.boot.context.properties.ConfigurationProperties;

@ConfigurationProperties(prefix = "crm")
public record CrmProperties(String welcomeMessage, int maxResults) {
}
```

To use this, add the following to your application.properties:

Listing 2-5. src/main/resources/application.properties

```
crm.welcome-message=Welcome to the Pro Spring Boot 4 CRM!
crm.max-results=50
```

Finally, you need to tell Spring to look for these properties. You can do this by adding @ConfigurationPropertiesScan to your main application class.

Listing 2-6. src/main/java/com/apress/crm/customer/CustomerApplication.java

```
@SpringBootApplication
@ConfigurationPropertiesScan
public class CustomerApplication {
    // ...
}
```

- This annotation tells Spring to scan for any class annotated with @ConfigurationProperties.

Now you can inject CrmProperties anywhere in your application, just like any other bean.

Listing 2-7. src/main/java/com/apress/crm/customer/CustomerController.java

```
@RestController
@RequestMapping("/api/v1/customers")
public class CustomerController {

    private final Repository<Customer, UUID> repository;
    private final CrmProperties crmProperties;

    public CustomerController(Repository<Customer, UUID> repository,
    CrmProperties crmProperties) {
        this.repository = repository;
        this.crmProperties = crmProperties;
    }

    @GetMapping("/welcome")
    public String welcome() {
        return crmProperties.welcomeMessage();
    }

}
```

Key keywords and concepts:

- **`@ConfigurationProperties`**: Maps external properties to a Java object. It supports relaxed binding, meaning `crm.welcome-message`, `crm.welcome_message`, and `crm.WELCOME_MESSAGE` all map to the same field.
- **`@ConfigurationPropertiesScan`**: Automatically discovers classes annotated with `@ConfigurationProperties` and registers them as beans.
- **Prefixing**: The `prefix` attribute organizes properties into logical groups, making your configuration easier to manage as the application grows.

Profiles

Spring Profiles provide a way to segregate parts of your application configuration and make it available only in certain environments. You can have separate bean definitions or property files for development, testing, and production.

Profile-Specific Properties

Spring Boot loads properties from `application.properties` (or YAML) by default. If a profile is active, it also loads properties from `application-{profile}.properties`, overriding the defaults.

Let's say we want a different welcome message for our "development" environment. Create a file named `application-dev.properties` in `src/main/resources`:

Listing 2-8. src/main/resources/application-dev.properties

```
crm.welcome-message=Dev Mode: Fast and furious CRM!
```

To activate this profile, you can use the `spring.profiles.active` property. When running the JAR or using the command line:

Listing 2-9. Running with dev profile

```
./mvnw spring-boot:run -Dspring-boot.run.profiles=dev
```

Or, set it in your `application.properties` to make it the default for now:

Listing 2-10. src/main/resources/application.properties

```
spring.profiles.active=dev
```

When you restart the application and hit the `/api/v1/customers/welcome` endpoint, you will see the development message.

Profile-Specific Beans

You can also restrict bean creation to specific profiles using the `@Profile` annotation. For example, maybe we only want to load our dummy data when we are **not** in production.

Modify the CustomerConfiguration class from Chapter 1:

Listing 2-11. src/main/java/com/apress/crm/customer/CustomerConfiguration.java

```
@Configuration
@Profile("!prod")
public class CustomerConfiguration {
    @Bean
    ApplicationListener<ApplicationReadyEvent>
            customerAppReady(Repository<Customer, UUID>
            customerRepository) {
        // ... loading dummy data ...
    }
}
```

- The `!prod` expression means this bean will be created in any profile **except** “prod”.

If you start the application with the `prod` profile (`-Dspring.profiles.active=prod`), the dummy data will not be loaded.

Key concepts:

- **`application-{profile}.properties`**: Naming convention for profile-specific configuration files.
- **`spring.profiles.active`**: The property used to switch active profiles.
- **`@Profile`**: Annotation to conditionally enable beans based on the active profile. It supports logical expressions like `dev | test` or `!prod`.

Logging

Spring Boot uses Commons Logging for all internal logging but leaves the underlying log implementation open. Default configurations are provided for Java Util Logging, Log4j2, and **Logback**. In most cases, you will use Logback, which is included by default.

Logs are routed to the console by default. If you use a starter dependency, Logback is automatically configured to produce high-quality logs.

Configuring Log Levels

You can set log levels for any logger directly in `application.properties`. This is incredibly useful for debugging specific parts of your application without changing code.

Listing 2-12. src/main/resources/application.properties

```
# Set the root logging level
logging.level.root=INFO

# Set a specific level for our CRM package
logging.level.com.apress.crm.customer=DEBUG

# You can even set levels for Spring framework categories
logging.level.org.springframework.web=INFO
```

Using Log Groups

To keep your configuration clean, you can group related loggers together. Spring Boot provides a few built-in groups like `web` and `sql`, but you can create your own.

Listing 2-13. src/main/resources/application.properties

```
logging.group.crm-debug=com.apress.crm.customer,com.apress.crm.customer.
repository logging.level.crm-debug=DEBUG
```

Adding Logging to the CRM

To use a logger in your code, the standard approach is to use the **SLF4J** `LoggerFactory`.

Let's add some logging to our `CustomerRepository` to see when data is being saved.

Listing 2-14. src/main/java/com/apress/crm/customer/CustomerRepository.java

```
package com.apress.crm.customer;

import org.slf4j.Logger;
import org.slf4j.LoggerFactory;
import org.springframework.stereotype.Component;
```

```
import java.util.UUID;

@Component
public class CustomerRepository implements Repository<Customer, UUID> {

    private static final Logger log = LoggerFactory.
    getLogger(CustomerRepository.class);

    // ... map definition ...

    @Override
    public Customer save(Customer entity) {
        log.debug("Saving customer: {}", entity.name());
        // ... save logic ...
        return entity;
    }
}
```

- We create a static logger instance for the class.
- We use a parameterized message. SLF4J will only evaluate the string if the DEBUG level is enabled, which is more efficient than string concatenation.

Key logging levels:

- **ERROR**: Serious issues that might crash the application.
- **WARN**: Potential problems or important runtime warnings.
- **INFO**: (Default) General informative messages about application progress.
- **DEBUG**: Detailed information useful for debugging.
- **TRACE**: Very fine-grained diagnostic information.

Internationalization (i18n)

Internationalization (i18n) allows your application to support multiple languages and locales. Spring Boot makes this easy by automatically configuring a `MessageSource` bean if it finds a resource bundle in your classpath.

Creating Message Bundles

By default, Spring Boot looks for files named `messages.properties` in the `src/main/resources` folder. You can create different versions of this file for each language you want to support.

Let's create a default message and a Spanish translation for our CRM.

In `src/main/resources/messages.properties`:

Listing 2-15. src/main/resources/messages.properties

```
welcome.message=Hello, {0}! Welcome to our CRM.
```

In `src/main/resources/messages_es.properties`:

Listing 2-16. src/main/resources/messages_es.properties

```
welcome.message=¡Hola, {0}! Bienvenido a nuestro CRM.
```

Using MessageSource in the Controller

To retrieve these messages, you can inject the `MessageSource` bean into your components. We'll update our `CustomerController` to provide a localized greeting based on the `Accept-Language` header sent by the client.

Listing 2-17. src/main/java/com/apress/crm/customer/CustomerController.java

```
package com.apress.crm.customer;

import org.springframework.context.MessageSource;
import org.springframework.context.i18n.LocaleContextHolder;
import org.springframework.web.bind.annotation.*;
import java.util.Locale;
```

```
@RestController
@RequestMapping("/api/v1/customers")
public class CustomerController {

    private final MessageSource messageSource;

    public CustomerController(MessageSource messageSource) {
        this.messageSource = messageSource;
    }

    @GetMapping("/greet/{name}")
    public String greet(@PathVariable String name) {
        Locale locale = LocaleContextHolder.getLocale();
        return messageSource.getMessage("welcome.message", new Object[]
        {name}, locale);
    }
}
```

- `LocaleContextHolder.getLocale()` automatically retrieves the current locale, which by default is extracted from the `Accept-Language` HTTP header.
- `getMessage` takes the message key, an array of arguments for placeholders, and the locale.

To test this, you can use `curl`:

Listing 2-18. Testing i18n with curl

```
# Default (English if your system is English)
curl http://localhost:8080/api/v1/customers/greet/Felipe

# Request Spanish
curl -H "Accept-Language: es" http://localhost:8080/api/v1/customers/
greet/Felipe
```

Key concepts:

- **MessageSource**: The interface used to resolve messages, supporting parameterization and internationalization.

- **Resource Bundles**: Properties files that hold the translated strings. The naming convention `messages_{language}_{country}.properties` is used.
- **`LocaleContextHolder`**: A utility class to access the locale associated with the current thread/request.

Aspect-Oriented Programming (AOP)

Aspect-oriented programming (AOP) allows you to separate "cross-cutting concerns" from your business logic. Common examples include logging, transaction management, and security. Instead of adding logging code to every method, you can define an "aspect" that applies to many methods at once.

To use AOP, you need to add the `spring-boot-starter-aspectj` dependency to your `pom.xml` (or `build.gradle`).

Listing 2-19. pom.xml

```
<dependency>
    <groupId>org.springframework.boot</groupId>
    <artifactId>spring-boot-starter-aspectj</artifactId>
</dependency>
```

Creating a Logging Aspect

Let's create an aspect that logs the execution time of every method in our `CustomerController`. This helps us monitor performance without polluting the controller code.

Create a new class named `ControllerLoggingAspect`:

Listing 2-20. src/main/java/com/apress/crm/customer/ControllerLoggingAspect.java

```
package com.apress.crm.customer;

import org.aspectj.lang.ProceedingJoinPoint;
import org.aspectj.lang.annotation.Around;
```

```
import org.aspectj.lang.annotation.Aspect;
import org.slf4j.Logger;
import org.slf4j.LoggerFactory;
import org.springframework.stereotype.Component;

@Aspect
@Component
public class ControllerLoggingAspect {

    private static final Logger log = LoggerFactory.getLogger
    (ControllerLoggingAspect.class);

    @Around("execution(* com.apress.crm.customer.
    CustomerController.*(..))")
    public Object logExecutionTime(ProceedingJoinPoint joinPoint) throws
    Throwable {
        long start = System.currentTimeMillis();
        Object proceed = joinPoint.proceed();
        long executionTime = System.currentTimeMillis() - start;
        log.info("{} executed in {}ms", joinPoint.getSignature(),
        executionTime);
        return proceed;
    }
}
```

- The **Pointcut** expression defines where this aspect applies. Here, it targets any method (*) inside `CustomerController`, regardless of arguments (`..`).
- `joinPoint.proceed()` executes the actual target method. We capture the time before and after this call.

When you run your application and call any endpoint in the `CustomerController`, you will see a log entry similar to:

```
INFO ... : String com.apress.crm.customer.CustomerController.greet(String)
executed in 5ms
```

Key concepts:

- **Aspect**: A modularization of a concern that cuts across multiple classes.
- **Advice**: The action taken by an aspect at a particular join point. `@Around`, `@Before`, and `@After` are common advice types.
- **Pointcut**: A predicate that matches join points (specific points in the execution of the program).

JSON Support

Spring Boot provides excellent integration with **Jackson**, the industry-standard library for processing JSON in Java. When you include `spring-boot-starter-webmvc`, Jackson is automatically configured to serialize and deserialize your Java objects.

Customizing JSON Serialization

Sometimes the default JSON output isn't exactly what you need. You might want to rename a field or format a date differently. You can control this using Jackson annotations directly on your domain model.

Let's modify our `Customer` record to change how the name is displayed in the JSON response.

Listing 2-21. src/main/java/com/apress/crm/customer/Customer.java

```
package com.apress.crm.customer;
import com.fasterxml.jackson.annotation.JsonProperty;
import java.util.UUID;
public record Customer(
        UUID id,
        @JsonProperty("full_name") String name,
        String email,
        String phone) {
    // ... constructor ...
}
```

- The @JsonProperty annotation tells Jackson to use full_name as the key in the JSON output instead of the field name name.

Now, the JSON response for a customer will look like this:

Listing 2-22. Custom JSON output

```
{
  "id": "...",
  "full_name": "John Doe",
  "email": "john.doe@example.com",
  "phone": "..."
}
```

Advanced Configuration

If you need global configuration (like changing the naming strategy for all fields to snake_case), you can do so in application.properties:

Listing 2-23. src/main/resources/application.properties

```
spring.jackson.property-naming-strategy=SNAKE_CASE
```

Or, if you need full control, you can define a JsonMapperBuilderCustomizer bean:

Listing 2-24. src/main/java/com/apress/crm/customer/CustomerConfiguration.java

```
@Bean
JsonMapperBuilderCustomizer jsonCustomizer() {
    return builder -> builder.enable(SerializationFeature.INDENT_OUTPUT);
    // Pretty-print JSON
}
```

Key concepts:

- **Jackson**: The default JSON processor in Spring Boot.
- **@JsonProperty**: Used to customize the name of a property in JSON.

- **@JsonIgnore**: Used to exclude a field from serialization (e.g., passwords).
- **JsonMapper**: The core class in Jackson that handles the conversion between Java objects and JSON.

Task Execution and Scheduling

In many enterprise applications, you need to run tasks in the background or at specific intervals—for example, generating reports, cleaning up temporary files, or synchronizing data with external systems. Spring Boot makes this easy with its scheduling support.

Enabling Scheduling

To enable scheduling in your Spring Boot application, you simply need to add the `@EnableScheduling` annotation to any configuration class, typically your main application class.

Listing 2-25. src/main/java/com/apress/crm/customer/CustomerApplication.java

```
@SpringBootApplication
@EnableScheduling
public class CustomerApplication {
    // ...
}
```

- This annotation enables Spring's scheduled task execution capability.

Creating a Scheduled Task

Once scheduling is enabled, you can use the `@Scheduled` annotation on any method of a Spring bean. Let's create a task that logs the total number of customers in our CRM every minute.

Create a new class named `CustomerStatsTask`:

Listing 2-26. src/main/java/com/apress/crm/customer/CustomerStatsTask.java

```
package com.apress.crm.customer;

import org.slf4j.Logger;
import org.slf4j.LoggerFactory;
import org.springframework.scheduling.annotation.Scheduled;
import org.springframework.stereotype.Component;
import java.util.stream.StreamSupport;

@Component
public class CustomerStatsTask {

    private static final Logger log = LoggerFactory.
    getLogger(CustomerStatsTask.class);
    private final Repository<Customer, ?> repository;

    public CustomerStatsTask(Repository<Customer, ?> repository) {
        this.repository = repository;
    }

    @Scheduled(fixedRate = 60000)
    public void reportCustomerCount() {
        long count = StreamSupport.stream(repository.findAll().
          spliterator(), false).count();
        log.info("CRM Stats: Total customers currently in system:
        {}", count);
    }

}
```

- `fixedRate = 60000` tells Spring to run this method every 60,000 milliseconds (1 minute).

Scheduling Options

The `@Scheduled` annotation supports several ways to define the interval:

- **`fixedRate`**: Executes the task at a fixed interval from the start of the previous execution.
- **`fixedDelay`**: Executes the task at a fixed interval between the end of the previous execution and the start of the next.
- **`cron`**: Uses a cron expression (e.g., `"0 0 * * * *"` for every hour) for complex timing requirements.

You can also externalize these values to your `application.properties`:

Listing 2-27. src/main/java/com/apress/crm/customer/CustomerStatsTask.java

```
@Scheduled(fixedRateString = "${crm.stats.rate:60000}")
public void reportCustomerCount() { ... }
```

Key concepts:

- **`@EnableScheduling`**: The “switch” to turn on scheduling support.
- **`@Scheduled`**: Marks a method to be executed periodically.
- **TaskScheduler**: The underlying abstraction that Spring uses to manage scheduled tasks. By default, it uses a single-threaded executor, but this can be customized if you have many tasks.

Kotlin Support

Spring Boot provides first-class support for **Kotlin**, a modern, statically typed language that runs on the JVM. Kotlin offers concise syntax, null safety, and full interoperability with Java, making it an excellent choice for Spring Boot applications.

If you chose Kotlin when generating your project on Spring Initializr, you would see a significant reduction in boilerplate code.

A Kotlin Comparison

Let's look at how our `Customer` domain model and `CustomerController` would look if written in Kotlin.

The Domain Model:

In Java, we used a `record`. In Kotlin, we use a `data class`, which is even more concise.

Listing 2-28. src/main/kotlin/com/apress/crm/customer/Customer.kt

```kotlin
import java.util.UUID

data class Customer(
    val id: UUID = UUID.randomUUID(), // Default value for ID
    val name: String,
    val email: String,
    val phone: String
)
```

The Controller:

Listing 2-29. src/main/kotlin/com/apress/crm/customer/CustomerController.kt

```kotlin
@RestController
@RequestMapping("/api/v1/customers")
class CustomerController(private val repository: CustomerRepository) {

    @GetMapping
    fun findAll() = repository.findAll()

    @GetMapping("/{id}")
    fun findById(@PathVariable id: UUID) = repository.findById(id)

    @PostMapping
    fun save(@RequestBody customer: Customer) = repository.save(customer)

}
```

Notice the differences:

- **Primary Constructors**: Dependencies like `CustomerRepository` are declared directly in the class header.
- **Type Inference**: The return types of methods like `findAll` are automatically inferred.
- **Conciseness**: No need for explicit getters, setters, or `toString` methods; they are generated automatically.

Spring Framework 5+ and Spring Boot 2+ have introduced dedicated Kotlin extensions (like `reified` type parameters) that make the APIs feel even more natural to Kotlin developers.

Summary

In this chapter, we went beyond the basics and explored the powerful features that make Spring Boot a robust platform for enterprise development. We customized the **Customer CRM** application to demonstrate:

- **Auto-Configuration**: Understanding the "magic" behind `@EnableAutoConfiguration` and startup detection.
- **SpringApplication**: Customizing the startup process and banner.
- **Externalized Configuration**: Using `@ConfigurationProperties` for type-safe settings.
- **Profiles**: managing environment-specific configurations for Dev and Prod.
- **Logging**: Configuring log levels and groups for debugging.
- **Internationalization**: Supporting multiple languages in our API.
- **AOP**: implementing cross-cutting concerns like logging execution time.
- **JSON Support**: Customizing serialization with Jackson.

- **Scheduling**: Automating background tasks.
- **Kotlin**: Understanding the benefits of using Kotlin with Spring Boot.

These features form the toolkit you will use daily as a Spring Boot developer. In the next chapter, we will focus deeply on **web development**, exploring Spring MVC, RESTful API design, and exception handling in greater detail.

CHAPTER 3

Web Development with Spring Boot

In the previous chapters, we laid the foundation of our **Customer CRM** application and explored the core internals of Spring Boot. Now, it is time to build a professional-grade web layer. In this chapter, we will evolve our simple REST API into a robust, production-ready service.

Spring Boot 4, built on Spring Framework 7 and Jakarta EE 11, introduces significant improvements for web developers. We will explore these new features firsthand, including:

- **Native API Versioning**: Using the framework's new built-in support for managing API evolution.
- **Declarative HTTP Clients**: Creating clients for external services with zero configuration using `@HttpExchange`.
- **Jackson 3 Integration**: Leveraging the latest JSON processing standards for our Java Records.
- **The New RestTestClient**: Adopting a unified, fluent API for all our testing needs, replacing the older `MockMvc` and `WebTestClient` patterns.

By the end of this chapter, you will not only have a fully functional CRUD API for customer management but also a deep understanding of the modern Spring MVC architecture and how to design APIs that are easy to maintain and test.

F. Gutierrez and D. Carter, *Pro Spring Boot 4*, https://doi.org/10.1007/979-8-8688-2640-5_3

Infrastructure and Serialization Improvements

Spring Boot 4 sits on a modernized stack that brings performance improvements and better support for contemporary Java features. Understanding these infrastructure changes is essential for leveraging the full power of the framework.

Jakarta EE 11 and Servlet 6.1

Spring Boot 4 aligns with **Jakarta EE 11**, which includes significant updates to core specifications:

- **Servlet 6.1**: Provides improved support for asynchronous processing and more efficient HTTP header handling.
- **Bean Validation 3.1**: Enhances the declarative validation model with better support for Java records and more expressive constraints.

Jackson 3: Modern JSON Processing

The default JSON processor, **Jackson**, has been upgraded to version 3. This version is a major step forward, particularly for Spring Boot applications:

- **Native Record Support**: Jackson 3 understands Java 17+ records out of the box, handling their unique constructor and property access patterns more efficiently.
- **ISO-8601 Defaults**: Date and time serialization now defaults to the ISO-8601 standard, making your APIs more interoperable by default.
- **Improved Performance**: Architectural changes in Jackson 3 reduce memory overhead and improve serialization speed for complex object graphs.

Efficient Path Matching with PathPattern

For years, Spring MVC used the `AntPathMatcher` for mapping HTTP requests to controller methods. While flexible, it could be slow for applications with many routes.

Spring Boot 4 completes the transition to **PathPattern** as the default and only recommended matching strategy. PathPattern is more efficient because it parses and caches the patterns at startup, resulting in faster request routing at runtime.

If you are migrating from older versions of Spring, be aware that some AntPathMatcher syntax (like certain uses of double asterisks **) may behave slightly differently or be restricted in PathPattern to ensure better performance and security.

Spring MVC Architecture Deep Dive

Before we dive into coding, it is important to understand the machinery that powers Spring MVC. While Spring Boot makes everything look simple with annotations, there is a well-orchestrated process happening behind the scenes for every HTTP request.

The Request Lifecycle

The heart of Spring MVC is the **DispatcherServlet**. It acts as a front controller, meaning all incoming requests pass through it. Here is the journey of a request:

1. **Incoming Request**: An HTTP request reaches the DispatcherServlet.
2. **Handler Mapping**: The DispatcherServlet asks the HandlerMapping (configured with our PathPattern logic) to find the appropriate controller for the requested URL.
3. **Handler Adapter**: Once the controller is found, the DispatcherServlet uses a HandlerAdapter to actually call the controller's method. The adapter is responsible for resolving method arguments (like @PathVariable or @RequestBody).
4. **Controller Execution**: Your controller method is executed, typically calling a service and returning a result.
5. **Message Conversion**: For REST APIs (annotated with @RestController), the return value is passed to a HttpMessageConverter (like Jackson). This converter transforms your Java object (or record) into JSON or XML.

6. **Response**: The converted data is sent back to the client as the HTTP response body.

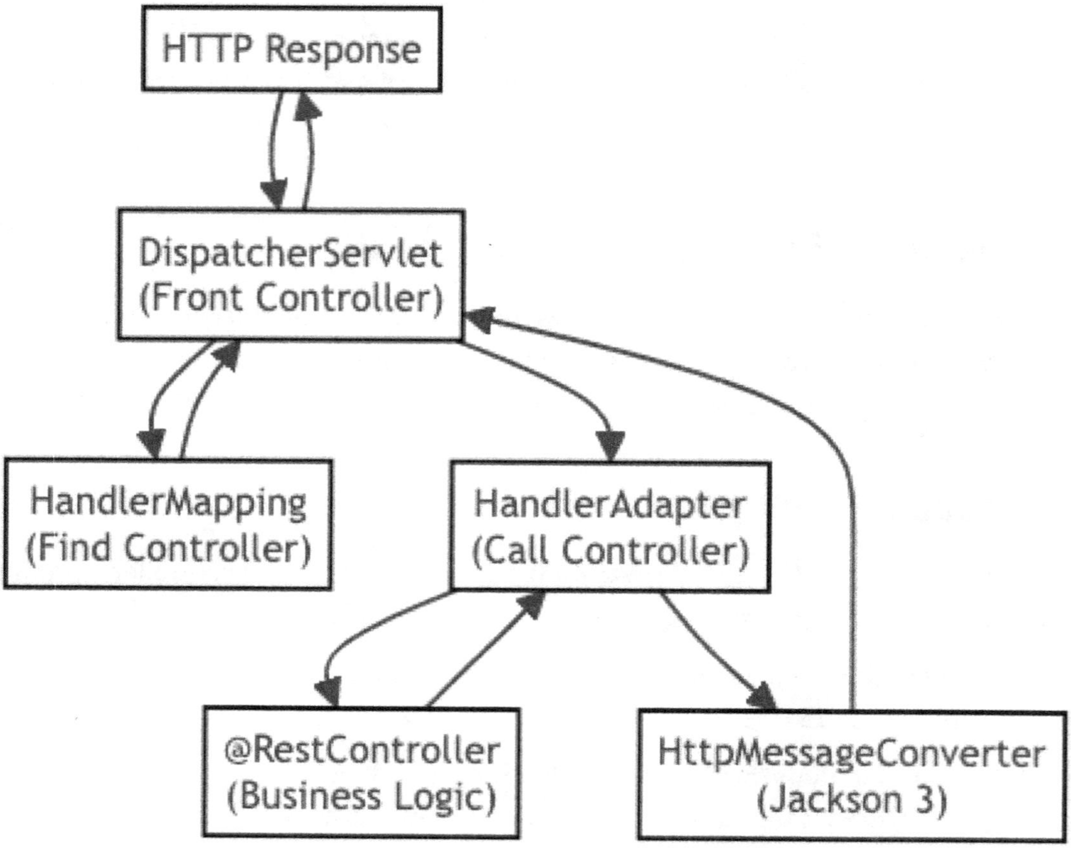

Figure 3-1. *Spring MVC Request Lifecycle*

Annotations Uncovered

The annotations we use daily are more than just labels; they are instructions for the `HandlerAdapter` and the `DispatcherServlet`.

- **`@RestController`**: This is a combination of `@Controller` and `@ResponseBody`. It tells Spring that every method in this class will return data directly to the response body instead of rendering an HTML template.

- **`@RequestMapping`**: This annotation registers a method as a web handler. Internally, Spring creates a `RequestMappingInfo` object at startup for every annotated method, which is then used by the `HandlerMapping` to route requests.
- **`@RequestBody`**: This signals that the body of the HTTP request should be deserialized into the method parameter. Spring uses an `HttpMessageConverter` (Jackson 3 by default) to perform this magic.
- **`@PathVariable`**: This instructs the `HandlerAdapter` to extract a variable from the URI template and bind it to the method parameter.

In Spring Boot 4, these annotations leverage **Runtime Hints** and improved reflection metadata to ensure they work efficiently even when the application is compiled to a native image with GraalVM.

RESTful API Design and Native Versioning

REST (Representational State Transfer) is the architectural style that governs how our web API should behave. Designing a good REST API is about consistency, predictability, and leveraging the full power of HTTP.

Core REST Principles

When designing our Customer CRM API, we follow these key principles:

- **Resources as Nouns**: Endpoints should represent resources (nouns), not actions (verbs). Use `/api/v1/customers`, not `/api/v1/getCustomers`.
- **Standard HTTP Methods**:
  - `GET`: Retrieve a resource or collection. (Safe and Idempotent)
  - `POST`: Create a new resource. (Not Safe, Not Idempotent)
  - `PUT`: Update an existing resource (Full update). (Not Safe, Idempotent)
  - `PATCH`: Update part of a resource. (Not Safe, Not Idempotent)
  - `DELETE`: Remove a resource. (Not Safe, Idempotent)

- **Meaningful Status Codes**: Use `201 Created` for successful POSTs, `204 No Content` for successful DELETEs, and `404 Not Found` when a resource doesn't exist.

API Versioning Strategy

As your application grows, you will inevitably need to change your API. Versioning allows you to introduce breaking changes without breaking existing clients.

Spring Boot 4 and Spring Framework 7 support various versioning strategies (URL path, header, media type). For our CRM, we will use **URL Path Versioning** because it is the most explicit and easiest for clients to explore.

We will define two distinct controllers for our different API versions.

Version 1 (Legacy): `/api/v1_1/customers` **Version 2 (Modern):** `/api/v2_0/customers`

This approach keeps our codebase clean and avoids "magic" routing configurations that can lead to ambiguous mapping errors.

Implementing Full CRUD

Now let's implement the full set of CRUD operations for our **Customer CRM**. We will update the `CustomerController` we started in Chapter 1 to be fully compliant with the principles we just discussed.

We will also integrate **Input Validation** using Jakarta Validation 3.1 to ensure we don't save invalid data.

Validating the Domain Model

To use validation annotations, you need to add the `spring-boot-starter-validation` dependency to your `pom.xml`:

Listing 3-1. pom.xml

```
<dependency>
    <groupId>org.springframework.boot</groupId>
        <artifactId>spring-boot-starter-validation</artifactId>
    </dependency>
```

First, let's update our Customer record to include validation constraints.

Listing 3-2. src/main/java/com/apress/crm/customer/Customer.java

```
package com.apress.crm.customer;

import jakarta.validation.constraints.Email;
import jakarta.validation.constraints.NotBlank;
import jakarta.validation.constraints.Pattern;
import java.util.UUID;

public record Customer(
    UUID id,

    @NotBlank(message = "Name cannot be empty")
    String name,

    @Email(message = "Invalid email format")
    @NotBlank(message = "Email cannot be empty")
    String email,

    @Pattern(regexp = "^\\+?[0-9. ()-]{7,25}$", message = "Invalid phone
    number")
    String phone) {

    public Customer(String name, String email, String phone) {
        this(null, name, email, phone);
    }

}
```

We have annotated our record components with standard Jakarta Bean Validation constraints:

- **@NotBlank**: Ensures the string is not null and the trimmed length is greater than zero. This is essential for required fields like name and email.
- **@Email**: Validates that the string follows a valid email address format (e.g., user@domain.com).
- **@Pattern**: Applies a regular expression to the field. Here, we enforce a flexible international phone number format.

Best Practices:

- **Fail Fast**: Validation prevents invalid data from ever reaching your service layer or database, saving resources and ensuring data integrity.
- **Specific Messages**: Always provide custom `message` attributes. "Invalid email format" is much more helpful to an API consumer than a generic "must be well-formed email address."
- **DTOs vs. Entities**: In larger applications, prefer applying validation on Data Transfer Objects (DTOs) specifically designed for incoming requests, keeping your internal domain entities clean.

The Complete CustomerController

Now, here is the complete controller implementation handling all HTTP verbs.

Listing 3-3. src/main/java/com/apress/crm/customer/CustomerController.java

```
package com.apress.crm.customer;

import jakarta.validation.Valid;
import org.springframework.http.ResponseEntity;
import org.springframework.web.bind.annotation.*;
import org.springframework.web.servlet.support.ServletUriComponentsBuilder;
import java.net.URI;
import java.util.UUID;

@RestController
@RequestMapping("/api/v1/customers")
public class CustomerController {

    private final Repository<Customer, UUID> repository;

    public CustomerController(Repository<Customer, UUID> repository) {
        this.repository = repository;
    }
```

```
@GetMapping
public Iterable<Customer> findAll() {
    return repository.findAll();
}

@GetMapping("/{id}")
public ResponseEntity<Customer> findById(@PathVariable UUID id) {
    Customer customer = repository.findById(id);
    return customer != null ? ResponseEntity.ok(customer) :
    ResponseEntity.notFound().build();
}

@PostMapping
public ResponseEntity<Customer> create(@Valid @RequestBody Customer
customer) {
    Customer saved = repository.save(customer);
    URI location = ServletUriComponentsBuilder.fromCurrentRequest()
            .path("/{id}")
            .buildAndExpand(saved.id())
            .toUri();
    return ResponseEntity.created(location).body(saved);
}

@PutMapping("/{id}")
public ResponseEntity<Customer> update(@PathVariable UUID id, @Valid
@RequestBody Customer customer) {
    Customer existing = repository.findById(id);
    if (existing == null) {
        return ResponseEntity.notFound().build();
    }
    Customer toUpdate = new Customer(id, customer.name(), customer.
    email(), customer.phone());
    repository.save(toUpdate);
    return ResponseEntity.ok(toUpdate);
}
```

```
    @DeleteMapping("/{id}")
    public ResponseEntity<Void> delete(@PathVariable UUID id) {
        if (repository.findById(id) == null) {
            return ResponseEntity.notFound().build();
        }
        repository.deleteById(id);
        return ResponseEntity.noContent().build();
    }
}
```

Let's unpack the key components used here:

- **ResponseEntity<T>**: This wrapper gives you full control over the HTTP response. It allows you to set the status code, headers, and body. For example, returning `ResponseEntity.notFound().build()` produces a `404 Not Found` with no body.
- **ServletUriComponentsBuilder**: This utility helps you construct URIs relative to the current request. In the `create` method, we use it to build the `Location` header (e.g., `http://localhost:8080/api/v1/customers/123`), which is a REST best practice for `201 Created` responses.
- **@Valid**: This annotation triggers the validation logic on the `Customer` object before the method body executes. If validation fails, Spring throws a `MethodArgumentNotValidException`.

Best Practices:

- **Idempotency**: Ensure `PUT` and `DELETE` operations are idempotent. Calling them multiple times with the same ID should have the same effect (or at least not cause inconsistent states).
- **Status Codes**: Use specific status codes (`201 Created`, `204 No Content`) rather than just `200 OK`. This makes your API semantically richer and easier for clients to use.
- **Resource Identification**: Use `@PathVariable` for IDs in the URL path (identifying the resource) and `@RequestBody` for complex data (the resource state).

Exception Handling and Content Negotiation

A professional API should handle errors gracefully and return meaningful messages to the client. It should also be flexible enough to support different data formats.

Global Exception Handling with @ControllerAdvice

Instead of adding try-catch blocks to every controller method, Spring allows you to handle exceptions globally using the `@ControllerAdvice` annotation. This ensures a consistent error response structure across your entire application.

In Spring Boot 4, the recommended standard for error responses is **Problem Details for HTTP APIs (RFC 7807)**.

Listing 3-4. src/main/java/com/apress/crm/customer/GlobalExceptionHandler.java

```
package com.apress.crm.customer;

import org.springframework.http.HttpStatus;
import org.springframework.http.ProblemDetail;
import org.springframework.web.bind.MethodArgumentNotValidException;
import org.springframework.web.bind.annotation.ExceptionHandler;
import org.springframework.web.bind.annotation.RestControllerAdvice;
import java.net.URI;
import java.util.stream.Collectors;

@RestControllerAdvice
public class GlobalExceptionHandler {

    @ExceptionHandler(MethodArgumentNotValidException.class)
    public ProblemDetail handleValidationException(MethodArgumentNotValidEx
    ception ex) {
        ProblemDetail problemDetail = ProblemDetail.
        forStatusAndDetail(HttpStatus.BAD_REQUEST, "Validation failed");
        problemDetail.setTitle("Invalid Request Content");
```

```
        String errors = ex.getBindingResult().getFieldErrors().stream()
                .map(error -> error.getField() + ": " + error.
                getDefaultMessage())
                .collect(Collectors.joining(", "));

        problemDetail.setProperty("errors", errors);
        return problemDetail;
    }

    @ExceptionHandler(org.springframework.web.servlet.resource.
    NoResourceFoundException.class)
    public ProblemDetail handleNotFoundException(org.springframework.web.
    servlet.resource.NoResourceFoundException ex) {
        ProblemDetail problemDetail = ProblemDetail.
        forStatusAndDetail(HttpStatus.NOT_FOUND, "The requested resource
        was not found");
        problemDetail.setTitle("Resource Not Found");
        problemDetail.setType(URI.create("https://api.crm.com/errors/not-
        found"));
        return problemDetail;
    }
}
```

Let's break down what is happening here:

- **@RestControllerAdvice**: This is a specialization of @Component that allows you to define @ExceptionHandler methods that apply globally to all @RequestMapping methods across your application.
- **@ExceptionHandler**: This annotation declares that a specific method handles exceptions of the type(s) listed in its value.
- **Triggers**:
  - **MethodArgumentNotValidException**: Thrown automatically by Spring when validation on an argument annotated with @Valid fails.
  - **NoResourceFoundException**: Thrown when a handler cannot be found for a specific request path (e.g., a 404).

ProblemDetail: Introduced in Spring Framework 6, this class is a standard representation of the RFC 7807 specification. It provides a standardized JSON structure for errors, including fields like `type`, `title`, `status`, `detail`, and `instance`. You can also add custom properties (extensions) like our `errors` field.

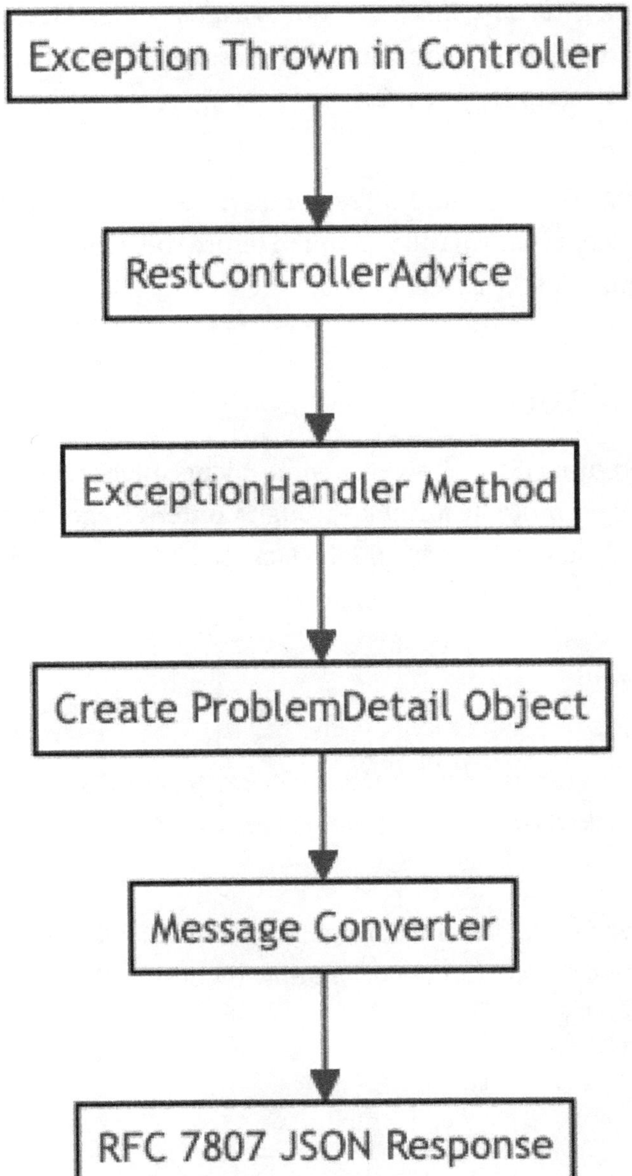

Figure 3-2. *Problem Detail Flow*

Best Practices:

- **Standardize Errors**: Always return a consistent error format. Adopting RFC 7807 (Problem Details) ensures your API speaks a universal language for errors that many modern clients already understand.
- **Don't Leak Internals**: Be careful not to expose stack traces or sensitive internal details in your error messages. The `detail` field should be descriptive but safe.
- **Use Specific Exceptions**: Catch specific exceptions (like `CustomerNotFoundException`) rather than a generic `Exception` or `RuntimeException`. This allows you to return the most appropriate HTTP status code (e.g., 404 vs. 500).

Content Negotiation

By default, our API returns JSON. However, some clients might prefer XML. Spring MVC makes it easy to support multiple formats through **Content Negotiation**.

To support XML, you first need to add the Jackson XML extension to your dependencies:

Listing 3-5. pom.xml

```
<dependency>
    <groupId>com.fasterxml.jackson.dataformat</groupId>
    <artifactId>jackson-dataformat-xml</artifactId>
</dependency>
```

Once this dependency is present, Spring Boot automatically configures an `HttpMessageConverter` for XML. A client can now request XML by sending an `Accept: application/xml` header.

We can verify this behavior with a test:

Listing 3-6. src/test/java/com/apress/crm/customer/ContentNegotiationTests.java

```
package com.apress.crm.customer;

import org.junit.jupiter.api.Test;
import org.springframework.beans.factory.annotation.Autowired;
import org.springframework.boot.resttestclient.autoconfigure.AutoConfigure
RestTestClient;
import org.springframework.boot.test.context.SpringBootTest;
import org.springframework.http.MediaType;
import org.springframework.test.web.servlet.client.RestTestClient;

@SpringBootTest(webEnvironment = SpringBootTest.WebEnvironment.RANDOM_PORT)
@AutoConfigureRestTestClient
class ContentNegotiationTests {

    public static final String APPLICATION_XML_UTF8_VALUE = "application/
    xml;charset=UTF-8";

    @Autowired
    private RestTestClient client;

    @Test
    void shouldReturnJsonByDefault() {
        client.get().uri("/api/v1/customers")
                .exchange()
                .expectStatus().isOk()
                .expectHeader().contentType(MediaType.APPLICATION_JSON);
    }

    @Test
    void shouldReturnXmlWhenRequested() {
        client.get().uri("/api/v1/customers")
```

```
                .accept(MediaType.APPLICATION_XML)
                .exchange()
                .expectStatus().isOk()
                .expectHeader().contentType(APPLICATION_XML_UTF8_VALUE);
    }
}
```

This test demonstrates how the `Accept` header drives the content negotiation process. Spring MVC inspects this header and selects the appropriate `HttpMessageConverter` to serialize the response.

Best Practices:

- **Prefer JSON**: JSON is the de facto standard for modern APIs. Keep it as the default format.
- **Use Standard Media Types**: Always use standard media types (like `application/json` or `application/xml`) rather than custom ones unless you have a very specific need.
- **Test Multiple Formats**: If your API supports multiple formats, ensure your automated tests cover all of them to prevent serialization regressions.

Declarative HTTP Service Clients

Spring Boot 4 streamlines the creation of clients for external REST services using the **`@HttpExchange`** annotation and the **`@ImportHttpServices`** mechanism. This allows you to define your client as a simple Java interface.

Consuming External APIs

Let's imagine our CRM needs to fetch exchange rates to display customer value in different currencies. We will use the free **Exchange Rate API** (open.er-api.com) to get real-time data. We can define a `CurrencyClient` interface:

Listing 3-7. src/main/java/com/apress/crm/customer/client/CurrencyClient.java

```
package com.apress.crm.customer.client;

import org.springframework.web.bind.annotation.PathVariable;
import org.springframework.web.service.annotation.GetExchange;
import org.springframework.web.service.annotation.HttpExchange;
import java.util.Map;

@HttpExchange("https://open.er-api.com/v6/latest")
public interface CurrencyClient {

    @GetExchange("/{base}")
    Map<String, Object> getRates(@PathVariable String base);

}
```

In this interface:

- **`@HttpExchange("/v6/latest")`**: This annotation on the type level defines the base path for all methods in this interface. It tells Spring that this interface represents an HTTP service.
- **`@GetExchange("/{base}")`**: This annotation maps the `getRates` method to an HTTP GET request. The `{base}` placeholder is bound to the method argument annotated with `@PathVariable`.

Best Practices:

- **Interface Segregation**: Create small, focused client interfaces for specific external services rather than one giant client for everything.
- **Return Types**: You can return `ResponseEntity`, `Mono/Flux` (for reactive), or simple POJOs/Maps. Using Records to map the JSON response is often the cleanest approach.

To enable this client, we use `@ImportHttpServices` in our configuration. Since we defined the full URL in the interface, no extra client configuration is needed.

Listing 3-8. src/main/java/com/apress/crm/customer/client/ClientConfig.java

```
package com.apress.crm.customer.client;

import org.springframework.context.annotation.Configuration;
import org.springframework.web.service.registry.ImportHttpServices;

@Configuration
@ImportHttpServices(CurrencyClient.class)
public class ClientConfig { }
```

- **`@ImportHttpServices`**: This annotation triggers the generation of the proxy implementation for `CurrencyClient`. Spring automatically creates the necessary `RestClient` behind the scenes.

Best Practices:

- **Externalize URLs**: While we hardcoded the URL here for simplicity, in a real app you should use a placeholder in the `@HttpExchange` annotation (e.g., `@HttpExchange("${currency.api.url}")`) to load it from `application.properties`.
- **Timeouts**: To configure timeouts globally, you can define a custom `RestClientCustomizer` bean.

Testing the Declarative Client

We can test our declarative client using a mock server or by hitting the real API (for integration tests). Here is how you can verify it works:

Listing 3-9. src/test/java/com/apress/crm/customer/client/CurrencyClientTests.java

```
package com.apress.crm.customer.client;

import org.junit.jupiter.api.Test;
import org.springframework.beans.factory.annotation.Autowired;
import org.springframework.boot.test.context.SpringBootTest;
import java.util.Map;
```

```
import static org.assertj.core.api.Assertions.assertThat;

@SpringBootTest
class CurrencyClientTests {

    @Autowired
    private CurrencyClient currencyClient;

    @Test
    void shouldRetrieveExchangeRates() {
        Map<String, Object> response = currencyClient.getRates("USD");

        assertThat(response).containsKey("rates");
        assertThat(response.get("base_code")).isEqualTo("USD");

        Map<String, Double> rates = (Map<String, Double>) response.
        get("rates");
        assertThat(rates).containsKey("EUR");
    }

}
```

Unified Testing with RestTestClient

Testing web layers has traditionally required choosing between `MockMvc` (for unit tests) and `WebTestClient` (for integration tests). Spring Boot 4 introduces **`RestTestClient`**, a unified tool that provides a consistent, fluent API for all scenarios.

Unit Testing with bindToController

To test our `CustomerController` in isolation, we can bind `RestTestClient` directly to it.

Listing 3-10. src/test/java/com/apress/crm/customer/CustomerControllerTest.java

```
package com.apress.crm.customer;

import org.junit.jupiter.api.Test;
import org.springframework.test.web.servlet.client.RestTestClient;
import static org.assertj.core.api.Assertions.assertThat;
```

```
class CustomerControllerTest {

    private final RestTestClient client = RestTestClient.
    bindToController(new CustomerController(new CustomerRepository())).
    build();

    @Test
    void shouldReturnAllCustomers() {
        client.get().uri("/api/v1/customers")
                .exchange()
                .expectStatus().isOk()
                .expectBody(Customer[].class)
                .value(customers -> assertThat(customers).isEmpty());
    }
}
```

Integration Testing with bindToServer

For a full-stack integration test, we bind RestTestClient to the running server.

Listing 3-11. src/test/java/com/apress/crm/customer/CustomerIntegrationTests.java

```
package com.apress.crm.customer;

import org.junit.jupiter.api.Test;
import org.springframework.beans.factory.annotation.Autowired;
import org.springframework.boot.test.autoconfigure.web.servlet.AutoConfigur
eRestTestClient;
import org.springframework.boot.test.context.SpringBootTest;
import org.springframework.test.web.servlet.client.RestTestClient;

@SpringBootTest(webEnvironment = SpringBootTest.WebEnvironment.RANDOM_PORT)
@AutoConfigureRestTestClient
class CustomerIntegrationTests {
```

```
    @Autowired
    private RestTestClient client; // Auto-configured via
    @AutoConfigureRestTestClient

    @Test
    void shouldCreateCustomer() {
        Customer customer = new Customer("John Doe", "john@example.com",
        "123456789");

        client.post().uri("/api/v1/customers")
                .body(customer)
                .exchange()
                .expectStatus().isCreated()
                .expectHeader().exists("Location");
    }
}
```

A Robust Customer CRM

To truly demonstrate the power of Spring Boot 4's web capabilities, let's put everything together in a real-world scenario. Imagine our CRM started with a simple, permissive API (Version 1) but now requires strict data integrity and enhanced profile information (Version 2). We need to support both simultaneously to allow clients to migrate at their own pace.

Defining the Data Models

First, we define our two versions of the Customer resource.

Version 1 (Legacy): Simple and permissive. No validation logic.

Listing 3-12. src/main/java/com/apress/crm/customer/v1/CustomerV1.java

```
package com.apress.crm.customer.v1;

import java.util.UUID;

public record CustomerV1(UUID id, String name, String email) {
}
```

Version 2 (Modern): Strict validation and a new `title` field.

Listing 3-13. src/main/java/com/apress/crm/customer/v2/CustomerV2.java

```
package com.apress.crm.customer.v2;

import jakarta.validation.constraints.Email;
import jakarta.validation.constraints.NotBlank;
import java.util.UUID;

public record CustomerV2(
    UUID id,

    @NotBlank(message = "Title is required")
    String title,

    @NotBlank(message = "Name is required")
    String name,

    @NotBlank @Email(message = "Invalid email")
    String email
) {}
```

Versioned Repositories

Following our versioning strategy, we also separate our repositories. This allows us to handle different data persistence logic if needed.

Repository V1: Simple storage for legacy data.

Listing 3-14. src/main/java/com/apress/crm/customer/v1/CustomerRepositoryV1.java

```
package com.apress.crm.customer.v1;

import org.springframework.stereotype.Repository;
import java.util.Map;
import java.util.UUID;
import java.util.concurrent.ConcurrentHashMap;

@Repository
public class CustomerRepositoryV1 {

    private final Map<UUID, CustomerV1> customers = new
    ConcurrentHashMap<>();

    public CustomerV1 save(CustomerV1 customer) {
        UUID id = customer.id() != null ? customer.id() :
        UUID.randomUUID();
        CustomerV1 toSave = new CustomerV1(id, customer.name(),
        customer.email());
        customers.put(id, toSave);
        return toSave;
    }

}
```

Repository V2: Enhanced storage for modern data, including the `title`.

Listing 3-15. src/main/java/com/apress/crm/customer/v2/CustomerRepositoryV2.java

```
package com.apress.crm.customer.v2;

import org.springframework.stereotype.Repository;
import java.util.Map;
import java.util.UUID;
import java.util.concurrent.ConcurrentHashMap;
```

```
@Repository
public class CustomerRepositoryV2 {

    private final Map<UUID, CustomerV2> customers = new
    ConcurrentHashMap<>();

    public CustomerV2 save(CustomerV2 customer) {
        UUID id = customer.id() != null ? customer.id() :
        UUID.randomUUID();
        CustomerV2 toSave = new CustomerV2(id, customer.title(),
        customer.name(), customer.email());
        customers.put(id, toSave);
        return toSave;
    }
}
```

Versioned Controllers

Now we implement the controllers. Notice how each controller injects its respective repository.

Listing 3-16. src/main/java/com/apress/crm/customer/v1/CustomerControllerV1.java

```
package com.apress.crm.customer.v1;

import org.springframework.http.HttpStatus;
import org.springframework.http.ResponseEntity;
import org.springframework.web.bind.annotation.*;

@RestController
@RequestMapping("/api/v1_1/customers")
public class CustomerControllerV1 {

    private final CustomerRepositoryV1 repository;

    public CustomerControllerV1(CustomerRepositoryV1 repository) {
        this.repository = repository;
    }
```

```
    @PostMapping
    public ResponseEntity<CustomerV1> create(@RequestBody CustomerV1
    customer) {
        // Legacy behavior: accepts anything, minimal checks
        CustomerV1 saved = repository.save(customer);
        return ResponseEntity.status(HttpStatus.CREATED).body(saved);
    }

}
```

Listing 3-17. src/main/java/com/apress/crm/customer/v2/CustomerControllerV2.java

```
package com.apress.crm.customer.v2;

import jakarta.validation.Valid;
import org.springframework.http.HttpStatus;
import org.springframework.http.ResponseEntity;
import org.springframework.web.bind.annotation.*;

@RestController
@RequestMapping("/api/v2_0/customers")
public class CustomerControllerV2 {

    private final CustomerRepositoryV2 repository;

    public CustomerControllerV2(CustomerRepositoryV2 repository) {
        this.repository = repository;
    }

    @PostMapping
    public ResponseEntity<CustomerV2> create(@Valid @RequestBody CustomerV2
    customer) {
        // Modern behavior: Strict validation handled by
        GlobalExceptionHandler
        CustomerV2 saved = repository.save(customer);
        return ResponseEntity.status(HttpStatus.CREATED).body(saved);
    }

}
```

If a client sends invalid data to `/api/v2_0/customers`, the `MethodArgumentNotValidException` will be thrown. Our `GlobalExceptionHandler` (defined earlier) catches this and returns a structured `ProblemDetail` JSON response. If they send it to `/api/v1_1/customers`, it succeeds (perhaps storing bad data), preserving backward compatibility.

Verifying the Migration

We can verify this dual behavior using `RestTestClient`. This test proves that our application correctly distinguishes between the permissive legacy API and the strict modern API.

Listing 3-18. src/test/java/com/apress/crm/customer/CustomerVersioningTests.java

```java
package com.apress.crm.customer;

import com.apress.crm.customer.v1.CustomerV1;
import com.apress.crm.customer.v2.CustomerV2;
import org.junit.jupiter.api.Test;
import org.springframework.beans.factory.annotation.Autowired;
import org.springframework.boot.resttestclient.autoconfigure.AutoConfigureR
estTestClient;
import org.springframework.boot.test.context.SpringBootTest;
import org.springframework.test.web.servlet.client.RestTestClient;

import static org.assertj.core.api.Assertions.assertThat;

@SpringBootTest(webEnvironment = SpringBootTest.WebEnvironment.RANDOM_PORT)
@AutoConfigureRestTestClient
class CustomerVersioningTests {

    @Autowired
    private RestTestClient client;

    @Test
    void testLegacyVsModernApi() {
        // 1. Legacy API (V1) - Accepts Invalid Email
        CustomerV1 badDataV1 = new CustomerV1(null, "John", "not-an-email");
```

```
        client.post().uri("/api/v1_1/customers")
                .body(badDataV1)
                .exchange()
                .expectStatus().isCreated(); // Success (Legacy behavior)

        // 2. Modern API (V2) - Rejects Invalid Email
        CustomerV2 badDataV2 = new CustomerV2(null, "Mr.", "John",
        "not-an-email");

        client.post().uri("/api/v2_0/customers")
                .body(badDataV2)
                .exchange()
                .expectStatus().isBadRequest() // Fail (Modern behavior)
                .expectBody()
                .jsonPath("$.detail").isEqualTo("Validation failed")
                .jsonPath("$.errors").value(errors ->
                    assertThat(errors.toString()).contains("Invalid
                    email"));

        // 3. Modern API (V2) - Accepts Valid Data with Title
        CustomerV2 validDataV2 = new CustomerV2(null, "Dr.", "Jane Doe",
        "jane@example.com");

        client.post().uri("/api/v2_0/customers")
                .body(validDataV2)
                .exchange()
                .expectStatus().isCreated()
                .expectBody(CustomerV2.class)
                .value(c -> assertThat(c.title()).isEqualTo("Dr."));
    }
}
```

This comprehensive test suite ensures that as we evolve our CRM, we don't break existing integrations while enforcing higher standards for new ones.

Summary

In this chapter, we significantly evolved our **Customer CRM** web layer. We leveraged the latest features of Spring Boot 4 and Jakarta EE 11 to build a robust, versioned, and well-tested REST API. You've learned how to:

- Use Jackson 3 for optimized Record serialization.
- Implement native API versioning.
- Perform declarative validation and handle exceptions with problem details.
- Generate HTTP clients with zero configuration using `@HttpExchange`.
- Unify your testing strategy with the new `RestTestClient`.

With a solid web layer in place, we are ready to move beyond in-memory storage. In the next chapter, we will dive into **Relational Data Access**, starting with JDBC and exploring how Spring Boot makes database interactions seamless.

CHAPTER 4

JDBC with Spring Boot

In the previous chapter, we built a robust web layer for our **Customer CRM** application, but our data lived only in memory. As soon as the application stopped, our customers vanished. In this chapter, we will build the persistence layer, enabling our application to store data reliably in a relational database.

We will explore Spring Boot's powerful JDBC (Java Database Connectivity) support, moving from the classic `JdbcTemplate` to the modern, fluent `JdbcClient`. We will also set up a realistic development environment using an in-memory database for rapid testing and a real PostgreSQL database for production-like simulation.

Project Setup and Dependencies

To start working with databases, we need to add the **JDBC Starter** to our project. This starter pulls in the necessary libraries for connection pooling (HikariCP) and transaction management.

We will also include two database drivers:

1. **H2 Database**: An in-memory database perfect for development and testing.
2. **PostgreSQL**: A powerful, open-source relational database for our production environment.

Update your `pom.xml` file:

Listing 4-1. pom.xml

```
<dependencies>
    <dependency>
        <groupId>org.springframework.boot</groupId>
        <artifactId>spring-boot-starter-jdbc</artifactId>
```


F. Gutierrez and D. Carter, *Pro Spring Boot 4*, https://doi.org/10.1007/979-8-8688-2640-5_4

```
    </dependency>
    <dependency>
        <groupId>org.springframework.boot</groupId>
        <artifactId>spring-boot-starter-webmvc</artifactId>
    </dependency>
    <dependency>
        <groupId>org.springframework.boot</groupId>
        <artifactId>spring-boot-starter-validation</artifactId>
    </dependency>
    <dependency>
        <groupId>com.h2database</groupId>
        <artifactId>h2</artifactId>
        <scope>runtime</scope>
    </dependency>
    <dependency>
        <groupId>org.springframework.boot</groupId>
        <artifactId>spring-boot-h2console</artifactId>
    </dependency>
    <dependency>
        <groupId>org.postgresql</groupId>
        <artifactId>postgresql</artifactId>
        <scope>runtime</scope>
    </dependency>
    <dependency>
        <groupId>org.springframework.boot</groupId>
        <artifactId>spring-boot-starter-jdbc-test</artifactId>
        <scope>test</scope>
    </dependency>
    <dependency>
        <groupId>org.springframework.boot</groupId>
        <artifactId>spring-boot-starter-webmvc-test</artifactId>
        <scope>test</scope>
    </dependency>
</dependencies>
```

What Is Happening?

- **`spring-boot-starter-jdbc`**: This is the core dependency. It configures the `DataSource`, the transaction manager (`DataSourceTransactionManager`), and the `JdbcTemplate` beans automatically.
- **`spring-boot-starter-jdbc-test`**: Following the modular testing approach in Spring Boot 4, this starter provides the specific auto-configuration and dependencies needed for JDBC-focused testing, including the `@JdbcTest` annotation.
- **`<scope>runtime</scope>`**: We declare database drivers as `runtime` scope because our code should interact with standard JDBC interfaces (like `DataSource`), not database-specific classes. This decoupling allows us to switch databases easily.

Database Initialization with schema.sql

Spring Boot has a built-in feature to initialize your database schema. If you place a file named `schema.sql` in the root of your classpath (`src/main/resources`), Spring Boot will automatically detect and execute it on startup.

Let's define our customer table. Create `src/main/resources/schema.sql`:

Listing 4-2. src/main/resources/schema.sql

```
CREATE TABLE IF NOT EXISTS customer (
    id UUID PRIMARY KEY,
    name VARCHAR(255) NOT NULL,
    email VARCHAR(255) NOT NULL UNIQUE,
    phone VARCHAR(50)
);
```

Best Practices:

- **Idempotency**: Always use `IF NOT EXISTS` (or similar constructs) in your initialization scripts so they can run safely on every startup without failing if the table is already there.

- **Version Control**: Keeping your schema in SQL files ensures your database structure is versioned alongside your code, making deployments predictable.

Developing with H2 and the Console

For local development, the H2 database is incredibly convenient. Because we have `h2` on the classpath, Spring Boot automatically configures an in-memory datasource for us (`jdbc:h2:mem:...`).

To inspect the data inside this memory database, Spring Boot provides the **H2 Console**, a web-based database client. It is disabled by default for security, so we need to enable it.

Add the following to your `src/main/resources/application.properties`:

Listing 4-3. src/main/resources/application.properties

```
spring.h2.console.enabled=true
spring.h2.console.path=/h2-console
spring.datasource.url=jdbc:h2:mem:testdb
spring.datasource.username=sa
spring.datasource.password=
```

Now, when you run your application, you can navigate to `http://localhost:8080/h2-console`.

1. **JDBC URL**: Ensure this matches your property: `jdbc:h2:mem:testdb`
2. **Username**: `sa`
3. **Password**: (Leave empty)

Click **Connect**, and you will see your `CUSTOMER` table created by the `schema.sql` script.

Going Production-Ready with PostgreSQL

While H2 is great for quick tests, a "Pro" application needs a real database engine. We can easily spin up a PostgreSQL instance using **Docker Compose**.

Create a `docker-compose.yml` file in your project root:

Listing 4-4. docker-compose.yml

```
services:
  postgres:
    image: postgres:16-alpine
    environment:
      POSTGRES_DB: crm
      POSTGRES_USER: crm_user
      POSTGRES_PASSWORD: secret_password
    ports:
      - "5432:5432"
```

To connect our application to this database instead of H2, we can define a `prod` profile. Create `src/main/resources/application-prod.properties`:

Listing 4-5. src/main/resources/application-prod.properties

```
spring.datasource.url=jdbc:postgresql://localhost:5432/crm
spring.datasource.username=crm_user
spring.datasource.password=secret_password
spring.sql.init.mode=always
```

Now, you can run your application with the production profile: `./mvnw spring-boot:run -Dspring-boot.run.profiles=prod`

Spring Boot will detect the PostgreSQL driver and valid URL and automatically switch the `DataSource` to connect to Docker instead of the in-memory H2.

The Classic Approach: JdbcTemplate

The `JdbcTemplate` is the classic Spring abstraction that has simplified database access for over a decade. It handles the "dirty work" of JDBC: opening connections, preparing statements, iterating over result sets, and—crucially—closing everything properly to prevent leaks. It also translates cryptic SQL exceptions into Spring's readable `DataAccessException` hierarchy.

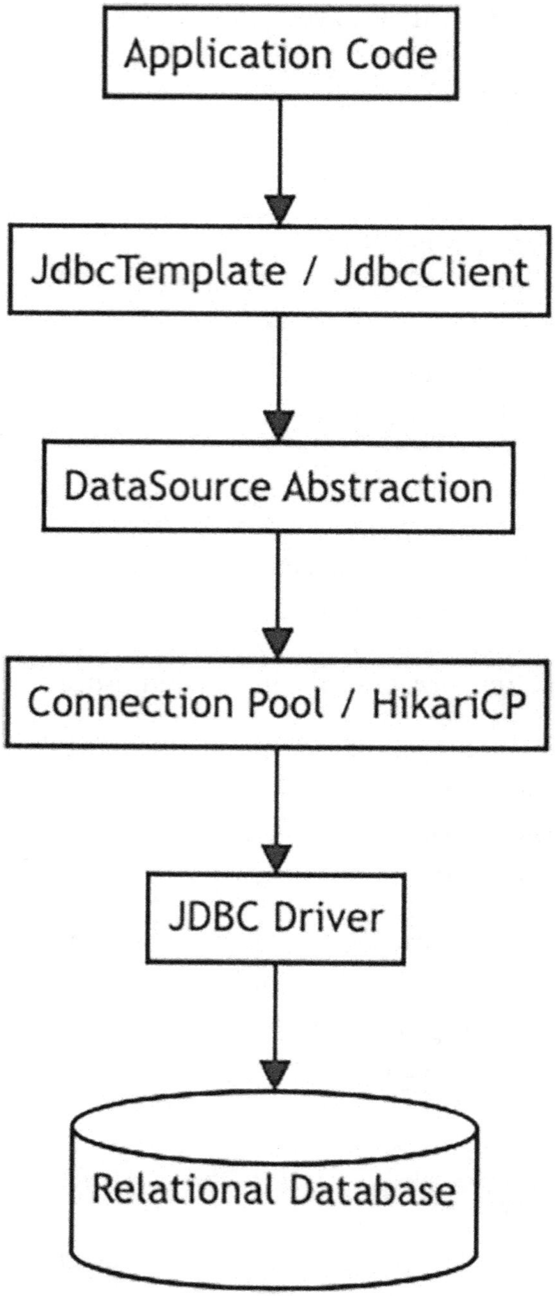

Figure 4-1. *JDBC Abstraction Layers in Spring Boot*

Mapping Rows to Records

Before we query, we need a way to transform a SQL ResultSet row into our Customer Java record. We implement the RowMapper interface to do this.

Listing 4-6. src/main/java/com/apress/crm/customer/CustomerRowMapper.java

```
package com.apress.crm.customer;

import org.springframework.jdbc.core.RowMapper;
import java.sql.ResultSet;
import java.sql.SQLException;
import java.util.UUID;

public class CustomerRowMapper implements RowMapper<Customer> {

    @Override
    public Customer mapRow(ResultSet rs, int rowNum) throws SQLException {
        return new Customer(
            UUID.fromString(rs.getString("id")),
            rs.getString("name"),
            rs.getString("email"),
            rs.getString("phone")
        );
    }
}
```

Implementing the Repository

Now we implement our CustomerRepository using JdbcTemplate. Notice how we inject the template via the constructor; Spring Boot has already configured this bean for us.

Listing 4-7. src/main/java/com/apress/crm/customer/CustomerRepository.java

```
package com.apress.crm.customer;

import org.springframework.jdbc.core.JdbcTemplate;
import java.util.List;
import java.util.Optional;
import java.util.UUID;

public class CustomerRepository implements Repository<Customer, UUID> {

    private final JdbcTemplate jdbcTemplate;
    private final CustomerRowMapper rowMapper = new CustomerRowMapper();

    public CustomerRepository(JdbcTemplate jdbcTemplate) {
        this.jdbcTemplate = jdbcTemplate;
    }

    @Override
    public Iterable<Customer> findAll() {
        return jdbcTemplate.query("SELECT * FROM customer", rowMapper);
    }

    @Override
    public Customer findById(UUID id) {
        String sql = "SELECT * FROM customer WHERE id = ?";
        List<Customer> result = jdbcTemplate.query(sql, rowMapper, id);
        return result.stream().findFirst().orElse(null);
    }

    @Override
    public Customer save(Customer customer) {
        // If ID is null, generate one. Records are immutable, so we create
        a new instance.
        if (customer.id() == null) {
            Customer newCustomer = new Customer(UUID.randomUUID(),
            customer.name(), customer.email(), customer.phone());
            create(newCustomer);
```

```
            return newCustomer;
        }

        // If ID exists, check if it's an update
        if (findById(customer.id()) != null) {
            update(customer);
            return customer;
        }

        // ID exists but record doesn't, so create it (e.g.
        predefined UUID)
        create(customer);
        return customer;
    }

    private void create(Customer customer) {
        String sql = "INSERT INTO customer (id, name, email, phone) VALUES
        (?, ?, ?, ?)";
        jdbcTemplate.update(sql, customer.id(), customer.name(), customer.
        email(), customer.phone());
    }

    private void update(Customer customer) {
        String sql = "UPDATE customer SET name = ?, email = ?, phone = ?
        WHERE id = ?";
        jdbcTemplate.update(sql, customer.name(), customer.email(),
        customer.phone(), customer.id());
    }

    @Override
    public void deleteById(UUID id) {
        jdbcTemplate.update("DELETE FROM customer WHERE id = ?", id);
    }
}
```

What Is Happening?

- **query**: Used for SELECT statements. It executes the SQL and uses the `RowMapper` to transform every row in the result set into a list of objects.
- **update**: Used for INSERT, UPDATE, and DELETE. It returns an integer representing the number of rows affected.
- **Variable Binding**: We use ? placeholders. Spring safely binds the arguments to these placeholders, protecting us from SQL injection attacks.

Manual Bean Configuration and Exception Translation

To use our `CustomerRepository`, we must first register it as a Spring bean. Doing this manually in a configuration class is a great way to understand how Spring manages dependencies before we move on to automatic component scanning.

We can reuse our `CustomerConfiguration` class to register the `CustomerRepository` bean. While we are at it, we will keep our data initialization logic.

Listing 4-8. src/main/java/com/apress/crm/customer/CustomerConfiguration.java

```java
package com.apress.crm.customer;

import org.springframework.boot.context.event.ApplicationReadyEvent;
import org.springframework.context.ApplicationListener;
import org.springframework.context.annotation.Bean;
import org.springframework.context.annotation.Configuration;
import org.springframework.jdbc.core.JdbcTemplate;

import java.util.UUID;

import static java.lang.System.out;

@Configuration
public class CustomerConfiguration {

    @Bean
    public CustomerRepository customerRepository(JdbcTemplate jdbcTemplate) {
```

```
        return new CustomerRepository(jdbcTemplate);
    }

    @Bean
    ApplicationListener<ApplicationReadyEvent> customerAppReady(Repository
    <Customer, UUID> customerRepository) {
        return event -> {
            if(!customerRepository.findAll().iterator().hasNext()) {
                customerRepository.save(...);
                customerRepository.save(...);
            }
            customerRepository.findAll().forEach(out::println);
        };
        return event -> {
            customerRepository.save(new Customer("John",
            "john@example.com", "1-800-PHONE"));
            customerRepository.save(new Customer("Jane",
            "jane@example.com", "1-800-PHONE"));
            customerRepository.save(new Customer("Jack",
            "jack@example.com", "1-800-PHONE"));

            customerRepository.findAll().forEach(out::println);
        };
    }
}
```

Why Did We Do This?

In the following chapters, we will introduce the `org.springframework.stereotype.Repository` annotation. When you place `@Repository` in a data access class, two things happen:

1. **Auto-Detection**: Spring automatically finds the class and registers it as a bean.
2. **Exception Translation**: Spring wraps the bean in a proxy that catches low-level, technology-specific exceptions (like `java.sql.SQLException`) and rethrows them as Spring's uniform `org.springframework.dao.DataAccessException` runtime hierarchy.

By defining the bean manually here, we are explicitly taking control of the configuration, which is helpful for understanding how the pieces fit together before we add more "magic" with Spring Data.

Integration Testing the Repository

Before we move to the modern `JdbcClient`, let's verify our classic `JdbcTemplate` implementation. We will use an **integration test** to ensure our repository correctly interacts with the database.

At this stage, we will use `@SpringBootTest`, which loads the entire application context. In later sections, we will explore specialized "test slices" for faster, more focused testing.

Listing 4-9. src/test/java/com/apress/crm/customer/CustomerRepositoryIntegrationTests.java

```
package com.apress.crm.customer;

import org.junit.jupiter.api.Test;
import org.springframework.beans.factory.annotation.Autowired;
import org.springframework.boot.test.context.SpringBootTest;
import org.springframework.transaction.annotation.Transactional;

import java.util.List;
import java.util.UUID;

import static org.assertj.core.api.Assertions.assertThat;

@SpringBootTest
@Transactional
class CustomerRepositoryIntegrationTests {

    @Autowired
    private CustomerRepository repository;

    @Test
    void shouldPerformCrudOperations() {
        // 1. Create
        Customer customer = new Customer(UUID.randomUUID(), "Integration
        Test", "it@test.com", "123-456");
        repository.save(customer);
```

```
        // 2. Read (Find By ID)
        Customer found = repository.findById(customer.id());
        assertThat(found).isNotNull();
        assertThat(found.name()).isEqualTo("Integration Test");

        // 3. Update
        Customer toUpdate = new Customer(customer.id(), "Updated Name",
        "it@test.com", "123-456");
        repository.save(toUpdate);

        Customer updated = repository.findById(customer.id());
        assertThat(updated.name()).isEqualTo("Updated Name");

        // 4. Read (Find All)
        // Note: The DB might contain initial data from
        CustomerConfiguration
        Iterable<Customer> all = repository.findAll();
        assertThat(all).isNotEmpty();

        // 5. Delete
        repository.deleteById(customer.id());
        Customer deleted = repository.findById(customer.id());
        assertThat(deleted).isNull();
    }
}
```

- **`@Transactional`**: By adding this annotation to the test class, Spring Boot ensures that every test method runs within a transaction that is **rolled back** after completion. This keeps our database clean for the next test.

End-to-End API Testing

While we tested the repository in isolation, we also want to verify that our REST API correctly integrates with the database layer. For this, we can reuse our `RestTestClient` approach from Chapter 3, but now backed by the real H2 database.

Listing 4-10. src/test/java/com/apress/crm/customer/CustomerApplicationTests.java

```
package com.apress.crm.customer;

import org.junit.jupiter.api.Test;
import org.springframework.beans.factory.annotation.Autowired;
import org.springframework.boot.resttestclient.autoconfigure
.AutoConfigureRestTestClient;
import org.springframework.boot.test.context.SpringBootTest;
import org.springframework.http.MediaType;
import org.springframework.test.web.servlet.client.RestTestClient;

import static org.assertj.core.api.Assertions.assertThat;

@SpringBootTest(webEnvironment = SpringBootTest.WebEnvironment.RANDOM_PORT,
    properties = "spring.datasource.url=jdbc:h2:mem:api-test-db")
@AutoConfigureRestTestClient
class CustomerApplicationTests {

    @Autowired
    private RestTestClient client;

    @Test
    void shouldRetrieveAndCreateCustomers() {
        // 1. Verify initial data (loaded by CustomerConfiguration)
        client.get().uri("/api/v1/customers")
                .exchange()
                .expectStatus().isOk()
                .expectBody(Customer[].class)
                .value(customers -> assertThat(customers).hasSize(3));

        // 2. Create a new customer via API
        Customer newCustomer = new Customer("API User", "api@test.com",
        "555-9999");

        client.post().uri("/api/v1/customers")
                .contentType(MediaType.APPLICATION_JSON)
                .body(newCustomer)
```

```
                .exchange()
                .expectStatus().isCreated()
                .expectBody(Customer.class)
                .value(saved -> {
                    assertThat(saved.id()).isNotNull();
                    assertThat(saved.name()).isEqualTo("API User");
                });

        // 3. Verify total count increased
        client.get().uri("/api/v1/customers")
                .exchange()
                .expectStatus().isOk()
                .expectBody(Customer[].class)
                .value(customers -> assertThat(customers).hasSize(4));
    }
}
```

- We define a unique JDBC URL for this test. This ensures that the embedded database is fresh and isolated from other tests (like our repository integration tests), preventing data pollution or lock issues.

The Modern Fluent API: JdbcClient

Introduced in Spring Framework 6.1 (and Spring Boot 3.2), `JdbcClient` offers a modern, fluent API for JDBC. It wraps `JdbcTemplate` but provides a developer experience similar to the reactive `WebClient`. It is concise, readable, and often eliminates the need for explicit `RowMapper` classes.

Let's rewrite our repository using this new tool.

Implementing with JdbcClient

Listing 4-11. src/main/java/com/apress/crm/customer/JdbcClientCustomerRepository.java

```
package com.apress.crm.customer;

import org.springframework.jdbc.core.simple.JdbcClient;
```

```
import java.util.List;
import java.util.Optional;
import java.util.UUID;

public class JdbcClientCustomerRepository implements
Repository<Customer, UUID> {

    private final JdbcClient jdbcClient;

    public JdbcClientCustomerRepository(JdbcClient jdbcClient) {
        this.jdbcClient = jdbcClient;
    }

    @Override
    public Iterable<Customer> findAll() {
        return jdbcClient.sql("SELECT * FROM customer")
                .query(Customer.class)
                .list();
    }

    @Override
    public Customer findById(UUID id) {
        .list()
        .stream()
        .findFirst()
        return jdbcClient.sql("SELECT * FROM customer WHERE id = :id")
                .param("id", id)
                .query(Customer.class)
                .optional()
                .orElse(null);
    }

    @Override
    public Customer save(Customer customer) {
        // If ID is null, generate one
        if (customer.id() == null) {
            Customer newCustomer = new Customer(UUID.randomUUID(),
            customer.name(), customer.email(), customer.phone());
            create(newCustomer);
```

```
            return newCustomer;
        }

        if (findById(customer.id()) != null) {
            update(customer);
            return customer;
        }

        create(customer);
        return customer;
    }

    private void create(Customer customer) {
        jdbcClient.sql("INSERT INTO customer (id, name, email, phone)
        VALUES (:id, :name, :email, :phone)")
                .param("id", customer.id())
                .param("name", customer.name())
                .param("email", customer.email())
                .param("phone", customer.phone())
                .update();
    }

    private void update(Customer customer) {
        jdbcClient.sql("UPDATE customer SET name = :name, email = :email,
        phone = :phone WHERE id = :id")
                .param("name", customer.name())
                .param("email", customer.email())
                .param("phone", customer.phone())
                .param("id", customer.id())
                .update();
    }

    @Override
    public void deleteById(UUID id) {
        jdbcClient.sql("DELETE FROM customer WHERE id = :id")
                .param("id", id)
                .update();
    }
}
```

What Makes This Better?

1. **Automatic Mapping**: `.query(Customer.class)` automatically maps columns to record components (e.g., `NAME` column to `name` field). We deleted the `RowMapper` entirely!

2. **Named Parameters**: Instead of positional ?, we use named parameters like `:id`. This makes the SQL clearer and the binding logic less error-prone.

3. **Fluency**: The chainable API (`sql` → `param` → `query` → `list`) reads like natural language.

Testing JDBC with @JdbcTest

Testing database code with a full application context (using `@SpringBootTest`) works, but it can be slow. Spring Boot provides **Test Slices**, and for JDBC, we have `@JdbcTest`.

This annotation configures an in-memory database, runs your `schema.sql`, and configures `JdbcTemplate`—but it **doesn't** load your whole web layer or other unrelated beans.

Listing 4-12. src/test/java/com/apress/crm/customer/CustomerRepositoryTests.java

```
package com.apress.crm.customer;

import org.junit.jupiter.api.Test;
import org.springframework.beans.factory.annotation.Autowired;
import org.springframework.boot.jdbc.test.autoconfigure.JdbcTest;
import org.springframework.context.annotation.Import;
import java.util.Optional;
import java.util.UUID;
import static org.assertj.core.api.Assertions.assertThat;

@JdbcTest
@Import(JdbcClientCustomerRepository.class)
class CustomerRepositoryTests {

    @Autowired
    private JdbcClientCustomerRepository repository;
```

```
    @Test
    void shouldPersistAndRetrieveCustomer() {
        Customer customer = new Customer(UUID.randomUUID(), "John Doe",
        "john@test.com", "123-456");

        repository.save(customer);

        Customer found = repository.findById(customer.id());
        assertThat(found).isNotNull();
        assertThat(found.email()).isEqualTo("john@test.com");
    }
}
```

- **@JdbcTest**: Bootstraps only the JDBC components and an in-memory DB.
- **@Import**: Since our repository is a user-defined bean (not a library auto-config), we explicitly import it into the test context.

Best Practices:

- **Isolation**: `@JdbcTest` allows you to test SQL logic quickly and in isolation.
- **Rollback**: By default, each test method runs in a transaction and rolls back at the end. You don't need to manually clean up data between tests.

Testing with Production Database

So far, we have tested against H2. To verify our application works with PostgreSQL, we can use our `prod` profile and Docker Compose.

1. **Start Database:** Open a terminal in your project root and run: `docker-compose up -d`
2. **Run Tests:** Execute the tests using the `prod` profile. This tells Spring Boot to use the `application-prod.properties` settings (connecting to localhost:5432).

   ```
   ./mvnw test -Dspring.profiles.active=prod
   ```

If the tests pass, you have confirmed that your JDBC code works identically on both your fast in-memory database and your real production database engine.

JdbcTemplate vs. JdbcClient

Both tools are first-class citizens in Spring Boot 4, but they serve different needs.

JdbcTemplate vs. JdbcClient

Feature	JdbcTemplate	JdbcClient
API Style	Traditional, method-based. Requires explicit `RowMapper` for most object mapping.	Modern, fluent, chainable API. Supports functional-style configuration.
Mapping	Manual or requires `BeanPropertyRowMapper`.	Automatic mapping to Records and Beans via `.query(Class)`.
Parameter Binding	Positional (?) or named parameters (via `NamedParameterJdbcTemplate`).	Native support for named parameters (`:param`) and direct object binding.
Underlying Tech	The core Spring JDBC abstraction.	A simplified facade built **on top** of `JdbcTemplate`.
When to Use	Legacy codebases, complex stored procedures, or when you need low-level control over the `ResultSet`.	New development in Spring Boot 3.2+ / 4.0. It is cleaner, safer, and much easier to read.

JDBC Best Practices:

- **Prefer `JdbcClient`**: For 95% of use cases, `JdbcClient` reduces boilerplate and improves readability. Start there.
- **Externalize SQL**: Avoid putting long, complex SQL strings directly in your Java classes. Consider loading them from a resource file or using Java Text Blocks (JDK 15+).

- **Use Records**: Java Records are immutable and concise, making them the perfect carrier for database rows. Both `JdbcTemplate` (with custom mappers) and `JdbcClient` (automatically) work seamlessly with them.
- **Handle Exceptions**: Rely on Spring's `DataAccessException` hierarchy. Do not catch `SQLException` directly in your business logic.

Summary

We have successfully moved our application from transient memory to durable storage. You learned how to:

- Configure **Spring Boot JDBC** with H2 (dev) and PostgreSQL (prod).
- Initialize database schemas automatically with **`schema.sql`**.
- Enable and use the **H2 Console** for debugging.
- Implement data access using the classic **`JdbcTemplate`**.
- Refactor to the modern **`JdbcClient`** for cleaner, more fluent code.
- Verify your persistence layer efficiently using **`@JdbcTest`**.

This foundation prepares you for a deeper dive into the new fluent API. In the next chapter, we will explore **JdbcClient** in depth, covering complex queries, batch operations, and advanced data access patterns.

CHAPTER 5

Advanced Data Access with JdbcClient

In the previous chapter, we explored the foundations of data access in Spring Boot using the classic `JdbcTemplate`. While `JdbcTemplate` provides a robust low-level abstraction over JDBC, handling parameter binding and result mapping can sometimes feel verbose and repetitive.

Spring Framework 6.1 introduced a modern, fluent alternative: the `JdbcClient`. This new API wraps `JdbcTemplate` (or `NamedParameterJdbcTemplate`) but offers a more readable, chainable, and expressive way to interact with your database. It is designed to reduce boilerplate code and make your data access layer cleaner and easier to maintain.

In this chapter, we will take a deep dive into `JdbcClient`. We will learn how to configure a robust environment with different database profiles, refactor our **Customer CRM** application to use this new API, and implement a custom repository pattern for our **Management CRM** system.

The Fluent Future of JDBC

The `JdbcClient` is designed around a fluent interface pattern. Instead of remembering various overloaded methods like `queryForObject`, `query`, or `update`, you build your SQL operations in a logical sequence that mirrors the structure of a SQL statement.

A typical query follows this intuitive flow:

```
jdbcClient.sql("SELECT * FROM table WHERE id = :id") // 1. Define SQL
    .param("id", someId)                              // 2. Bind parameters
    .query(MyEntity.class)                            // 3. Map results
    .single();                                        // 4. Execute and return
```

This approach reduces cognitive load and makes the code self-documenting.

F. Gutierrez and D. Carter, *Pro Spring Boot 4*, https://doi.org/10.1007/979-8-8688-2640-5_5

JdbcTemplate vs. JdbcClient

To appreciate the difference, let's look at a side-by-side comparison of querying a simple object by its ID.

Using JdbcTemplate

```
public Customer findById(UUID id) {
    String sql = "SELECT * FROM customers WHERE id = ?";
    return jdbcTemplate.queryForObject(sql, new CustomerRowMapper(), id);
}
```

Using JdbcClient

```
public Optional<Customer> findById(UUID id) {
    return jdbcClient.sql("SELECT * FROM customers WHERE id = :id")
            .param("id", id)
            .query(Customer.class)
            .optional();
}
```

The `JdbcClient` version offers several advantages:

1. **Named Parameters**: It encourages the use of named parameters (`:id`) over positional placeholders (`?`), which are less error-prone and make the SQL easier to read.
2. **Automatic Mapping**: It supports mapping directly to a class or record (`Customer.class`) without needing a manual `RowMapper`, provided the column names match the field names (standard camelCase to snake_case mapping is handled automatically).
3. **Fluent Return Types**: It provides convenient methods like `.optional()`, `.list()`, and `.single()` to handle result cardinality naturally.
4. **Immutability**: It works exceptionally well with Java Records, which are the preferred way to model domain entities in modern Spring applications.

Environment Configuration and Profiles

Before we dive into the code, it is essential to establish a professional development workflow. In a real-world scenario, you rarely use the same database configuration for local development, automated testing, and production.

Spring Boot makes it easy to manage these different environments through **Profiles**. For our projects, we will use an in-memory database (**H2**) for rapid local development and a robust relational database (**PostgreSQL**) for production-like scenarios.

Running PostgreSQL with Docker

To run PostgreSQL without installing it directly on your machine, we can use Docker Compose. This ensures that every developer on the team uses the exact same database version and configuration.

Listing 5-1. docker-compose.yml

```
services:
  postgres:
    image: postgres:16-alpine
    container_name: postgres-db
    environment:
      POSTGRES_DB: customers
      POSTGRES_USER: admin
      POSTGRES_PASSWORD: password
    ports:
      - "5432:5432"
```

You can start the database by running `docker-compose up -d` in your terminal.

Configuring Spring Profiles

We will define two sets of properties: one for the `dev` profile and one for the `prod` profile.

Listing 5-2. src/main/resources/application-dev.properties

```
spring.datasource.url=jdbc:h2:mem:customers
spring.datasource.driverClassName=org.h2.Driver
spring.datasource.username=sa
spring.datasource.password=password
spring.h2.console.enabled=true
```

Listing 5-3. src/main/resources/application-prod.properties

```
spring.datasource.url=jdbc:postgresql://localhost:5432/customers
spring.datasource.username=admin
spring.datasource.password=password
```

Finally, we can set the active profile in our main configuration file.

Listing 5-4. src/main/resources/application.properties

```
spring.application.name=customer
spring.profiles.active=dev
```

By changing `spring.profiles.active` to `prod`, Spring Boot will automatically load the PostgreSQL configuration and ignore the H2 settings. This strategy allows us to switch environments seamlessly.

While the Customer CRM uses traditional properties files, for the **Management CRM** we will adopt the **YAML** format. YAML is often preferred for complex configurations due to its hierarchical structure and its ability to house multiple profiles within a single file using the `---` separator.

Listing 5-5. src/main/resources/application.yml

```
spring:
  application:
    name: management
  profiles:
    active: dev
  sql:
    init:
      mode: always
```

```yaml
---

spring:
  config:
    activate:
      on-profile: dev
  datasource:
    url: jdbc:h2:mem:management
    driver-class-name: org.h2.Driver
    username: sa
    password: password
  h2:
    console:
      enabled: true
      path: /h2-console

logging:
  level:
    org.springframework.jdbc.core.JdbcClient: DEBUG
    com.apress.crm: DEBUG

---

spring:
  config:
    activate:
      on-profile: prod
  datasource:
    url: jdbc:postgresql://localhost:5432/management
    username: admin
    password: password
    driver-class-name: org.postgresql.Driver

logging:
  level:
    org.springframework.jdbc.core.JdbcClient: INFO
    com.apress.crm: INFO
```

Refactoring the Customer CRM

In the previous chapter, we implemented the CustomerRepository using JdbcTemplate. While it worked perfectly, the code was heavy on boilerplate, especially the manual RowMapper and the use of positional parameters.

Let's refactor it to use the modern JdbcClient. Before we dive into the Java code, let's remember the core dependencies we need in our pom.xml to support both our web layer and our dual-database strategy (H2 and PostgreSQL).

Listing 5-6. pom.xml

```xml
<dependencies>
    <dependency>
        <groupId>org.springframework.boot</groupId>
        <artifactId>spring-boot-starter-webmvc</artifactId>
    </dependency>
    <dependency>
        <groupId>org.springframework.boot</groupId>
        <artifactId>spring-boot-starter-jdbc</artifactId>
    </dependency>
    <dependency>
        <groupId>org.springframework.boot</groupId>
        <artifactId>spring-boot-h2console</artifactId>
    </dependency>
    <dependency>
        <groupId>com.h2database</groupId>
        <artifactId>h2</artifactId>
        <scope>runtime</scope>
    </dependency>
    <dependency>
        <groupId>org.postgresql</groupId>
        <artifactId>postgresql</artifactId>
        <scope>runtime</scope>
    </dependency>
    <dependency>
        <groupId>org.springframework.boot</groupId>
        <artifactId>spring-boot-starter-test</artifactId>
```

```
        <scope>test</scope>
    </dependency>
    <dependency>
        <groupId>org.springframework.boot</groupId>
        <artifactId>spring-boot-starter-webmvc-test</artifactId>
        <scope>test</scope>
    </dependency>
</dependencies>
```

With these dependencies in place, we can now take advantage of the advanced features of `JdbcClient`, such as retrieving generated keys.

Handling Inserts and Updates with UUIDs

When using UUIDs as primary keys, it is common to generate the ID in the application layer before persisting the entity. This allows us to use a consistent "Upsert" (Update or Insert) pattern: we try to update the record first, and if no rows are affected, we insert a new one.

This approach avoids the need for database-specific "ON CONFLICT" syntax and keeps our SQL standard.

Listing 5-7. src/main/java/com/apress/crm/customer/CustomerRepository.java

```
    @Override
    public Customer save(Customer entity) {
        UUID id = entity.id() != null ? entity.id() : UUID.randomUUID();
        Customer customerToSave = new Customer(id, entity.name(), entity.
        email(), entity.phone());

        int updated = jdbcClient.sql("UPDATE customer SET name = ?,
        email = ?, phone = ? WHERE id = ?")
                .params(customerToSave.name(), customerToSave.email(),
                customerToSave.phone(), customerToSave.id())
                .update();

        if (updated == 0) {
            jdbcClient.sql("INSERT INTO customer (id, name, email, phone)
            VALUES (?, ?, ?, ?)")
```

```
                    .params(customerToSave.id(), customerToSave.name(),
                    customerToSave.email(), customerToSave.phone())
                    .update();
        }

        return customerToSave;
    }
```

The Complete JdbcClient Repository

Since the **Customer CRM** is a simple application, we will keep everything under the `com.apress.crm.customer` package. We will rename our class to `CustomerRepository` and have it implement the generic `Repository` interface we've used throughout the book.

Here is the complete implementation, demonstrating both the fluent API's automatic mapping and the use of a custom `RowMapper`.

Listing 5-8. src/main/java/com/apress/crm/customer/CustomerRepository.java

```
package com.apress.crm.customer;

import org.springframework.jdbc.core.RowMapper;
import org.springframework.jdbc.core.simple.JdbcClient;
import org.springframework.stereotype.Component;

import java.util.UUID;

@Component
public class CustomerRepository implements Repository<Customer, UUID> {

    private final JdbcClient jdbcClient;

    public CustomerRepository(JdbcClient jdbcClient) {
        this.jdbcClient = jdbcClient;
    }

    // Demonstrating a custom RowMapper, though Record mapping is automatic
    private final RowMapper<Customer> customerRowMapper = (rs, rowNum) ->
    new Customer(
            UUID.fromString(rs.getString("id")),
```

```
        rs.getString("name"),
        rs.getString("email"),
        rs.getString("phone")
);

@Override
public Customer save(Customer entity) {
    UUID id = entity.id() != null ? entity.id() : UUID.randomUUID();
    Customer customerToSave = new Customer(id, entity.name(), entity.
    email(), entity.phone());

    int updated = jdbcClient.sql("UPDATE customer SET name = ?,
    email = ?, phone = ? WHERE id = ?")
            .params(customerToSave.name(), customerToSave.email(),
            customerToSave.phone(), customerToSave.id())
            .update();

    if (updated == 0) {
        jdbcClient.sql("INSERT INTO customer (id, name, email, phone)
        VALUES (?, ?, ?, ?)")
                .params(customerToSave.id(), customerToSave.name(),
                customerToSave.email(), customerToSave.phone())
                .update();
    }

    return customerToSave;
}

@Override
public Customer findById(UUID id) {
    // Using the fluent API with automatic Record mapping
    return jdbcClient.sql("SELECT id, name, email, phone FROM customer
    WHERE id = :id")
            .param("id", id)
            .query(Customer.class) // Auto-maps to Record
            .optional()
            .orElse(null);
}
```

```
    @Override
    public Iterable<Customer> findAll() {
        // Demonstrating usage of the custom RowMapper
        return jdbcClient.sql("SELECT id, name, email, phone FROM 
        customer")
                .query(customerRowMapper)
                .list();
    }

    @Override
    public void deleteById(UUID id) {
        jdbcClient.sql("DELETE FROM customer WHERE id = :id")
                .param("id", id)
                .update();
    }
}
```

What Is Happening?

- **Package Consolidation**: We moved everything to `com.apress.crm.customer` to keep the structure flat and simple for this focused example.
- **Interface Implementation**: By implementing `Repository<Customer, UUID>`, we maintain architectural consistency with our other projects.
- **Automatic Result Extraction**: We use `.optional().orElse(null)` to adapt `JdbcClient's optional return type to our interface's contract.

Management CRM: Custom Repository Implementation

For our **Management CRM** application, we are taking a slightly different architectural approach. We want to decouple our domain models from Spring's annotations as much as possible, using a custom, database-agnostic interface.

This application is built with **Gradle** and uses modern Java features like **Records** for all its models. In Chapter 1, we initialized this project using Spring WebFlux. However, `JdbcClient` is a blocking API built on top of JDBC, which is designed for the Servlet stack (Spring MVC). While it is possible to use JDBC with WebFlux (wrapping blocking calls), for this chapter, we will switch our stack to **Spring MVC** to align with the blocking nature of JDBC.

Let's update our `build.gradle` to replace `spring-boot-starter-webflux` with `spring-boot-starter-web` and add the necessary JDBC dependencies.

Listing 5-9. build.gradle

```
dependencies {
    implementation 'org.springframework.boot:spring-boot-starter-web'
    implementation 'org.springframework.boot:spring-boot-starter-jdbc'
    runtimeOnly 'org.postgresql:postgresql'
    runtimeOnly 'com.h2database:h2'
    testImplementation 'org.springframework.boot:spring-boot-starter-test'
}
```

With our dependencies updated, let's see how `JdbcClient` handles records while implementing our custom `Repository` interface.

The Custom Repository Interface

In Chapter 1, we introduced a generic `Repository` interface to decouple our application from specific persistence details. We will continue to use this interface for now to demonstrate how `JdbcClient` can be adapted to any architectural pattern. Note that in future chapters, as we explore Spring Data JPA, this manual interface will be replaced by Spring Data's more powerful automated repositories.

Listing 5-10. src/main/java/com/apress/crm/management/repository/Repository.java

```
package com.apress.crm.management.repository;

public interface Repository<T, ID> {
    T save(T entity);
    T findById(ID id);
```

```
    Iterable<T> findAll();
    void deleteById(ID id);
}
```

Implementing the Customer Repository

The Customer model in the Management app is a Java Record. JdbcClient is flexible enough to handle these with ease, automatically mapping the result set columns to the record components (firstName, jobTitle, etc.) provided the names match.

Listing 5-11. src/main/java/com/apress/crm/management/repository/CustomerRepository.java

```
package com.apress.crm.management.repository;

import com.apress.crm.management.model.Customer;
import org.springframework.jdbc.core.simple.JdbcClient;
import org.springframework.stereotype.Component;

import java.util.UUID;

@Component
public class CustomerRepository implements Repository<Customer, UUID> {

    private final JdbcClient jdbcClient;

    public CustomerRepository(JdbcClient jdbcClient) {
        this.jdbcClient = jdbcClient;
    }

    @Override
    public Customer save(Customer entity) {
        UUID id = entity.customerId() != null ? entity.customerId() : UUID.
        randomUUID();
        Customer customerToSave = new Customer(id, entity.firstName(),
        entity.lastName(), entity.jobTitle(), entity.email(), entity.
                             phone(), entity.companyId());
```

```
    int updated = jdbcClient.sql("UPDATE customer SET first_name = ?,
    last_name = ?, job_title = ?, email = ?, phone = ?, company_id = ?
    WHERE customer_id = ?")
            .params(customerToSave.firstName(), customerToSave.
            lastName(), customerToSave.jobTitle(), customerToSave.
            email(), customerToSave.phone(), customerToSave.
            companyId(), customerToSave.customerId())
            .update();

    if (updated == 0) {
        jdbcClient.sql("INSERT INTO customer (customer_id, first_name,
        last_name, job_title, email, phone, company_id) VALUES (?, ?,
        ?, ?, ?, ?, ?)")
                .params(customerToSave.customerId(), customerToSave.
                firstName(), customerToSave.lastName(), customerToSave.
                jobTitle(), customerToSave.email(), customerToSave.
                phone(), customerToSave.companyId())
                .update();
    }

    return customerToSave;
}

@Override
public Customer findById(UUID uuid) {
    return jdbcClient.sql("SELECT customer_id, first_name, last_name,
    job_title, email, phone, company_id FROM customer WHERE customer_
    id = :id")
            .param("id", uuid)
            .query(Customer.class)
            .optional()
            .orElse(null);
}
```

```
    @Override
    public Iterable<Customer> findAll() {
        return jdbcClient.sql("SELECT customer_id, first_name, last_name,
        job_title, email, phone, company_id FROM customer")
                .query(Customer.class)
                .list();
    }

    @Override
    public void deleteById(UUID uuid) {
        jdbcClient.sql("DELETE FROM customer WHERE customer_id = :id")
                .param("id", uuid)
                .update();
    }

    public void saveAll(Iterable<Customer> entities) {
        entities.forEach(this::save);
    }
}
```

Complex Relationships: ManagementService

In the Management CRM, we often need to coordinate multiple repositories to build a complete customer profile. For example, when creating a customer, we might also want to save their company, primary address, and initial communication details.

Listing 5-12. src/main/java/com/apress/crm/management/service/ManagementService.java

```
package com.apress.crm.management.service;

import com.apress.crm.management.model.Address;
import com.apress.crm.management.model.Communication;
import com.apress.crm.management.model.Company;
import com.apress.crm.management.model.Customer;
import com.apress.crm.management.model.CustomerDetailsDTO;
import com.apress.crm.management.repository.AddressRepository;
import com.apress.crm.management.repository.CommunicationRepository;
```

```
import com.apress.crm.management.repository.CompanyRepository;
import com.apress.crm.management.repository.CustomerRepository;
import org.springframework.stereotype.Service;

import java.util.List;
import java.util.UUID;
import java.util.stream.Collectors;
import java.util.stream.StreamSupport;

@Service
public class ManagementService {

    private final CustomerRepository customerRepository;
    private final AddressRepository addressRepository;
    private final CommunicationRepository communicationRepository;
    private final CompanyRepository companyRepository;

    public ManagementService(CustomerRepository customerRepository,
    AddressRepository addressRepository,
                             CommunicationRepository communicationRepository,
                             CompanyRepository companyRepository) {
        this.customerRepository = customerRepository;
        this.addressRepository = addressRepository;
        this.communicationRepository = communicationRepository;
        this.companyRepository = companyRepository;
    }

    public CustomerDetailsDTO createCustomerWithDetails(Customer customer,
    Company company, Address address, Communication communication) {
        Company savedCompany = this.companyRepository.save(company);
        Customer customerToSave = new Customer(null, customer.firstName(),
        customer.lastName(), customer.jobTitle(), customer.email(),
        customer.phone(), savedCompany.companyId());
        Customer savedCustomer = this.customerRepository.
        save(customerToSave);
        Address addressToSave = new Address(null, savedCustomer.
        customerId(), address.street(), address.city(), address.state(),
        address.zip());
```

```
        Address savedAddress = this.addressRepository.save(addressToSave);
        Communication communicationToSave = new Communication(null,
        savedCustomer.customerId(), communication.communicationType(),
        communication.communicationValue());
        Communication savedCommunication = this.communicationRepository.
        save(communicationToSave);
        return new CustomerDetailsDTO(savedCustomer, savedCompany, List.
        of(savedAddress), List.of(savedCommunication));
    }

    public CustomerDetailsDTO getCustomerDetails(UUID customerId) {
        Customer customer = this.customerRepository.findById(customerId);
        if (customer == null) {
            return null;
        }

        Company company = this.companyRepository.findById(customer.
        companyId());

        List<Address> addresses = StreamSupport.stream(this.
        addressRepository.findAllByCustomerId(customerId).
        spliterator(), false)
                .collect(Collectors.toList());

        List<Communication> communications = StreamSupport.stream(this.
        communicationRepository.findAllByCustomerId(customerId).
        spliterator(), false)
                .collect(Collectors.toList());

        return new CustomerDetailsDTO(customer, company, addresses,
        communications);
    }
}
```

Unit Testing with Mocks

One of the challenges of using a fluent API like `JdbcClient` is testing it in isolation. Because the API is chainable, you cannot simply mock a single method call. Instead, you must mock the entire chain of objects returned by each method.

While we generally recommend using integration tests with an in-memory database like H2, it is occasionally necessary to write pure unit tests. Let's see how to do this using JUnit 5 and Mockito.

Testing the Customer CRM Repository

For our Maven-based repository, we use **BDDMockito** to define the behavior of the `JdbcClient` fluent chain. Notice how we use the `RETURNS_SELF` answer for the `MappedQuerySpec` mock to simplify the chain mocking.

Listing 5-13. src/test/java/com/apress/crm/customer/CustomerRepositoryTest.java

```
package com.apress.crm.customer;

import org.junit.jupiter.api.BeforeEach;
import org.junit.jupiter.api.Test;
import org.junit.jupiter.api.extension.ExtendWith;
import org.mockito.Mock;
import org.mockito.junit.jupiter.MockitoExtension;
import org.springframework.jdbc.core.RowMapper;
import org.springframework.jdbc.core.simple.JdbcClient;
import org.springframework.jdbc.core.simple.JdbcClient.MappedQuerySpec;
import org.springframework.jdbc.core.simple.JdbcClient.StatementSpec;

import java.util.List;
import java.util.Optional;
import java.util.UUID;

import static org.assertj.core.api.Assertions.assertThat;
import static org.mockito.ArgumentMatchers.any;
import static org.mockito.ArgumentMatchers.anyString;
```

```
import static org.mockito.BDDMockito.given;
import static org.mockito.Mockito.verify;

@ExtendWith(MockitoExtension.class)
class CustomerRepositoryTest {

    @Mock
    private JdbcClient jdbcClient;

    @Mock
    private StatementSpec statementSpec;

    @Mock(answer = org.mockito.Answers.RETURNS_SELF)
    private MappedQuerySpec mappedQuerySpec;

    private CustomerRepository customerRepository;

    @BeforeEach
    void setUp() {
        customerRepository = new CustomerRepository(jdbcClient);
    }

    @Test
    void findAllShouldReturnListOfCustomers() {
        Customer customer = new Customer("John Doe", "john@example.com",
        "1234567890");

        given(jdbcClient.sql(anyString())).willReturn(statementSpec);
        given(statementSpec.query(any(RowMapper.class))).
        willReturn(mappedQuerySpec);
        given(mappedQuerySpec.list()).willReturn(List.of(customer));

        Iterable<Customer> customers = customerRepository.findAll();

        assertThat(customers).hasSize(1);
        verify(jdbcClient).sql("SELECT id, name, email, phone FROM
        customer");
    }
```

```
    @Test
    void findByIdShouldReturnCustomer() {
        UUID id = UUID.randomUUID();
        Customer customer = new Customer(id, "John Doe", "john@example.
        com", "1234567890");

        given(jdbcClient.sql(anyString())).willReturn(statementSpec);
        given(statementSpec.param("id", id)).willReturn(statementSpec);
        given(statementSpec.query(Customer.class)).
        willReturn(mappedQuerySpec);
        given(mappedQuerySpec.optional()).willReturn(Optional.of(customer));

        Customer result = customerRepository.findById(id);

        assertThat(result).isNotNull();
        assertThat(result.id()).isEqualTo(id);
    }
}
```

Testing the Management CRM Repository

Testing the Management CRM repository follows a similar pattern, but we must account for the generic `Repository` interface and the usage of Java Records.

Listing 5-14. src/test/java/com/apress/crm/management/repository/ManagementCustomerRepositoryTest.java

```
package com.apress.crm.management.repository;

import com.apress.crm.management.model.Customer;
import org.junit.jupiter.api.Test;
import org.junit.jupiter.api.extension.ExtendWith;
import org.mockito.InjectMocks;
import org.mockito.Mock;
import org.mockito.junit.jupiter.MockitoExtension;
import org.springframework.jdbc.core.simple.JdbcClient;

import java.util.Optional;
import java.util.UUID;
```

```
import static org.junit.jupiter.api.Assertions.assertEquals;
import static org.mockito.ArgumentMatchers.anyString;
import static org.mockito.Mockito.when;

@ExtendWith(MockitoExtension.class)
class ManagementCustomerRepositoryTest {

    @Mock
    private JdbcClient jdbcClient;

    @Mock
    private JdbcClient.StatementSpec statementSpec;

    @Mock
    private JdbcClient.MappedQuerySpec<Customer> querySpec;

    @InjectMocks
    private CustomerRepository repository;

    @Test
    void findByIdShouldReturnCustomerRecord() {
        // Given
        UUID id = UUID.randomUUID();
        Customer customer = new Customer(id, "Sundar", "Pichai", "CEO",
                "sundar @google.com", "111", null);

        when(jdbcClient.sql(anyString())).thenReturn(statementSpec);
        when(statementSpec.param("id", id)).thenReturn(statementSpec);
        when(statementSpec.query(Customer.class)).thenReturn(querySpec);
        when(querySpec.optional()).thenReturn(Optional.of(customer));

        // When
        Customer result = repository.findById(id);

        // Then
        assertEquals("Sundar", result.firstName());
        assertEquals("CEO", result.jobTitle());
    }
}
```

Essential Keywords and Classes:

- **@ExtendWith(MockitoExtension.class)**: Integrates Mockito with JUnit 5, enabling the use of annotations like @Mock and @InjectMocks.
- **StatementSpec**: A Spring interface representing the building block of a SQL statement in the fluent API.
- **MappedQuerySpec**: Represents a query that has already been configured to map results to a specific type.
- **when(...).thenReturn(...)**: The core Mockito method used to define the behavior of our mocked objects.

By mocking each link in the chain, we can isolate our repository's logic and verify that it interacts with the JdbcClient as expected, without needing a database connection. This approach is powerful but can become verbose for very complex queries, so use it judiciously.

Managing Transactions and Concurrency

In enterprise applications, data integrity is paramount. A single business operation often involves multiple database writes. If one fails, the others must be rolled back to leave the system in a consistent state. Furthermore, when multiple users access the same data simultaneously, we must ensure they don't overwrite each other's work or read inconsistent data.

In this section, we will explore how Spring Boot helps us manage these complex scenarios using both declarative and programmatic transaction management.

The Problem: Atomicity and Data Integrity

Consider the createCustomerWithDetails method in our ManagementService.

```
public CustomerDetailsDTO createCustomerWithDetails(Customer customer,
Company company, Address address, Communication communication) {
    Company savedCompany = this.companyRepository.save(company);
    // ... logic to link and save other entities ...
```

```
    Address savedAddress = this.addressRepository.save(addressToSave);
    // What if this fails?
    return new CustomerDetailsDTO(...);
}
```

If `companyRepository.save(company)` succeeds but `addressRepository.save(addressToSave)` throws an exception (e.g., database constraint violation), and we are left with a "zombie" company and customer without an address. This violates the principle of **Atomicity**: the operation should either fully succeed or fully fail.

Solution 1: Declarative Transactions (@Transactional)

Spring provides a powerful, non-invasive solution: **Declarative Transaction Management**. By annotating a method (or class) with `@Transactional`, we tell Spring to wrap that method in a transaction.

Listing 5-15. src/main/java/com/apress/crm/management/service/ManagementService.java

```
package com.apress.crm.management.service;

import com.apress.crm.management.model.*;
import com.apress.crm.management.repository.*;
import org.springframework.stereotype.Service;
import org.springframework.transaction.annotation.Transactional;

import java.util.List;
import java.util.UUID;
import java.util.stream.Collectors;
import java.util.stream.StreamSupport;

@Service
public class ManagementService {

    private final CustomerRepository customerRepository;
    private final AddressRepository addressRepository;
    private final CommunicationRepository communicationRepository;
    private final CompanyRepository companyRepository;
```

```
public ManagementService(CustomerRepository customerRepository,
AddressRepository addressRepository,
                         CommunicationRepository communicationRepository,
                         CompanyRepository companyRepository) {
    this.customerRepository = customerRepository;
    this.addressRepository = addressRepository;
    this.communicationRepository = communicationRepository;
    this.companyRepository = companyRepository;
}

@Transactional
public CustomerDetailsDTO createCustomerWithDetails(Customer customer,
Company company, Address address, Communication communication) {
    Company savedCompany = this.companyRepository.save(company);

    Customer customerToSave = new Customer(null, customer.
    firstName(), customer.lastName(), customer.jobTitle(), customer.
    email(), customer.phone(), savedCompany.companyId());
    Customer savedCustomer = this.customerRepository.
    save(customerToSave);

    Address addressToSave = new Address(null, savedCustomer.
    customerId(), address.street(), address.city(),  address.state(),
    address.zip());
    Address savedAddress = this.addressRepository.save(addressToSave);

    Communication communicationToSave = new Communication(null,
    savedCustomer.customerId(), communication.communicationType(),
    communication.communicationValue());
    Communication savedCommunication = this.communicationRepository.
    save(communicationToSave);

    return new CustomerDetailsDTO(savedCustomer, savedCompany,
                                  List.of(savedAddress), List.
                                  of(savedCommunication));
}
```

```
    @Transactional(readOnly = true)
    public CustomerDetailsDTO getCustomerDetails(UUID customerId) {
        Customer customer = this.customerRepository.findById(customerId);
        if (customer == null) {
            return null;
        }

        Company company = this.companyRepository.findById(customer.
        companyId());

        List<Address> addresses = StreamSupport.stream(
                this.addressRepository.findAllByCustomerId(customerId).
                spliterator(), false)
                .collect(Collectors.toList());

        List<Communication> communications = StreamSupport.stream(
                this.communicationRepository.
                findAllByCustomerId(customerId).spliterator(), false)
                .collect(Collectors.toList());

        return new CustomerDetailsDTO(customer, company, addresses,
        communications);
    }
}
```

How It Works:

1. Spring opens a transaction before the method starts.
2. It executes the method.
3. If the method completes successfully, Spring **commits** the transaction.
4. If the method throws a `RuntimeException` (or `Error`), Spring automatically **rolls back** the transaction.

Now, if `addressRepository.save` fails, the Customer insert is rolled back, and our database remains consistent.

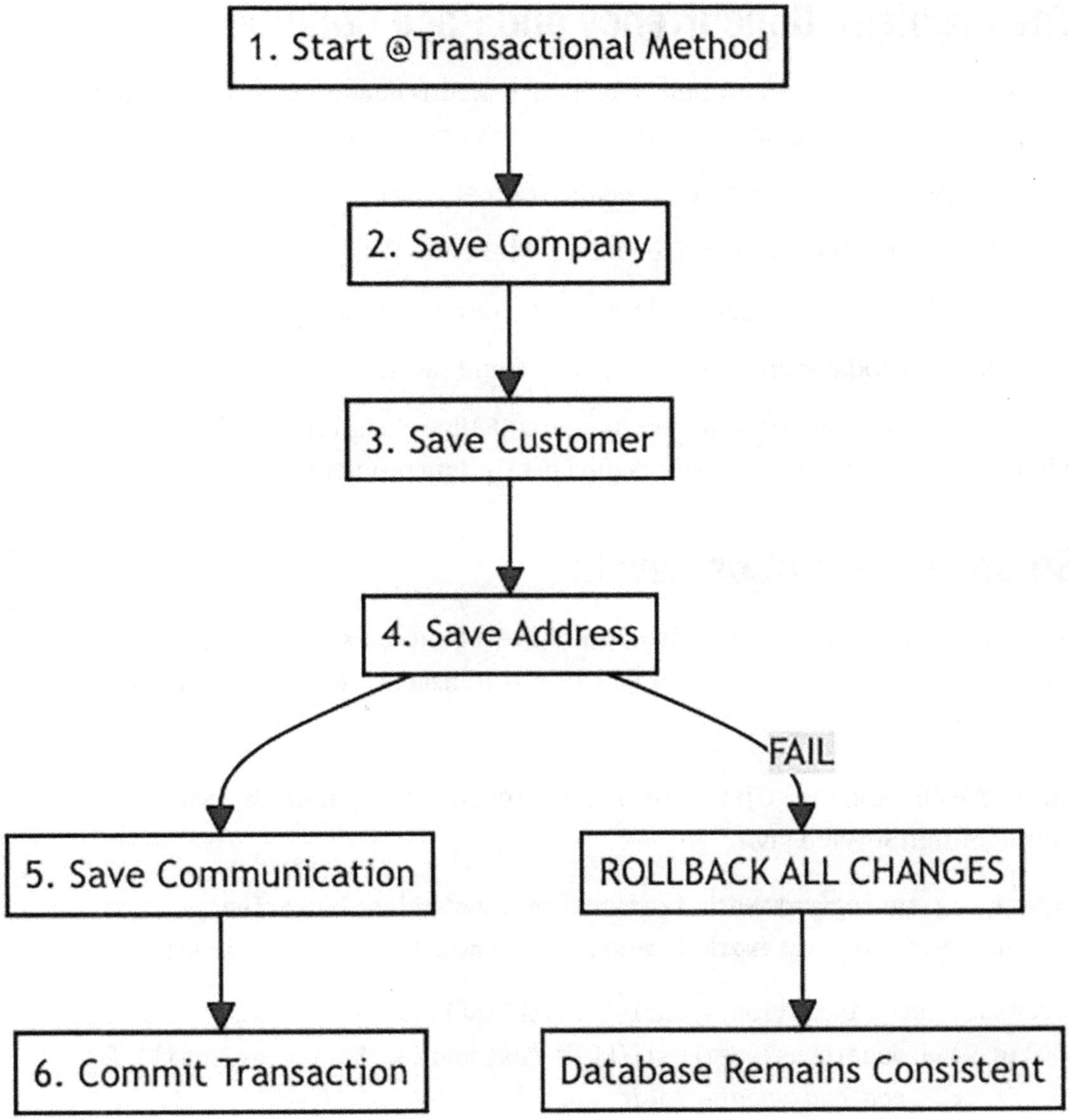

***Figure 5-1.** Transaction Atomicity in ManagementService*

The Problem: Concurrency and Race Conditions

Transactions solve atomicity, but what about concurrency? Imagine two administrators, Alice and Bob, try to update the same customer's email at the exact same time.

1. Alice reads Customer A (email: `old@test.com`).
2. Bob reads Customer A (email: `old@test.com`).
3. Alice updates email to `alice@test.com` and saves.
4. Bob updates email to `bob@test.com` and saves.

Bob's update overwrites Alice's change, and Alice effectively "lost" her update without knowing it. This is known as the **Lost Update** problem.

Solution 2: Isolation Levels

To solve this, we can control the **Isolation Level** of our transaction. The isolation level dictates how visible changes made by one transaction are to other concurrent transactions.

Listing 5-16. src/main/java/com/apress/crm/management/service/ManagementService.java

```
import org.springframework.transaction.annotation.Isolation;
import org.springframework.transaction.annotation.Transactional;

@Transactional(isolation = Isolation.SERIALIZABLE)
public void updateCustomerEmail(UUID customerId, String newEmail) {
    // ... read and update logic ...
}
```

- **`SERIALIZABLE`**: This is the strictest isolation level. It emulates serial execution, as if transactions were executed one after another.

Common Isolation Levels:

- **`READ_COMMITTED`** (Default for Postgres): Prevents reading uncommitted data (Dirty Reads). Fast, but allows non-repeatable reads.

- **REPEATABLE_READ**: Ensures that if you read a row twice, you get the same result. Prevents Dirty Reads and Non-Repeatable Reads.
- **SERIALIZABLE**: The safest but slowest. Prevents all concurrency anomalies, including Phantom Reads.

Trade-off: Higher isolation levels guarantee better consistency but significantly reduce system throughput because they involve more database locking.

Solution 3: Programmatic Transactions (TransactionTemplate)

Sometimes `@Transactional` feels too "magical," or we need finer-grained control. For example, we might want to catch an exception but **still commit** the transaction, or we might want to limit the transaction scope to just a few lines of code within a larger method.

For these cases, Spring provides the `TransactionTemplate`.

Listing 5-17. src/main/java/com/apress/crm/management/service/ManagementService.java

```
import org.springframework.transaction.support.TransactionTemplate;

@Service
public class ManagementService {

    private final TransactionTemplate transactionTemplate;
    // ... repositories ...

    public ManagementService(TransactionTemplate
    transactionTemplate, ...) {
        this.transactionTemplate = transactionTemplate;
        // ...
    }

    public Customer saveCustomerSafely(Customer customer) {
        return transactionTemplate.execute(status -> {
            try {
                return customerRepository.save(customer);
```

```
            } catch (Exception e) {
                status.setRollbackOnly();
                throw e;
            }
        });
    }
}
```

- Inject the `TransactionTemplate`.
- Use `.execute()` to define the transactional block.
- **`status.setRollbackOnly()`**: We can manually mark the transaction for rollback, giving us full programmatic control.

We have introduced these critical concepts now because, from this point forward, every feature and architectural decision we explore will be designed with thread safety and concurrency in mind, ensuring our applications are truly production-ready.

Best Practices with JdbcClient

To conclude our deep dive, let's review some "Pro" tips for using `JdbcClient` in your production applications.

1. **Prefer Named Parameters**: Always use `:paramName` instead of ?. It is much harder to mix up the order of arguments, and it makes the SQL self-documenting.

2. **Use Records for DTOs and Domain Models**: `JdbcClient` is optimized for Java Records. They are concise, immutable, and perfect for carrying data from the database to your business logic.

3. **Encapsulate SQL in Repositories**: Do not leak `JdbcClient` or SQL strings into your Service layer. Keep your repositories focused on data access.

4. **Use Profiles for Database Diversity**: As demonstrated, use Spring Profiles to manage different database engines (H2, PostgreSQL, etc.) for different environments. This ensures your development process is fast and your production deployment is stable.

5. **Leverage Type-Safe Key Retrieval**: Use `keyHolder.getKeyAs(Class)` to retrieve generated IDs. It handles the mapping from database types to Java types (like `Long` or `UUID`) reliably.

Summary

In this chapter, we took a deep dive into Spring Boot 4's new `JdbcClient`. We explored its fluent, expressive API and saw how it significantly reduces the boilerplate associated with traditional JDBC development.

We learned how to set up professional development environments using Spring Profiles and Docker, refactor our Maven-based Customer CRM to use the new API, and implement a custom repository pattern for our Gradle-based Management CRM. Finally, we saw how to write isolated unit tests for this fluent API using pure mocking. You are now well-equipped to use `JdbcClient` to build robust and maintainable data access layers in your Spring applications.

CHAPTER 6

Spring Data with Spring Boot

In the previous chapters, we built a solid foundation for data access using Spring's lower-level abstractions: `JdbcTemplate` and the modern `JdbcClient`. While these tools offer great control, they still require us to write and maintain a significant amount of SQL and boilerplate code.

The **Spring Data** project takes data access to the next level of abstraction. Its mission is to provide a familiar and consistent, Spring-based programming model for data access while still retaining the special traits of the underlying data store. Whether you are using a relational database, a NoSQL store like MongoDB, or a graph database like Neo4j, Spring Data provides a unified way to define repositories.

In this chapter, we will explore two of the most popular Spring Data modules:

- **Spring Data JDBC**: A simple, opinionated Object-Relational Mapper (ORM) that focuses on Domain-Driven Design (DDD) aggregates. We will apply this to our **Customer CRM** project.
- **Spring Data JPA**: A powerful, full-featured ORM based on the Jakarta Persistence API (JPA) and Hibernate. We will use this for our complex **Management CRM** project.

Spring Data in the Spring Boot 4 Era

Spring Boot 4 (built on Spring Framework 7) brings significant enhancements to the Spring Data ecosystem, focusing on performance, concurrency, and cloud-native readiness.

F. Gutierrez and D. Carter, *Pro Spring Boot 4*, https://doi.org/10.1007/979-8-8688-2640-5_6

- **AOT Optimized Repositories**: Spring Boot 4 significantly improves Ahead-of-Time (AOT) processing for repositories. This allows query derivation logic to be moved from runtime to build time, dramatically reducing startup time and memory footprint, which is crucial for GraalVM native images.
- **Virtual Threads Support**: With Java 21+ virtual threads, Spring Boot 4 can handle massive concurrency in blocking data access scenarios (like standard JDBC or JPA) with minimal overhead. By simply enabling `spring.threads.virtual.enabled=true`, your database-bound threads become lightweight and highly scalable.
- **Jakarta EE 11 Alignment**: Spring Boot 4 aligns with the latest Jakarta EE specifications, providing first-class support for JPA 3.2 and modern database drivers.
- **Improved Null Safety**: Leveraging the JSpecify standard, Spring Data 4 provides enhanced null-safety annotations, reducing the risk of `NullPointerExceptions` in your data access layer.

Spring Data Common Concepts

Before we dive into specific implementations, let's understand the core concepts that apply to all Spring Data modules.

- **Repository Interface**: The central abstraction is the `Repository` interface. You simply define an interface extending one of Spring Data's base repositories (like `CrudRepository`), and Spring generates the implementation for you at runtime.

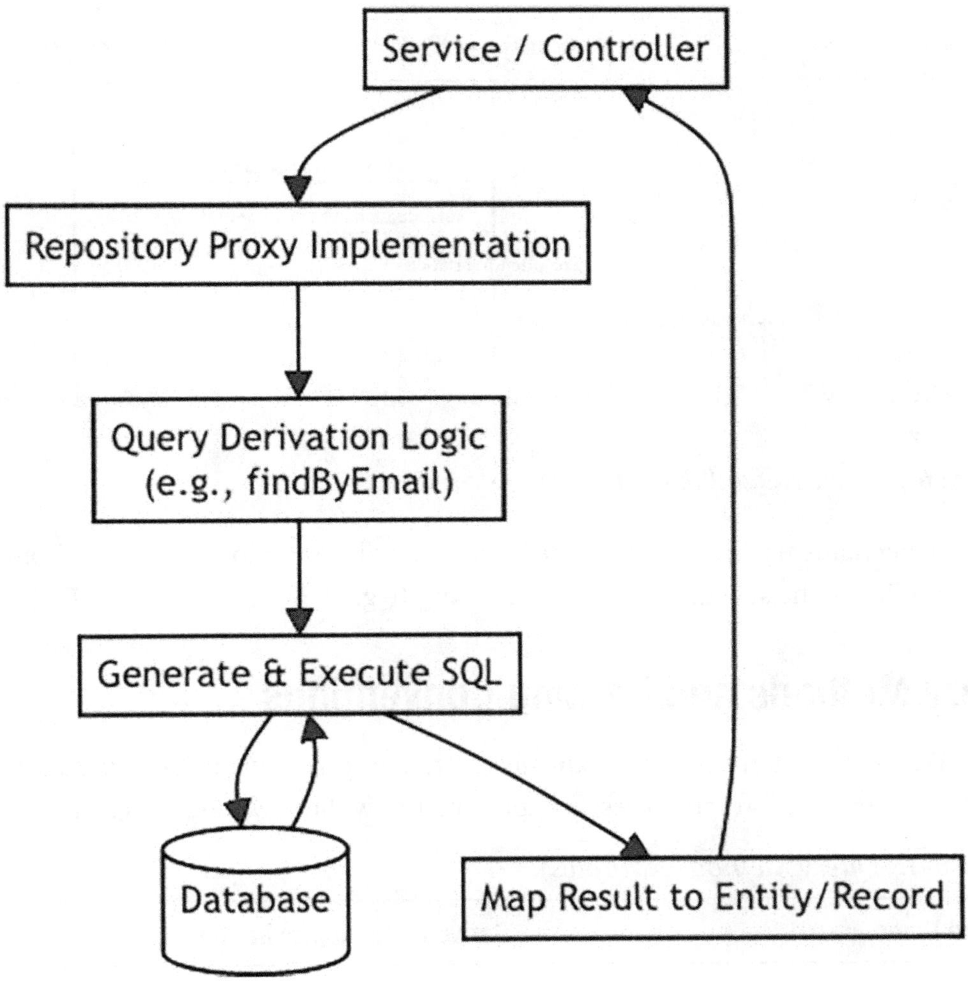

Figure 6-1. *Spring Data Proxy Repository Pattern*

- **Query Methods**: You can define queries simply by declaring method names. For example, `findByEmail(String email)` is automatically translated into the correct SQL query (`SELECT ... WHERE email = ?`).
- **Centralized Exception Translation**: All Spring Data modules automatically translate low-level datastore exceptions into Spring's uniform `DataAccessException` hierarchy.

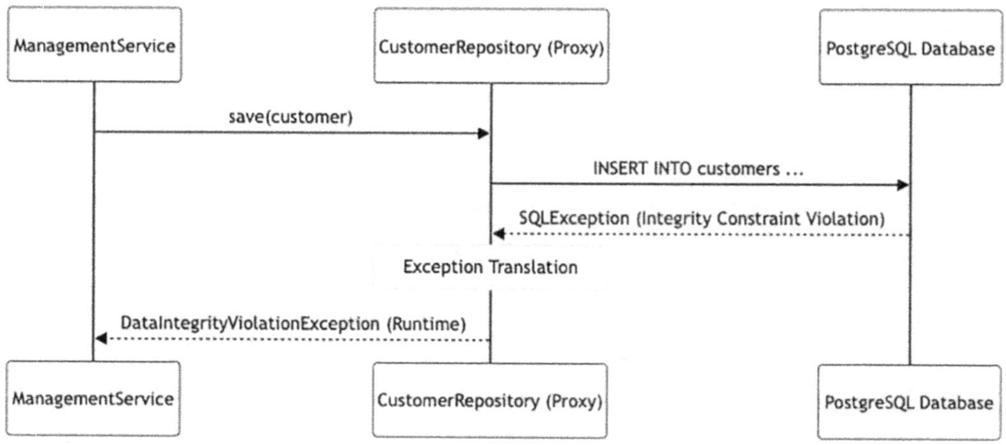

Figure 6-2. *Centralized Exception Translation*

This mechanism allows your service layer to handle exceptions cleanly without being coupled to the specific database technology (e.g., JDBC, JPA, or MongoDB).

Query Methods and Naming Conventions

Spring Data's query derivation mechanism is incredibly powerful. By following a simple naming convention, you can express complex queries without writing a single line of SQL.

Table 6-1. *Query Method Examples*

Method Name	Derived SQL (approximate)
`findByEmail(String email)`	`SELECT * FROM table WHERE email = ?`
`findByLastNameAndFirstName(String last, String first)`	`SELECT * FROM table WHERE last_name = ? AND first_name = ?`
`findByAgeGreaterThan(int age)`	`SELECT * FROM table WHERE age > ?`
`findByStartDateBetween(Date start, Date end)`	`SELECT * FROM table WHERE start_date BETWEEN ? AND ?`
`findByLastNameLike(String pattern)`	`SELECT * FROM table WHERE last_name LIKE ?`
`findByActiveTrue()`	`SELECT * FROM table WHERE active = true`
`findFirst3ByOrderByLastNameAsc()`	`SELECT * FROM table ORDER BY last_name ASC LIMIT 3`

Spring Data JDBC with the Customer CRM

Spring Data JDBC is often described as a "middle ground" between the manual control of `JdbcClient` and the complexity of JPA. It provides a simple, opinionated ORM that maps your domain objects to relational database tables without the overhead of a heavy persistence context.

Key Features

- **Aggregate-Oriented**: Spring Data JDBC is built around the concept of aggregates. An aggregate is a cluster of domain objects that can be treated as a single unit. When you save the root of an aggregate, Spring Data JDBC saves the entire object graph.
- **No Lazy Loading**: It fetches all data eagerly. This eliminates the dreaded `LazyInitializationException` but requires you to model your aggregates carefully to avoid loading too much data.
- **No Caching**: There is no first-level cache or dirty checking. Every `save()` triggers an `INSERT` or `UPDATE`, and every `find()` triggers a `SELECT`. This makes the behavior predictable and easy to debug.
- **Simple Annotations**: It uses a minimal set of annotations (e.g., `@Id`, `@Table`, `@Column`) that are separate from JPA, keeping your domain model clean.

When to Use It

Spring Data JDBC is an excellent choice for:

- **Microservices**: Where domain models are bounded and aggregates are naturally small.
- **High-Throughput Systems**: Where the overhead of JPA's dirty checking and state management is undesirable.
- **Clean Architecture**: When you want to keep your domain model decoupled from complex ORM specifications.

Let's refactor our **Customer CRM** (Maven) project to use Spring Data JDBC.

Dependencies

First, we need to update our pom.xml to include the spring-boot-starter-data-jdbc dependency and spring-boot-starter-validation.

Listing 6-1. pom.xml

```
<dependencies>
    <dependency>
        <groupId>org.springframework.boot</groupId>
        <artifactId>spring-boot-starter-webmvc</artifactId>
    </dependency>
    <dependency>
        <groupId>org.springframework.boot</groupId>
        <artifactId>spring-boot-starter-validation</artifactId>
    </dependency>
    <dependency>
        <groupId>org.springframework.boot</groupId>
        <artifactId>spring-boot-starter-data-jdbc</artifactId>
    </dependency>
    <dependency>
        <groupId>com.h2database</groupId>
        <artifactId>h2</artifactId>
        <scope>runtime</scope>
    </dependency>
    <dependency>
        <groupId>org.postgresql</groupId>
        <artifactId>postgresql</artifactId>
        <scope>runtime</scope>
    </dependency>
    <dependency>
        <groupId>org.springframework.boot</groupId>
        <artifactId>spring-boot-starter-test</artifactId>
        <scope>test</scope>
    </dependency>
</dependencies>
```

Domain Model Annotation

Spring Data JDBC works exceptionally well with immutable aggregates. Unlike JPA, which often requires mutable entities with no-arg constructors, Spring Data JDBC is designed to map data directly to immutable objects. Therefore, we will switch our `Customer` model from a standard Java class to a **Java Record**.

A critical detail when using manually assigned primary keys (like UUIDs generated in the application) is the use of the `Persistable` interface. By default, Spring Data determines if an entity is new by checking if its ID is `null`. If we assign the ID ourselves before saving, Spring Data might mistakenly try to perform an `UPDATE` instead of a direct `INSERT`. Implementing `Persistable` allows us to explicitly tell Spring Data when an entity is new, optimizing performance and ensuring correct behavior.

Listing 6-2. src/main/java/com/apress/crm/customer/Customer.java

```
package com.apress.crm.customer;

import jakarta.validation.constraints.Email;
import jakarta.validation.constraints.NotBlank;
import org.springframework.data.annotation.Id;
import org.springframework.data.domain.Persistable;
import org.springframework.data.relational.core.mapping.Table;

import java.util.UUID;

@Table("customers")
public record Customer(
    @Id UUID id,
    @NotBlank(message = "Name is required") String name,
    @NotBlank(message = "Email is required") @Email(message =
    "Invalid email format") String email, String phone) implements
    Persistable<UUID> {

    @Override
    public UUID getId() {
        return id;
    }
```

```
    @Override
    public boolean isNew() {
        return id == null;
    }
}
```

The Repository Interface

Instead of writing a class that manually constructs SQL queries, we simply extend `ListCrudRepository`.

Listing 6-3. src/main/java/com/apress/crm/customer/CustomerRepository.java

```
package com.apress.crm.customer;

import org.springframework.data.repository.ListCrudRepository;
import java.util.UUID;
import java.util.List;

public interface CustomerRepository extends
ListCrudRepository<Customer, UUID> {

    List<Customer> findByEmail(String email);

    List<Customer> findByName(String name);

    List<Customer> findByEmailEndingWith(String domain);
}
```

Using the Repository in a Controller

With the repository defined, our web layer becomes extremely lean. We can inject the `CustomerRepository` directly into our controller.

Listing 6-4. src/main/java/com/apress/crm/customer/CustomerController.java

```
package com.apress.crm.customer;

import org.springframework.http.HttpStatus;
import org.springframework.web.bind.annotation.*;
import org.springframework.web.server.ResponseStatusException;

import java.util.UUID;

@RestController @RequestMapping("/api/v1/customers")
public class CustomerController {

    private final CustomerRepository repository;

    public CustomerController(CustomerRepository repository) {
        this.repository = repository;
    }

    @GetMapping
    Iterable<Customer> findAll() {
        return repository.findAll();
    }

    @GetMapping("/{id}")
    Customer findById(@PathVariable UUID id) {
        return repository.findById(id)
                .orElseThrow(() -> new ResponseStatusException(HttpStatus.
                NOT_FOUND, "Customer not found"));
    }

    @PostMapping @ResponseStatus(HttpStatus.CREATED)
    Customer save(@RequestBody @jakarta.validation.Valid Customer
    customer) {
        return repository.save(customer);
    }

    @DeleteMapping("/{id}")
    @ResponseStatus(HttpStatus.NO_CONTENT)
```

```
    void deleteById(@PathVariable UUID id) {
        repository.deleteById(id);
    }
}
```

Testing with @SpringBootTest

While `@DataJdbcTest` is excellent for testing the repository in isolation, sometimes you want to test within the full application context. We can use `@SpringBootTest` for a complete integration test.

Listing 6-5. src/test/java/com/apress/crm/customer/CustomerRepositoryTest.java

```
package com.apress.crm.customer;

import org.junit.jupiter.api.Test;
import org.springframework.beans.factory.annotation.Autowired;
import org.springframework.boot.test.context.SpringBootTest;
import org.springframework.transaction.annotation.Transactional;

import java.util.List;
import java.util.Optional;
import java.util.UUID;

import static org.assertj.core.api.Assertions.assertThat;

@SpringBootTest(properties = "spring.datasource.url=jdbc:h2:mem:customer_
repo_test")
@Transactional
class CustomerRepositoryTest {

    @Autowired
    private CustomerRepository repository;

    @Test
    void shouldSaveAndFindCustomer() {
        Customer customer = new Customer(null, "John Doe", "john.doe@
        example.com", "1234567890");
```

```
        Customer saved = repository.save(customer);

        assertThat(saved.id()).isNotNull();

        Optional<Customer> found = repository.findById(saved.id());
        assertThat(found).isPresent();
        assertThat(found.get().name()).isEqualTo("John Doe");
    }

    @Test
    void shouldFindAllCustomers() {
        repository.save(new Customer(null, "User 1", "user1@example.com",
        "111"));
        repository.save(new Customer(null, "User 2", "user2@example.com",
        "222"));

        Iterable<Customer> all = repository.findAll();
        assertThat(all).hasSizeGreaterThanOrEqualTo(2);
    }

    @Test
    void shouldDeleteCustomer() {
        Customer saved = repository.save(new Customer(null, "To Delete",
        "delete@example.com", "000"));
        UUID id = saved.id();

        repository.deleteById(id);

        assertThat(repository.findById(id)).isEmpty();
    }

    @Test
    void shouldFindByName() {
        repository.save(new Customer(null, "Felipe", "felipe@example.com",
        "123"));
        List<Customer> result = repository.findByName("Felipe");
        assertThat(result).isNotEmpty();
        assertThat(result.get(0).name()).isEqualTo("Felipe");
    }
```

```
    @Test
    void shouldFindByEmailEndingWith() {
        repository.save(new Customer(null, "Josh", "josh@spring.io", "123"));
        List<Customer> result = repository.findByEmailEndingWith
        ("%spring.io");
        assertThat(result).isNotEmpty();
        assertThat(result.get(0).name()).isEqualTo("Josh");
    }
}
```

Spring Data JPA with the Management CRM

While Spring Data JDBC is great for simple aggregates, **Spring Data JPA** shines when you need full Object-Relational Mapping (ORM) capabilities for complex domain models.

Dependencies

Update your `build.gradle` to use `spring-boot-starter-data-jpa` and `spring-boot-starter-validation`.

Listing 6-6. build.gradle

```
dependencies {
    implementation 'org.springframework.boot:spring-boot-starter-web'
    implementation 'org.springframework.boot:spring-boot-starter-
    validation'
    implementation 'org.springframework.boot:spring-boot-starter-data-jpa'
    runtimeOnly 'org.postgresql:postgresql'
    runtimeOnly 'com.h2database:h2'
    testImplementation 'org.springframework.boot:spring-boot-starter-test'
}
```

Annotating Entities with JPA

Note that for JPA entities, we typically use standard Java **Classes** because JPA providers require mutability and proxying.

Listing 6-7. src/main/java/com/apress/crm/management/model/Customer.java

```
package com.apress.crm.management.model;

import jakarta.persistence.*;
import jakarta.validation.constraints.Email;
import jakarta.validation.constraints.NotBlank;
import java.util.UUID;
import java.util.List;

@Entity
@Table(name = "customer")
public class Customer {

    @Id
    @GeneratedValue(strategy = GenerationType.UUID)
    private UUID customerId;

    @NotBlank(message = "First name is required")
    private String firstName;

    @NotBlank(message = "Last name is required")
    private String lastName;

    private String jobTitle;

    @NotBlank(message = "Email is required")
    @Email(message = "Email must be valid")
    private String email;

    private String phone;

    @ManyToOne
    @JoinColumn(name = "company_id")
    private Company company;
```

```
    @OneToMany(mappedBy = "customer", cascade = CascadeType.ALL,
    orphanRemoval = true)
    private List<Address> addresses;

    // Constructors, Getters, and Setters omitted
}
```

Key Annotations:

- **@Entity**: Marks the class as a JPA entity.
- **@GeneratedValue**: Instructs the provider to generate the ID (automatically handling UUIDs).
- **@ManyToOne/@OneToMany**: Defines the relationships between tables.
- **@JoinColumn**: Specifies the foreign key column in the database table. It is used on the "owning side" of a relationship (usually the ManyToOne side) to indicate which column links back to the target entity. For example, in our Address entity, `@JoinColumn(name = "customer_id")` tells JPA that the `customer_id` column in the `addresses` table holds the reference to the `Customer` primary key.

Listing 6-8. src/main/java/com/apress/crm/management/model/Address.java

```
package com.apress.crm.management.model;

import jakarta.persistence.*;
import jakarta.validation.constraints.NotBlank;
import java.util.UUID;

@Entity
@Table(name = "address")
public class Address {

    @Id
    @GeneratedValue(strategy = GenerationType.UUID)
    private UUID addressId;

    @ManyToOne
    @JoinColumn(name = "customer_id")
    private Customer customer;
```

```
    @NotBlank(message = "Street is required")
    private String street;

    @NotBlank(message = "City is required")
    private String city;

    @NotBlank(message = "State is required")
    private String state;

    @NotBlank(message = "Zip is required")
    private String zip;

    // Constructors, Getters, and Setters omitted
}
```

To keep our examples focused, we only show key entities here. You can download the complete source code for all models (including `Company` and `Communication`) and services from the Apress website.

The JPA Repository

Extend `JpaRepository` to unlock JPA-specific features.

Listing 6-9. src/main/java/com/apress/crm/management/repository/CustomerRepository.java

```
package com.apress.crm.management.repository;

import com.apress.crm.management.model.Customer;
import org.springframework.data.domain.Page;
import org.springframework.data.domain.Pageable;
import org.springframework.data.jpa.repository.JpaRepository;
import org.springframework.data.jpa.repository.Query;
import java.util.UUID;
import java.util.List;

public interface CustomerRepository extends JpaRepository<Customer, UUID> {

    List<Customer> findByLastName(String lastName);
```

```
    @Query("SELECT c FROM Customer c WHERE c.email LIKE %:domain")
    List<Customer> findByEmailDomain(String domain);

    @Query("SELECT c FROM Customer c JOIN FETCH c.company WHERE c.email =
    :email")

    Customer findByEmailWithCompany(String email);

    Page<Customer> findByCompanyCompanyId(UUID companyId, Pageable
    pageable);
}
```

Listing 6-10. src/main/java/com/apress/crm/management/repository/AddressRepository.java

```
package com.apress.crm.management.repository;

import com.apress.crm.management.model.Address;
import org.springframework.data.jpa.repository.JpaRepository;
import org.springframework.data.jpa.repository.Query;
import java.util.UUID;
import java.util.List;

public interface AddressRepository extends JpaRepository<Address, UUID> {

    @Query("SELECT a FROM Address a JOIN FETCH a.customer WHERE a.city
    = :city")
    List<Address> findByCityWithCustomer(String city);

    List<Address> findByCustomerCustomerId(UUID customerId);
}
```

Listing 6-11. src/main/java/com/apress/crm/management/repository/CommunicationRepository.java

```
package com.apress.crm.management.repository;

import com.apress.crm.management.model.Communication;
import org.springframework.data.jpa.repository.JpaRepository;
import java.util.UUID;
import java.util.List;
```

```
public interface CommunicationRepository extends
JpaRepository<Communication, UUID> {

    List<Communication> findByCustomerCustomerId(UUID customerId);
}
```

Simplifying Business Logic with JPA

With JPA's **Cascading** feature, coordinating multiple writes becomes trivial. The following service demonstrates how we can persist an entire object graph in a single transactional method.

Listing 6-12. src/main/java/com/apress/crm/management/service/ManagementService.java

```
package com.apress.crm.management.service;

import com.apress.crm.management.model.Address;
import com.apress.crm.management.model.Communication;
import com.apress.crm.management.model.Company;
import com.apress.crm.management.model.Customer;
import com.apress.crm.management.model.CustomerDetailsDTO;
import com.apress.crm.management.repository.AddressRepository;
import com.apress.crm.management.repository.CommunicationRepository;
import com.apress.crm.management.repository.CompanyRepository;
import com.apress.crm.management.repository.CustomerRepository;
import org.springframework.stereotype.Service;
import org.springframework.transaction.annotation.Transactional;

import java.util.List;
import java.util.UUID;
import java.util.stream.Collectors;
import java.util.stream.StreamSupport;

@Service
public class ManagementService {

    private final CustomerRepository customerRepository;
    private final AddressRepository addressRepository;
```

```
    private final CommunicationRepository communicationRepository;
    private final CompanyRepository companyRepository;

    public ManagementService(CustomerRepository customerRepository,
    AddressRepository addressRepository,
                             CommunicationRepository communicationRepository,
                             CompanyRepository companyRepository) {
        this.customerRepository = customerRepository;
        this.addressRepository = addressRepository;
        this.communicationRepository = communicationRepository;
        this.companyRepository = companyRepository;
    }

    @Transactional
    public CustomerDetailsDTO createCustomerWithDetails(Customer customer,
    Company company, Address address, Communication communication) {
        // We save the company first to ensure it has a generated ID
        Company savedCompany = this.companyRepository.save(company);

        // Update customer with saved company
        customer.setCompany(savedCompany);

        // We assume ID is generated if null. JPA usually ignores
        set ID for
        // generated strategy unless we merge.
        Customer customerToSave = new Customer(null, customer.
        getFirstName(),
                   customer.getLastName(), customer.getJobTitle(),
                   customer.getEmail(), customer.getPhone(), savedCompany);
                   Customer savedCustomer = this.customerRepository.
                   save(customerToSave);

        // Coordination of multiple repository calls within a single
        transaction
        Address addressToSave = new Address(null, savedCustomer, address.
        getStreet(), address.getCity(), address.getState(), address.
        getZip());
        Address savedAddress = this.addressRepository.save(addressToSave);
```

```
        Communication communicationToSave = new Communication(null,
        savedCustomer, communication.getCommunicationType(), communication.
        getCommunicationValue());
        Communication savedCommunication = this.communicationRepository.
        save(communicationToSave);

        return new CustomerDetailsDTO(savedCustomer, savedCompany,
                                      List.of(savedAddress), List.
                                      of(savedCommunication));
    }

    @Transactional(readOnly = true)
    public CustomerDetailsDTO getCustomerDetails(UUID customerId) {
        Customer customer = this.customerRepository.findById(customerId).
        orElse(null);
        if (customer == null) {
            return null;
        }

        // Company is accessible via the entity relationship
        Company company = customer.getCompany();

        List<Address> addresses = StreamSupport.stream(
                this.addressRepository.findByCustomerCustomerId(customer
                Id).spliterator(), false)
                .collect(Collectors.toList());

        List<Communication> communications = StreamSupport.stream(
                this.communicationRepository.findByCustomerCustomerId(
                customerId).spliterator(), false)
                .collect(Collectors.toList());

        return new CustomerDetailsDTO(customer, company, addresses,
        communications);
    }
}
```

Key Implementation Points:

- **Repository Coordination**: Even though JPA can handle cascading, sometimes manual coordination is clearer. Here we save the `Company` first to ensure its foreign key is available for the `Customer`.
- **Generated IDs**: Note that we pass `null` for IDs. Spring Data JPA and the underlying provider (Hibernate) will automatically generate UUIDs based on our `@GeneratedValue` configuration.
- **Transactional Boundaries**: The entire `createCustomerWithDetails` method is atomic. If saving the address fails, the company and customer inserts will be rolled back.

Pagination and Sorting

Handling large datasets is straightforward with `Pageable`.

Listing 6-13. src/main/java/com/apress/crm/management/service/ManagementService.java

```java
public Page<Customer> getCustomersByCompany(UUID companyId, int page,
int size) {
    Pageable pageable = PageRequest.of(page, size, Sort.by("lastName").
    ascending());
    return customerRepository.findByCompanyId(companyId, pageable);
}
```

Testing with @SpringBootTest

While Spring Data provides specialized test slices like `@DataJpaTest`, in complex projects like the **Management CRM**, we often need to test the interaction between multiple repositories and services within the full application context. Using `@SpringBootTest` allows us to verify our data access layer while ensuring all custom configurations and beans are correctly loaded.

Listing 6-14. src/test/java/com/apress/crm/management/repository/ManagementCustomerRepositoryTest.java

```
package com.apress.crm.management.repository;

import com.apress.crm.management.model.Company;
import com.apress.crm.management.model.Customer;
import org.junit.jupiter.api.Test;
import org.springframework.beans.factory.annotation.Autowired;
import org.springframework.boot.test.context.SpringBootTest;
import org.springframework.data.domain.Page;
import org.springframework.data.domain.PageRequest;
import org.springframework.transaction.annotation.Transactional;

import java.util.List;
import java.util.Optional;
import java.util.UUID;

import static org.assertj.core.api.Assertions.assertThat;

@SpringBootTest @Transactional
class ManagementCustomerRepositoryTest {

    @Autowired
    private CustomerRepository repository;

    @Autowired
    private CompanyRepository companyRepository;

    @Test
    void findByIdShouldReturnCustomer() {
        // Given
        Customer customer = new Customer(null, "Sundar", "Pichai", "CEO",
                "sundar@google.com", "111-222-3333", null);
        Customer saved = repository.save(customer);

        // When
        Optional<Customer> result = repository.findById(saved.
        getCustomerId());
```

```
        // Then
        assertThat(result).isPresent();
        assertThat(result.get().getFirstName()).isEqualTo("Sundar");
        assertThat(result.get().getJobTitle()).isEqualTo("CEO");
    }

    @Test
    void shouldFindAllCustomers() {
        // Given
        repository.save(new Customer(null, "John", "Doe", "Dev", "john@
        example.com", "123", null));
        repository.save(new Customer(null, "Jane", "Doe", "Mgr", "jane@
        example.com", "456", null));

        // When
        Iterable<Customer> customers = repository.findAll();

        // Then
        assertThat(customers).hasSizeGreaterThanOrEqualTo(2);
    }

    @Test
    void shouldFindByLastName() {
        // Given
        repository.save(new Customer(null, "Felipe", "Gutierrez", "Author",
        "felipe@example.com", "123", null));

        // When
        List<Customer> result = repository.findByLastName("Gutierrez");

        // Then
        assertThat(result).isNotEmpty();
        assertThat(result.get(0).getFirstName()).isEqualTo("Felipe");
    }

    @Test
    void shouldFindByEmailDomain() {
        // Given
```

```
        repository.save(new Customer(null, "Josh", "Long", "Advocate",
        "josh@spring.io", "123", null));

        // When
        List<Customer> result = repository.findByEmailDomain("spring.io");

        // Then
        assertThat(result).isNotEmpty();
        assertThat(result.get(0).getFirstName()).isEqualTo("Josh");
    }

    @Test
    void shouldFindByEmailWithCompany() {
        // Given
        Company company = companyRepository.save(new Company(null,
        "Google", "Tech", "google.com"));
        repository.save(new Customer(null, "Sundar", "Pichai", "CEO",
        "sundar@google.com", "111", company));

        // When
        Customer result = repository.findByEmailWithCompany("sundar@
        google.com");

        // Then
        assertThat(result).isNotNull();
        assertThat(result.getCompany()).isNotNull();
        assertThat(result.getCompany().getCompanyName()).
        isEqualTo("Google");
    }

    @Test
    void shouldFindByCompanyCompanyIdWithPagination() {
        // Given
        Company company = companyRepository.save(new Company(null,
        "Apress", "Publishing", "apress.com"));
        repository.save(new Customer(null, "User 1", "Test", "Dev", "user1@
        apress.com", "1", company));
```

```
        repository.save(new Customer(null, "User 2", "Test", "Dev", "user2@
        apress.com", "2", company));
        repository.save(new Customer(null, "User 3", "Test", "Dev", "user3@
        apress.com", "3", company));

        // When
        Page<Customer> page = repository.findByCompanyCompanyId(company.
        getCompanyId(), PageRequest.of(0, 2));

        // Then
        assertThat(page.getContent()).hasSize(2);
        assertThat(page.getTotalElements()).isEqualTo(3);
    }
}
```

We also verify the relationship traversal in our AddressRepository.

Listing 6-15. src/test/java/com/apress/crm/management/repository/ManagementAddressRepositoryTest.java

```
package com.apress.crm.management.repository;

import com.apress.crm.management.model.Address;
import com.apress.crm.management.model.Customer;
import org.junit.jupiter.api.Test;
import org.springframework.beans.factory.annotation.Autowired;
import org.springframework.boot.test.context.SpringBootTest;
import org.springframework.transaction.annotation.Transactional;

import java.util.List;

import static org.assertj.core.api.Assertions.assertThat;

@SpringBootTest @Transactional
class ManagementAddressRepositoryTest {

    @Autowired
    private AddressRepository addressRepository;
```

```
    @Autowired
    private CustomerRepository customerRepository;

    @Test
    void shouldFindByCityWithCustomer() {
        // Given
        Customer customer = customerRepository.save(new Customer(null,
        "John", "Doe", "Dev", "john@example.com", "123", null));
        addressRepository.save(new Address(null, customer, "123 Main St",
        "TestCity", "NY", "10001"));

        // When
        List<Address> result = addressRepository.findByCityWithCustomer
        ("TestCity");

        // Then
        assertThat(result).isNotEmpty();
        assertThat(result.get(0).getCustomer()).isNotNull();
        assertThat(result.get(0).getCustomer().getFirstName()).
        isEqualTo("John");
    }
}
```

Key Implementation Points:

- **`@SpringBootTest`**: Bootstraps the entire application context, providing a real-world testing environment where all services and configurations are active.
- **Transactional Rollback**: By using `@Transactional` at the class level, every test method runs within its own transaction, which is automatically rolled back at the end. This ensures a clean state for each test without needing manual cleanup.
- **Relationship Verification**: These tests explicitly verify that JPA correctly handles entity links (e.g., between `Customer` and `Company`) during both save and retrieve operations.

- **Pagination Verification**: We use PageRequest to verify that our repositories correctly return paginated subsets of data, a crucial feature for enterprise-grade APIs.

Comparison: Spring Data Common vs. JDBC vs. JPA

Table 6-2. *Spring Data Module Comparison*

Feature	Spring Data Common	Spring Data JDBC	Spring Data JPA
Role	Base infrastructure	Simple, DDD-focused ORM	Full-featured ORM
Core Interfaces	`Repository`, `CrudRepository`	`ListCrudRepository`	`JpaRepository`
Annotations	`@Id`, `@CreatedBy`, `@Version`	`@Table`, `@Column`, `@Query`	`@Entity`, `@Table`, `@OneToMany`
Query Logic	Definition via method name	Direct SQL generation	JPQL, Criteria API, SQL
Best Use Case	Shared across all modules	Microservices, simple aggregates	Complex graphs, legacy databases

Advanced AOT: Optimizing for Native Images

One of the most significant advancements in Spring Boot 4 is the deepened support for GraalVM Native Images. While basic AOT support has been present since Spring Boot 3, Spring Data 4 introduces specialized **AOT Repository processing**.

While we introduce the concept of AOT here in the context of data access, we will explore the internal mechanics of Ahead-of-Time compilation and GraalVM Native Images in much greater depth in Chapter 14.

Pre-generating Repositories

In a standard JVM execution, Spring Data repositories are implemented at runtime using dynamic proxies and reflection. This is flexible but starts slowly.

For Native Images, reflection is costly. Spring Data AOT processing now inspects your repository interfaces at **build time**. It pre-generates the backing implementation classes and even pre-computes the SQL or JPQL queries derived from method names. This means:

1. **Faster Startup**: No runtime parsing of query methods.
2. **Reduced Memory**: Less metadata is required at runtime.
3. **Compile-Time Safety**: Some query errors can be caught during the build process rather than at runtime.

This happens automatically when you build with the native profile (`./gradlew nativeCompile`), but knowing it helps you understand why your build times might be slightly longer for the benefit of instant startup.

Explicit Hints with @RegisterReflectionForBinding

Sometimes, you might return a DTO or a Record from a query that isn't a managed Entity. If this DTO is only used in a custom `@Query` and nowhere else, the AOT processor might miss it, leading to a runtime error in the native image.

Spring Framework 7 introduces `@RegisterReflectionForBinding` to easily solve this without complex configuration files.

Listing 6-16. src/main/java/com/apress/crm/management/repository/CustomerRepository.java

```java
import org.springframework.aot.hint.annotation.RegisterReflectionForBinding;

@Repository
public interface CustomerRepository extends JpaRepository<Customer, UUID> {

    @Query("SELECT new com.apress.crm.dto.CustomerSummary(c.firstName,
    c.email) FROM Customer c")
    @RegisterReflectionForBinding(CustomerSummary.class)
    List<CustomerSummary> findSummaries();
}
```

- **`@RegisterReflectionForBinding`**: Explicitly tells the AOT processor to generate reflection hints for the `CustomerSummary` record, ensuring it can be instantiated by the persistence provider at runtime.

Summary

In this chapter, we ascended the ladder of abstraction. We moved from writing manual SQL with `JdbcClient` to leveraging the automated power of **Spring Data**.

We refactored our **Customer CRM** to use **Spring Data JDBC**, enjoying a simpler code base that focuses on domain aggregates. We then implemented the data layer for our **Management CRM** using **Spring Data JPA**, unlocking the full power of Object-Relational Mapping for handling complex entity relationships.

By understanding the strengths and trade-offs of each approach, you can now make informed decisions about which data access technology best fits the specific requirements of your Spring Boot applications.

CHAPTER 7

NoSQL with Spring Boot

In the previous chapters, we focused on relational databases and how Spring Data simplifies interactions with them. However, the modern data landscape is diverse. Nowadays, applications frequently require the horizontal scalability of document stores, the lightning speed of in-memory key-value caches, or the complex relationship traversal of graph databases.

In this chapter, we will explore how Spring Boot 4 and Spring Data provide a consistent programming model for NoSQL technologies. We will refactor our projects to leverage MongoDB, Redis, and Neo4j, while also touching upon the burgeoning trend of Vector Search for AI applications.

Document Persistence with Spring Data MongoDB

MongoDB is the leading document-oriented NoSQL database. Instead of tables and rows, it stores data in flexible, JSON-like BSON documents. This schema-less nature makes it ideal for rapid development and evolving domain models.

Key Features

- **`MongoRepository`**: Extends the standard Spring Data repository model with MongoDB-specific operations like geo-spatial queries.
- **`MongoTemplate`**: Provides a lower-level, fluent API for complex aggregations and custom updates.
- **GridFS Support**: A specification for storing and retrieving large files (like images or videos) that exceed the BSON-document size limit.
- **Transaction Support**: Full multi-document ACID transactions, allowing MongoDB to handle complex business logic similar to relational databases.

F. Gutierrez and D. Carter, *Pro Spring Boot 4*, https://doi.org/10.1007/979-8-8688-2640-5_7

Best Practices

1. **Use Records**: MongoDB maps exceptionally well to Java Records, promoting immutability in your document structure.
2. **Implement `Persistable`**: As with JDBC, when using manually assigned IDs, implementing `Persistable` prevents unnecessary "existence checks" (SELECTs) before an insert.
3. **Index Management**: Use the `@Indexed` annotation to define indexes directly in your Java code, ensuring queries remain performant as your dataset grows.

Implementation: Customer CRM (Maven)

Let's refactor the **Customer CRM** to use MongoDB. We start by updating the dependencies in the `pom.xml`.

Listing 7-1. pom.xml

```xml
<dependencies>
    <dependency>
        <groupId>org.springframework.boot</groupId>
        <artifactId>spring-boot-starter-data-mongodb</artifactId>
    </dependency>
    <dependency>
        <groupId>org.springframework.boot</groupId>
        <artifactId>spring-boot-starter-validation</artifactId>
    </dependency>
    <dependency>
        <groupId>org.springframework.boot</groupId>
        <artifactId>spring-boot-starter-test</artifactId>
        <scope>test</scope>
    </dependency>
    <dependency>
        <groupId>org.springframework.boot</groupId>
        <artifactId>spring-boot-testcontainers</artifactId>
        <scope>test</scope>
```

```
    </dependency>
    <dependency>
        <groupId>org.testcontainers</groupId>
        <artifactId>mongodb</artifactId>
        <scope>test</scope>
    </dependency>
    <dependency>
        <groupId>org.testcontainers</groupId>
        <artifactId>junit-jupiter</artifactId>
        <scope>test</scope>
    </dependency>
</dependencies>
```

Next, we annotate our `Customer` Record. Notice the use of `@Document` and the implementation of `Persistable`. In this implementation, we use a `String` for the identifier to match MongoDB's natural `ObjectId` or any custom string ID.

Listing 7-2. src/main/java/com/apress/crm/customer/Customer.java

```java
package com.apress.crm.customer;

import jakarta.validation.constraints.Email;
import jakarta.validation.constraints.NotBlank;
import org.springframework.data.annotation.Id;
import org.springframework.data.domain.Persistable;
import org.springframework.data.mongodb.core.mapping.Document;

@Document(collection = "customers")
public record Customer(
    @Id String id,
    @NotBlank(message = "Name is required") String name,
    @NotBlank(message = "Email is required") @Email(message = "Email must
    be valid") String email, String phone
) implements Persistable<String> {

    public Customer(String name, String email, String phone) {
        this(null, name, email, phone);
    }
```

```
    @Override
    public String getId() { return id; }

    @Override
    public boolean isNew() { return id == null; }
}
```

The repository interface remains consistent with our previous Spring Data examples, providing several derived query methods.

Listing 7-3. src/main/java/com/apress/crm/customer/CustomerRepository.java

```
package com.apress.crm.customer;

import org.springframework.data.mongodb.repository.MongoRepository;
import java.util.List;

public interface CustomerRepository extends MongoRepository<Customer,
String> {
    List<Customer> findByName(String name);
    List<Customer> findByEmailEndingWith(String domain);
}
```

Key Implementation Points:

- **`@Document`**: Maps the Record to the `customers` collection.
- **`Persistable<String>`**: Crucial for performance when using application-generated IDs. It tells Spring Data whether to perform an `insert` or `update` without an extra database lookup.
- **Query Derivation**: Spring Data MongoDB automatically implements the `findByName` and `findByEmailEndingWith` methods by parsing their names and generating the appropriate BSON query filters.

Testing with Testcontainers

While `@DataMongoTest` can use an embedded MongoDB, the professional approach in Spring Boot 4 is using **Testcontainers**.

Why Testcontainers? Relying on "embedded" versions of databases can lead to false positives in your tests. Embedded databases often implement only a subset of the real database's features and may behave differently in edge cases. Testcontainers allows you to spin up a real, containerized version of MongoDB, ensuring your tests run against the exact same engine you use in production.

While we introduce Testcontainers here, we will take a much deeper dive into its advanced configurations in Chapter 10.

Listing 7-4. src/test/java/com/apress/crm/customer/CustomerRepositoryTest.java

```
package com.apress.crm.customer;

import org.junit.jupiter.api.Test;
import org.springframework.beans.factory.annotation.Autowired;
import org.springframework.boot.test.autoconfigure.data.mongo.Data
MongoTest;
import org.springframework.boot.testcontainers.service.connection.Service
Connection;
import org.testcontainers.containers.MongoDBContainer;
import org.testcontainers.junit.jupiter.Container;
import org.testcontainers.junit.jupiter.Testcontainers;

import java.util.List;
import java.util.Optional;

import static org.assertj.core.api.Assertions.assertThat;

@DataMongoTest @Testcontainers
class CustomerRepositoryTest {

    @Container @ServiceConnection
    static MongoDBContainer mongo = new MongoDBContainer("mongo:7.0");

    @Autowired
    private CustomerRepository repository;
```

```
@Test
void shouldSaveAndFindCustomer() {
    Customer customer = new Customer("John Doe", "john.doe@example.
    com", "1234567890");
    Customer saved = repository.save(customer);

    assertThat(saved.id()).isNotNull();

    Optional<Customer> found = repository.findById(saved.id());
    assertThat(found).isPresent();
    assertThat(found.get().name()).isEqualTo("John Doe");
}

@Test
void shouldFindAllCustomers() {
    repository.save(new Customer("User 1", "user1@example.com", "111"));
    repository.save(new Customer("User 2", "user2@example.com", "222"));

    List<Customer> all = repository.findAll();
    assertThat(all).hasSizeGreaterThanOrEqualTo(2);
}

@Test
void shouldDeleteCustomer() {
    Customer saved = repository.save(new Customer("To Delete",
        "delete@example.com", "000"));
    String id = saved.id();

    repository.deleteById(id);

    assertThat(repository.findById(id)).isEmpty();
}

@Test
void shouldFindByName() {
    repository.save(new Customer("Felipe", "felipe@example.com", "123"));
    List<Customer> result = repository.findByName("Felipe");
    assertThat(result).isNotEmpty();
    assertThat(result.get(0).name()).isEqualTo("Felipe");
}
```

```
    @Test
    void shouldFindByEmailEndingWith() {
        repository.save(new Customer("Josh", "josh@spring.io", "123"));
        List<Customer> result = repository.findByEmailEndingWith(
        "spring.io");
        assertThat(result).isNotEmpty();
        assertThat(result.get(0).name()).isEqualTo("Josh");
    }
}
```

Understanding the Annotations:

1. **`@Testcontainers`**: This JUnit 5 extension automates the lifecycle of your containers. It looks for any fields annotated with `@Container` and ensures they are started before your tests run and stopped immediately after.

2. **`@Container`**: Marks the specific container instance (in this case, `MongoDBContainer`) that should be managed by the `@Testcontainers` extension.

3. **`@ServiceConnection`**: This is a game-changing feature introduced in Spring Boot 3.1 and refined in version 4.0. Historically, you had to manually extract the container's dynamic port and set a Spring property (like `spring.mongodb.uri`). `@ServiceConnection` does this automatically. It detects the type of container and configures the relevant Spring Data properties, allowing for zero-configuration integration testing.

Key-Value Persistence with Spring Data Redis

Redis is a high-performance, in-memory data structure store. While often used as a cache, it can also serve as a primary database for specific use cases like session management.

In our **Management CRM**, we will not replace our relational database with Redis. Instead, we will adopt a **Polyglot Persistence** strategy. We keep our core entities (Customer, Address, etc.) in PostgreSQL for durability and complex relationship management, while using Redis to handle highly transient, fast-changing data like user sessions and activity tracking. This allows us to leverage the unique strengths of each technology.

Key Features

- **`RedisTemplate`**: The primary entry point for low-level operations on Redis strings, lists, sets, and hashes.
- **`@RedisHash`**: Allows you to map Java objects to Redis Hashes automatically.
- **Reactive Support**: `ReactiveRedisTemplate` for non-blocking architectures.
- **TTL (Time To Live)**: Built-in support for expiring keys, making it the perfect tool for temporary data storage.
- **Pub/Sub**: Native messaging capabilities for event-driven architectures.

Best Practices

1. **Serialization**: Use `Jackson2JsonRedisSerializer` for human-readable data.
2. **Reactive Logic**: In WebFlux applications, always use `ReactiveRedisOperations`.
3. **Memory Management**: Always define an eviction policy or use TTL for temporary data.

Implementation: Management CRM (Gradle)

In our **Management CRM**, we utilize **Spring WebFlux**. To maintain a fully non-blocking stack, we must use the reactive support provided by Spring Data Redis.

Listing 7-5. build.gradle

```
dependencies {
    implementation 'org.springframework.boot:spring-boot-starter-webflux'
    implementation 'org.springframework.boot:spring-boot-starter-data-jpa'
    implementation 'org.springframework.boot:spring-boot-starter-data-
    redis-reactive'
    implementation 'org.springframework.boot:spring-boot-starter-data-neo4j'
    implementation 'org.springframework.boot:spring-boot-starter-
    validation'
    runtimeOnly 'org.postgresql:postgresql'
    testImplementation 'org.springframework.boot:spring-boot-starter-test'
    testImplementation 'org.springframework.boot:spring-boot-starter-
    webflux-test'
    testImplementation 'org.springframework.boot:spring-boot-
    testcontainers'
    testImplementation 'org.testcontainers:neo4j:1.20.4'
    testImplementation 'org.testcontainers:postgresql:1.20.4'
    testImplementation 'com.redis:testcontainers-redis:2.2.3'
    testImplementation 'org.testcontainers:junit-jupiter:1.20.4'
    testImplementation 'io.projectreactor:reactor-test'
    testRuntimeOnly 'org.junit.platform:junit-platform-launcher'
}
```

We model our session data as a **Java Record**.

Listing 7-6. src/main/java/com/apress/crm/management/model/CustomerSession.java

```
package com.apress.crm.management.model;

import java.util.UUID;

public record CustomerSession(
    String sessionId,
    UUID customerId,
    String lastAction
) {}
```

The Need for Session Management

You might wonder why a CRM needs a `CustomerSession` in Redis when we already have the customer data in Postgres. In a distributed, cloud-native environment, managing user state is a challenge. By offloading session data (like the last viewed customer, temporary authentication tokens, or transient UI state) to Redis, we achieve several goals:

1. **Stateless Applications**: Our Spring Boot application instances become truly stateless. Any instance can handle a request because the session data is shared in a central Redis store.
2. **Horizontal Scalability**: We can spin up or down dozens of application instances without losing user state (Session Persistence).
3. **Performance**: We avoid expensive relational database writes for data that changes every few seconds (like "last activity" timestamps) and automatically expires.

Orchestrating NoSQL in the Service Layer

Our **ManagementService** updates the Redis session whenever a customer detail is accessed.

Listing 7-7. src/main/java/com/apress/crm/management/service/ManagementService.java

```
@Service
public class ManagementService {
    private final CustomerRepository customerRepository;
    private final ReactiveRedisOperations<String, CustomerSession>
    sessionOps;
    private final ReferralRepository referralRepository;

    public ManagementService(CustomerRepository customerRepo,
                             ReactiveRedisOperations<String,
                                CustomerSession> ops,
```

```
                     ReferralRepository referralRepo) {
    this.customerRepository = customerRepo;
    this.sessionOps = ops;
    this.referralRepository = referralRepo;
}

/* Other methods */

@Transactional(readOnly = true)
public Mono<CustomerDetailsDTO> getCustomerWithSession(UUID
customerId) {
    return Mono.fromCallable(() -> customerRepository.
    findById(customerId))
            .subscribeOn(Schedulers.boundedElastic())
            .flatMap(customerOpt -> {
                if (customerOpt.isEmpty()) return Mono.empty();
                Customer customer = customerOpt.get();
                String key = "session:" + customerId;
                CustomerSession session = new CustomerSession(key,
                customerId, "View Details");
                return sessionOps.opsForValue()
                        .set(key, session, Duration.ofMinutes(30))
                        .thenReturn(new CustomerDetailsDTO(
                        customer, ...));
            });
}

public Mono<CustomerSession> startSession(UUID customerId) {
    String key = "session:" + customerId;
    CustomerSession session = new CustomerSession(key, customerId,
    "Login");
    return sessionOps.opsForValue()
            .set(key, session, Duration.ofMinutes(30))
            .thenReturn(session);
}
```

```
    public Mono<CustomerSession> getSession(UUID customerId) {
        return sessionOps.opsForValue().get("session:" + customerId);
    }

    public Mono<CustomerNode> addReferral(UUID customerId, UUID
    referrerId) {
        return Mono.fromCallable(() -> {
            CustomerNode node = new CustomerNode(customerId, "New
            Customer");
            referralRepository.findById(referrerId).ifPresent(referrer -> {
                referrer.getReferrals().add(node);
                referralRepository.save(referrer);
            });
            return node;
        }).subscribeOn(Schedulers.boundedElastic());
    }
}
```

Key Implementation Points:

- **Reactive Redis Operations**: We use `ReactiveRedisOperations` to perform non-blocking key-value operations. This is essential for maintaining the performance benefits of our WebFlux-based architecture.
- **Context Bridging**: The `Mono.fromCallable` combined with `subscribeOn(Schedulers.boundedElastic())` is a vital pattern for integrating blocking code (like our JPA repository or blocking Neo4j calls) into a reactive stream without blocking the main event loop.
- **Polyglot Orchestration**: The service now acts as the coordinator between the relational data (Postgres), transient session data (Redis), and relationship data (Neo4j).

Reactive Handlers and Routing

We separate the logic into a **Handler** and the mapping into a **Router**.

Listing 7-8. src/main/java/com/apress/crm/management/reactive/ManagementHandlers.java

```
package com.apress.crm.management.reactive;

import com.apress.crm.management.service.CorporateService;
import com.apress.crm.management.service.ManagementService;
import org.springframework.stereotype.Component;
import org.springframework.web.reactive.function.server.ServerRequest;
import org.springframework.web.reactive.function.server.ServerResponse;
import reactor.core.publisher.Mono;
import reactor.core.scheduler.Schedulers;
import java.util.UUID;

@Component
public class ManagementHandlers {

    private final ManagementService managementService;
    private final CorporateService corporateService;

    public ManagementHandlers(ManagementService managementService,
    CorporateService corporateService) {
        this.managementService = managementService;
        this.corporateService = corporateService;
    }

    public Mono<ServerResponse> getCustomerDetails(ServerRequest request) {
        UUID customerId = UUID.fromString(request.pathVariable("id"));
        return managementService.getCustomerWithSession(customerId)
                .flatMap(dto -> ServerResponse.ok().bodyValue(dto))
                .switchIfEmpty(ServerResponse.notFound().build());
    }

    public Mono<ServerResponse> linkCompanies(ServerRequest request) {
        String parent = request.queryParam("parent").orElseThrow();
        String subsidiary = request.queryParam("subsidiary").orElseThrow();

        return Mono.fromRunnable(() -> corporateService.
        linkSubsidiary(parent, subsidiary))
```

```
                .subscribeOn(Schedulers.boundedElastic())
                .then(ServerResponse.ok().build());
    }
}
```

Listing 7-9. src/main/java/com/apress/crm/management/configuration/ManagementConfiguration.java

```
package com.apress.crm.management.configuration;

import com.apress.crm.management.model.*;
import com.apress.crm.management.reactive.ManagementHandlers;
import com.apress.crm.management.service.ManagementService;
import org.springframework.boot.context.event.ApplicationReadyEvent;
import org.springframework.context.ApplicationListener;
import org.springframework.context.annotation.Bean;
import org.springframework.context.annotation.Configuration;
import org.springframework.web.reactive.function.server.RouterFunction;
import org.springframework.web.reactive.function.server.ServerResponse;

import static org.springframework.web.reactive.function.server.Request
Predicates.GET;
import static org.springframework.web.reactive.function.server.Request
Predicates.POST;
import static org.springframework.web.reactive.function.server.Router
Functions.route;

@Configuration
public class ManagementConfiguration {

    @Bean
    public RouterFunction<ServerResponse> managementRoutes(Management
    Handlers handlers) {
        return route(GET("/api/v1/management/customers/{id}"),
        handlers::getCustomerDetails)
                .andRoute(POST("/api/v1/management/corporate/link"),
                handlers::linkCompanies);
    }
```

```
    @Bean
    public ApplicationListener<ApplicationReadyEvent> managementReady(
    ManagementService managementService) {
        return event -> {
            // ... polyglot data initialization ...
        };
    }
}
```

Key Implementation Points:

- **Functional Endpoints**: Instead of `@RestController`, we use the functional routing model. The configuration class defines the path mapping, while the `ManagementHandlers` contains the logic.
- **Immutability and Streams**: The handler returns `Mono<ServerResponse>`, which represents a promise of an HTTP response. This allows the framework to handle the response asynchronously.

Testing with Testcontainers

For reactive applications, we combine Testcontainers with `StepVerifier`.

Listing 7-10. src/test/java/com/apress/crm/management/reactive/CustomerSessionTest.java

```
package com.apress.crm.management.reactive;

import com.apress.crm.management.BaseTest;
import com.apress.crm.management.model.CustomerSession;
import org.junit.jupiter.api.Test;
import org.springframework.beans.factory.annotation.Autowired;
import org.springframework.data.redis.core.ReactiveRedisOperations;
import reactor.core.publisher.Mono;
import reactor.test.StepVerifier;
import java.util.UUID;
```

```
class CustomerSessionTest extends BaseTest {

    @Autowired
    private ReactiveRedisOperations<String, CustomerSession> sessionOps;

    @Test
    void shouldSaveAndRetrieveSessionReactively() {
        UUID customerId = UUID.randomUUID();
        String key = "session:" + customerId;
        CustomerSession session = new CustomerSession(key, customerId,
        "Login");

        var saveAndGet = sessionOps.opsForValue()
                .set(key, session)
                .then(sessionOps.opsForValue().get(key));

        StepVerifier.create(saveAndGet)
                .expectNext(session)
                .verifyComplete();
    }
}
```

Graph Databases with Spring Data Neo4j

While relational and document databases excel at storing data, graph databases like **Neo4j** excel at traversing the **connections** between data. In a B2B Management CRM, knowing the legal structure of companies—who owns whom—is a vital requirement.

While Spring Data provides a repository abstraction for Neo4j, many professional developers prefer the **`Neo4jClient`**. This modern, fluent API allows you to write Cypher queries directly, providing maximum flexibility and avoiding the complexities of Object-Graph Mapping (OGM).

Key Features of Neo4jClient

- **Fluent API**: A chainable interface (`query()`, `bind()`, `fetch()`) that mirrors the style of `JdbcClient`.

- **Direct Cypher Control**: Execute complex pattern-matching queries without worrying about how an ORM will translate them.
- **Resource Management**: Automatically handles database connections and transaction boundaries within the Spring ecosystem.

Implementation: Corporate Hierarchy Service

To track company relationships, we'll create a `CorporateService`. This service uses Cypher's `MERGE` keyword to ensure nodes and relationships are created only if they don't already exist.

Listing 7-11. src/main/java/com/apress/crm/management/service/CorporateService.java

```
package com.apress.crm.management.service;

import org.springframework.data.neo4j.core.Neo4jClient;
import org.springframework.stereotype.Service;
import java.util.Collection;
import java.util.Map;

@Service
public class CorporateService {

    private final Neo4jClient neo4jClient;

    public CorporateService(Neo4jClient neo4jClient) {
        this.neo4jClient = neo4jClient;
    }

    public void linkSubsidiary(String parentName, String subsidiaryName) {
        String cypher = """
                MERGE (p:Company {name: $parentName})
                MERGE (s:Company {name: $subsidiaryName})
                MERGE (p)-[:OWNS]->(s)
                """;
```

```
        neo4jClient.query(cypher)
                .bind(parentName).to("parentName")
                .bind(subsidiaryName).to("subsidiaryName")
                .run();
    }

    public Collection<Map<String, Object>> getCorporateTree(String
    rootCompanyName) {
        String cypher = """
                MATCH (root:Company {name: $rootName})-[:OWNS*1..]->
                (subsidiary)
                RETURN root.name as Parent, subsidiary.name as Subsidiary
                """;

        return neo4jClient.query(cypher)
                .bind(rootCompanyName).to("rootName")
                .fetch()
                .all();
    }

    public Long countCompanies() {
        return neo4jClient.query("MATCH (c:Company) RETURN count(c)")
                .fetchAs(Long.class)
                .one()
                .orElse(0L);
    }
}
```

Key Implementation Points:

- **MERGE**: This Cypher keyword is an "upsert" for graphs. It matches existing nodes or creates new ones if they are missing.
- **Variable Binding**: `.bind(name).to("param")` protects against Cypher injection, similar to how we handled SQL in earlier chapters.
- **Path Traversal**: The `[:OWNS*1..]` syntax allows Neo4j to recursively follow ownership links to any depth, a task that would require complex recursive CTEs in a relational database.

A "Pro" Strategy for Testing Polyglot Applications

In a project using multiple NoSQL stores, starting containers in every test class is slow. A better approach is to create a `BaseTest` that manages the lifecycle of all required containers.

Listing 7-12. src/test/java/com/apress/crm/management/BaseTest.java

```
package com.apress.crm.management;

import com.redis.testcontainers.RedisContainer;
import org.springframework.boot.test.context.SpringBootTest;
import org.springframework.test.context.ActiveProfiles;
import org.springframework.test.context.DynamicPropertyRegistry;
import org.springframework.test.context.DynamicPropertySource;
import org.testcontainers.containers.Neo4jContainer;
import org.testcontainers.utility.DockerImageName;

@SpringBootTest(webEnvironment = SpringBootTest.WebEnvironment.RANDOM_PORT)
@ActiveProfiles("test")
public abstract class BaseTest {

    static final Neo4jContainer<?> neo4j;
    static final RedisContainer redis;

    static {
        neo4j = new Neo4jContainer<>(DockerImageName.parse("neo4j:5.26.0"))
                .withRandomPassword();
        redis = new RedisContainer(DockerImageName.parse("redis:alpine"));
        neo4j.start();
        redis.start();
    }

    @DynamicPropertySource
    static void configureProperties(DynamicPropertyRegistry registry) {
        registry.add("spring.neo4j.uri", neo4j::getBoltUrl);
        registry.add("spring.neo4j.authentication.username", () ->
        "neo4j");
```

```
        registry.add("spring.neo4j.authentication.password",
        neo4j::getAdminPassword);
        registry.add("spring.data.redis.host", redis::getHost);
        registry.add("spring.data.redis.port", () -> redis.
        getMappedPort(6379));
    }
}
```

- **Singleton Container Pattern**: By using a static initializer block and calling `.start()` manually, we ensure these containers are shared across all test classes that extend `BaseTest`.
- **Manual Property Mapping**: Since we aren't using `@ServiceConnection` in this pattern, we explicitly map the container's dynamic connection details to Spring's configuration properties.

Now, our specific tests can remain focused and clean by simply extending `BaseTest`.

Listing 7-13. src/test/java/com/apress/crm/management/service/CorporateStructureTest.java

```
package com.apress.crm.management.service;

import com.apress.crm.management.BaseTest;
import org.junit.jupiter.api.Test;
import org.springframework.beans.factory.annotation.Autowired;
import java.util.Collection;
import java.util.Map;
import static org.assertj.core.api.Assertions.assertThat;

class CorporateStructureTest extends BaseTest {

    @Autowired
    private CorporateService corporateService;

    @Test
    void shouldLinkAndRetrieveCorporateStructure() {
        // Link some companies
```

```
        corporateService.linkSubsidiary("Apress", "Spring");
        corporateService.linkSubsidiary("Apress", "CockroachLabs");
        corporateService.linkSubsidiary("Spring", "ProjectReactor");

        // Verify total nodes
        Long count = corporateService.countCompanies();
        assertThat(count).isEqualTo(4);

        // Verify recursive tree
        Collection<Map<String, Object>> tree = corporateService.
        getCorporateTree("Apress");
        assertThat(tree).hasSize(3); // Spring, CockroachLabs,
        ProjectReactor (via Spring)
    }
}
```

Listing 7-14. src/test/java/com/apress/crm/management/ManagementApplicationTests.java

```
package com.apress.crm.management;

import com.apress.crm.management.model.*;
import com.apress.crm.management.repository.jpa.CustomerRepository;
import com.apress.crm.management.service.ManagementService;
import org.junit.jupiter.api.BeforeEach;
import org.junit.jupiter.api.Test;
import org.springframework.beans.factory.annotation.Autowired;
import org.springframework.boot.test.autoconfigure.web.reactive.
AutoConfigureWebTestClient;
import org.springframework.test.web.reactive.server.WebTestClient;
import reactor.test.StepVerifier;
import java.util.UUID;
import static org.assertj.core.api.Assertions.assertThat;

@AutoConfigureWebTestClient
class ManagementApplicationTests extends BaseTest {

    @Autowired
    private WebTestClient webTestClient;
```

```
    @Autowired
    private CustomerRepository customerRepository;

    @Autowired
    private ManagementService managementService;

    private Customer testCustomer;

    @BeforeEach
    void setUp() {
        customerRepository.deleteAll();
        Company company = new Company(null, "Test Corp", "Tech",
        "test.com");
        Customer customer = new Customer(null, "Test", "User", "Tester",
        "t@t.com", "123", null);
        Address address = new Address(null, null, "123 St", "City", "ST",
        "12345");
        Communication comm = new Communication(null, null, "email",
        "t@t.com");

        CustomerDetailsDTO details = managementService.createCustomerWith
        Details(customer, company, address, comm);
        testCustomer = details.customer();
    }

    @Test
    void shouldRetrieveCustomerDetails() {
        webTestClient.get().uri("/api/v1/management/customers/" +
        testCustomer.getCustomerId())
                .exchange()
                .expectStatus().isOk()
                .expectBody(CustomerDetailsDTO.class)
                .value(dto -> {
                    assertThat(dto.customer().getCustomerId()).
                    isEqualTo(testCustomer.getCustomerId());
                });
    }
```

```
    @Test
    void shouldVerifyRedisSession() {
        UUID id = testCustomer.getCustomerId();
        var verifySession = managementService.startSession(id)
                .then(managementService.getSession(id));

        StepVerifier.create(verifySession)
                .expectNextMatches(s -> s.lastAction().equals("Login"))
                .verifyComplete();
    }
}
```

The AI Frontier: Vector Search in NoSQL

Nowadays, one of the most critical features of modern NoSQL databases is **Vector Search**. This allows databases like MongoDB and Redis to store and query high-dimensional data, known as **embeddings**, which are generated by large language models (LLMs). While traditional databases excel at keyword matching (e.g., finding a customer by "name"), Vector Search enables **semantic search**—finding data based on **meaning** and **context**.

The CRM Use Case: Semantic Feedback Analysis

In a standard CRM, searching through customer feedback or support notes is limited to exact keywords. If a customer writes "I am frustrated with the delay," a keyword search for "unhappy" or "slow" might miss it. By vectorizing this feedback, our **Management CRM** can:

1. **Find Similar Issues**: Instantly locate other customers who expressed similar sentiments, even if they used completely different words.
2. **Automated Categorization**: Group feedback into clusters (e.g., "Performance Issues," "Billing Complaints") without manual tagging.
3. **Lookalike Discovery**: Identify prospective customers who "look" like your most successful existing clients based on their qualitative interactions.

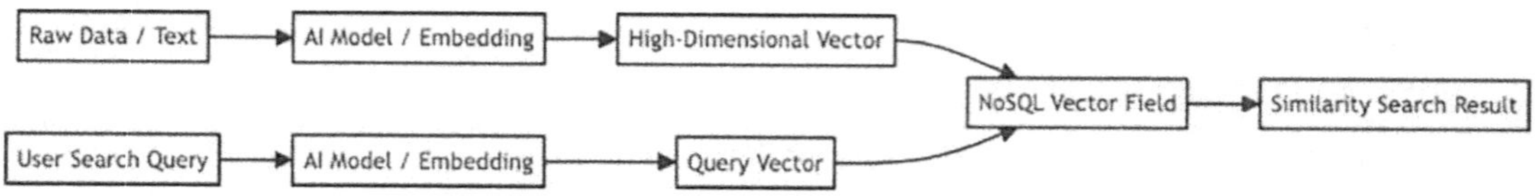

Figure 7-1. *AI Vector Search Workflow*

The Vectorization Workflow

Implementing Vector Search involves three essential steps:

1. **Vectorization (Embedding)**: Raw text (like a support note) is sent to an AI model (e.g., OpenAI, HuggingFace, or a local Llama model). The model transforms the text into a **Vector**—an array of hundreds or thousands of floating-point numbers that represent the "semantic essence" of the text.
2. **Storage**: The resulting vector is stored in a specialized field in your NoSQL database. Both MongoDB and Redis now provide native support for these high-dimensional arrays.
3. **Semantic Querying**: When a user performs a search, their query is also vectorized. The database then performs a **Similarity Search** (using algorithms like Cosine Similarity or Euclidean Distance) to find the "nearest neighbors"—the documents whose vectors are most similar to the query vector.

Listing 7-15. src/main/java/com/apress/crm/customer/CustomerFeedback.java

```
@Document(collection = "customer_feedback")
public record CustomerFeedback(
    @Id String id,
    UUID customerId,
    String rawText,
    float[] vector
) {}
```

- **The Vector Field**: This field stores the numerical representation of the feedback, enabling high-speed semantic matching.

Spring Data 4 and Spring AI provide seamless integration for these capabilities, allowing you to build these AI-powered features directly on top of your existing NoSQL infrastructure. We will explore the actual implementation of AI agents and vector stores in depth in Chapter 16.

Comparison: NoSQL Database Types

Choosing the right NoSQL database requires understanding the trade-offs between flexibility, performance, and the complexity of your data relationships.

Table 7-1. *Comparison of NoSQL Database Types*

Feature	Document (MongoDB)	Key-Value (Redis)	Graph (Neo4j)	Vector (AI-Enabled)
Data Model	Flexible BSON documents	Simple key-value/ hashes	Nodes and relationships	High-dimensional arrays
Primary Strength	Schema flexibility and scaling	In-memory speed (low latency)	Complex connection traversal	Semantic/contextual matching
Typical Usage	Content management, web APIs	Caching, session management	Social networks, referrals	AI search, recommendations
Scalability	Horizontal (sharding)	Vertical/clusters	Vertical (traversal-centric)	Horizontal (index-centric)
Query Language	JSON-based/Mongo Query	Key-lookup/API calls	Cypher (pattern matching)	Similarity search/KNN

Summary

In this chapter, we expanded our horizons beyond the relational world, exploring the rich variety of tools available in the modern NoSQL ecosystem.

Through our **Customer CRM**, we saw how **Spring Data MongoDB** offers a flexible document-oriented model, perfect for evolving datasets. We refactored our **Management CRM** to leverage **Reactive Redis**, demonstrating that even in high-performance, non-blocking architectures, Spring Data provides a consistent and familiar programming model. We also introduced **Neo4j** to manage complex referral networks, highlighting the power of graph-native path traversals.

Key takeaways include:

- **Polyglot Persistence**: The "Pro" strategy of using multiple specialized databases (Postgres for master data, Redis for sessions, Neo4j for relationships) within a single application.
- **Reactive Readiness**: The importance of using non-blocking drivers and templates (like `ReactiveRedisTemplate`) when working with Spring WebFlux.
- **Future-Proofing with Vectors**: How NoSQL stores are evolving into Vector databases, providing the necessary foundation for building next-generation AI agents.

By mastering these diverse persistence strategies, you are now equipped to select and integrate the optimal data store for any architectural challenge, ensuring your Spring Boot applications remain scalable, performant, and intelligent.

CHAPTER 8

NewSQL: Distributed SQL Transactions with Spring Boot

In the previous chapters, we navigated the landscape of relational databases and NoSQL stores. However, as applications scale globally, they face a daunting challenge: the "Speed of Light" problem. Relational databases like PostgreSQL are excellent for consistency but hard to scale across regions. NoSQL databases like MongoDB scale easily but often at the cost of strict ACID compliance.

Nowadays, a new category of database has emerged to bridge this gap: **NewSQL**. In this chapter, we will explore **CockroachDB**, a cloud-native, distributed SQL database that provides horizontal scalability while maintaining the gold standard of data integrity: **SERIALIZABLE** isolation.

One of the key reasons CockroachDB integrates so easily with the Spring ecosystem is its **PostgreSQL wire-protocol compatibility**. By implementing the PostgreSQL protocol layer, CockroachDB appears to your application as a standard PostgreSQL database. This allows you to use the mature PostgreSQL JDBC drivers and tools while enjoying the benefits of a globally distributed system.

The Challenge of Distributed Systems

Moving from a single-node database to a distributed system introduces a set of complexities that every "Pro" developer must master. As highlighted in the report **Understanding Multi-Region Application Architecture**, we must design for several key factors:

F. Gutierrez and D. Carter, *Pro Spring Boot 4*, https://doi.org/10.1007/979-8-8688-2640-5_8

- **Resilience**: A distributed system must survive not just disk failures but the loss of entire nodes, racks, or availability zones (AZs).
- **Scalability**: We need the ability to scale **out** (adding more nodes) rather than just **up** (adding more RAM/CPU), without the operational nightmare of manual sharding.
- **Latency**: The speed of light is constant. Accessing data across continents adds hundreds of milliseconds of delay. We must use **data locality** to keep data close to the user.
- **Operational Overhead**: Traditional RDBMS require significant human effort to maintain replicas and backups. A NewSQL database should automate these tasks.
- **Regulatory Compliance**: Laws like GDPR or the US Federal Wire Act often require that data about individuals reside and be processed within specific borders. **Geo-partitioning** is the technical solution to this legal requirement.
- **Load Balancing**: In a distributed cluster, every node should be capable of handling requests, ensuring no single node becomes a bottleneck.

Setting Up a Local Multi-Region Infrastructure

To truly understand distributed transactions, we need a running cluster. Following the practices used in large-scale deployments, we can simulate a multi-region environment locally using the CockroachDB binary.

Starting a Three-Node Local Cluster

We will start three nodes, each simulating a different "locality." First, download the appropriate binary for your operating system from the official Cockroach Labs website:

`https://www.cockroachlabs.com/docs/releases/#downloads`

The `--locality` flag is the most important part here, as it tells the cluster how the nodes are geographically distributed.

In the following commands, we explicitly set the `--http-addr` to use ports starting at **8081**. This is a deliberate choice to avoid port conflicts with our Spring Boot applications, which by default listen on port **8080**.

While we provide the raw commands here for educational purposes, the source code for both sample applications includes two shell scripts to automate this process: **`start-crdb.sh`** to launch the three-node cluster and **`stop-crdb.sh`** to shut it down and clean up the data. There is no need to copy these commands manually; you can simply execute the provided scripts.

Listing 8-1. Starting three local nodes with locality

```
# Node 1: US-East
cockroach start --insecure --store=node1 --listen-addr=localhost:26257 \
  --http-addr=localhost:8081 --join=localhost:26257,localhost:26258,
  localhost:26259 \
  --locality=region=us-east,zone=us-east-1 --background

# Node 2: US-West
cockroach start --insecure --store=node2 --listen-addr=localhost:26258 \
  --http-addr=localhost:8082 --join=localhost:26257,localhost:26258,
  localhost:26259 \
  --locality=region=us-west,zone=us-west-1 --background

# Node 3: EU-West
cockroach start --insecure --store=node3 --listen-addr=localhost:26259 \
  --http-addr=localhost:8083 --join=localhost:26257,localhost:26258,
  localhost:26259 \
  --locality=region=eu-west,zone=eu-west-1 --background

# Initialize the cluster
cockroach init --insecure --host=localhost:26257
```

The **`cockroach init`** command is essential and mandatory. While the previous `start` commands launch the individual processes, the cluster remains in a "joining" state and will not accept SQL connections until it is initialized. You only need to run this command once against any single node in the cluster.

Understanding the Startup Flags:

- **`--insecure`**: Disables TLS encryption and password authentication. This is suitable only for local development and testing.
- **`--store`**: Specifies the directory where the node will store its data.
- **`--listen-addr`**: The network address and port where the node listens for SQL and internal cluster traffic.
- **`--http-addr`**: The port for the web-based CockroachDB Console (Admin UI). We moved this to 9080+ to avoid conflicts with our web applications.
- **`--join`**: A list of addresses used by the node to find other nodes and join the cluster.
- **`--locality`**: Defines the geographical location of the node. CockroachDB uses this metadata to optimize data placement and satisfy survival goals.
- **`--background`**: Runs the cockroach process in the background, allowing you to use the same terminal window for subsequent commands.

Once the cluster is initialized, you can access the **CockroachDB Console** at `http://localhost:9080` to see the live nodes and their simulated regions.

Configuring the Database for Multi-Region

By default, a database doesn't know it should be multi-region. We must explicitly configure our SQL databases to use these localities. In our case, we will create two databases: `customer_db` and `management_db`, which will serve as our production environments.

Listing 8-2. src/main/resources/multi-region-setup.sql

```sql
-- Create our production databases
CREATE DATABASE customer_db;
CREATE DATABASE management_db;
```

```sql
-- Set the regions available to the databases
ALTER DATABASE customer_db PRIMARY REGION "us-east";
ALTER DATABASE customer_db ADD REGION "us-west";
ALTER DATABASE customer_db ADD REGION "eu-west";

ALTER DATABASE management_db PRIMARY REGION "us-east";
ALTER DATABASE management_db ADD REGION "us-west";
ALTER DATABASE management_db ADD REGION "eu-west";

-- Set the survival goal (survive a whole region failure)
ALTER DATABASE customer_db SURVIVE REGION FAILURE;
ALTER DATABASE management_db SURVIVE REGION FAILURE;
```

With these settings, CockroachDB will automatically ensure that data is replicated in a way that the loss of an entire region (e.g., all nodes in `us-east`) will not result in data loss or downtime.

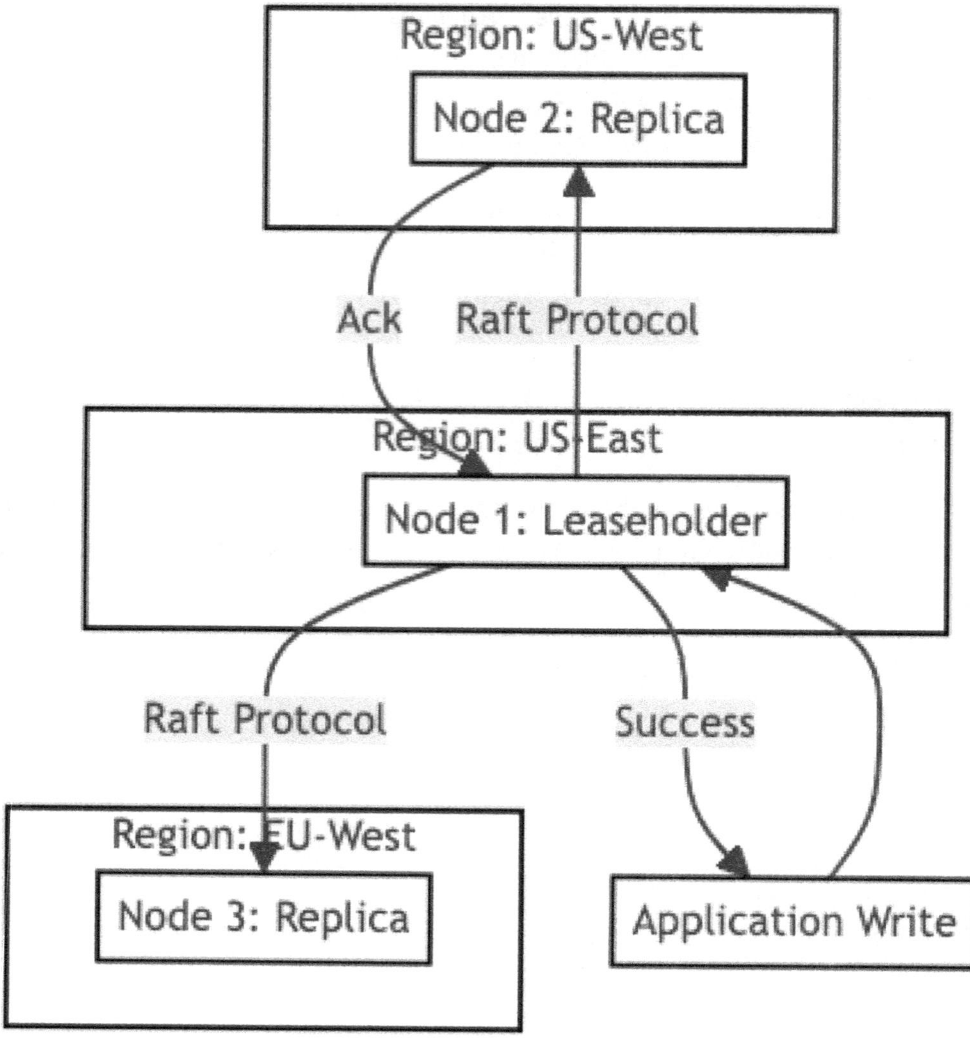

Figure 8-1. *Multi-Region Data Replication*

Distributed Schema Design: Avoiding Hotspots

In a traditional single-node database, using an auto-incrementing integer (like `SERIAL` or `BIGSERIAL`) for primary keys is common practice. However, in a distributed database like CockroachDB, this pattern becomes a major performance bottleneck known as a **hotspot**.

The Sequential ID Bottleneck

CockroachDB stores data in ordered "ranges" of about 512MB. If you use a monotonically increasing value (1, 2, 3...) for your primary key, all new rows will be appended to the same range—the one at the "top" of the keyspace. In a distributed cluster, this means only one node (the "Leaseholder" for that range) will handle all the write traffic, while the rest of the nodes sit idle. This negates the primary benefit of horizontal scaling.

Professional Alternatives

To achieve true horizontal scalability, we must ensure that writes are distributed across as many nodes as possible.

- **UUIDs (Universally Unique Identifiers)**: The most common solution. UUIDv4 values are randomly generated, ensuring that new rows are scattered across the entire cluster. CockroachDB has a native `UUID` data type that is highly optimized.
- **UUIDv7 (Ordered UUIDs)**: A modern alternative that includes a timestamp. It provides enough randomness to avoid hotspots while keeping data roughly sorted by time, which is helpful for "last 100 entries" style queries.
- **Hash-Sharded Indexes**: If your business logic strictly requires sequential integers, you can use a `HASH SHARDED` index. CockroachDB will internally hash the ID to distribute the data, while your application still sees the integer.

When using Spring Data, define your primary keys as `java.util.UUID`. In Spring Data JDBC, you can use the `@Id` annotation on a `UUID` field and let the database generate the value using `DEFAULT gen_random_uuid()`.

Listing 8-3. src/main/resources/schema.sql

```
CREATE TABLE customers (
    id UUID PRIMARY KEY DEFAULT gen_random_uuid(),
    first_name STRING NOT NULL,
    last_name STRING NOT NULL,
```

```
    email STRING UNIQUE NOT NULL,
    created_at TIMESTAMP DEFAULT now()
);
```

We can verify that CockroachDB is correctly generating these random UUIDs using a simple integration test.

Listing 8-4. src/test/java/com/apress/crm/customer/CustomerRepositoryTest.java

```
@Test
void shouldGenerateUUIDWithCockroachDB() {
    // CockroachDB uses gen_random_uuid() for UUIDv4 generation
    Customer customer1 = repository.save(new Customer(null, "UUID",
    "Test1", "Dev", "uuid1@example.com", "111", testCompany));
    Customer customer2 = repository.save(new Customer(null, "UUID",
    "Test2", "Dev", "uuid2@example.com", "222", testCompany));

    assertThat(customer1.getCustomerId()).isNotNull();
    assertThat(customer2.getCustomerId()).isNotNull();
    assertThat(customer1.getCustomerId()).isNotEqualTo(customer2.
    getCustomerId());

    // Verify UUIDs are version 4 (random)
    assertThat(customer1.getCustomerId().version()).isEqualTo(4);
    assertThat(customer2.getCustomerId().version()).isEqualTo(4);
}
```

Mandatory SERIALIZABLE Isolation

Unlike traditional databases that default to READ COMMITTED, CockroachDB enforces SERIALIZABLE isolation—the highest level defined by the SQL standard.

Why does this matter? In a distributed environment, "Write Skew" and "Phantom Reads" can lead to catastrophic data corruption. In `READ COMMITTED` mode, two transactions can read the same data, make independent decisions, and both commit, resulting in a state that violates business rules.

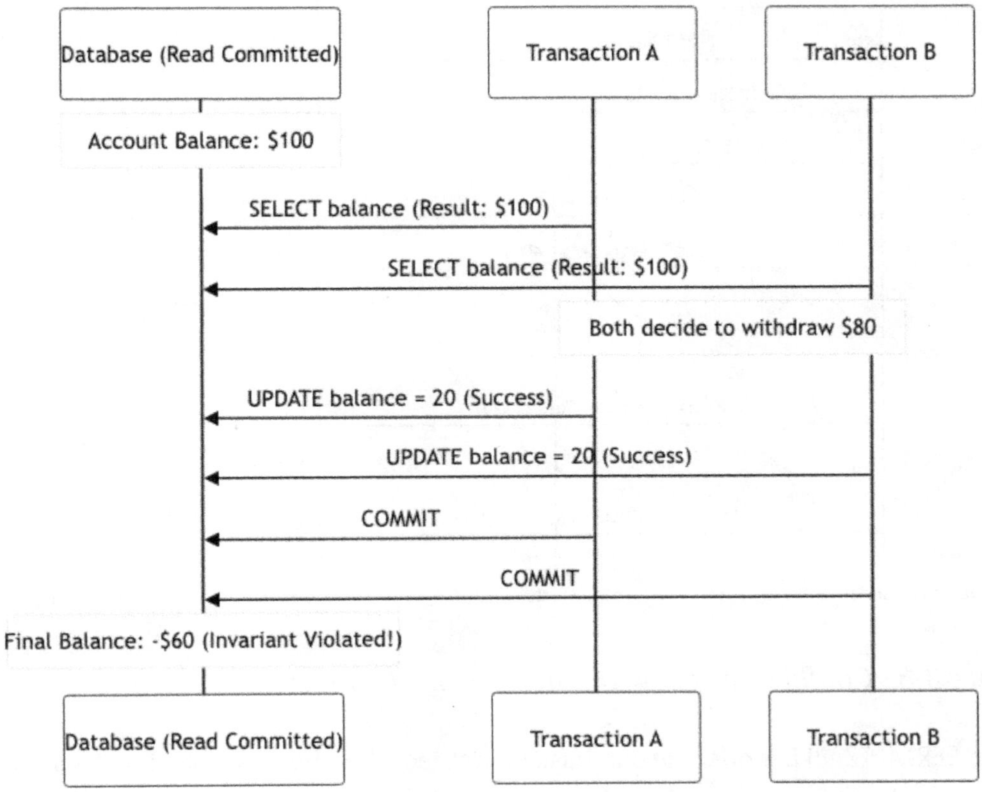

Figure 8-2. *Write Skew Anomaly in READ COMMITTED*

`SERIALIZABLE` isolation ensures that the result of several concurrent transactions is the same as if they had executed one after another. If the database detects that a transaction is about to commit based on "stale" data that was modified by another committed transaction, it will abort the second one.

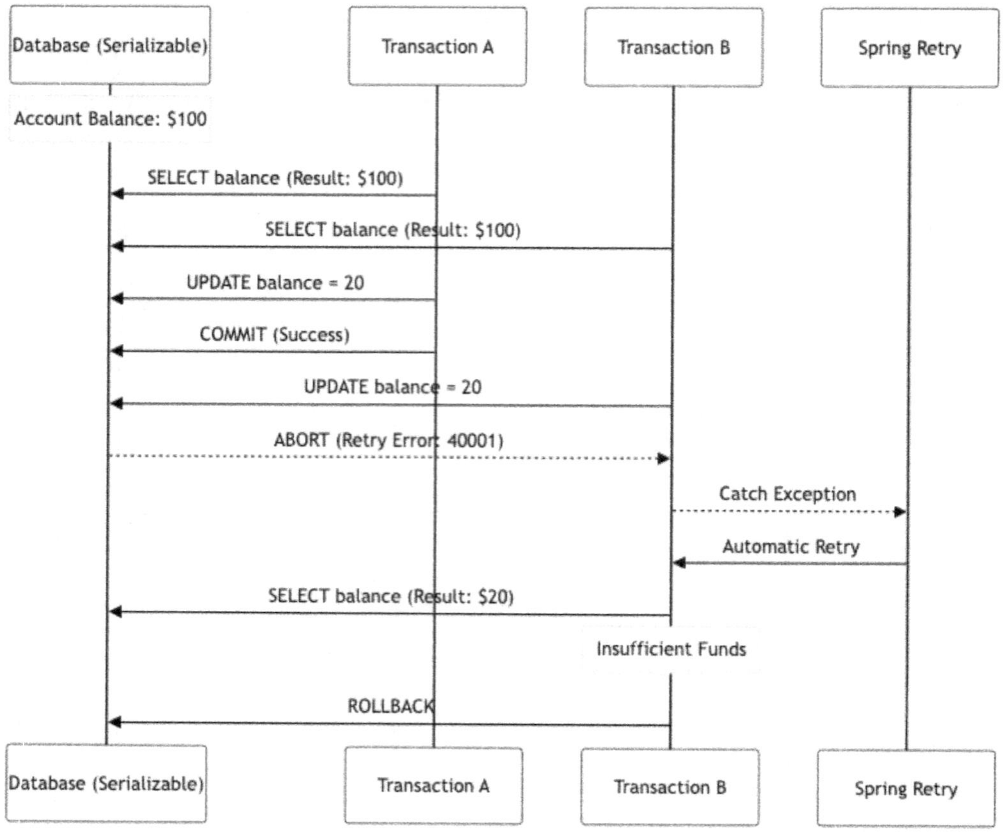

Figure 8-3. *Conflict Detection and Retry in SERIALIZABLE*

In `SERIALIZABLE` mode, the database guarantees that the final state is consistent, but it is the application's responsibility to handle and retry aborted transactions.

We can verify this behavior with a test that ensures concurrent operations are handled correctly without data corruption.

Listing 8-5. src/test/java/com/apress/crm/customer/CustomerRepositoryTest.java

```
@Test
void shouldHandleSerializableIsolationLevel() {
    // CockroachDB uses SERIALIZABLE isolation by default
    Customer customer = new Customer(null, "Isolation", "Test",
    "Developer", "isolation@example.com", "999", testCompany);
```

```
    Customer saved = repository.save(customer);
    entityManager.flush();

    assertThat(saved.getCustomerId()).isNotNull();

    // Retrieve and verify
    Optional<Customer> found = repository.findById(saved.getCustomerId());
    assertThat(found).isPresent();
    assertThat(found.get().getFirstName()).isEqualTo("Isolation");
}
```

However, this strictness comes with a trade-off: **Transaction Contention**. If two transactions overlap in a way that violates serializability, the database will abort one of them. It is then the application's responsibility to **retry** that transaction.

Handling Contention with Spring Retry

To make our application resilient to these aborted transactions, we use **Spring Retry**. This allows us to transparently re-execute logic when a specific exception occurs.

Dependencies and Configuration

First, we update the `build.gradle` for our **Management CRM** to include the retry and AspectJ starters.

Listing 8-6. build.gradle

```
dependencies {
    implementation 'org.springframework.retry:spring-retry:2.0.7'
    implementation 'org.springframework:spring-aspects'
    runtimeOnly 'org.postgresql:postgresql'
}
```

We enable the retry mechanism by adding `@EnableRetry` to our configuration.

Listing 8-7. src/main/java/com/apress/crm/management/configuration/ManagementConfiguration.java

```java
@Configuration
@EnableRetry
public class ManagementConfiguration {
    // ... routes and beans ...
}
```

- **`@EnableRetry`**: This annotation instructs Spring to look for `@Retryable` annotations and create the necessary proxies to handle the retry logic.

Configuring the Connection Pool (HikariCP)

For a distributed database like CockroachDB, tuning your connection pool is critical. Following the official best practices, we configure **HikariCP** to ensure low-latency connectivity and efficient resource utilization.

Listing 8-8. src/main/resources/application.properties

```
# Datasource Configuration
spring.datasource.url=jdbc:postgresql://localhost:26257/management_
db?sslmode=disable
spring.datasource.username=root
spring.datasource.password=

# HikariCP Best Practices for CockroachDB
spring.datasource.hikari.maximum-pool-size=25
spring.datasource.hikari.minimum-idle=5
spring.datasource.hikari.idle-timeout=600000
spring.datasource.hikari.max-lifetime=1800000
spring.datasource.hikari.connection-timeout=30000
spring.datasource.hikari.leak-detection-threshold=2000
```

- **Maximum Pool Size**: Setting this to roughly 2-4x the number of CPU cores in your cluster is a common starting point.

Retrying the Service Layer

We apply the @Retryable annotation to our service methods. For CockroachDB, we specifically look for the state code 40001 (Serialization Failure).

Listing 8-9. src/main/java/com/apress/crm/management/service/ManagementService.java

```
@Service
public class ManagementService {

    private final CustomerRepository customerRepository;
    private final AddressRepository addressRepository;
    private final CommunicationRepository communicationRepository;
    private final CompanyRepository companyRepository;

    // ... constructor ...

    @Transactional
    @Retryable(
        retryFor = SQLException.class,
        maxAttempts = 3,
        backoff = @Backoff(delay = 1000)
    )
    public CustomerDetailsDTO createCustomerWithDetails(Customer customer,
    Company company, Address address, Communication communication) {
        Company savedCompany = this.companyRepository.save(company);

        customer.setCompany(savedCompany);
        Customer savedCustomer = this.customerRepository.save(customer);

        address.setCustomerId(savedCustomer.getCustomerId());
        Address savedAddress = this.addressRepository.save(address);

        communication.setCustomerId(savedCustomer.getCustomerId());
        Communication savedCommunication = this.
        communicationRepository.save(
            new Communication(null, savedCustomer.getCustomerId(),
```

```
                                communication.getType(), communication.
                                getCommValue()));

        return new CustomerDetailsDTO(savedCustomer, savedCompany,
                                      List.of(savedAddress), List.
                                      of(savedCommunication));
    }
}
```

- **Exception Mapping**: We target `SQLException` directly, as CockroachDB's serialization errors (code `40001`) are propagated as SQL exceptions.
- **Backoff Strategy**: We wait 1 second for the first retry, allowing the competing transaction time to finish.

Key Implementation Points:

- **Idempotency**: Ensure that the method being retried is idempotent or wrapped in a single transaction. Since we use `@Transactional`, Spring will roll back the partial changes of the failed attempt before retrying.
- **Max Attempts**: We limit retries to 3. If it fails after that, the exception propagates to the caller (e.g., the Handler), who can return a `503 Service Unavailable`.

Multi-Region Optimization with Spring Cache

Cross-region database calls are expensive due to the speed of light. To build a "Pro" application, we must mitigate this latency using **Spring Cache**.

Why Spring Cache?

The Spring Cache abstraction allows you to transparently add caching to your methods. By storing the results of expensive operations in a fast, local memory store (like Redis), you can serve subsequent requests in sub-millisecond time.

Key Features

- **Provider Agnostic**: Switch between providers (Redis, Caffeine, Ehcache) with zero changes to your business logic.
- **Declarative Annotations**: Use annotations like `@Cacheable` to manage your cache without polluting your code with boilerplate.
- **Cache Management**: Built-in support for cache eviction (`@CacheEvict`) and updates (`@CachePut`).

Best Practices for Distributed Caching

1. **Manage TTL Carefully**: Always define a **Time-To-Live (TTL)** for your cache entries to ensure they eventually refresh.
2. **Avoid Cache Stampede**: Use the `sync = true` attribute in `@Cacheable` to ensure that if multiple threads request the same missing key, only one hits the database.
3. **Cache the "Follower Read"**: Caching data in a local Redis instance effectively implements a high-speed "Follower Read" pattern.

Implementation: Regional Speed in the Management CRM

Listing 8-10. build.gradle

```
dependencies {
    // Standard Spring Boot caching abstraction
    implementation 'org.springframework.boot:spring-boot-starter-
    data-redis'
}
```

Listing 8-11. src/main/java/com/apress/crm/management/service/ManagementService.java

```
@Transactional(readOnly = true)
@Cacheable(value = "customers", key = "#customerId")
public CustomerDetailsDTO getCustomerDetails(UUID customerId) {
    Customer customer = this.customerRepository.findById(customerId).
    orElse(null);
    if (customer == null) {
        return null;
    }

    Company company = customer.getCompany();
    List<Address> addresses = this.addressRepository.
    findByCustomerId(customerId);
    List<Communication> communications = this.communicationRepository.
    findByCustomerId(customerId);

    return new CustomerDetailsDTO(customer, company, addresses,
    communications);
}

@Transactional
@CacheEvict(value = "customers", allEntries = true)
@Retryable(retryFor = SQLException.class, maxAttempts = 3, backoff =
@Backoff(delay = 1000))
public CustomerDetailsDTO createCustomerWithDetails(Customer customer,
Company company, Address address, Communication communication) {
    // ... repository saves as shown in Listing 8-7 ...
    return new CustomerDetailsDTO(savedCustomer, savedCompany,
                    List.of(savedAddress), List.of(savedCommunication));
}
```

- **@Cacheable**: First checks the "customers" cache. If missing, it executes the method and stores the result.

- **`@CacheEvict`**: Since creating a new customer affects the overall collection and specific lookups, we invalidate the "customers" cache to ensure consistency.

Native Follower Reads and Time-Travel Queries

While Spring Cache is excellent for application-level performance, CockroachDB offers a powerful native feature for read-only workloads: **Follower Reads**. This allows you to perform low-latency reads from the closest replica, even if it's not the "Leaseholder" (the primary writer) for that data.

Reducing Cross-Region Latency

In a multi-region cluster, the Leaseholder for a range might be in `us-east`, while a user in `eu-west` is trying to read it. Normally, this would require a cross-atlantic trip. With Follower Reads, the `eu-west` node can serve the read request from its local replica, provided the application can tolerate a small amount of staleness (usually 4.8 seconds).

Implementing Time-Travel Queries

Follower reads are implemented using the `AS OF SYSTEM TIME` clause. This allows you to query the state of the database as it was at a specific point in the past.

Listing 8-12. Querying with Follower Reads (SQL)

```sql
USE customer_db;

-- Read data from the closest replica as of 5 seconds ago
SELECT * FROM customers AS OF SYSTEM TIME '-5s';
```

In Spring Boot, you can easily integrate this into your repositories using native queries.

Listing 8-13. src/main/java/com/apress/crm/customer/CustomerRepository.java

```
public interface CustomerRepository extends JpaRepository<Customer, UUID> {

    Page<Customer> findByLastName(String lastName, Pageable pageable);

    Customer findByEmail(String email);

    /**
     * CockroachDB Follower Reads - Read data as of 5 seconds ago.
     */
    @Query(value = "SELECT * FROM customers AS OF SYSTEM TIME '-5s'",
           nativeQuery = true)
    List<Customer> findAllAsOfSystemTime();

    /**
     * CockroachDB Follower Reads with a parameterized query.
     */
    @Query(value = "SELECT * FROM customers AS OF SYSTEM TIME '-5s' " +
                   "WHERE last_name = :lastName", nativeQuery = true)
    List<Customer> findByLastNameAsOfSystemTime(@Param("lastName") String
    lastName);
}
```

Understanding the Query:

- **`nativeQuery = true`**: We must use a native query because standard JPQL (Java Persistence Query Language) does not support vendor-specific clauses like `AS OF SYSTEM TIME`. By setting this flag to true, we tell Spring Data JPA to bypass its parser and send the raw SQL directly to the database.
- **`AS OF SYSTEM TIME '-5s'`**: This is the magic clause. It instructs CockroachDB to perform a "Time-Travel Query," returning the data as it existed exactly 5 seconds ago. By accepting this small window of staleness, the database is no longer required to contact the Leaseholder (primary) to confirm the absolute latest state. Instead, it can serve the read immediately from the nearest local replica (Follower), drastically reducing cross-region latency.

Follower reads are ideal for dashboards, analytics, or product catalogs where absolute real-time consistency is less important than sub-millisecond latency.

The following test demonstrates the trade-off of follower reads: they provide extremely low latency but may return slightly stale data (from 5 seconds ago).

Listing 8-14. src/test/java/com/apress/crm/customer/CustomerRepositoryTest.java

```
@Test
@Transactional(propagation = Propagation.NOT_SUPPORTED)
void shouldDemonstrateFollowerReadStaleData() throws InterruptedException {
    // 1. Create initial customer
    Customer initial = repository.save(new Customer(null, "Stale",
    "DataTest", "Dev", "stale@example.com", "555-1111", null));
    UUID customerId = initial.getCustomerId();

    // 2. Wait for follower read window (> 5s)
    Thread.sleep(6000);

    // 3. Delete the customer NOW
    repository.deleteById(customerId);

    // 4. Follower read still sees it (stale data from -5s)
    List<Customer> stillVisibleViaFollower = repository.
    findAllAsOfSystemTime();
    boolean stillVisible = stillVisibleViaFollower.stream()
            .anyMatch(c -> c.getCustomerId().equals(customerId));

    assertThat(stillVisible).isTrue();

    // 5. But a current read correctly shows it's gone
    assertThat(repository.findById(customerId)).isEmpty();
}
```

Change Data Capture (CDC) and Webhooks

A powerful feature of CockroachDB is its ability to stream real-time changes using **Changefeeds**. While we will focus on **Webhooks** for this integration, it is important to note that CockroachDB supports a variety of enterprise-grade "sinks," including **Apache Kafka**, **AWS S3**, and **Cloud Pub/Sub**.

Why CDC Is Vital for Integration

CDC solves the brittle "Dual-Write" problem by reading directly from the database's transaction log, ensuring that events are emitted only when a change is successfully committed. It is an essential tool for:

- **Service Decoupling**: Services can stay synchronized without knowing about each other's internal logic.
- **Eventual Consistency**: Maintaining data across different specialized stores.
- **Resilience**: Events are generated from the log, so you never miss a change.

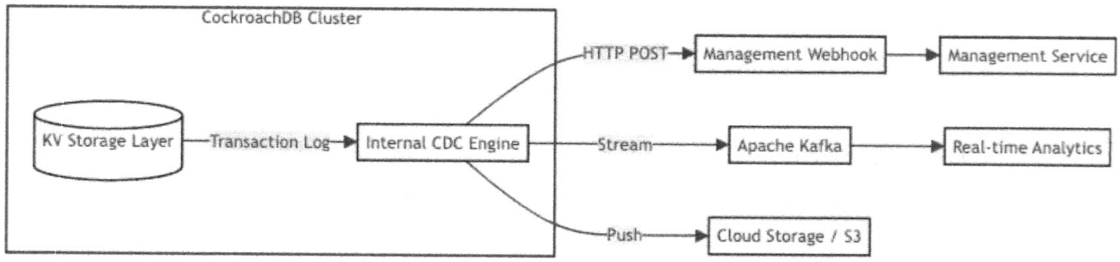

***Figure 8-4.** CockroachDB Native Change Data Capture (CDC) Architecture*

We will take a much deeper dive into **Apache Kafka** and event-driven patterns in Chapter 12, where we will connect our CDC Changefeeds to a robust message broker.

Step 1: Receiving the Event (Management CRM)

Listing 8-16. src/main/java/com/apress/crm/management/reactive/ManagementHandlers.java

```
public Mono<ServerResponse> handleCustomerSync(ServerRequest request) {
    return request.bodyToMono(Map.class)
            .doOnNext(payload -> log.info("Received CDC Sync: {}",
            payload))
            .flatMap(payload -> ServerResponse.ok().build());
}
```

Step 2: Creating the Changefeed (CockroachDB)

You don't need to write Java code in the Customer CRM to emit events. You simply execute a SQL command in the CockroachDB console:

Listing 8-17. SQL for Changefeed creation

```
USE customer_db;

SET CLUSTER SETTING kv.rangefeed.enabled = true;

CREATE CHANGEFEED FOR TABLE customers
INTO 'webhook-http://management-crm:8080/api/v1/management/webhooks/
customer-sync'
WITH updated;
```

Modern Concurrency with Virtual Threads

In a distributed environment where we wait for cross-region network calls and transaction retries, the efficiency of our thread management becomes paramount. Spring Boot 4, running on Java 21+, introduces a paradigm shift in how we handle concurrency: **Virtual Threads**.

The High-Concurrency Challenge

Historically, Java threads (Platform Threads) were thin wrappers around operating system threads. They are "heavy" assets, consuming significant memory and taking time to create. In a distributed B2B CRM, if thousands of users are concurrently accessing hierarchical data across regions, a traditional application would quickly run out of threads, leading to "Thread Starvation."

Virtual Threads solve this by being extremely lightweight. You can spawn millions of them on a single JVM, as they are managed by the Java runtime rather than the OS.

Key Features

- **Cheap to Create**: Unlike platform threads, creating a virtual thread has near-zero overhead.
- **Non-Blocking I/O Integration**: When a virtual thread performs a blocking I/O operation (like a CockroachDB query), the underlying platform thread is released to do other work, while the virtual thread waits efficiently.
- **Seamless Compatibility**: They implement the standard `java.lang.Thread` API, meaning your existing code and libraries work without modification.

Best Practices for Distributed Apps

1. **Don't Pool Virtual Threads**: Virtual threads are disposable. Pooling them (like we do with platform threads) is an anti-pattern. Just create a new one for every task.
2. **Focus on I/O-Bound Tasks**: They are ideal for applications that spend time waiting for databases, caches, or external APIs (like our multi-region CRM).
3. **Avoid Thread Locals**: Since you might have millions of threads, storing large amounts of data in `ThreadLocal` can lead to excessive memory consumption.

Enabling Virtual Threads in Spring Boot

One of the most remarkable features of Spring Boot 4 is how easily you can adopt this technology. You don't need to rewrite your services; you simply enable a global flag in your `application.properties`.

Listing 8-18. src/main/resources/application.properties

```
spring.threads.virtual.enabled=true
```

With this single line, Spring Boot automatically configures the embedded Tomcat server and the task executors to use virtual threads for every incoming request and background task. This allows our application to handle massive concurrent load while waiting for distributed CockroachDB transactions to complete.

Testing Distributed Transactions and Retries

To verify our distributed logic, we must test against our running local CockroachDB cluster.

For these tests to run, you must have the CockroachDB cluster up and running. You can use the provided **`start-crdb.sh`** script to launch it. Once your tests are finished, you can stop the cluster using **`stop-crdb.sh`**.

Integration Testing Infrastructure

A "Pro" testing strategy involves a clean base class and a simplified configuration for the test environment. We use a dedicated **`TestCacheConfiguration`** to avoid the need for a full Redis container during our CockroachDB-focused tests.

Listing 8-19. src/test/java/com/apress/crm/management/TestCacheConfiguration.java

```
@TestConfiguration
@EnableCaching
public class TestCacheConfiguration {

    @Bean @Primary
    public CacheManager cacheManager() {
```

```
        // Use a simple in-memory cache for tests instead of Redis
        return new ConcurrentMapCacheManager("customers");
    }
}
```

Listing 8-20. src/test/java/com/apress/crm/management/BaseTest.java

```
@SpringBootTest(webEnvironment = SpringBootTest.WebEnvironment.RANDOM_PORT)
@ActiveProfiles("test")
@Import(TestCacheConfiguration.class)
public abstract class BaseTest {
    // Base test class for all integration tests
    // Uses local CockroachDB at localhost:26257/defaultdb
}
```

Verifying Concurrency with Virtual Threads

The ultimate test for our distributed CRM is handling massive concurrent load. We use the `Executors.newVirtualThreadPerTaskExecutor()` to simulate many simultaneous users hitting our multi-table transactions.

Listing 8-21. src/test/java/com/apress/crm/management/ManagementServiceConcurrencyTest.java

```
class ManagementServiceConcurrencyTest extends BaseTest {

    @Autowired
    private ManagementService managementService;

    @Test
    void shouldHandleConcurrentCustomerCreationsWithVirtualThreads() throws
    Exception {
        int threads = 20;
        CountDownLatch startLatch = new CountDownLatch(1);
        CountDownLatch endLatch = new CountDownLatch(threads);
        AtomicInteger successCount = new AtomicInteger();
```

```
try (var executor = Executors.newVirtualThreadPerTaskExecutor()) {
    for (int i = 0; i < threads; i++) {
        final int index = i;
        executor.submit(() -> {
            try {
                startLatch.await();
                Company company = new Company(null, "Concurrent Co
                " + index, "Tech", "concurrent" + index + ".com");
                Customer customer = new Customer(null,
                "Concurrent", "User" + index,
                                       "Dev", "concurrent" + index
                                       + "@example.com",
                                       "555-" + index, null);
                Address address = new Address(null, null, index + "
                St", "City", "ST", "1000" + index);
                Communication communication = new Communication
                (null, null, "email", "concurrent" + index +
                "@example.com");

                managementService.createCustomerWithDetails(
                customer, company, address, communication);
                successCount.incrementAndGet();
            } catch (Exception e) {
                // CockroachDB SERIALIZABLE isolation handles
                contention
            } finally {
                endLatch.countDown();
            }
        });
    }
```

```
            startLatch.countDown();
            endLatch.await(30, TimeUnit.SECONDS);
        }

        // Verify that CockroachDB and Spring Retry handled the
        concurrent load
        assertThat(successCount.get()).isGreaterThan(threads / 2);
    }
}
```

Analyzing the Concurrency Test

In our test, we use the `Executors.newVirtualThreadPerTaskExecutor()` factory method. Unlike traditional thread pools that reuse a limited number of "heavy" OS threads, this executor creates a new, lightweight virtual thread for every task submitted. This is the most professional way to test distributed concurrency because:

- **Isolation**: Each update operation runs in its own dedicated thread, ensuring that one doesn't wait for the other due to pool starvation.
- **Realistic Simulation**: It mimics how Spring Boot 4 handles incoming web requests when `spring.threads.virtual.enabled=true`.
- **Automatic Synchronization**: By using a `try-with-resources` block, the executor automatically waits for all submitted tasks to complete before closing, simplifying our test orchestration.

Handling Maxed-Out Retries in Production

When your retry strategy fails, it is a signal that your system is under extreme contention. In a professional application, you should:

- **Log with Context**: Use structured logging to capture the specific IDs and operations that failed.
- **Return a 503 or 429**: Inform the user or the calling service that the operation could not be completed and they should try again later.
- **Dead-Letter Queue (DLQ)**: For background tasks, offload the failed event to a queue for later processing or manual review.

Observability: Monitoring Distributed Transactions

In a distributed environment, "silent" retries can mask performance issues. If your transaction contention is too high, your application will spend more time retrying than doing productive work. Spring Boot Actuator, combined with Micrometer, allows us to monitor these events.

Tracking Retry Metrics

By using Spring Retry, we can automatically capture metrics about how many times our methods are being re-executed.

We will explore Spring Boot Actuator, Micrometer, and custom metrics in much greater detail in Chapter 13, where we build a complete observability stack for our microservices.

Listing 8-22. src/main/resources/application.properties

```
# Enable Spring Retry metrics
management.metrics.export.prometheus.enabled=true
management.endpoint.metrics.enabled=true
```

Once enabled, you can query your metrics endpoint (e.g., `/actuator/metrics/spring.retry`) to see the count of successful retries vs. exhausted ones.

CockroachDB-Specific Monitoring

CockroachDB also provides internal metrics that are vital for "Pro" developers. You can query the `crdb_internal` virtual tables to find which queries are causing the most contention.

Listing 8-23. Finding contentious queries (SQL)

```
SELECT
    query,
    contention_count,
    max_retries
```

```
FROM crdb_internal.node_statement_statistics
ORDER BY contention_count DESC
LIMIT 5;
```

If you see high contention on specific tables, consider using the **Hash-Sharded Index** strategy mentioned earlier in the chapter or re-evaluating your transaction boundaries to keep them as short as possible.

Table 8-1. *Comparison: SQL vs. NoSQL vs. NewSQL*

Feature	Traditional SQL (Postgres)	NoSQL (MongoDB)	NewSQL (CockroachDB)
Consistency	ACID (single node)	Eventual/tunable	ACID (global/distributed)
Isolation	Read committed (typical)	N/A	SERIALIZABLE (mandatory)
Scalability	Vertical (hard to scale out)	Horizontal (easy)	Horizontal (native)
Multi-Region	Manual sharding/read replicas	Native sharding	Native geo-partitioning

Summary

In this chapter, we stepped into the high-stakes world of distributed SQL. We learned that **CockroachDB** provides the familiar SQL interface but with the "superpowers" of a global, multi-region architecture.

We addressed the core challenges of distributed systems:

- **Design**: Avoiding performance hotspots with **UUIDs** and **Hash-Sharded Indexes**.
- **Consistency**: Leveraging mandatory `SERIALIZABLE` isolation to prevent distributed anomalies.
- **Resilience**: Using **Spring Retry** to handle transaction contention gracefully.
- **Performance**: Enabling **Virtual Threads** for high concurrency and using **Spring Cache** to mitigate regional latency.

- **Read Scalability**: Utilizing **Follower Reads** and `AS OF SYSTEM TIME` for sub-millisecond local reads.
- **Connectivity**: Using **CDC Changefeeds** to build a robust, event-driven link between our microservices.
- **Observability**: Monitoring retries and database contention using **Spring Boot Actuator** and CockroachDB internal statistics.

With these "Pro" patterns, your applications are now ready to "Scale fast, Survive disaster, and Thrive globally," as envisioned in modern multi-region architectures.

Even though the code examples in this chapter focused primarily on the **Management CRM**, the **Customer CRM** has also been fully updated to utilize these professional patterns—including caching, Spring Retry, and CockroachDB-native features. We highly encourage you to explore the `customer-crm` source code to see how these concepts are applied in a different context.

CHAPTER 9

Going Reactive with Spring Boot

In the previous chapters, we built robust applications using the traditional Spring MVC model, where each request is handled by a dedicated thread. While simple and effective for many use cases, this "Thread-per-Request" model can hit scalability limits under heavy concurrent loads or when dealing with slow I/O operations (like network calls or database queries). Threads are expensive resources; blocking them while waiting for I/O is inefficient.

This chapter introduces the **Reactive Programming** paradigm, designed to build resilient, elastic, and responsive applications that can handle massive concurrency with a small, fixed number of threads.

We will explore the **Spring Reactive Stack**, which includes

- **Project Reactor**: The reactive foundation providing `Mono` and `Flux`.
- **Spring WebFlux**: The non-blocking web framework, offering both annotation-based and functional programming models.
- **Spring Data R2DBC**: The Reactive Relational Database Connectivity specification, allowing non-blocking SQL access.

We will refactor our two core applications to fully embrace the reactive stack, using **CockroachDB** as our backing store for both:

1. **Customer CRM**: Will implement the **Annotation-based** model (familiar `@RestController` style).
2. **Management System**: Will implement the **Functional Endpoints** model (Router functions and Handler functions).

F. Gutierrez and D. Carter, *Pro Spring Boot 4*, https://doi.org/10.1007/979-8-8688-2640-5_9

Why Reactive?

In a traditional blocking application, if a database query takes 500ms, the thread handling that request sits idle for 500ms. If you have a pool of 200 threads, you can handle at most 200 concurrent requests. Once the pool is exhausted, the application becomes unresponsive.

Reactive programming inverts this model. It uses an **Event Loop** architecture (similar to Node.js). When a request involves I/O, the thread dispatches the operation and immediately goes back to handle other requests. When the I/O completes, a callback (or event) signals the thread to resume processing. This allows a few threads (usually equal to the number of CPU cores) to handle thousands of concurrent requests.

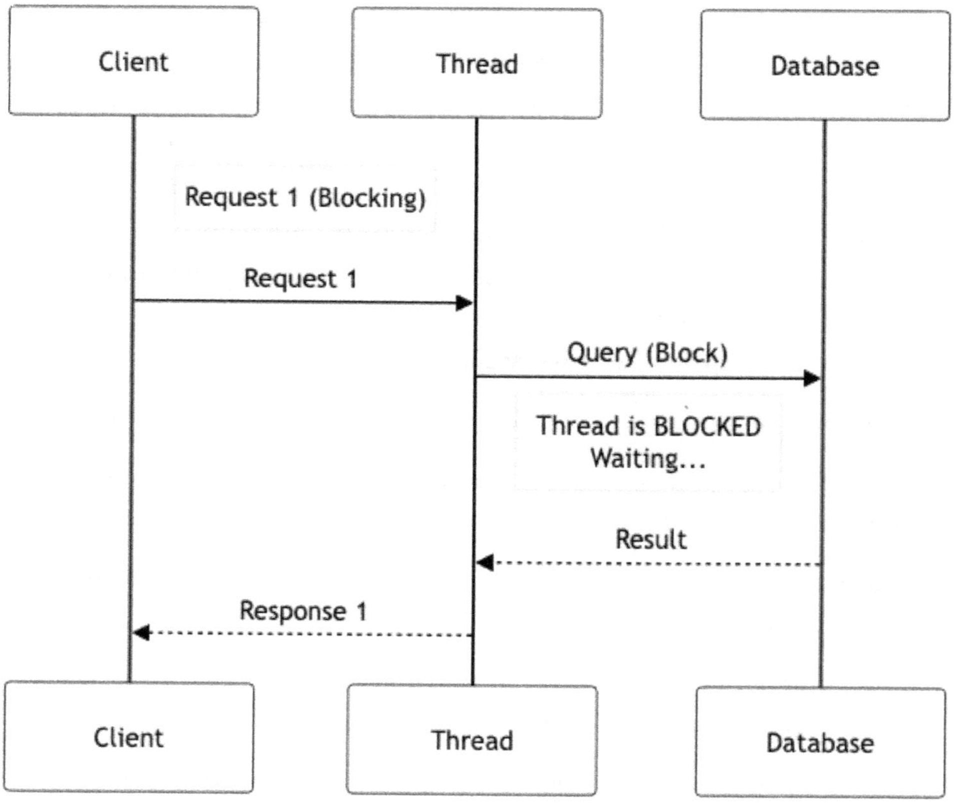

Figure 9-1. *Traditional Blocking I/O Model*

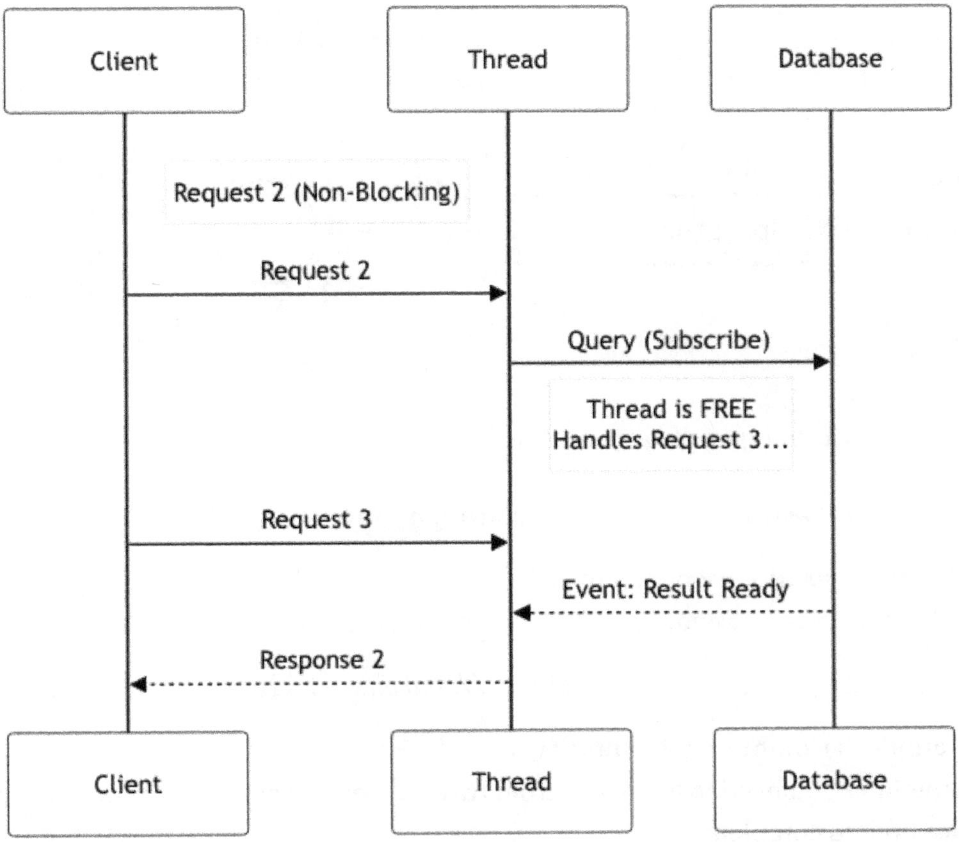

***Figure 9-2.** Reactive Non-Blocking I/O Model*

Project Reactor Essentials

Spring WebFlux is built on top of **Project Reactor**, a reactive library for building non-blocking applications on the JVM. It implements the Reactive Streams specification.

The two core types you must master are `Mono` and `Flux`.

Mono: 0 or 1 Item

A `Mono<T>` is a publisher that produces at most **one** item. It is the reactive equivalent of `Optional<T>` or a single-result `CompletableFuture<T>`.

- **Use Cases:** Fetching a user by ID, checking if a record exists, or an operation that returns `void` (a completion signal only).

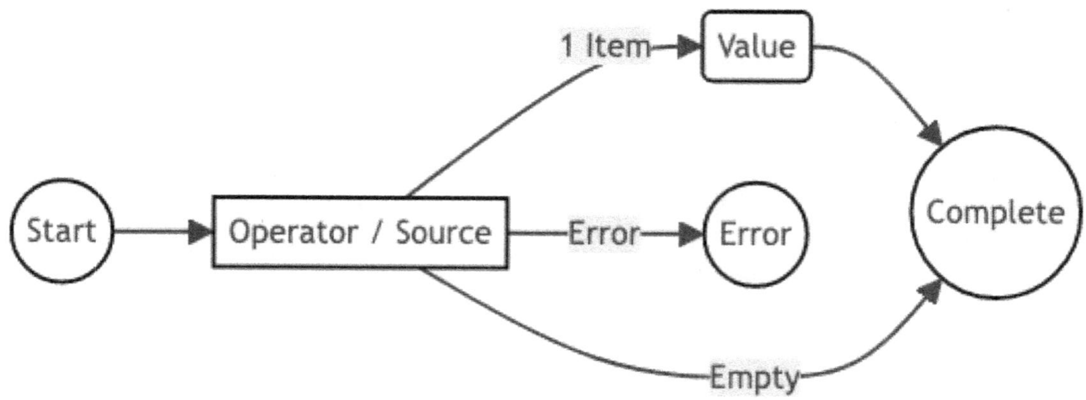

Figure 9-3. *Mono Lifecycle*

Example 1: Basic Creation and Subscription

```
Mono<String> noData = Mono.empty();
Mono<String> data = Mono.just("Hello Reactive World");

data.subscribe(System.out::println); // Output: Hello Reactive World
```

Example 2: Combining Results (Zip)

Sometimes you need to fetch data from two sources and combine them. `Mono.zip` waits for both to complete.

```
Mono<String> firstName = Mono.just("John");
Mono<String> lastName = Mono.just("Doe");

Mono.zip(firstName, lastName)
    .map(tuple -> tuple.getT1() + " " + tuple.getT2())
    .subscribe(System.out::println); // Output: John Doe
```

Example 3: Handling Errors

You can gracefully handle errors by returning a default value or switching to another Mono.

```
Mono<String> result = Mono.error(new RuntimeException("Database down"))
    .onErrorReturn("Default Value")
    .cast(String.class);

result.subscribe(System.out::println); // Output: Default Value
```

Example 4: Wrapping Legacy Blocking Code

If you must use a blocking library, wrap it in `fromCallable` to defer execution until subscription.

```
Mono<String> blockingWrapper = Mono.fromCallable(() -> {
    // Simulate blocking I/O
    Thread.sleep(100);
    return "Legacy Data";
});
```

Flux: 0 to N Items

A `Flux<T>` is a publisher that produces **0 to N** items. It is the reactive equivalent of a `Stream<T>` or `Iterable<T>`, but potentially infinite.

- **Use Cases:** Fetching all customers, reading a file line-by-line, or processing a live stream of stock prices.

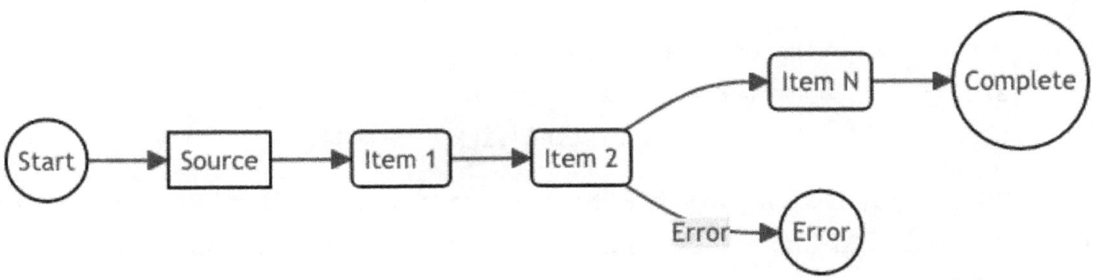

Figure 9-4. *Flux Lifecycle*

Example 1: Basic Transformation

```
Flux<String> flux = Flux.just("Spring", "Boot", "Reactor");

flux.map(String::toUpperCase) .subscribe(System.out::println);
// Output:
// SPRING
// BOOT
// REACTOR
```

Example 2: Filtering and Logic

You can filter items just like a Java Stream.

```
Flux.range(1, 10) // 1 to 10
    .filter(i -> i % 2 == 0) // Evens only
    .map(i -> "Even: " + i)
    .subscribe(System.out::println);
```

Example 3: Processing a Stream from an Iterable

Ideally used when you have an existing list that you want to process reactively.

```
List<String> names = List.of("Alice", "Bob", "Charlie");

Flux.fromIterable(names)
    .map(String::length)
    .subscribe(System.out::println); // Output: 5, 3, 7
```

Example 4: Infinite Streams (Interval)

Reactive streams can be infinite. Here we emit a value every second.

```
Flux.interval(Duration.ofSeconds(1))
    .take(5) // Stop after 5 items
    .subscribe(i -> System.out.println("Tick: " + i));
```

Nothing happens until you subscribe. Reactive streams are "lazy." Defining a `Flux` just describes the pipeline. The data only flows when a subscriber (like the web server) requests it.

Spring Data R2DBC: The Non-Blocking SQL Standard

For decades, Java developers have relied on **JDBC** (Java Database Connectivity) to talk to relational databases. JDBC is stable and mature, but it has a fatal flaw for reactive programming: it is **blocking**. When a JDBC thread sends a query, it is stuck waiting until the database responds. In a reactive application, where a few threads handle thousands of requests, blocking even one thread is unacceptable.

Enter **R2DBC** (Reactive Relational Database Connectivity). R2DBC is an open specification designed from the ground up to be fully non-blocking and reactive.

Key Features

Spring Data R2DBC brings the familiar Spring Data programming model to this new world:

- **Reactive Repositories**: Interfaces like `R2dbcRepository` that return `Mono` and `Flux` instead of `List` or `Optional`.
- **DatabaseClient**: A powerful, fluent API for executing SQL, similar to the `JdbcClient` but strictly non-blocking.
- **Reactive Transactions**: Full support for `@Transactional`, managed asynchronously without thread binding.
- **Connection Pooling**: Integration with `r2dbc-pool` to manage reactive connections efficiently.

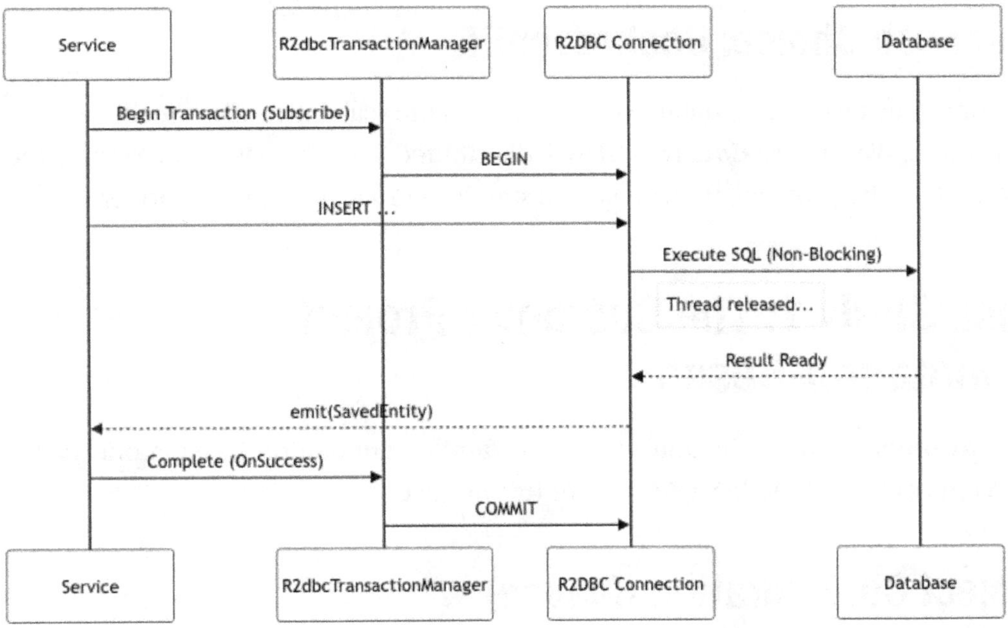

***Figure 9-5.** Reactive Transaction Flow*

Best Practices

1. **Never Block**: Avoid calling `.block()` or `.blockFirst()` within your reactive chain. This negates all benefits of R2DBC.
2. **Use Connection Pooling**: Unlike JDBC, creating R2DBC connections is expensive. Always use `r2dbc-pool` in production.
3. **Prefer `DatabaseClient` for Complex Queries**: While Repositories are great for CRUD, the `DatabaseClient` offers more control over mapping and execution for complex joins or reports.
4. **Handle Backpressure**: If you are reading millions of rows, ensure your subscriber (e.g., the HTTP client) can handle the flow, or use operators like `limitRate`.

Database Choice: CockroachDB

For our project, we need a database that matches the scalability of our reactive application. We will use **CockroachDB**, a distributed SQL database. Since it uses the PostgreSQL wire protocol, we can use the standard `r2dbc-postgresql` driver.

Case Study 1: The Customer Project (Annotation-Based)

The **Customer CRM** application will use the familiar annotation-based model (`@RestController`). We will use **Maven** for this project.

Project Configuration (Maven)

First, add the reactive dependencies to your `pom.xml`.

Listing 9-1. pom.xml—Customer Project

```
<project xmlns="http://maven.apache.org/POM/4.0.0" ...>
    <properties>
        <java.version>21</java.version>
```

```
    <testcontainers.version>1.20.4</testcontainers.version>
</properties>

<dependencyManagement>
    <dependencies>
        <dependency>
            <groupId>org.testcontainers</groupId>
            <artifactId>testcontainers-bom</artifactId>
            <version>${testcontainers.version}</version>
            <type>pom</type>
            <scope>import</scope>
        </dependency>
    </dependencies>
</dependencyManagement>

<dependencies>
    <dependency>
        <groupId>org.springframework.boot</groupId>
        <artifactId>spring-boot-starter-webflux</artifactId>
    </dependency>
    <dependency>
        <groupId>org.springframework.boot</groupId>
        <artifactId>spring-boot-starter-validation</artifactId>
    </dependency>
    <dependency>
        <groupId>org.springframework.boot</groupId>
        <artifactId>spring-boot-starter-data-r2dbc</artifactId>
    </dependency>
    <dependency>
        <groupId>org.postgresql</groupId>
        <artifactId>r2dbc-postgresql</artifactId>
        <scope>runtime</scope>
    </dependency>
    <dependency>
        <groupId>io.r2dbc</groupId>
        <artifactId>r2dbc-pool</artifactId>
    </dependency>
```

```
        <dependency>
            <groupId>org.springframework.boot</groupId>
            <artifactId>spring-boot-starter-webflux-test</artifactId>
            <scope>test</scope>
        </dependency>
        <dependency>
            <groupId>org.springframework.boot</groupId>
            <artifactId>spring-boot-testcontainers</artifactId>
            <scope>test</scope>
        </dependency>
        <dependency>
            <groupId>org.testcontainers</groupId>
            <artifactId>cockroachdb</artifactId>
            <scope>test</scope>
        </dependency>
        <dependency>
            <groupId>org.testcontainers</groupId>
            <artifactId>junit-jupiter</artifactId>
            <scope>test</scope>
        </dependency>
        <dependency>
            <groupId>io.projectreactor</groupId>
            <artifactId>reactor-test</artifactId>
            <scope>test</scope>
        </dependency>
    </dependencies>
</project>
```

Next, configure the connection in application.properties.

Listing 9-2. src/main/resources/application.properties—Customer DB

```
spring.r2dbc.url=r2dbc:postgresql://localhost:26257/customer_db
spring.r2dbc.username=root
spring.r2dbc.password=
```

```
spring.r2dbc.pool.enabled=true
spring.r2dbc.pool.initial-size=5
spring.r2dbc.pool.max-size=20
```

Database Initialization

For Spring Data R2DBC in 2025, you generally need to provide a `schema.sql` or use an external migration tool because R2DBC does not support automatic schema generation from domain classes like Spring Data JPA does.

Why You Need a Schema Script:

- **No Auto-DDL**: Unlike Hibernate/JPA, Spring Data R2DBC cannot automatically create or update your database tables based on annotations.
- **Manual Mapping**: You must manually ensure the database structure exists.

Create a file named `schema.sql` in `src/main/resources`:

Listing 9-3. src/main/resources/schema.sql

```sql
CREATE TABLE IF NOT EXISTS customers (
    id UUID PRIMARY KEY,
    first_name VARCHAR(255),
    last_name VARCHAR(255),
    email VARCHAR(255),
    phone VARCHAR(255)
);
```

Domain Model

We use a Java Record for the domain model. We implement `Persistable<UUID>` to control the `isNew` check manually.

Listing 9-4. src/main/java/com/apress/crm/customer/Customer.java

```
package com.apress.crm.customer;

import jakarta.validation.constraints.Email;
import jakarta.validation.constraints.NotBlank;
import org.springframework.data.annotation.Id;
import org.springframework.data.annotation.PersistenceCreator;
import org.springframework.data.annotation.Transient;
import org.springframework.data.domain.Persistable;
import org.springframework.data.relational.core.mapping.Table;

import java.util.UUID;

@Table("customers")
public record Customer(
        @Id UUID id,
        @NotBlank String firstName,
        @NotBlank String lastName,
        @Email @NotBlank String email,
        String phone,
        @Transient boolean isNew) implements Persistable<UUID> {

    public Customer(String firstName, String lastName, String email, String
    phone) {
        this(UUID.randomUUID(), firstName, lastName, email, phone, true);
    }

    @PersistenceCreator
    public Customer(UUID id, String firstName, String lastName, String
    email, String phone) {
        this(id, firstName, lastName, email, phone, false);
    }

    @Override
    public UUID getId() { return id; }

    @Override
    public boolean isNew() { return isNew; }
}
```

Reactive Repository

The repository extends R2dbcRepository, returning reactive types.

Listing 9-5. src/main/java/com/apress/crm/customer/CustomerRepository.java

```
package com.apress.crm.customer;

import org.springframework.data.r2dbc.repository.R2dbcRepository;
import reactor.core.publisher.Flux;
import java.util.UUID;

public interface CustomerRepository extends
R2dbcRepository<Customer, UUID> {
    Flux<Customer> findByLastName(String lastName);
}
```

Reactive Controller with Resilience

Here we use standard @RestController annotations. We apply a **Retry Strategy** to handle potential concurrency conflicts from CockroachDB (SERIALIZABLE isolation).

Listing 9-6. src/main/java/com/apress/crm/customer/CustomerController.java

```
package com.apress.crm.customer;

import io.r2dbc.spi.R2dbcException;
import jakarta.validation.Valid;
import org.springframework.http.HttpStatus;
import org.springframework.http.ResponseEntity;
import org.springframework.web.bind.annotation.*;
import reactor.core.publisher.Flux;
import reactor.core.publisher.Mono;
import reactor.util.retry.Retry;

import java.time.Duration;
import java.util.UUID;
```

```
@RestController @RequestMapping("/api/v1/customers")
public class CustomerController {

    private final CustomerRepository repository;

    public CustomerController(CustomerRepository repository) {
        this.repository = repository;
    }

    @GetMapping
    Flux<Customer> findAll() {
        return repository.findAll();
    }

    @GetMapping("/{id}")
    Mono<ResponseEntity<Customer>> findById(@PathVariable UUID id) {
        return repository.findById(id)
                .map(ResponseEntity::ok)
                .defaultIfEmpty(ResponseEntity.notFound().build());
    }

    @PostMapping @ResponseStatus(HttpStatus.CREATED)
    Mono<Customer> save(@Valid @RequestBody Customer customer) {
        return repository.save(customer)
                .retryWhen(Retry.backoff(3, Duration.ofMillis(100))
                        .filter(throwable -> throwable instanceof
                        R2dbcException &&
                                "40001".equals(((R2dbcException)
                                throwable).getSqlState())));
    }

    @DeleteMapping("/{id}")
    Mono<Void> deleteById(@PathVariable UUID id) {
        return repository.deleteById(id);
    }
}
```

Let's break down the resilience pattern used in the `save` method:

- **`retryWhen`**: This operator allows us to resubscribe to the upstream source (re-execute the save) if an error occurs. Unlike the blocking `@Retryable` annotation, this happens entirely within the reactive stream, preserving the non-blocking nature of the application.
- **`Retry.backoff(3, ...)`**: We configure an exponential backoff strategy. If a conflict occurs, we wait (100ms, then 200ms, etc.), giving the competing transaction time to finish.
- **`filter(...)`**: We don't want to retry **every** error (e.g., validation errors should fail immediately). We specifically filter for `R2dbcException` with SQL state **`40001`**. This is the standard code for **Serialization Failure** in PostgreSQL and CockroachDB, indicating that the transaction was aborted due to contention and is safe to retry.

Seed Configuration and Error Handling

To round out our annotation-based project, we need a way to initialize data and handle validation errors gracefully in a reactive context.

Listing 9-7. src/main/java/com/apress/crm/customer/CustomerConfiguration.java

```
package com.apress.crm.customer;

import org.springframework.boot.context.event.ApplicationReadyEvent;
import org.springframework.context.ApplicationListener;
import org.springframework.context.annotation.Bean;
import org.springframework.context.annotation.Configuration;
import reactor.core.publisher.Flux;

@Configuration
public class CustomerConfiguration {

    @Bean
```

```
    ApplicationListener<ApplicationReadyEvent> customerAppReady(CustomerRep
    ository customerRepository) {
        return event -> {
            customerRepository.deleteAll()
                    .thenMany(
                            Flux.just(
                                    new Customer("John", "Doe", "john@
                                    example.com", "1-800-PHONE"),
                                    new Customer("Jane", "Doe", "jane@
                                    example.com", "1-800-PHONE"),
                                    new Customer("Jack", "Smith", "jack@
                                    example.com", "1-800-PHONE")
                            )
                    )
                    .flatMap(customerRepository::save)
                    .subscribe(c -> System.out.println("Saved: " + c));
        };
    }
}
```

This configuration class demonstrates a reactive approach to data seeding:

- **ApplicationListener<ApplicationReadyEvent>**: This ensures our logic runs only after the Spring context is fully initialized and the database connection is ready.
- **deleteAll().thenMany(...)**: We start by cleaning the database. The `.thenMany()` operator ensures that the subsequent insertion only happens **after** the delete completes successfully.
- **Flux.just(...)**: We create a static stream of `Customer` objects.
- **flatMap(customerRepository::save)**: For each customer in the stream, we asynchronously call the repository's save method.
- **subscribe()**: Nothing happens in a reactive stream until you subscribe. This terminal operation triggers the entire chain (Delete → Create Stream → Save → Print).

Listing 9-8. src/main/java/com/apress/crm/customer/CustomerControllerAdvice.java

```
package com.apress.crm.customer;

import org.springframework.http.HttpStatus;
import org.springframework.http.ProblemDetail;
import org.springframework.web.bind.annotation.ExceptionHandler;
import org.springframework.web.bind.annotation.RestControllerAdvice;
import org.springframework.web.bind.support.WebExchangeBindException;

import java.net.URI;
import java.util.stream.Collectors;

@RestControllerAdvice
public class CustomerControllerAdvice {

    @ExceptionHandler(WebExchangeBindException.class)
    public ProblemDetail handleBindException(WebExchangeBindException ex) {
        ProblemDetail problemDetail = ProblemDetail.
        forStatusAndDetail(HttpStatus.BAD_REQUEST, "Validation failed");
        problemDetail.setType(URI.create("https://api.crm.com/errors/
        validation"));
        problemDetail.setTitle("Validation Error");

        var errors = ex.getBindingResult().getFieldErrors().stream()
                .map(error -> error.getField() + ": " + error.
                getDefaultMessage())
                .collect(Collectors.toList());

        problemDetail.setProperty("errors", errors);
        return problemDetail;
    }
}
```

In a reactive WebFlux application, validation errors trigger a `WebExchangeBindException`.

- **`@ExceptionHandler`**: Intercepts the exception before it reaches the client.
- **`ProblemDetail`**: We construct a standardized RFC 7807 error response. This ensures that clients receive a consistent error format.
- **`ex.getBindingResult()`**: We extract the specific field errors and add them as a custom property to the response.

Case Study 2: The Management Project (Functional Endpoints)

For the **Management Project**, we will use the **Functional Web Framework** and **Gradle**. This model offers more explicit control over request routing.

Project Configuration (Gradle)

Update your `build.gradle` to include the reactive starters and Testcontainers.

Listing 9-9. build.gradle

```
plugins {
    id 'java'
    id 'org.springframework.boot' version '4.0.0'
    id 'io.spring.dependency-management' version '1.1.7'
}

group = 'com.apress.crm'
version = '0.0.1-SNAPSHOT'

java {
    toolchain {
        languageVersion = JavaLanguageVersion.of(21)
    }
}
```

```
repositories {
    mavenCentral()
}

dependencyManagement {
    imports {
        mavenBom "org.testcontainers:testcontainers-bom:1.20.4"
    }
}

dependencies {
    implementation 'org.springframework.boot:spring-boot-starter-webflux'
    implementation 'org.springframework.boot:spring-boot-starter-
    validation'
    implementation 'org.springframework.boot:spring-boot-starter-
    data-r2dbc'
    implementation 'io.r2dbc:r2dbc-pool'
    runtimeOnly 'org.postgresql:r2dbc-postgresql'
    testImplementation 'org.springframework.boot:spring-boot-starter-
    webflux-test'
    testImplementation 'org.springframework.boot:spring-boot-
    testcontainers'
    testImplementation 'org.testcontainers:cockroachdb'
    testImplementation 'org.testcontainers:junit-jupiter'
    testImplementation 'io.projectreactor:reactor-test'
}
```

For the management project, we prefer YAML configuration.

Listing 9-10. src/main/resources/application.yml—Management DB

```
spring:
  r2dbc:
    url: r2dbc:postgresql://localhost:26257/management_db
    username: root
    password:
    pool:
      enabled: true
```

```
      initial-size: 5
      max-size: 20
---
spring:
  config:
    activate:
      on-profile: test
  r2dbc:
    url: r2dbc:postgresql://localhost:26257/defaultdb
```

Resilience and Caching Service

In this service, we combine **Transactions**, **Retries**, and **Caching** into a powerful reactive pipeline. Since Spring's @Cacheable is blocking, we implement a **Reactive Cache-Aside** pattern using an in-memory map.

Listing 9-11. src/main/java/com/apress/crm/management/service/ManagementService.java

```java
package com.apress.crm.management.service;

import com.apress.crm.management.model.*;
import com.apress.crm.management.repository.*;
import io.r2dbc.spi.R2dbcException;
import org.springframework.stereotype.Service;
import org.springframework.transaction.annotation.Transactional;
import reactor.core.publisher.Mono;
import reactor.util.retry.Retry;

import java.time.Duration;
import java.util.List;
import java.util.Map;
import java.util.UUID;
import java.util.concurrent.ConcurrentHashMap;
```

```
@Service
public class ManagementService {

    private final CustomerRepository customerRepository;
    private final AddressRepository addressRepository;
    private final CommunicationRepository communicationRepository;
    private final CompanyRepository companyRepository;

    private final Map<UUID, CustomerDetailsDTO> cache = new
    ConcurrentHashMap<>();

    public ManagementService(CustomerRepository customerRepository,
    AddressRepository addressRepository,
                             CommunicationRepository communicationRepository,
                             CompanyRepository companyRepository) {
        this.customerRepository = customerRepository;
        this.addressRepository = addressRepository;
        this.communicationRepository = communicationRepository;
        this.companyRepository = companyRepository;
    }

    @Transactional
    public Mono<CustomerDetailsDTO> createCustomerWithDetails(Cust
    omer customer, Company company, Address address, Communication
    communication) {
        return companyRepository.save(company)
                .flatMap(savedCompany -> {
                    Customer c = new Customer(null, customer.firstName(),
                    customer.lastName(), customer.jobTitle(), customer.
                    email(), customer.phone(), savedCompany.companyId());
                    return customerRepository.save(c)
                            .flatMap(savedCustomer -> {
                                Address a = new Address(null,
                                savedCustomer.customerId(), address.
                                street(), address.city(), address.state(),
                                address.zip());
```

```
                                    Communication comm = new
                                    Communication(null, savedCustomer.
                                    customerId(), communication.
                                    communicationType(), communication.
                                    communicationValue());

                                    return Mono.zip(
                                            addressRepository.save(a),
                                            communicationRepository.save(comm)
                                    ).map(tuple -> new CustomerDetailsDTO(sav
                                    edCustomer, savedCompany, List.of(tuple.
                                    getT1()), List.of(tuple.getT2())));
                                });
            })
            .doOnNext(dto -> cache.put(dto.customer().
            customerId(), dto))
            .retryWhen(Retry.backoff(3, Duration.ofMillis(100))
                    .filter(throwable -> throwable instanceof
                     R2dbcException &&
                            "40001".equals(((R2dbcException)
                            throwable).getSqlState())));
}

public Mono<CustomerDetailsDTO> getCustomerDetails(UUID customerId) {
    return Mono.justOrEmpty(cache.get(customerId))
            .switchIfEmpty(
                    customerRepository.findById(customerId)
                            .flatMap(customer -> companyRepository.
                            findById(customer.companyId())
                                    .zipWith(Mono.just(customer)))
                            .flatMap(tuple -> {
                                Company company = tuple.getT1();
                                Customer customer = tuple.getT2();
                                return Mono.zip(
```

```
                                        addressRepository.
                                        findAllByCustomerId(
                                        customerId).collectList(),
                                        communicationRepository.
                                        findAllByCustomerId(
                                        customerId).collectList()
                                ).map(details -> new
                                CustomerDetailsDTO(customer, company,
                                details.getT1(), details.getT2()));
                        })
                        .doOnNext(dto -> cache.
                        put(customerId, dto))
                );
        }
}
```

Let's analyze the `ManagementService`:

- **Transactional Orchestration**: Even in a reactive world, transactions are essential. We use `@Transactional` to ensure that saving the company, the customer, and the associated addresses and communications either all succeed or all fail together.
- **`Mono.zip`**: This operator is used to run multiple asynchronous operations in parallel and wait for all of them to complete.
- **Programmatic Cache Update**: We manually manage the cache using `doOnNext`. After a successful save, we update the `ConcurrentHashMap`.
- **Resilient Retries**: Just like the controller, we apply `retryWhen` to handle the specific CockroachDB serialization errors.

Handler Function

The handler takes a `ServerRequest` and returns a `Mono<ServerResponse>`.

Listing 9-12. src/main/java/com/apress/crm/management/reactive/ManagementHandlers.java

```java
package com.apress.crm.management.reactive;

import com.apress.crm.management.model.*;
import com.apress.crm.management.service.ManagementService;
import org.springframework.stereotype.Component;
import org.springframework.web.reactive.function.server.ServerRequest;
import org.springframework.web.reactive.function.server.ServerResponse;
import reactor.core.publisher.Mono;

import java.net.URI;
import java.util.UUID;

@Component
public class ManagementHandlers {

    private final ManagementService managementService;

    public ManagementHandlers(ManagementService managementService) {
        this.managementService = managementService;
    }

    public Mono<ServerResponse> getCustomerDetails(ServerRequest request) {
        String id = request.pathVariable("id");
        return managementService.getCustomerDetails(UUID.fromString(id))
                .flatMap(details -> ServerResponse.ok().bodyValue(details))
                .switchIfEmpty(ServerResponse.notFound().build());
    }

    public Mono<ServerResponse> createCustomer(ServerRequest request) {
        return request.bodyToMono(Customer.class)
                .flatMap(managementService::createWithAudit)
                .flatMap(details -> ServerResponse.created(URI.create("/
                  api/v1/customers/" + details.customer().customerId()))
                        .bodyValue(details.customer()));
    }
}
```

What's happening here? The handler bridges the web layer and the service. It extracts the `Customer` object from the request body and delegates the complex transactional orchestration (creating the company, address, and audit logs) to the `ManagementService`. Finally, it transforms the result into a `ServerResponse` with a `201 Created` status.

Router Function

The Router maps URL patterns to Handler functions.

Listing 9-13. src/main/java/com/apress/crm/management/configuration/ManagementConfiguration.java

```
package com.apress.crm.management.configuration;

import com.apress.crm.management.model.Address;
import com.apress.crm.management.model.Communication;
import com.apress.crm.management.model.Company;
import com.apress.crm.management.model.Customer;
import com.apress.crm.management.reactive.ManagementHandlers;
import com.apress.crm.management.service.ManagementService;
import org.springframework.boot.context.event.ApplicationReadyEvent;
import org.springframework.context.ApplicationListener;
import org.springframework.context.annotation.Bean;
import org.springframework.context.annotation.Configuration;
import org.springframework.web.reactive.function.server.RouterFunction;
import org.springframework.web.reactive.function.server.ServerResponse;

import static org.springframework.web.reactive.function.server.Request
Predicates.GET;
import static org.springframework.web.reactive.function.server.Request
Predicates.POST;
import static org.springframework.web.reactive.function.server.Router
Functions.route;
```

```
@Configuration
public class ManagementConfiguration {

    @Bean
    ApplicationListener<ApplicationReadyEvent> managementReady(ManagementSe
    rvice managementService) {
        return event -> {
            // Customer 1
            Company company1 = new Company(null, "Apress", "Publishing",
            "apress.com");
            Customer customer1 = new Customer(null, "Felipe", "Gomez",
            "Author", "felipe.gomez@apress.com", "123-456-7890", null);
            Address address1 = new Address(null, null, "123 Main St", "New
            York", "NY", "10001");
            Communication communication1 = new Communication(null, null,
            "email", "felipe.gomez@apress.com");

            managementService.createCustomerWithDetails(customer1,
            company1, address1, communication1)
                    .subscribe(dto -> System.out.println("Created customer
                    1: " + dto));

            // Customer 2
            Company company2 = new Company(null, "Spring", "Software",
            "spring.io");
            Customer customer2 = new Customer(null, "Josh",
            "Long", "Developer Advocate", "josh.long@spring.io",
            "098-765-4321", null);
            Address address2 = new Address(null, null, "456 Oak Ave", "San
            Francisco", "CA", "94102");
            Communication communication2 = new Communication(null, null,
            "twitter", "@starbuxman");

            managementService.createCustomerWithDetails(customer2,
            company2, address2, communication2)
                    .subscribe(dto -> System.out.println("Created customer
                    2: " + dto));
```

```
            // Customer 3
            Company company3 = new Company(null, "Google", "Technology",
            "google.com");
            Customer customer3 = new Customer(null, "Sundar", "Pichai",
            "CEO", "sundar.pichai@google.com", "111-222-3333", null);
            Address address3 = new Address(null, null, "789 Pine Ln",
            "Mountain View", "CA", "94043");
            Communication communication3 = new Communication(null, null,
            "email", "sundar.pichai@google.com");

            managementService.createCustomerWithDetails(customer3,
            company3, address3, communication3)
                    .subscribe(dto -> System.out.println("Created customer
                    3: " + dto));
        };
    }

    @Bean
    RouterFunction<ServerResponse> managementRoutes(ManagementHandlers
    handlers) {
        return route(GET("/api/v1/customers/{id}"),
        handlers::getCustomerDetails)
                .andRoute(POST("/api/v1/customers"),
                handlers::createCustomer);
    }
}
```

Let's analyze this class: it defines the functional routes for the management system and seeds the database with initial data. Note how each `subscribe()` triggers the asynchronous save pipeline for our complex customer entities.

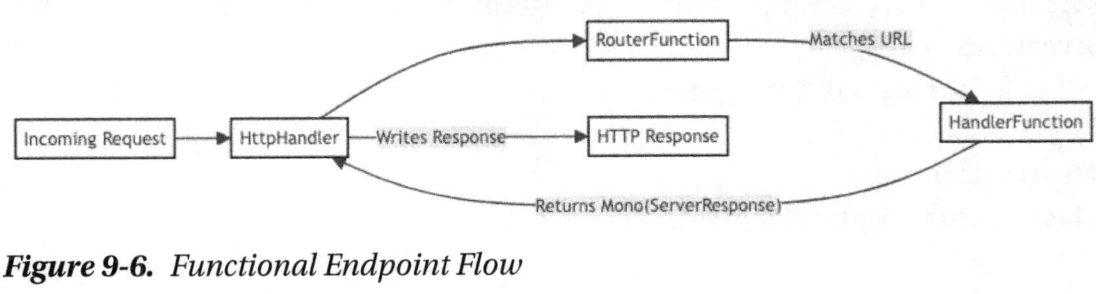

Figure 9-6. *Functional Endpoint Flow*

Testing Reactive Applications

Testing in WebFlux is a joy thanks to `WebTestClient`. We use **Testcontainers** for the database and **Java 21 Virtual Threads** to simulate massive concurrency.

Testing the Annotation-Based Controller

Listing 9-14. src/test/java/com/apress/crm/customer/CustomerApplicationTests.java

```
package com.apress.crm.customer;

import org.junit.jupiter.api.BeforeEach;
import org.junit.jupiter.api.Test;
import org.springframework.boot.test.context.SpringBootTest;
import org.springframework.context.ApplicationContext;
import org.springframework.test.context.DynamicPropertyRegistry;
import org.springframework.test.context.DynamicPropertySource;
import org.springframework.test.web.reactive.server.WebTestClient;
import org.testcontainers.containers.CockroachContainer;
import org.testcontainers.junit.jupiter.Container;
import org.testcontainers.junit.jupiter.Testcontainers;

import java.util.concurrent.CountDownLatch;
import java.util.concurrent.Executors;
import java.util.concurrent.TimeUnit;
import java.util.concurrent.atomic.AtomicInteger;

import static org.assertj.core.api.Assertions.assertThat;

@SpringBootTest(webEnvironment = SpringBootTest.WebEnvironment.RANDOM_PORT,
properties = {
        "spring.sql.init.mode=always"
})
@Testcontainers
class CustomerApplicationTests {
```

```
@Container
static CockroachContainer cockroach = new
CockroachContainer("cockroachdb/cockroach:v25.4.0");

@DynamicPropertySource
static void r2dbcProperties(DynamicPropertyRegistry registry) {
    registry.add("spring.r2dbc.url", () -> String.format("r2dbc:p
    ostgresql://%s:%d/defaultdb", cockroach.getHost(), cockroach.
    getMappedPort(26257)));
    registry.add("spring.r2dbc.username", cockroach::getUsername);
    registry.add("spring.r2dbc.password", cockroach::getPassword);
}

private WebTestClient webTestClient;

@BeforeEach
void setUp(ApplicationContext context) {
    this.webTestClient = WebTestClient.bindToApplicationContext(context
    ).build();
}

@Test
void shouldHandleConcurrentWritesWithVirtualThreads() throws
InterruptedException {
    int concurrentUsers = 10;
    CountDownLatch latch = new CountDownLatch(concurrentUsers);
    AtomicInteger successCount = new AtomicInteger();

    try (var executor = Executors.newVirtualThreadPerTaskExecutor()) {
        for (int i = 0; i < concurrentUsers; i++) {
            int index = i;
            executor.submit(() -> {
                try {
                    Customer newCustomer = new Customer("User",
                    "" + index, "user" + index + "@test.com",
                    "1-800-PHONE");

                    webTestClient.post()
```

```
                        .uri("/api/v1/customers")
                        .bodyValue(newCustomer)
                        .exchange()
                        .expectStatus().isCreated();

                    successCount.incrementAndGet();
                } catch (Throwable e) {
                    System.err.println("Error for user " + index + ": "
                    + e.getMessage());
                } finally {
                    latch.countDown();
                }
            });
        }
    }

    latch.await(15, TimeUnit.SECONDS);
    assertThat(successCount.get()).isEqualTo(concurrentUsers);
  }
}
```

Let's analyze this test class:

- **Concurrency Simulation**: We use a `CountDownLatch` to coordinate multiple threads, ensuring the test waits for all concurrent operations to finish.
- **Virtual Threads**: The use of `Executors.newVirtualThreadPerTaskExecutor()` is a key feature of Spring Boot 4 and Java 21. It creates a new, lightweight **Virtual Thread** for every single task, allowing us to simulate hundreds of concurrent users with negligible overhead.
- **Non-blocking Verification**: By hammering the `@PostMapping` endpoint, we verify that our `retryWhen` logic and the R2DBC driver can handle the typical contention found in distributed databases like CockroachDB.

Testing Functional Endpoints and Caching

Listing 9-15. src/test/java/com/apress/crm/management/ManagementApplicationTests.java

```
package com.apress.crm.management;

import com.apress.crm.management.model.Customer;
import com.apress.crm.management.model.CustomerDetailsDTO;
import org.junit.jupiter.api.BeforeEach;
import org.junit.jupiter.api.Test;
import org.springframework.boot.test.context.SpringBootTest;
import org.springframework.context.ApplicationContext;
import org.springframework.test.context.DynamicPropertyRegistry;
import org.springframework.test.context.DynamicPropertySource;
import org.springframework.test.web.reactive.server.WebTestClient;
import org.testcontainers.containers.CockroachContainer;
import org.testcontainers.junit.jupiter.Container;
import org.testcontainers.junit.jupiter.Testcontainers;

import java.util.UUID;
import java.util.concurrent.Executors;
import java.util.stream.IntStream;

import static org.assertj.core.api.Assertions.assertThat;

@SpringBootTest(webEnvironment = SpringBootTest.WebEnvironment.RANDOM_PORT,
properties = {
        "spring.sql.init.mode=always"
})
@Testcontainers
class ManagementApplicationTests {

    @Container
    static CockroachContainer cockroach = new
    CockroachContainer("cockroachdb/cockroach:v25.4.0");
```

```
    @DynamicPropertySource
    static void r2dbcProperties(DynamicPropertyRegistry registry) {
        registry.add("spring.r2dbc.url", () -> String.format("r2dbc:p
        ostgresql://%s:%d/defaultdb", cockroach.getHost(), cockroach.
        getMappedPort(26257)));
        registry.add("spring.r2dbc.username", cockroach::getUsername);
        registry.add("spring.r2dbc.password", cockroach::getPassword);
    }

    private WebTestClient webTestClient;

    @BeforeEach
    void setUp(ApplicationContext context) {
        this.webTestClient = WebTestClient.bindToApplicationContext(context
        ).build();
    }

    @Test
    void shouldServeConcurrentReadsFromCache() {
        // 1. Setup: Create a customer
        Customer newCustomer = new Customer(null, "Cache", "Target",
        "Manager", "cache@test.com", "555-CACHE", null);

        Customer created = webTestClient.post()
            .uri("/api/v1/customers")
            .bodyValue(newCustomer)
            .exchange()
            .expectStatus().isCreated()
            .returnResult(Customer.class)
            .getResponseBody()
            .blockFirst();

        assertThat(created).isNotNull();
        UUID id = created.customerId();

        // 2. Simulate 100 concurrent users reading the same customer
        try (var executor = Executors.newVirtualThreadPerTaskExecutor()) {
            IntStream.range(0, 100).forEach(i ->
```

```
                executor.submit(() -> {
                    webTestClient.get()
                        .uri("/api/v1/customers/" + id)
                        .exchange()
                        .expectStatus().isOk()
                        .expectBody(CustomerDetailsDTO.class)
                        .value(dto -> {
                            assertThat(dto.customer().customerId()).
                            isEqualTo(id);
                            assertThat(dto.customer().firstName()).
                            isEqualTo("Cache");
                        });
                })
            );
        }
    }
}
```

Let's analyze this test class:

- **`@DynamicPropertySource`**: In modern Spring Boot testing, we don't always know which port a container will use. This annotation allows us to map the CockroachDB container's dynamic port to the `spring.r2dbc.url` property programmatically.
- **`blockFirst()`**: During test setup, we use `.blockFirst()` to wait for the created customer ID. This bridges the reactive response to our imperative test orchestration.
- **Virtual Threads Hammering the Cache**: We simulate 100 concurrent users. Since each request first hits the cache in `ManagementService`, this test proves our non-blocking cache implementation correctly scales without blocking the main event loops.

Reactive Type Comparison

To wrap up, let's compare the core reactive types against their traditional blocking counterparts.

Table 9-1. *Mono vs. Flux vs. Blocking*

Feature	Mono (`0..1`)	Flux (`0..N`)	Blocking Equivalent
Cardinality	Zero or One item.	Zero to Infinite items.	T or `List<T>`
Java Equivalent	`Optional<T>` or `CompletableFuture<T>`	`Stream<T>` or `Iterable<T>`	T (POJO) or `Collection<T>`
Behavior	Emits a single value (or error) and completes.	Emits a stream of values over time. Supports backpressure.	Returns the entire dataset at once (blocks until ready).
Use Case	`findById`, `exists`, `save` (return entity), `delete` (return void).	`findAll`, `streaming updates`, `file processing`, `infinite feeds`.	Standard CRUD where concurrency is low and simplicity is key.
Example	`Mono.just("User")`	`Flux.fromIterable(users)`	`return new User("User")`

To React or Not to React?

Reactive programming is powerful, but it is **not a silver bullet**. It introduces a paradigm shift that comes with significant trade-offs. As a professional developer, you must choose the right tool for the job.

The Cost of Reactive

- **Learning Curve**: Shifting from imperative (step-by-step) to declarative (stream-based) programming is difficult. Operators like `flatMap`, `switchMap`, and `concatMap` have distinct nuances that can trip up even experienced developers.

- **Debugging**: Stack traces in reactive streams often point to the framework internals rather than your business logic, making standard debugging harder.
- **Complexity**: Simple logic can become verbose when wrapped in reactive operators.

The Impact of Virtual Threads

With **Java 21** and **Spring Boot 4**, Virtual Threads (Project Loom) have changed the calculation. Virtual Threads allow traditional blocking code (Servlet stack) to handle massive concurrency, similar to Reactive, but without the complex API.

- **If You Are Starting a New Project**: Consider using **Spring MVC with Virtual Threads** (`spring.threads.virtual.enabled=true`). It gives you the scalability of reactive with the simplicity of blocking code.
- **If You Need Streaming/Backpressure**: Spring WebFlux is still the king. Features like infinite streams, Server-Sent Events (SSE), and WebSocket orchestration are native to the reactive model.

Table 9-2. *Choosing Your Reactive Stack*

Scenario	Recommended Stack	Why?
High Concurrency HTTP API	Spring MVC + Virtual Threads	Simple code, massive scalability, easy debugging.
Streaming / Real-time Data	Spring WebFlux	Native support for backpressure and infinite streams.
Edge Service / Gateway	Spring Cloud Gateway (WebFlux)	High throughput with low resource footprint.
Complex Data Orchestration	Spring WebFlux	Operators like `zip` and `merge` make composing parallel calls easy.
CPU-Intensive Tasks	Spring MVC (Platform Threads)	Reactive does not help with CPU-bound work; it blocks the event loop.

Summary

In this chapter, we performed a deep dive into the world of reactive programming with Spring Boot 4. We started by understanding the fundamental shift from the traditional blocking thread-per-request model to the non-blocking event-loop architecture, which allows a small number of threads to handle thousands of concurrent connections.

We explored the core of Project Reactor, mastering the `Mono` and `Flux` types and their rich set of operators. We then transitioned our persistence layer to **Spring Data R2DBC**, leveraging **CockroachDB** to build a fully non-blocking data access layer that supports reactive transactions.

Through our two case studies, we implemented the following:

- An **Annotation-Based** model in the Customer project, integrating resilient retry logic directly into our controllers to handle distributed transaction conflicts.
- A **Functional** model in the Management project, demonstrating the power of handler and router functions for explicit request orchestration and hierarchical data management.
- A **Reactive Cache-Aside** pattern to significantly optimize read performance while ensuring the main event loop remains non-blocking.

Finally, we verified the robustness of our systems using **WebTestClient** and **Testcontainers**, simulating extreme concurrency with **Java 21 Virtual Threads**. By mastering these patterns, you are now prepared to build the high-performance, resilient, and scalable systems required by modern, cloud-native environments. In the next chapter, we will expand our testing expertise by exploring comprehensive strategies for unit, integration, and contract testing across the entire Spring Boot ecosystem.

CHAPTER 10

Advanced Testing with Spring Boot

Building production-grade applications requires more than just functional code; it requires a comprehensive, high-performance testing suite. Spring Boot 4, leveraging Spring Framework 7 and Java 21/25, has revolutionized the testing landscape. The focus has shifted from monolithic integration tests to highly optimized "test slices," unified APIs, and deep integration with containerized infrastructure.

In this chapter, we will explore the cutting-edge testing features of Spring Boot 4, including:

- **Modularized Test Starters**: Using focused dependencies for specific layers.
- **Unified Testing with RestTestClient**: Adopting a single, fluent API for all REST tests.
- **Automatic Context Pausing**: A major performance breakthrough for large test suites.
- **JUnit 6 Baseline**: Embracing the next generation of the JVM's most popular testing framework.
- **Testcontainers 2.0**: Zero-config integration testing with real databases and services.

The Evolution of Testing in Spring Boot 4

Historically, testing a Spring Boot application often felt like a binary choice: write a lightweight unit test or load the entire application context with `@SpringBootTest`. The latter, while powerful, is slow and memory-intensive.

F. Gutierrez and D. Carter, *Pro Spring Boot 4*, https://doi.org/10.1007/979-8-8688-2640-5_10

Spring Boot 4 addresses this by doubling down on **Test Slices** and introducing **Automatic Context Pausing**. When you run a large suite, Spring now pauses inactive test contexts, releasing resources like background threads and scheduled tasks. This prevents the "resource exhaustion" commonly seen in CI/CD pipelines.

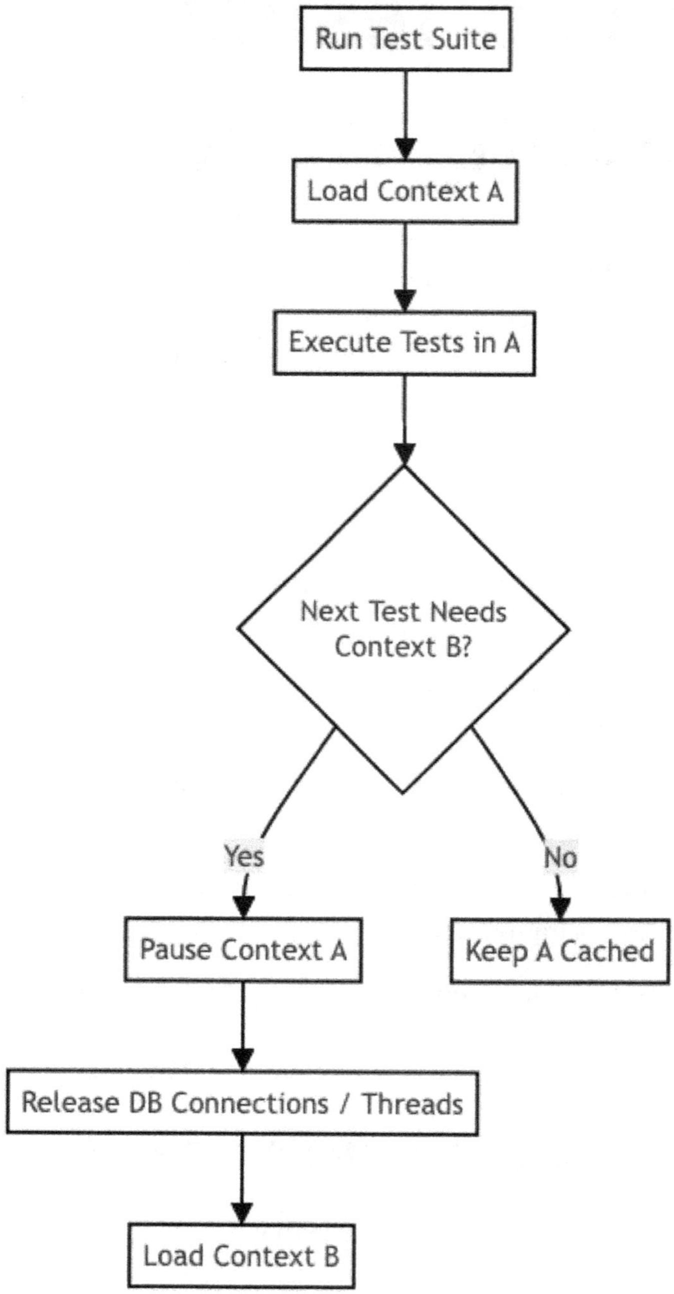

Figure 10-1. *Test Context Lifecycle in Spring Boot 4*

The Testing Pyramid and @SpringBootTest

Before diving into specific tools, it is crucial to understand where each test fits in a professional development lifecycle. A healthy test suite follows the **Testing Pyramid** principle: many fast unit tests at the base, fewer integration tests in the middle, and a small set of high-level smoke tests at the top.

Levels of Testing

- **Unit Tests**: Test a single class in isolation. They use pure JUnit 6 and Mockito (without Spring) and should execute in milliseconds.
- **Integration Tests**: Verify that multiple components work together. In Spring Boot, this is where **Test Slices** and **`@SpringBootTest`** shine.
- **Smoke Tests**: High-level checks to ensure the application starts and basic critical paths work (e.g., hitting a `/health` endpoint).
- **End-to-End (E2E) Tests**: Test the full system from the user's perspective, often involving real databases and external services.

Mastering @SpringBootTest

The **`@SpringBootTest`** annotation is the standard for integration testing. It tells Spring to search for your `@SpringBootApplication` class and load the **full ApplicationContext**.

Listing 10-1. src/test/java/com/apress/crm/ManagementIntegrationTests.java

```
@SpringBootTest(
    webEnvironment = WebEnvironment.RANDOM_PORT,
    properties = "spring.main.banner-mode=off"
)
class ManagementIntegrationTests {
    // Loads the full context: Controllers, Services, Repositories, etc.
}
```

Analyze the Configuration:

1. **webEnvironment**:
    - **MOCK (Default)**: Loads a web ApplicationContext and provides a mock servlet environment. Use this with MockMvc.
    - **RANDOM_PORT**: Starts a real embedded server (Tomcat/Netty) on an available port. Use this for "lifelike" tests with RestTestClient.
    - **NONE**: Loads the context but does not start any web server. Perfect for testing background services or batch jobs.
2. **properties**: Allows you to override specific application properties just for this test class.

When to Use It? Use @SpringBootTest for complex scenarios that involve cross-layer coordination. However, for testing individual layers (like a single repository), prefer **Test Slices** to keep your suite fast.

Modularized Test Starters

In previous versions, spring-boot-starter-test was a large, monolithic dependency. In Spring Boot 4, you should use granular starters to keep your test classpath clean and reduce startup time.

Listing 10-2. pom.xml

```xml
<dependencies>
    <!-- Core Testing (JUnit 6, AssertJ, Mockito) -->
    <dependency>
        <groupId>org.springframework.boot</groupId>
        <artifactId>spring-boot-starter-test</artifactId>
        <scope>test</scope>
    </dependency>

    <!-- Granular Starter for Spring MVC -->
    <dependency>
        <groupId>org.springframework.boot</groupId>
        <artifactId>spring-boot-starter-webmvc-test</artifactId>
```

```
        <scope>test</scope>
    </dependency>

    <!-- Granular Starter for Spring WebFlux -->
    <dependency>
        <groupId>org.springframework.boot</groupId>
        <artifactId>spring-boot-starter-webflux-test</artifactId>
        <scope>test</scope>
    </dependency>

    <!-- Integration with Testcontainers -->
    <dependency>
        <groupId>org.springframework.boot</groupId>
        <artifactId>spring-boot-testcontainers</artifactId>
        <scope>test</scope>
    </dependency>
</dependencies>
```

What's happening here? By splitting the starters, Spring Boot avoids loading the entire WebMvc infrastructure if you are only testing a Data R2DBC repository. Each module is optimized for its specific domain.

Embracing the JUnit 6 Baseline

Spring Boot 4 officially moves to **JUnit 6** as its baseline testing framework. JUnit 4 support has been removed, and the transition from JUnit 5 to 6 is seamless but significant for "Pro" developers. JUnit 6 focuses on a cleaner extension model and better support for hierarchical test structures.

Key Advantages of JUnit 6

- **Native `@Nested` Support**: You can organize tests into logical groups within a single class, with each group sharing specific setup logic.
- **Constructor Injection**: JUnit 6 allows you to inject dependencies (like `TestReporter` or custom Spring beans) directly into the test class constructor.

- **Cleaner Extension Model**: The older @RunWith (JUnit 4) and @ExtendWith (JUnit 5) logic is unified into a more powerful, annotation-based extension system that integrates deeply with Spring's TestContextFramework.

Listing 10-3. src/test/java/com/apress/crm/customer/CustomerLifecycleTests.java

```
@SpringBootTest
class CustomerLifecycleTests {

    @Nested
    @DisplayName("When creating a new customer")
    class CreationTests {
        @Test
        void shouldAssignValidUUID() { /* ... */ }

        @Test
        void shouldSendWelcomeEmail() { /* ... */ }
    }

    @Nested
    @DisplayName("When deleting a customer")
    class DeletionTests {
        @Test
        void shouldCleanupCache() { /* ... */ }
    }
}
```

Analyze the Pattern: By using @Nested, we create "living documentation" of our business rules. Each inner class represents a specific state or action, making the test output in your IDE or CI/CD pipeline much easier to read.

Mastering Test Slices

Test slices allow you to test a specific "slice" of the application by auto-configuring only the necessary components. Behind the scenes, this is powered by @TypeExcludeFilter, which prevents the regular component scanning from loading your entire application logic.

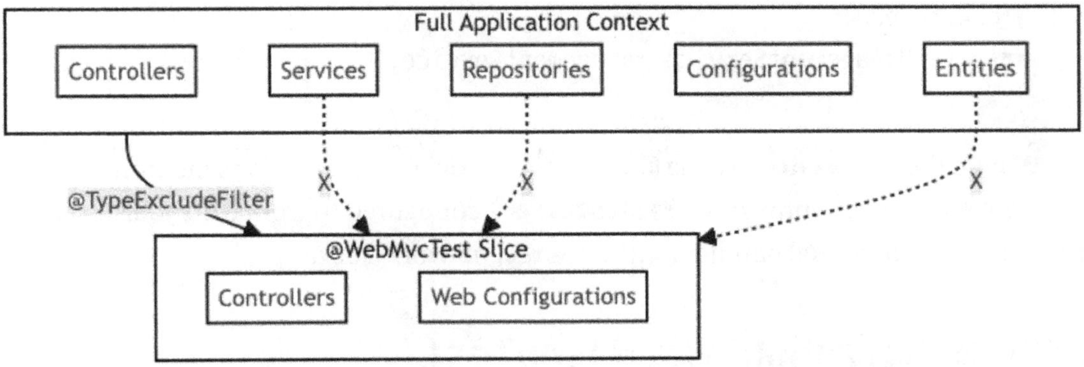

Figure 10-2. *Spring Boot Test Slice Architecture*

Web Layer Testing with @WebMvcTest

Use this when you want to verify your controller logic (mappings, validation, serialization) without starting a full HTTP server or connecting to a database.

Starter Required: To use this slice, you must include the **spring-boot-starter-webmvc-test** dependency in your project.

```
@WebMvcTest(CustomerController.class)
class CustomerControllerTest {
    // This slice loads: DispatcherServlet, Jackson, ControllerAdvice
    // This slice DOES NOT load: @Service, @Repository, @Component
}
```

Reactive Web Testing with @WebFluxTest

If your application uses the reactive stack (Spring WebFlux), you should use the **@WebFluxTest** slice. Similar to @WebMvcTest, it focuses only on the web layer but auto-configures the reactive infrastructure.

Starter Required: To use this slice, you must include the **spring-boot-starter-webflux-test** dependency.

```
@WebFluxTest(ManagementHandlers.class)
class ManagementHandlerTest {
    @Autowired
    private WebTestClient webTestClient; // Auto-configured for
    reactive testing
```

```
    @MockitoBean
    private ManagementService managementService;
}
```

What's the Difference? While `@WebMvcTest` provides `MockMvc` for synchronous testing, `@WebFluxTest` provides a **`WebTestClient`** configured to work with your reactive controllers or functional handlers without a real network stack.

JSON Serialization with `@JsonTest`

Testing complex JSON mapping logic is often overlooked. `@JsonTest` auto-configures `JacksonTester`, allowing you to verify that your Java Records are being transformed into the correct JSON structure.

Starter Required: This slice is included in the core **`spring-boot-starter-test`**, as it is a foundational utility for all JSON-based tests.

```
@JsonTest
class CustomerJsonTest {
    @Autowired
    private JacksonTester<Customer> json;

    // Verifies @JsonProperty, Date formats, and null-handling
}
```

Client-Side Testing with `@RestClientTest`

As seen in Chapter 3, declarative HTTP clients are the modern way to consume external APIs. `@RestClientTest` provides a mock server (`MockRestServiceServer`) to verify your client's outgoing requests.

Starter Required: To test declarative clients, you should use the **`spring-boot-starter-webmvc-test`** (for standard clients) or **`spring-boot-starter-webflux-test`** (for reactive clients).

```
@RestClientTest(CurrencyClient.class)
class CurrencyClientTest {
    // Simulates external API responses for the declarative client
}
```

Reactive Data Access with @DataR2dbcTest

For our CockroachDB-backed projects, this slice is essential. It configures the R2DBC infrastructure and provides an `R2dbcEntityTemplate` for testing queries in isolation.

Starter Required: To use this slice, you must include the **spring-boot-starter-data-r2dbc-test** dependency.

```
@DataR2dbcTest
class CustomerRepositoryTest {
    // Configures non-blocking database access infrastructure
}
```

Verification Strategies: Mockito and Hamcrest

While `RestTestClient` and AssertJ are the modern defaults, many "Pro" developers continue to leverage the power of **Mockito** for behavior verification and **Hamcrest** for expressive matching logic within `MockMvc`.

Listing 10-4. src/test/java/com/apress/crm/customer/CustomerControllerTest.java

```
@WebMvcTest(CustomerController.class)
class CustomerControllerTest {

    @Autowired
    private MockMvc mockMvc;

    @MockitoBean
    private CustomerService customerService;

    @Test
    void shouldReturnCustomerWithHamcrest() throws Exception {
        Customer mockCustomer = new Customer(UUID.randomUUID(), "Felipe",
        "Gutierrez", "felipe@test.com");

        // Mockito: Stubbing the behavior
        when(customerService.findById(any(UUID.class)))
            .thenReturn(Mono.just(mockCustomer));
```

```
        mockMvc.perform(get("/api/v1/customers/{id}", mockCustomer.id()))
            .andExpect(status().isOk())
            // Hamcrest: Expressive assertions
            .andExpect(jsonPath("$.firstName", is("Felipe")))
            .andExpect(jsonPath("$.email", containsString("@test.com")))
            .andExpect(jsonPath("$.lastName", notNullValue()));
    }
}
```

Let's Analyze This Code:

1. **`@MockitoBean`**: This is the modern Spring Boot 4 replacement for `@MockBean`. It automatically registers a Mockito mock into the test application context.
2. **Hamcrest Matchers**: By using static imports from `org.hamcrest.Matchers` (like `is`, `containsString`, and `notNullValue`), your assertions read like plain English sentences. This is particularly effective for verifying the structure and content of complex JSON payloads.

Unified API: `RestTestClient`

Spring Boot 4 introduces **`RestTestClient`**, a unified, fluent API that replaces the older `TestRestTemplate`. It provides a consistent developer experience whether you are testing against a mock environment (`MockMvc`) or a real running server.

Listing 10-5. src/test/java/com/apress/crm/customer/CustomerApiTests.java

```
@SpringBootTest(webEnvironment = RANDOM_PORT)
@AutoConfigureRestTestClient
class CustomerApiTests {

    @Autowired
    private RestTestClient client;
```

```
    @Test
    void shouldFindCustomer() {
        client.get().uri("/api/v1/customers/{id}", id)
            .exchange()
            .expectStatus().isOk()
            .expectBody()
            .jsonPath("$.firstName").isEqualTo("Felipe");
    }
}
```

Let's Analyze This Code: RestTestClient uses a non-blocking API inspired by the reactive WebClient. It is safer and more expressive than TestRestTemplate, particularly when using jsonPath to assert deep JSON structures.

Advanced Assertions: Awaitility and JsonPath

To build a truly professional test suite, you often need to assert beyond simple equality. Spring Boot 4 includes powerful libraries like **Awaitility** and **JsonPath** in its test starters to handle asynchronous logic and complex data structures.

Testing Asynchrony with Awaitility

In reactive or event-driven systems, some operations happen in the background. If you assert immediately after a call, the test might fail because the background thread hasn't finished. **Awaitility** provides a fluent DSL for polling until a condition is met.

Starter Required: Awaitility is typically included transitively in spring-boot-starter-test. However, if you need to add it manually or use it in a standalone module, use the following:

For Maven (pom.xml)

```
<dependency>
    <groupId>org.awaitility</groupId>
    <artifactId>awaitility</artifactId>
    <version>4.2.2</version>
    <scope>test</scope>
</dependency>
```

For Gradle (build.gradle)

```
testImplementation 'org.awaitility:awaitility:4.2.2'
```

Listing 10-6. src/test/java/com/apress/crm/customer/CustomerAsyncTests.java

```
@SpringBootTest
class CustomerAsyncTests {

    @Autowired
    private ManagementService service;

    @Test
    void shouldWaitForBackgroundCachePopulation() {
        UUID id = UUID.randomUUID();
        service.triggerBackgroundProcessing(id);

        // Awaitility: Poll until the cache is eventually populated
        await()
            .atMost(Duration.ofSeconds(5))
            .pollInterval(Duration.ofMillis(500))
            .until(() -> service.isCachePopulated(id));
    }
}
```

Let's Analyze This Code:

1. **Background Operation**: We trigger a task that runs on a separate thread (common in Chapter 9).
2. **Timeout Configuration**: We define a maximum wait time. If the condition isn't met in 5 seconds, the test fails.
3. **Polling Condition**: Awaitility will repeatedly execute this lambda until it returns `true`. This is much cleaner and more reliable than using `Thread.sleep()`.

Deep JSON Verification with JsonPath

When verifying REST responses, checking the entire string is brittle. **JsonPath** allows you to use a "query language" to assert specific parts of a JSON document.

```
client.get().uri("/api/v1/customers")
    .exchange()
    .expectBody()
    // JsonPath: Assert that the first customer in the array has the
    correct email
    .jsonPath("$[0].email").isEqualTo("felipe@test.com")
    // Assert that the 'id' field is a valid UUID string
    .jsonPath("$[0].id").exists()
    // Assert that no phone number is leaked if null
    .jsonPath("$[0].phone").doesNotExist();
```

Why Use It? JsonPath decouples your tests from the order of fields in the JSON. Even if you add new fields to your `Customer` Record later, these specific assertions will remain valid.

Advanced Bean Overriding

One of the most significant changes in Spring Boot 4 is the move toward a unified **Bean Overriding API**. The traditional annotations `@MockBean` and `@SpyBean` have been deprecated and replaced by cleaner, more robust alternatives that are now part of the core `spring-test` module.

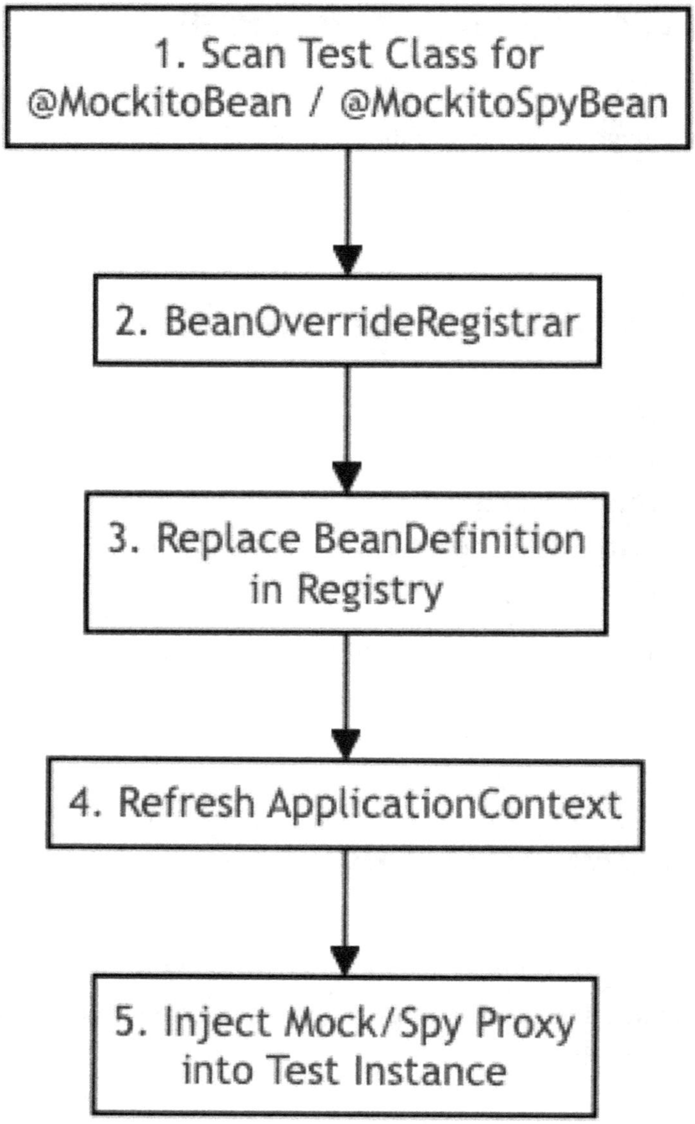

Figure 10-3. *Internal Flow of Bean Overriding*

Replacing Beans with `@MockitoBean`

Previously, overriding non-singleton beans resulted in an `IllegalStateException`. Spring Boot 4 now natively supports replacing these transient beans.

```
@SpringBootTest
class AnalyticsServiceTest {

    @MockitoBean // Replaces any @Bean (including Prototype scope) with a
    full mock
    private ExternalService mockService;
}
```

Partial Mocking with @MockitoSpyBean

If you need to mock only specific methods of a bean while keeping the original logic for others, you use a **Spy**. In Spring Boot 4, the traditional @SpyBean is replaced by **@MockitoSpyBean**.

Listing 10-7. src/test/java/com/apress/crm/management/ServiceSpyTests.java

```
@SpringBootTest
class ServiceSpyTests {

    @MockitoSpyBean
    private ManagementService managementService;

    @Test
    void shouldVerifySpecificMethodCall() {
        // We only mock one specific method
        doReturn(Mono.empty()).when(managementService).
        triggerBackgroundSync(any());

        managementService.getCustomerDetails(UUID.randomUUID());

        // We can verify interactions on the real bean
        verify(managementService, times(1)).getCustomerDetails(any());
    }
}
```

Analyze the Transition:

1. **Requirement**: Unlike the old @SpyBean, the new **@MockitoSpyBean** strictly requires the bean to already exist in the application context. It will not create one for you.
2. **Package Shift**: The new annotations move from org.springframework.boot.test.mock.mockito to the standardized org.springframework.test.context.bean.override.mockito package.
3. **Consistency**: This change aligns Spring Boot with the broader Spring Framework 7 strategy of providing a unified, framework-agnostic way to override beans in tests.

Decoupled Testing with @RecordApplicationEvents

Modern applications use events to decouple logic. Testing these flows used to require complex mocks. In Spring Boot 4, you can use the ApplicationEvents utility.

Listing 10-8. src/test/java/com/apress/crm/management/CustomerEventTests.java

```
@SpringBootTest
@RecordApplicationEvents
class CustomerEventTests {

    @Autowired
    private ApplicationEvents events;

    @Autowired
    private ManagementService service;

    @Test
    void shouldPublishEventWhenCustomerCreated() {
        service.createCustomerWithDetails(...);
```

```
        // Verify that exactly one event was published internally
        assertThat(events.stream(CustomerCreatedEvent.class)).hasSize(1);
    }
}
```

Analyze the Flow:

1. **@RecordApplicationEvents**: Tells Spring to start recording all events published within the ApplicationContext during the test.
2. **ApplicationEvents**: We inject this recorder to verify that our service correctly triggered the expected internal signals.

Testcontainers 2.0 and Development Mode

Spring Boot 4 features deep integration with **Testcontainers 2.0**. This allows you to run your integration tests against real databases like CockroachDB with zero manual configuration.

Zero-Config with @ServiceConnection

As we saw in Chapter 9, the @ServiceConnection annotation eliminates the need for manual property mapping.

Listing 10-9. src/test/java/com/apress/crm/BaseIntegrationTest.java

```
@Testcontainers
public abstract class BaseIntegrationTest {

    @Container
    @ServiceConnection
    static CockroachContainer cockroach = new
CockroachContainer("cockroachdb/cockroach:v25.4.0");
}
```

Analyze the Magic: Spring Boot detects the CockroachContainer and automatically sets spring.r2dbc.url, username, and password. You no longer need to write a @DynamicPropertySource block for standard containers.

Running the Application Against Testcontainers

A "Pro" tip for Spring Boot 4 is using **Testcontainers at development time**. You can create a specialized "Test Main" that starts your application but uses containerized infrastructure instead of your local DB.

Listing 10-10. src/test/java/com/apress/crm/TestCustomerApplication.java

```
public class TestCustomerApplication {
    public static void main(String[] args) {
        SpringApplication.from(CustomerApplication::main)
            .with(TestcontainersConfiguration.class)
            .run(args);
    }
}
```

What Is Happening Here?

1. **`SpringApplication.from(...)`**: This new API allows you to launch your production `main` method within a test-aware wrapper.
2. **`with(TestcontainersConfiguration.class)`**: You provide a configuration class that defines the containers you want to start. Spring Boot 4 will start these containers and automatically override your `application.properties` (like `spring.r2dbc.url`) to point to the temporary containerized instances.

This allows developers to run the entire application locally by simply executing this `main` method from their IDE, without ever installing a local database. It is the ultimate "Zero-Install" development experience.

Docker Compatibility Note: During the development of the samples for this book, I discovered that **Docker Engine v29** (included in Docker Desktop 4.52.0) has significant networking issues with the Testcontainers 2.0 bridge. If you encounter "Connection Refused" errors during test startup, I highly recommend downgrading your Docker engine to **v28.5.2** (Docker Desktop v4.51.0), which has been verified to work perfectly with Spring Boot 4.

Testing Tools Reference Table

Choosing the right testing tool is critical for maintaining a fast and reliable suite.

Table 10-1. *Spring Boot 4 Testing Toolbox*

Tool	Scope	Best Use Case
JUnit 6	Core Framework	Foundations, assertions, and test orchestration.
MockMvc	Server-side (Mock)	Fast, isolated web layer testing without a network stack.
RestTestClient	Unified (Mock or Real)	High-level API verification. Modern, fluent alternative to TestRestTemplate.
StepVerifier	Reactive	Testing asynchronous `Mono` and `Flux` streams and backpressure.
Testcontainers	Infrastructure	Integration tests against real databases, brokers, and cloud services.
JacksonTester	Serialization	Verifying complex JSON mappings and date/time formats.

The Extended Testing Toolbox

While we have focused on Web, R2DBC, and Testcontainers, Spring Boot 4 provides a vast array of specialized testing modules. The modular architecture allows you to pick exactly what you need for your specific stack.

Table 10-2. *Additional Spring Boot 4 Test Modules*

Module	Annotation	CRM Application Context
JDBC	`@JdbcTest`	Perfect for the Customer project if we stick to classic `JdbcClient` without the full Spring Data abstraction.
MongoDB	`@DataMongoTest`	Ideal if the Management project adds a "Support Notes" feature requiring a document store.
Redis	`@DataRedisTest`	Use this to verify that our `ConcurrentHashMap` cache could be safely migrated to a real Redis cluster.
GraphQL	`@GraphQlTest`	Use this if we expose a GraphQL API for complex hierarchical customer data traversal.
Cassandra	`@DataCassandraTest`	Highly relevant if the CRM needs to handle massive time-series activity logs for global customers.
Ldap	`@DataLdapTest`	Useful for testing authentication logic if the CRM integrates with a corporate Active Directory.

Wait, there's more! Spring Boot 4's modularity is truly extensive. Beyond these, you will find specialized support for **Apache Kafka**, **RabbitMQ**, **Spring AI**, and even **Elasticsearch**. Always check the latest documentation at `docs.spring.io` to find the exact starter that minimizes your test footprint.

Summary

In this chapter, we explored the advanced testing capabilities that make Spring Boot 4 the most robust framework for enterprise Java development.

- We mastered **Test Slices** to build fast, focused test suites.
- We adopted **RestTestClient** as our unified API for REST verification.
- We learned how **Automatic Context Pausing** and **Modular Starters** optimize resource usage.

- We explored advanced bean overriding with **`@MockitoBean`** and event verification with **`@RecordApplicationEvents`**.
- We leveraged **Testcontainers 2.0** to build lifelike integration tests and even run our applications in a "DB-less" local environment.

Testing is no longer a chore; it is an integrated part of the development workflow that ensures your Spring Boot 4 applications are resilient, scalable, and ready for production. In the next chapter, we will shift our focus to **Security**, learning how to protect our reactive and synchronous services using Spring Security 6 and OAuth2.

CHAPTER 11

Securing Spring Boot Applications

Security is no longer an optional "add-on" feature; it is a fundamental pillar of modern enterprise applications. In a world of increasing cyber threats and strict data privacy regulations, building secure systems by design is mandatory for any "Pro" developer. Spring Security 7, integrated into Spring Boot 4, provides a robust, modular, and highly flexible framework to handle authentication, authorization, and protection against common exploits.

In this chapter, we will explore the security advancements in Spring Boot 4, transitioning from foundational concepts to advanced OAuth2 and Reactive security patterns. We will cover:

- **Modular Security Architecture**: Reducing the attack surface by using focused starters.
- **Component-Based Configuration**: Mastering the Lambda DSL and the removal of legacy adapters.
- **Advanced Authorization**: Granular control using method-specific and role-based request matchers.
- **Fine-Grained Authorization**: RBAC and method-level security with `@PreAuthorize`.
- **Advanced Patterns**: Using custom **Meta-Annotations** for clean, type-safe security logic.
- **Exploit Protection**: Implementing robust **CORS** and **CSRF** strategies for REST APIs.

F. Gutierrez and D. Carter, *Pro Spring Boot 4*, https://doi.org/10.1007/979-8-8688-2640-5_11

- **Secure Storage**: Mastering **Password Encoding with BCrypt** and delegation.
- **Identity Contracts**: Implementing custom **UserDetailsService** for local database integration.
- **Modern Authentication**: Implementing One-Time Tokens (OTT), Passkeys, and **Two-Factor Authentication (2FA)**.
- **Zero Trust Architecture**: Securing service-to-service communication with **mTLS and SSL Bundles**.
- **Case Study 1 (Servlet)**: Securing the Customer CRM with OTT and modern SSL monitoring.
- **Case Study 2 (Reactive)**: Protecting the Management System with OAuth2, OIDC, and mTLS.

Modern Security Architecture

Spring Boot 4 aligns with **Spring Framework 7** and **Jakarta EE 11**, enforcing a strictly component-based security model. The framework has moved away from deep class hierarchies and inheritance-based configuration in favor of a more functional, bean-oriented approach.

One of the most significant changes is the further **modularization of starters**. Instead of using a single, heavy security starter, you can now include only the modules your project requires.

- **`spring-boot-starter-security`**: The core Servlet-based security starter.
- **`spring-boot-starter-oauth2-client`**: Focused logic for OAuth2 and OpenID Connect clients.
- **`spring-boot-starter-oauth2-resource-server`**: Lightweight support for securing APIs with JWTs.

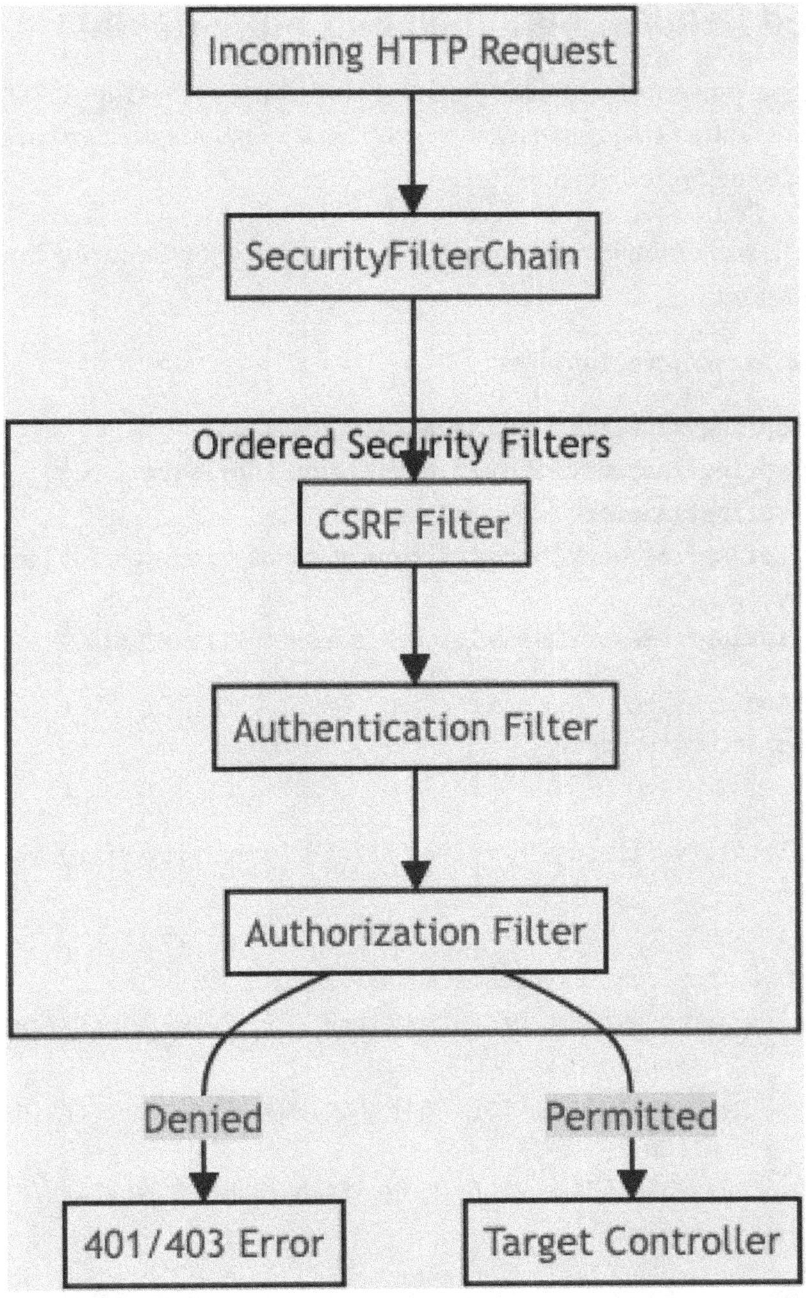

Figure 11-1. *The Security Filter Chain Logic*

The **Security Filter Chain** acts as the gatekeeper. Every request must pass through a series of filters before reaching your business logic. In Spring Boot 4, configuring this chain using the **Lambda DSL** is the standard.

Advanced Request Matching and Authorization

One of the most powerful features of the SecurityFilterChain is the ability to define granular access rules using requestMatchers. This allows you to secure specific parts of your API while keeping others public.

Listing 11-1. src/main/java/com/apress/crm/customer/SecurityConfig.java (Advanced Matching)

```
package com.apress.crm.customer;

import org.springframework.context.annotation.Bean;
import org.springframework.context.annotation.Configuration;
import org.springframework.http.HttpMethod;
import org.springframework.security.config.annotation.web.builders.
HttpSecurity;
import org.springframework.security.web.SecurityFilterChain;

@Configuration
public class SecurityConfig {

    @Bean
    public SecurityFilterChain filterChain(HttpSecurity http) throws
    Exception {
        http
            .authorizeHttpRequests(auth -> auth
                .requestMatchers(HttpMethod.GET, "/api/v1/customers/**").
                hasAuthority("SCOPE_read")
                .requestMatchers(HttpMethod.POST, "/api/v1/customers").
                hasRole("ADMIN")
                .requestMatchers("/api/v1/public/**", "/health/**").
                permitAll()
                .anyRequest().authenticated()
            );
        return http.build();
    }
}
```

Let's Analyze These Scenarios:

1. **Method-Specific Matching**: You can restrict access based on the HTTP verb. Here, anyone with the `SCOPE_read` authority can perform GET requests on all customer paths.
2. **Role-Based Control**: Creating a new customer (POST) is a sensitive operation restricted only to users with the `ADMIN` role. Note that `hasRole("ADMIN")` internally checks for the `ROLE_ADMIN` authority.
3. **Public Endpoints**: You can whitelist specific patterns (like a public API or Actuator health checks) using `permitAll()`.
4. **Catch-All Rule**: It is a security best practice to always end your configuration with `anyRequest().authenticated()`. This ensures that if you add a new controller later and forget to secure it, it remains protected by default.

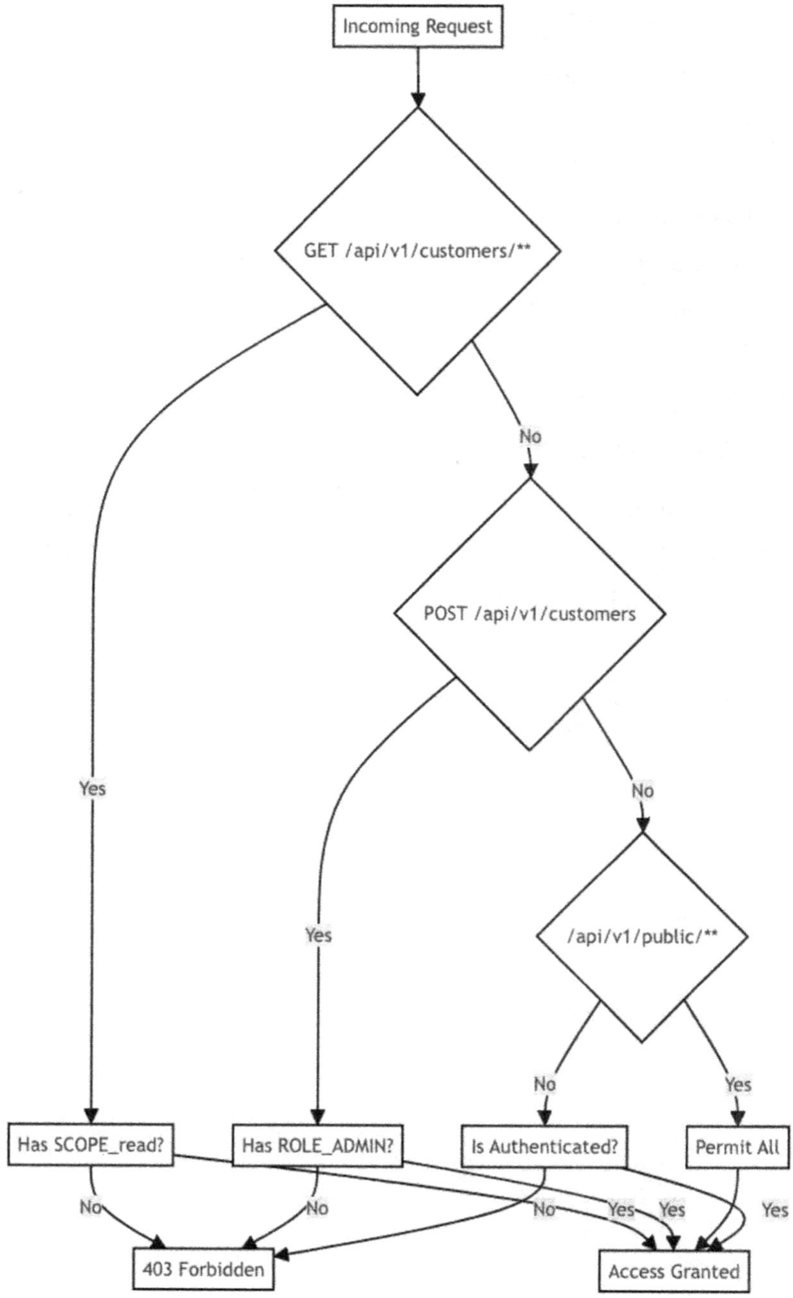

Figure 11-2. *Multi-Layered Request Authorization Flow*

Fine-Grained Authorization: RBAC and Method Security

While URL-based security is excellent for general access control, complex business logic often requires **Role-Based Access Control (RBAC)** enforced at the method level. This ensures that even if a URL is accessible, specific actions (like deleting a record) are restricted based on the user's granted authorities.

In Spring Security 7, method security is enabled by default in many starters, but it is best practice to be explicit.

Listing 11-2. src/main/java/com/apress/crm/customer/MethodSecurityConfig.java

```
package com.apress.crm.customer;

import org.springframework.context.annotation.Configuration;
import org.springframework.security.config.annotation.method.configuration.
EnableMethodSecurity;

@Configuration
@EnableMethodSecurity
public class MethodSecurityConfig {
}
```

- **`@EnableMethodSecurity`**: This replaces the legacy `@EnableGlobalMethodSecurity`. It enables the use of `@PreAuthorize`, `@PostAuthorize`, `@PreFilter`, and `@PostFilter`.

Using @PreAuthorize for Dynamic Rules

The most common annotation is **`@PreAuthorize`**, which uses Spring Expression Language (SpEL) to decide if a method should be executed.

Listing 11-3. src/main/java/com/apress/crm/customer/CustomerService.java

```
package com.apress.crm.customer;

import org.springframework.security.access.prepost.PreAuthorize;
import org.springframework.stereotype.Service;
import java.util.UUID;
```

```
@Service
public class CustomerService {

    @PreAuthorize("hasRole('ADMIN') or hasAuthority('SCOPE_
    customer:write')")
    public void deleteCustomer(UUID id) {
        // ... logic ...
    }

    @PreAuthorize("#customer.owner == authentication.name")
    public void updateCustomer(Customer customer) {
        // ... logic ...
    }
}
```

Let's Analyze These Authorization Patterns:

1. **Role vs. Authority**: `hasRole('ADMIN')` looks for an authority named `ROLE_ADMIN`. `hasAuthority('SCOPE_customer:write')` looks for the exact string match, typically used in OAuth2/OIDC scopes.
2. **Domain-Object Security**: SpEL can access method arguments. Here, we ensure that only the "owner" of the customer record (matching the authenticated username) can perform an update. This is a powerful way to implement **Instance-Level Security**.

Advanced Patterns: Custom Security Meta-Annotations

While `@PreAuthorize` is flexible, repeating the same string-based SpEL expressions throughout your codebase is error-prone. A "Pro" developer uses **Meta-Annotations** to create a custom security DSL for their project.

Listing 11-4. src/main/java/com/apress/crm/customer/IsAdmin.java (Security Shortcut)

```
package com.apress.crm.customer;

import org.springframework.security.access.prepost.PreAuthorize;
import java.lang.annotation.*;
```

```
@Target({ ElementType.METHOD, ElementType.TYPE })
@Retention(RetentionPolicy.RUNTIME)
@PreAuthorize("hasRole('ADMIN') or hasAuthority('SCOPE_customer:write')")
public @interface IsAdmin {
}
```

By creating this annotation, you can now secure your service methods with `@IsAdmin` instead of a long string. But we can go even further by mapping the **Principal** directly to our domain model.

Listing 11-5. src/main/java/com/apress/crm/customer/CRMUser.java (Principal Mapping)

```
package com.apress.crm.customer;

import
org.springframework.security.core.annotation.AuthenticationPrincipal;
import java.lang.annotation.*;

@Target({ ElementType.PARAMETER })
@Retention(RetentionPolicy.RUNTIME)
@AuthenticationPrincipal(expression = "#this instanceof T(org.
springframework.security.oauth2.core.oidc.user.OidcUser) ?
attributes['email'] : username")
public @interface CRMUser {
}
```

Analyze the Power of Custom Annotations:

1. **Reusable Logic**: The `@IsAdmin` annotation centralizes your authorization policy. If the "Admin" definition changes (e.g., you add a new scope), you only update it in one place.

2. **Clean Controllers**: With `@CRMUser`, your controller methods can now look like this: `public void save(@CRMUser String userEmail, ...)`. The annotation handles the complex logic of extracting the identity, whether the user logged in via Form, OTT, or OIDC.

Applying Custom Annotations in Practice

Let's see how these type-safe shortcuts simplify our code and improve readability.

Listing 11-6. src/main/java/com/apress/crm/customer/CustomerController.java (Using Annotations)

```
package com.apress.crm.customer;

import org.springframework.web.bind.annotation.*;
import org.springframework.http.ResponseEntity;
import static org.springframework.http.HttpStatus.CREATED;

@RestController
@RequestMapping("/api/v1/customers")
public class CustomerController {

    private final CustomerService customerService;

    public CustomerController(CustomerService customerService) {
        this.customerService = customerService;
    }

    @PostMapping
    @IsAdmin
    public ResponseEntity<Customer> create(@RequestBody Customer customer,
    @CRMUser String createdBy) {
        // ... logic ...
        return ResponseEntity.status(CREATED).body(customerService.
        save(customer));
    }
}
```

Analyze the Implementation:

1. **`@IsAdmin`**: Instead of a brittle string like `@PreAuthorize("hasRole('ADMIN')...")`, we use our custom meta-annotation. This makes the security requirement immediately obvious to any developer reading the code.

2. **@CRMUser**: Notice how we no longer need to manually cast the `Principal` or inspect the `SecurityContext`. Spring Security 7 resolves the email address automatically using our custom logic, resulting in a much cleaner method signature.

Exploit Protection: CSRF and CORS

Building a REST API requires protecting users from common web exploits. Spring Security 7 provides robust defaults for **CSRF** and **CORS**.

- **CSRF (Cross-Site Request Forgery)**: Prevents an attacker from tricking a user's browser into performing unwanted actions on a different site where they are authenticated. For traditional web apps, Spring uses a "Synchronizer Token Pattern." For SPAs (React/ Angular), it can be configured to use a cookie-based approach.
- **CORS (Cross-Origin Resource Sharing)**: A browser-enforced security mechanism that restricts how a web page from one domain can request resources from another domain.

Listing 11-7. src/main/java/com/apress/crm/customer/SecurityConfig.java (CORS/CSRF)

```
package com.apress.crm.customer;

import org.springframework.context.annotation.Bean;
import org.springframework.context.annotation.Configuration;
import org.springframework.security.config.annotation.web.builders.
HttpSecurity;
import org.springframework.security.web.SecurityFilterChain;
import org.springframework.security.web.csrf.CookieCsrfTokenRepository;
import org.springframework.web.cors.CorsConfiguration;
import java.util.List;

@Configuration
public class SecurityConfig {

    @Bean
```

```
    public SecurityFilterChain exploitFilterChain(HttpSecurity http) throws
    Exception {
        http
            .csrf(csrf -> csrf
                .csrfTokenRepository(CookieCsrfTokenRepository.
                withHttpOnlyFalse())
            )
            .cors(cors -> cors.configurationSource(request -> {
                CorsConfiguration config = new CorsConfiguration();
                config.setAllowedOrigins(List.of("https://trusted-
                frontend.com"));
                config.setAllowedMethods(List.of("GET", "POST", "PUT",
                "DELETE"));
                return config;
            }));
        return http.build();
    }
}
```

- **CSRF for SPAs**: By setting `withHttpOnlyFalse`, the JavaScript frontend can read the CSRF token from the cookie and include it in headers for state-changing requests (POST/PUT).
- **CORS Origin**: We explicitly whitelist the frontend domain that is allowed to consume our API.

Secure Credential Storage: Password Encoding

If your application manages its own users, you must **never** store passwords in plain text. Spring Security enforces the use of the `PasswordEncoder` interface.

BCrypt is the recommended standard. It is a slow, salted hashing algorithm that is resistant to rainbow table attacks and brute-force attempts.

Listing 11-8. src/main/java/com/apress/crm/customer/PasswordConfig.java

```
package com.apress.crm.customer;

import org.springframework.context.annotation.Bean;
import org.springframework.context.annotation.Configuration;
import
org.springframework.security.crypto.factory.PasswordEncoderFactories;
import org.springframework.security.crypto.password.PasswordEncoder;

@Configuration
public class PasswordConfig {

    @Bean
    public PasswordEncoder passwordEncoder() {
        // Uses BCrypt by default, but supports multiple formats for
           migration
        return PasswordEncoderFactories.createDelegatingPasswordEncoder();
    }
}
```

- **DelegatingPasswordEncoder**: This is a "Pro" best practice. It allows you to use BCrypt for new passwords while still supporting older hashes (like SHA-256) for legacy users, enabling a smooth migration path without forcing everyone to reset their passwords.

The Identity Contract: Custom User Management

Spring Security is designed to be identity-agnostic. It doesn't care if your users are stored in a relational database, an LDAP directory, or fetched via a REST API. To bridge your domain model (like our `Customer` entity) with the security framework, you implement the **UserDetailsService** interface.

This interface has a single method: `loadUserByUsername`. Its job is to find a user and wrap it in a **UserDetails** object that Spring Security understands.

Listing 11-9. src/main/java/com/apress/crm/customer/SecurityConfig.java (Custom UserDetailsService)

```
package com.apress.crm.customer;

import org.springframework.context.annotation.Bean;
import org.springframework.security.core.userdetails.User;
import org.springframework.security.core.userdetails.UserDetailsService;
import
org.springframework.security.core.userdetails.UsernameNotFoundException;

@Bean
public UserDetailsService userDetailsService(CustomerRepository
repository) {
    return username -> repository.findByEmail(username)
        .map(customer -> User.withUsername(customer.email())
            .password(customer.password()) // Must be encoded
            (e.g., BCrypt)
            .authorities("ROLE_USER")
            .build())
        .orElseThrow(() -> new UsernameNotFoundException("User not found: "
        + username));
}
```

Let's Analyze This Mapping:

1. **Repository Integration**: We use our existing `CustomerRepository` to fetch the record. This is why Spring Security is so powerful: it plugins directly into your existing data access layer.

2. **User Builder**: The `User.withUsername(...)` fluent API is the standard way to create a `UserDetails` implementation. It handles the mapping of your domain fields (email, password) to the security context.

Reactive Equivalents: For our management project, the contract is identical in spirit but uses the **`ReactiveUserDetailsService`**, which returns a `Mono<UserDetails>`. This ensures the identity lookup never blocks the event loop.

Case Study 1: The Customer Project (Servlet Security)

Our **Customer CRM** uses the standard Spring MVC Servlet stack. We will secure it using one of the most exciting new features in the Spring Security ecosystem: **One-Time Token (OTT) Login**. This allows users to log in via a "magic link" sent to their email, eliminating the need for complex password management for simple internal tools.

Project Configuration (Maven)

Add the focused security and validation starters to your `pom.xml`.

Listing 11-10. pom.xml

```
<dependencies>
    <dependency>
        <groupId>org.springframework.boot</groupId>
        <artifactId>spring-boot-starter-security</artifactId>
    </dependency>
    <!-- Required for One-Time Token Support -->
    <dependency>
        <groupId>org.springframework.security</groupId>
        <artifactId>spring-security-cas</artifactId>
    </dependency>
</dependencies>
```

What's happening here? We include the core security starter. For OTT, we also ensure our classpath has the necessary token generation utilities.

The Rise of Password-Less: One-Time Tokens

The traditional username/password model is increasingly seen as a liability. Users struggle with password fatigue, and databases full of hashed passwords are prime targets for hackers. **One-Time Token (OTT) Login**—often referred to as "Magic Links"—is a modern alternative that provides high security with minimal friction.

Key Features of OTT

- **Zero Password Storage**: Your application no longer needs to store or manage user passwords, eliminating an entire category of security risks.
- **Single-Use Assurance**: Each token is cryptographically generated and is immediately invalidated after its first successful use.
- **Time-Bound Security**: Tokens have a very short lifespan (typically 5-15 minutes), drastically reducing the window of opportunity for an attacker.
- **Seamless Integration**: Spring Security 7 provides native support for generating and validating these tokens via the `oneTimeTokenLogin()` DSL.

Ideal Use Cases

1. **Internal Administrative Tools**: For tools like our Customer CRM, where users are already part of a trusted corporate email system.
2. **Low-Friction Onboarding**: Reducing the barrier to entry for new users by not requiring them to create yet another password.
3. **Multi-Factor Fallback**: Using OTT as a reliable second factor or recovery method when a primary credential is lost.

Implementing One-Time Token (OTT) Login

In Spring Boot 4, we define a `SecurityFilterChain` bean. We will configure it to use OTT and permit access to the H2 console for development.

Listing 11-11. src/main/java/com/apress/crm/customer/SecurityConfig.java

```
package com.apress.crm.customer;

import org.springframework.context.annotation.Bean;
import org.springframework.context.annotation.Configuration;
```

```
import org.springframework.security.config.Customizer;
import org.springframework.security.config.annotation.web.builders.Htt
pSecurity;
import org.springframework.security.web.SecurityFilterChain;

@Configuration
public class SecurityConfig {

    @Bean
    public SecurityFilterChain filterChain(HttpSecurity http) throws
    Exception {
        http
            .authorizeHttpRequests(auth -> auth
                .requestMatchers("/h2-console/**").permitAll()
                .anyRequest().authenticated()
            )
            .csrf(csrf -> csrf.ignoringRequestMatchers("/h2-console/**"))
            .headers(headers -> headers.frameOptions(f -> f.sameOrigin()))
            .oneTimeTokenLogin(Customizer.withDefaults())
            .formLogin(Customizer.withDefaults());

        return http.build();
    }
}
```

Analyze the Configuration:

1. **Request Matching**: We use `requestMatchers` to explicitly permit access to the database console while requiring authentication for every other endpoint.
2. **CSRF/Headers**: For the H2 console to work properly, we must ignore CSRF for those paths and allow frames from the same origin.
3. **`oneTimeTokenLogin()`**: This enables the OTT flow. When a user enters their email, Spring will generate a token. You can provide a custom `OneTimeTokenGenerationSuccessHandler` to send this token via email or SMS.

Handling Token Success: Sending the Magic Link

By default, Spring Security generates the token but doesn't know how you want to deliver it. You must provide a **OneTimeTokenGenerationSuccessHandler** to bridge the gap between the security framework and your notification system (like JavaMail or Twilio).

Listing 11-12. src/main/java/com/apress/crm/customer/CrmOttSuccessHandler.java

```
package com.apress.crm.customer;

import org.springframework.security.authentication.ott.OneTimeToken;
import org.springframework.security.web.authentication.ott.OneTimeTokenGene
rationSuccessHandler;
import org.springframework.security.web.util.UrlUtils;
import org.springframework.stereotype.Component;
import org.springframework.web.util.UriComponentsBuilder;
import jakarta.servlet.http.HttpServletRequest;
import jakarta.servlet.http.HttpServletResponse;
import java.io.IOException;

@Component
public class CrmOttSuccessHandler implements
OneTimeTokenGenerationSuccessHandler {

    @Override
    public void handle(HttpServletRequest request, HttpServletResponse
    response, OneTimeToken ott) throws IOException {
        // Generate the full Magic Link URL
        String redirectUri = UriComponentsBuilder.fromUriString(UrlUtils.
        buildFullRequestUrl(request))
                .replacePath(request.getContextPath() + "/login/ott")
                .queryParam("token", ott.getTokenValue())
                .build().toUriString();

        // Pro Tip: In production, send this via email using JavaMailSender
        System.out.println("Magic Link sent to " + ott.getUsername() + ": "
        + redirectUri);
```

```
        // For this demo, we redirect to a success page
        response.sendRedirect("/ott-sent");
    }
}
```

Analyze the Success Handler: This class intercepts the token generation. It builds a "Magic Link" that points back to the `/login/ott` endpoint with the unique token as a query parameter. In a real-world CRM, you would inject a mail service here to send this link to the customer's verified email address.

Elevating Trust: Two-Factor Authentication (2FA)

In high-security environments, a single form of authentication is rarely enough. **Two-Factor Authentication (2FA)** adds a critical layer of defense by requiring users to provide two different types of evidence: something they know (a password or OTT) and something they have (a code from an Authenticator app or a hardware key).

2FA Strategies in Spring Boot 4

Spring Security 7 provides a flexible foundation for implementing MFA (Multi-Factor Authentication).

- **Time-Based One-Time Password (TOTP)**: Generating a 6-digit code that changes every 30 seconds, compatible with Google Authenticator or Authy.
- **SMS/Email Fallback**: Sending a numeric code via a separate communication channel (e.g., via Twilio).
- **Duo/FIDO2 Integration**: Supporting physical security keys for the highest level of protection.

Step-by-Step: Implementing TOTP Authentication

Let's implement a professional TOTP flow for our Customer Project. This allows our users to use any third-party authenticator app.

Step 1: Add the TOTP Library. Add the industry-standard GoogleAuth library to your `pom.xml`.

```xml
<dependency>
    <groupId>com.warrenstrange</groupId>
    <artifactId>googleauth</artifactId>
    <version>1.5.0</version>
</dependency>
```

Step 2: Create the MFA Verification Service. This service will handle generating secrets for new users and validating the 6-digit codes they provide.

Listing 11-13. src/main/java/com/apress/crm/customer/MfaService.java

```java
package com.apress.crm.customer;

import com.warrenstrange.googleauth.GoogleAuthenticator;
import org.springframework.stereotype.Service;

@Service
public class MfaService {
    private final GoogleAuthenticator gAuth = new GoogleAuthenticator();

    public String generateSecret() {
        return gAuth.createCredentials().getKey();
    }

    public boolean verifyCode(String secret, int code) {
        return gAuth.authorize(secret, code);
    }
}
```

Step 3: Configure Step-Up Authentication. Instead of forcing 2FA at login, we will implement **Step-Up Authentication**. This means users only need their second factor when they try to access sensitive administrative features.

Listing 11-14. src/main/java/com/apress/crm/customer/SecurityConfig.java (MFA Setup)

```java
package com.apress.crm.customer;

import org.springframework.context.annotation.Bean;
import org.springframework.context.annotation.Configuration;
```

```
import org.springframework.security.config.Customizer;
import org.springframework.security.config.annotation.web.builders.Htt
pSecurity;
import org.springframework.security.web.SecurityFilterChain;

@Configuration
public class SecurityConfig {

    @Bean
    public SecurityFilterChain mfaFilterChain(HttpSecurity http) throws
    Exception {
        http
            .authorizeHttpRequests(auth -> auth
                .requestMatchers("/api/v1/admin/**").hasRole("MFA_
                AUTHENTICATED")
                .anyRequest().authenticated()
            )
            .exceptionHandling(ex -> ex
                .accessDeniedHandler((request, response,
                accessDeniedException) -> {
                    // If authenticated but missing MFA role, redirect
                       to verify
                    response.sendRedirect("/mfa-verify");
                })
            )
            .formLogin(Customizer.withDefaults());
        return http.build();
    }
}
```

Let's Analyze the 2FA Flow:

1. **Elevated Authority**: We define a specific role (MFA_AUTHENTICATED) required for sensitive administrative paths. Users logged in with just a password have ROLE_USER but not this elevated role.

2. **Access Denied Redirect**: When a user hits a forbidden admin path, our custom handler catches the `AccessDeniedException` and sends them to the MFA verification page. Once they enter the correct TOTP code from their app, we update their authentication with the new role.

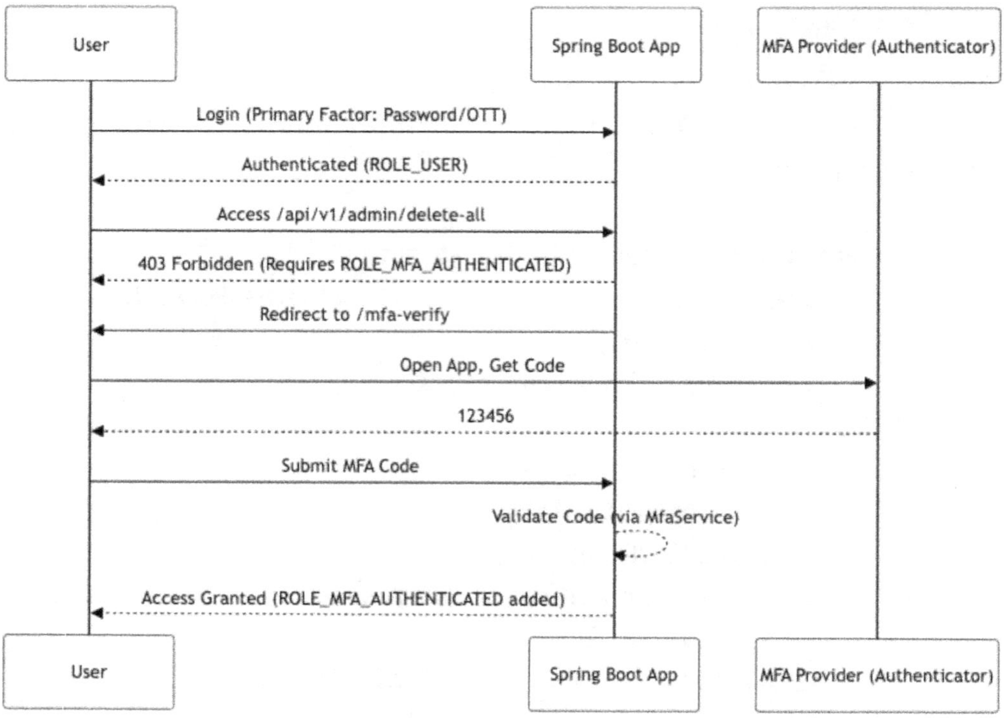

Figure 11-3. *Two-Factor Authentication (2FA) Flow*

Pro Tip For a truly modern experience, consider using **Passkeys (WebAuthn)**. This standard allows users to authenticate using biometric data (FaceID/TouchID) or hardware keys, providing a more secure and faster alternative to traditional 2FA methods. Spring Security 7 has native support for Passkey registration and login.

Advanced SSL Health Monitoring

Spring Boot 4 introduces enhanced monitoring for your security certificates. It now tracks the full chain and reports precisely when a certificate is nearing its end.

Listing 11-15. src/main/resources/application.properties

```
# Enable detailed SSL health info
management.health.ssl.enabled=true
# Notify if certificates expire within 30 days
management.health.ssl.certificate-validity-threshold=30d
```

When you access /actuator/health, the new **expiringChains** field will provide a detailed list of certificates that need rotation, allowing your SRE team to take action before a service interruption occurs.

We will take a much deeper dive into the health ecosystem, custom indicators, and advanced monitoring patterns in Chapter 13.

Modern Identity: OAuth2 and JWT

As we move toward distributed microservices and reactive architectures, traditional session-based security (using JSESSIONID cookies) becomes difficult to scale. Modern identity management relies on **OAuth2** for authorization and **OIDC (OpenID Connect)** for authentication, typically using **JWT (JSON Web Tokens)** as the secure transport for user information.

Why Stateless Security?

In a reactive, cloud-native system, your services should be stateless. This allows any instance of a service to handle any request without needing to share session data across a cluster.

Table 11-1. Stateful (Session) vs. Stateless (JWT) Security

Feature	Session-Based (Stateful)	Token-Based (JWT/Stateless)
Storage	Stored on the server (Memory/Redis).	Stored on the client (Browser/App).
Scalability	Requires session replication or "Sticky Sessions."	Horizontally scalable by design.
Revocation	Easy (delete the session from the server).	Complex (requires short TTL or block-lists).
Overhead	Small cookies, but server-side memory cost.	Larger tokens, but no server-side storage cost.

OAuth2 Actors and Flow

OAuth2 defines a standardized way for applications to obtain limited access to user accounts.

- **Resource Owner**: The user who owns the data.
- **Client**: The application (like our Management System) requesting access.
- **Authorization Server**: The system that authenticates the user and issues tokens (e.g., Keycloak).
- **Resource Server**: The API (like our Customer CRM) that accepts the tokens.

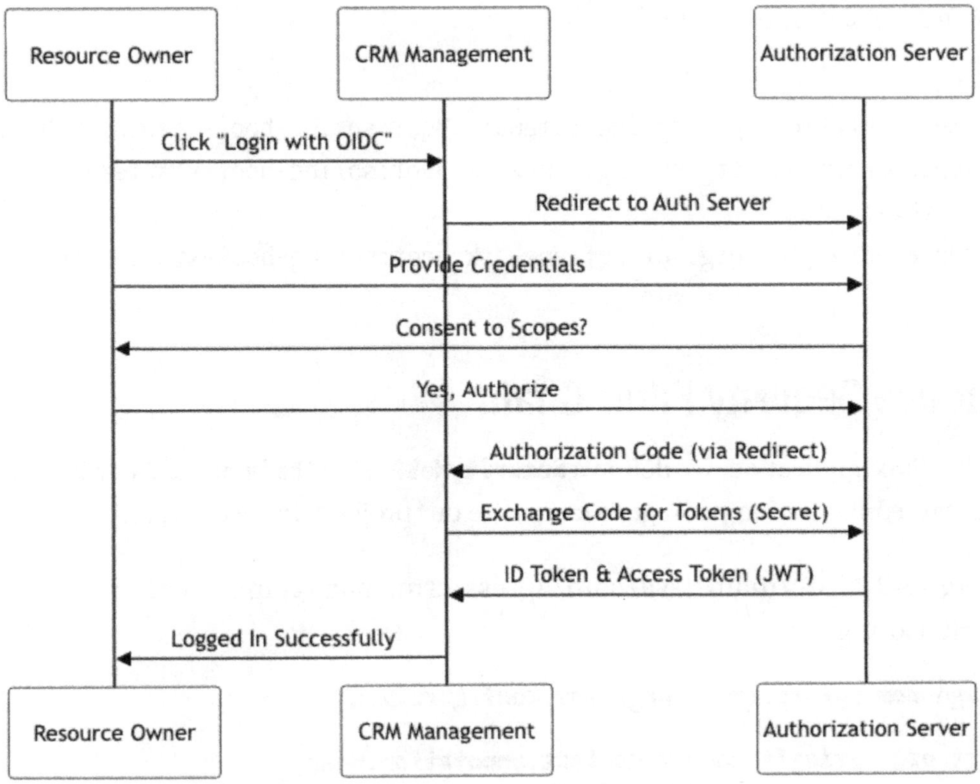

Figure 11-4. *OAuth2 Authorization Code Flow with OIDC*

Case Study 2: The Management Project (Reactive Security)

The **Management System** is built on the reactive stack (WebFlux). Reactive security requires a different mindset: threads are not bound to a single request, so the security context must be managed within the **Reactor Context**.

Project Configuration (Gradle)

For the management system, we will use **OAuth2 and OpenID Connect (OIDC)**, delegating authentication to an external Identity Provider (like Keycloak, Okta, or GitHub).

Listing 11-16. build.gradle

```
dependencies {
    implementation 'org.springframework.boot:spring-boot-starter-webflux'
    implementation 'org.springframework.boot:spring-boot-starter-
    oauth2-client'
    implementation 'org.springframework.boot:spring-boot-starter-security'
}
```

Reactive Security Filter Chain

In a WebFlux application, we define a **SecurityWebFilterChain** bean. We will organize this in our configuration package to centralize our project's infrastructure.

Listing 11-17. src/main/java/com/apress/crm/management/configuration/SecurityConfig.java

```
package com.apress.crm.management.configuration;

import org.springframework.context.annotation.Bean;
import org.springframework.context.annotation.Configuration;
import org.springframework.security.config.Customizer;
import org.springframework.security.config.web.server.ServerHttpSecurity;
import org.springframework.security.web.server.SecurityWebFilterChain;

@Configuration
public class SecurityConfig {

    @Bean
    public SecurityWebFilterChain springSecurityFilterChain(ServerHttpSecur
    ity http) {
        return http
            .authorizeExchange(ex -> exchanges
                .pathMatchers("/api/v1/management/public/**").permitAll()
                .anyExchange().authenticated()
            )
            .oauth2Login(Customizer.withDefaults())
            .oauth2Client(Customizer.withDefaults())
```

```
            .build();
    }
}
```

Let's Analyze This Reactive Chain:

- **ServerHttpSecurity**: This is the reactive equivalent of `HttpSecurity`, managing the security filters for the Netty-based stack.
- **authorizeExchange**: In WebFlux, we protect "exchanges" rather than "requests." This integrates directly with our Functional Router defined in `ManagementConfiguration`.

Accessing Security Context in Handlers

When using Functional Endpoints, you often need to access the authenticated user within your `ManagementHandlers`. Spring Security 7 makes this easy through the `ReactiveSecurityContextHolder`, which allows you to extract authentication details from the current Reactor stream without blocking the event loop.

Listing 11-18. src/main/java/com/apress/crm/management/reactive/ManagementHandlers.java

```
package com.apress.crm.management.reactive;

import com.apress.crm.management.model.*;
import com.apress.crm.management.service.ManagementService;
import
org.springframework.security.core.context.ReactiveSecurityContextHolder;
import org.springframework.security.core.context.SecurityContext;
import org.springframework.stereotype.Component;
import org.springframework.web.reactive.function.server.ServerRequest;
import org.springframework.web.reactive.function.server.ServerResponse;
import reactor.core.publisher.Mono;

import java.net.URI;
import java.util.UUID;
```

```
@Component
public class ManagementHandlers {

    private final ManagementService managementService;

    public ManagementHandlers(ManagementService managementService) {
        this.managementService = managementService;
    }

    public Mono<ServerResponse> getCurrentUser(ServerRequest request) {
        return ReactiveSecurityContextHolder.getContext()
                .map(SecurityContext::getAuthentication)
                .flatMap(auth -> ServerResponse.ok().bodyValue(auth.
                getPrincipal()));
    }

    public Mono<ServerResponse> getCustomerDetails(ServerRequest request) {
        String id = request.pathVariable("id");
        return managementService.getCustomerDetails(UUID.fromString(id))
                .flatMap(details -> ServerResponse.ok().bodyValue(details))
                .switchIfEmpty(ServerResponse.notFound().build());
    }

    public Mono<ServerResponse> createCustomer(ServerRequest request) {
        return request.bodyToMono(Customer.class)
                .flatMap(managementService::saveCustomer)
                .flatMap(saved -> ServerResponse.created(URI.create("/api/
                v1/customers/" + saved.customerId()))
                        .bodyValue(saved));
    }
}
```

Analyze the Handler Security:

- **`ReactiveSecurityContextHolder`**: Since WebFlux is non-blocking and doesn't use `ThreadLocal` for security storage, we use this utility to access the `SecurityContext` bound to the current Reactor stream.

- **Dynamic Orchestration**: The `createCustomer` method now correctly uses the dynamic data provided in the `ServerRequest` body. Security is applied at the **Router** level or via `@PreAuthorize` on the service method, ensuring that only authorized users can trigger the creation of new customer records.

Testing Your Security

A secure application must be verifiable. We will use **`RestTestClient`** for our Servlet project and **`WebTestClient`** with specialized security support for our Reactive project.

Testing One-Time Tokens (Customer CRM)

We want to verify that our `SecurityFilterChain` correctly requires authentication and redirects to the login page.

Listing 11-19. src/test/java/com/apress/crm/customer/CustomerSecurityTests.java

```
package com.apress.crm.customer;

import org.junit.jupiter.api.Test;
import org.springframework.beans.factory.annotation.Autowired;
import org.springframework.boot.test.context.SpringBootTest;
import org.springframework.boot.test.autoconfigure.web.servlet.
AutoConfigureRestTestClient;
import org.springframework.test.web.reactive.server.WebTestClient;
import static org.springframework.boot.test.context.SpringBootTest.
WebEnvironment.RANDOM_PORT;

@SpringBootTest(webEnvironment = RANDOM_PORT)
@AutoConfigureRestTestClient
class CustomerSecurityTests {

    @Autowired
    private WebTestClient client;
```

```
    @Test
    void shouldRedirectToLoginForProtectedPath() {
        client.get().uri("/api/v1/customers")
            .exchange()
            .expectStatus().isFound() // 302 Redirect to /login
            .expectHeader().location("/login");
    }
}
```

Testing OIDC Protected Routes (Management CRM)

For the reactive project, we use SecurityMockServerConfigurers to simulate an authenticated OIDC user without needing a real identity provider.

Listing 11-20. src/test/java/com/apress/crm/management/ManagementSecurityTests.java

```
package com.apress.crm.management;

import org.junit.jupiter.api.Test;
import org.springframework.beans.factory.annotation.Autowired;
import org.springframework.boot.test.context.SpringBootTest;
import org.springframework.security.test.context.support.WithMockUser;
import org.springframework.test.web.reactive.server.WebTestClient;
import org.springframework.security.core.authority.SimpleGrantedAuthority;
import static org.springframework.security.test.web.reactive.server.
SecurityMockServerConfigurers.mockOidcLogin;
import static org.springframework.boot.test.context.SpringBootTest.
WebEnvironment.RANDOM_PORT;

@SpringBootTest(webEnvironment = RANDOM_PORT)
class ManagementSecurityTests {

    @Autowired
    private WebTestClient webTestClient;

    @Test
    void shouldAllowAccessForAuthenticatedUser() {
```

```
        webTestClient
            .mutateWith(mockOidcLogin()
                .idToken(token -> token.claim("sub", "felipe"))
                .authorities(new SimpleGrantedAuthority("ROLE_ADMIN")))
            .get().uri("/api/v1/customers")
            .exchange()
            .expectStatus().isOk();
    }
}
```

Analyze the Testing Logic: 1. **`mutateWith(mockOidcLogin())`**: This is a powerful Spring Security utility that injects a mock `SecurityContext` into the reactive exchange. It allows you to test authorization logic (`@PreAuthorize`, roles, scopes) in complete isolation from the network.

Security Observability with OpenTelemetry

Spring Boot 4 introduces deep integration with **OpenTelemetry**. Security events, such as authentication failures or access denials, are now automatically correlated with your distributed traces.

Listing 11-21. src/main/resources/application.properties

```
# Enable OpenTelemetry Tracing
management.otlp.tracing.endpoint=http://localhost:4317
# Correlate security events with traces
management.observations.security.enabled=true
# Export all security-related spans
management.tracing.sampling.probability=1.0
```

Let's Analyze This Observability Stack:

If a login fails, Spring Boot emits a span attribute identifying the failure reason (e.g., `invalid_credentials` or `account_locked`). This allows you to visualize security bottlenecks or brute-force attempts in your monitoring dashboard (like Zipkin or Jaeger) alongside the performance data of your API. This correlation is vital for identifying if a performance lag is being caused by an expensive password hashing algorithm during a high-volume attack.

We will explore the full power of distributed tracing, metrics, and the OpenTelemetry ecosystem in Chapter 13.

Zero Trust: mTLS and SSL Bundles

In a traditional security model, we focus on protecting the "perimeter" (the edge of our network). However, modern cloud-native architectures assume a **Zero Trust** mindset: never trust, always verify. This means we must encrypt and authenticate every communication, even between internal services. **Mutual TLS (mTLS)** is the gold standard for this, and Spring Boot 4's **SSL Bundles** make it remarkably easy to implement.

Centralized Certificates with SSL Bundles

Historically, managing SSL in Spring involved a messy mix of `server.ssl.*` properties and manual `KeyStore` loading. Spring Boot 4 introduces **SSL Bundles**, which group keys, truststores, and passwords into a single, named logical unit that can be reused across the application.

Configuring the Server (Management Project)

First, we define an SSL bundle in the `application.yml` of our Management System. This bundle includes the server's identity and the Root CA used to verify clients.

Listing 11-22. src/main/resources/application.yml - Management SSL Bundle

```
spring:
  ssl:
    bundle:
      jks:
        management-bundle:
          key:
```

```
          alias: "management-sys"
        keystore:
          location: "classpath:management.jks"
          password: "changeit"
        truststore:
          location: "classpath:ca.jks"
  security:
    x509:
      enabled: true # Enable X.509 certificate authentication
```

Next, we update our security configuration to require a client certificate and extract the user's identity from it.

Listing 11-23. src/main/java/com/apress/crm/management/configuration/SecurityConfig.java (X.509)

```
@Bean
public SecurityWebFilterChain x509FilterChain(ServerHttpSecurity http) {
    return http
        .x509(Customizer.withDefaults())
        .authorizeExchange(ex -> ex.anyExchange().authenticated())
        .build();
}
```

- **x509()**: Tells Spring Security to look for a client certificate in the incoming request. It will automatically extract the **Common Name (CN)** from the certificate and use it as the username.

Configuring the Client (Customer Project)

To call the Management System, the Customer Project must provide its own certificate. First, we define a declarative HTTP interface that represents the Management System's API.

Listing 11-24. src/main/java/com/apress/crm/customer/ManagementClient.java

```
package com.apress.crm.customer;

import org.springframework.web.service.annotation.HttpExchange;
import org.springframework.web.service.annotation.PostExchange;

@HttpExchange("/api/v1/management")
public interface ManagementClient {

    @PostExchange("/customers")
    void createCustomer(Customer customer);
}
```

Next, we define a client bundle and apply it to our declarative REST client.

Listing 11-25. src/main/java/com/apress/crm/customer/ClientConfig.java (mTLS Integration)

```
package com.apress.crm.customer;

import org.springframework.boot.ssl.SslBundle;
import org.springframework.boot.ssl.SslBundles;
import org.springframework.context.annotation.Bean;
import org.springframework.context.annotation.Configuration;
import org.springframework.context.annotation.Profile;
import org.springframework.web.client.RestClient;
import org.springframework.web.client.support.RestClientAdapter;
import org.springframework.web.service.invoker.HttpServiceProxyFactory;

@Profile( "mtls")
@Configuration
public class ClientConfig {
```

```
    @Bean
    public ManagementClient managementClient(RestClient.Builder builder,
          SslBundles sslBundles) {

        // Apply the 'customer-client' SSL Bundle to the RestClient
        SslBundle bundle = sslBundles.getBundle("customer-client");

        return HttpServiceProxyFactory.builderFor(
                RestClientAdapter.create(
                        builder.apply(bundle.
                        createRestClientCustomizer()).build()
                )
        ).build().createClient(ManagementClient.class);
    }
}
```

- **`createRestClientCustomizer()`**: This is a powerful Spring Boot 4 feature. It automatically configures the underlying HTTP client (like Apache HC or Jetty) with the correct SSL context from the bundle.

Going Deeper with `ClientHttpRequestFactory`: While `createRestClientCustomizer()` provides a convenient shortcut for standard use cases, advanced production scenarios often require fine-grained control over the underlying connection pool or timeout settings. In these cases, you would manually extract the **`SslContext`** from the bundle and inject it into a specialized `ClientHttpRequestFactory` (such as `HttpComponentsClientHttpRequestFactory` for Apache HttpClient 5). This allows you to combine mTLS security with custom performance tuning, ensuring your secure communications are both robust and efficient.

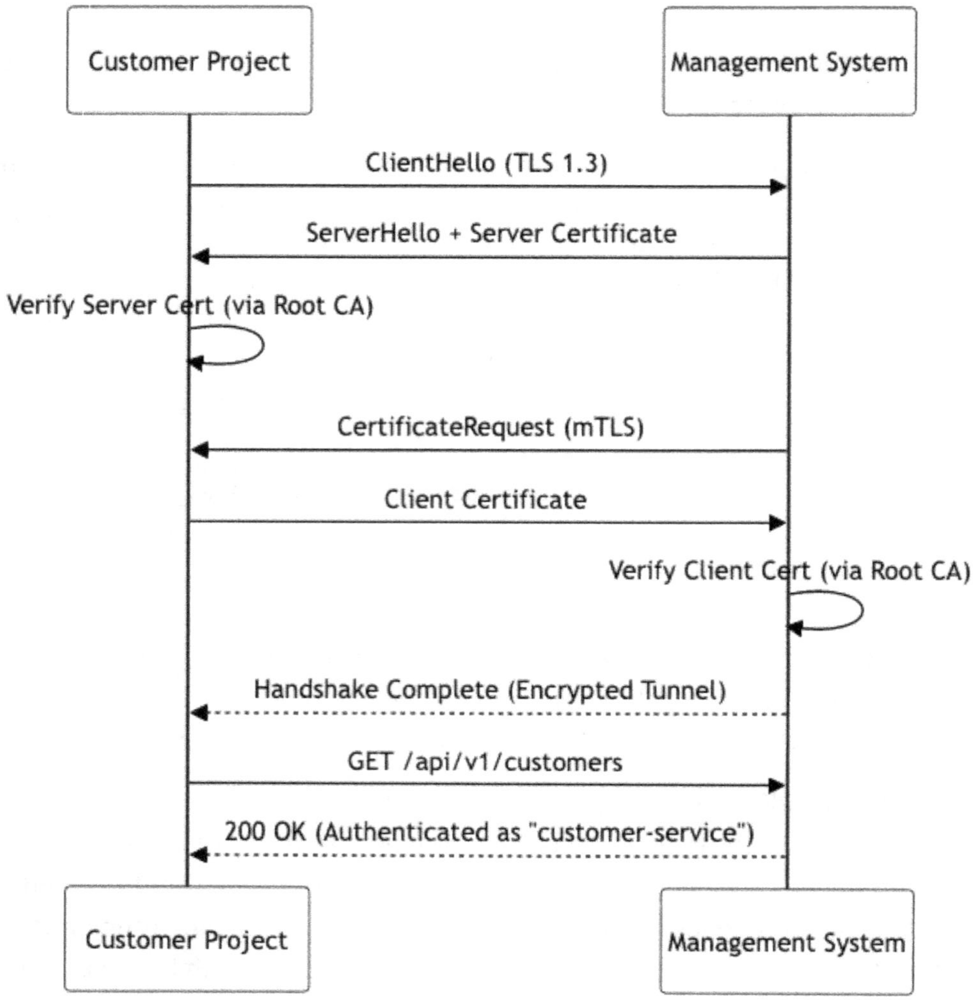

Figure 11-5. *Mutual TLS (mTLS) Handshake Flow*

Advanced: mTLS with Spring Authorization Server

For the ultimate security, we can use mTLS not just for encryption but as a method for **Client Authentication (RFC 8705)**. In this scenario, the Customer Project doesn't use a password (client secret) to talk to the Authorization Server. Instead, it presents its CA-signed certificate.

Step-by-Step: Creating Your PKI

To make this work, we need a "Chain of Trust." We will act as our own Certificate Authority (CA).

Listing 11-26. Terminal—Certificate Generation with keytool

```
# 1. Create a Root CA
keytool -genkeypair -alias root-ca -keyalg RSA -keysize 4096 -ext bc:c \
  -keystore root-ca.jks -storepass changeit -dname "CN=Internal-CA"

# 2. Create the Management System KeyStore
keytool -genkeypair -alias management-sys -keyalg RSA -keysize 2048 \
  -keystore management.jks -storepass changeit -dname
"CN=management-system"

# 3. Create the Customer Project KeyStore
keytool -genkeypair -alias customer-client -keyalg RSA -keysize 2048 \
  -keystore customer.jks -storepass changeit -dname "CN=customer-service"

# 4. Sign the Management & Customer certs with the Root CA...
# (Export CSR, sign with root-ca, and import back into keystores)
```

In a professional environment, you would never do this manually. You would use tools like **HashiCorp Vault** or **cert-manager** in Kubernetes to automate the issuance and rotation of these certificates.

Configuring the Authorization Server

In the **Spring Authorization Server**, we register the Customer Project to use `tls_client_auth`.

Listing 11-27. src/main/resources/application.yml - Auth Server Client Registration

```
spring:
  security:
    oauth2:
      authorizationserver:
        client:
```

```yaml
      customer-service:
        registration:
          client-id: "customer-service"
          client-authentication-methods:
            - "tls_client_auth"
          authorization-grant-types:
            - "client_credentials"
          scopes:
            - "customer:write"
```

- **tls_client_auth**: This tells the server to ignore passwords and instead look for a client certificate that matches the registered client identity.

Orchestrating the Save Operation

Now, let's look at how the Customer Project (Client) sends a new customer to the Management System (Resource Server) using this secure pipeline.

Listing 11-28. src/main/java/com/apress/crm/customer/ManagementOrchestrator.java

```java
package com.apress.crm.customer;

import org.springframework.stereotype.Service;

@Service
public class ManagementOrchestrator {

    private final ManagementClient managementClient; // mTLS-enabled
    RestClient

    public ManagementOrchestrator(ManagementClient managementClient) {
        this.managementClient = managementClient;
    }

    public void onboardNewCustomer(Customer customer) {
        // 1. The RestClient automatically performs the mTLS handshake
        // 2. It obtains an OAuth2 token using its certificate
```

```
        // 3. It POSTs the new customer to the management system
        managementClient.createCustomer(customer);
    }
}
```

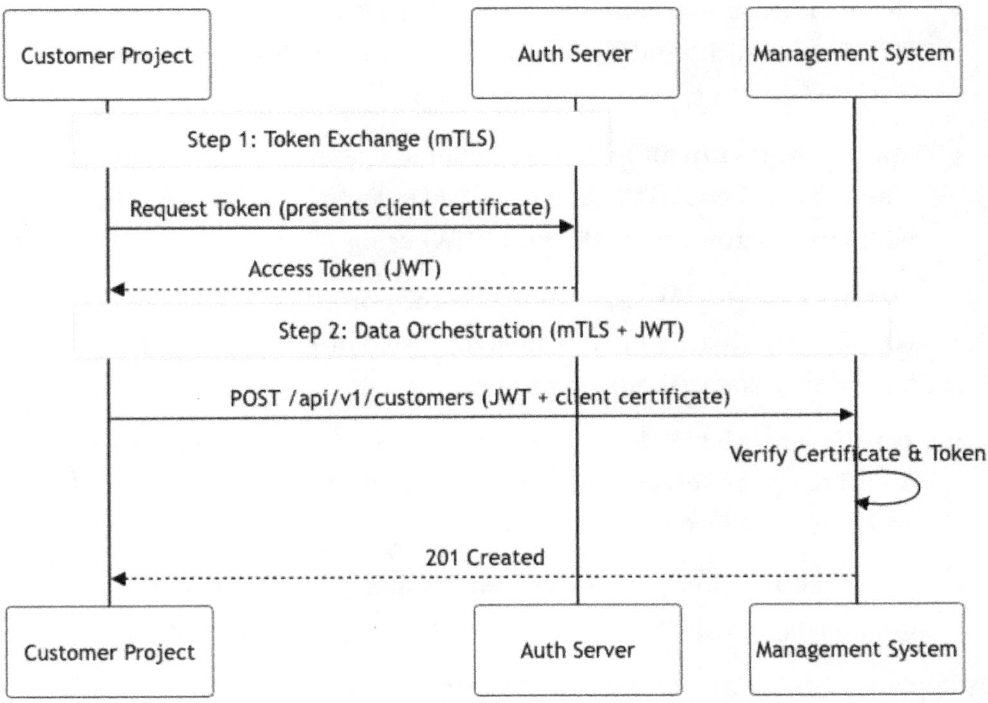

***Figure 11-6.** Zero-Trust Orchestration Flow*

Analyze the Orchestration: This is the pinnacle of modern security. The connection is encrypted via TLS 1.3, the client is verified via its hardware-bound certificate (mTLS), and the specific action is authorized via a scoped JWT.

Summary

In this chapter, we explored the vast and powerful security ecosystem of Spring Boot 4 and Spring Security 7. We transitioned from basic request matching to a sophisticated Zero-Trust architecture.

Key takeaways include:

- **Component-Based Security**: We moved away from legacy adapters to a modern, Lambda-based configuration model using `SecurityFilterChain`.
- **Granular Authorization**: We mastered `requestMatchers` for URL-level security and `@PreAuthorize` for fine-grained, method-level RBAC.
- **Modern Authentication**: We implemented password-less login with **One-Time Tokens (OTT)** and added an essential layer of protection with **Two-Factor Authentication (2FA)** using TOTP.
- **Stateless Identity**: We integrated **OAuth2 and OpenID Connect (OIDC)** to delegate authentication to trusted providers, using **JWTs** for scalable, stateless authorization.
- **Zero Trust with mTLS**: We leveraged the new **SSL Bundles** in Spring Boot 4 to secure service-to-service communication with Mutual TLS and X.509 certificates.
- **Observability**: We configured **OpenTelemetry** and SSL health monitoring to ensure our security posture is visible and proactive.

By applying these "Pro" patterns, you have transformed your applications from simple protected services into a resilient, production-ready ecosystem. Security is a continuous journey, but with Spring Boot 4, you have the tools to stay ahead of modern threats.

In the next chapter, we will shift our focus to **Messaging**, exploring how to build decoupled, event-driven systems using JMS, RabbitMQ, and Apache Kafka.

CHAPTER 12

Messaging with Spring Boot

Messaging is the backbone of modern distributed systems. While synchronous REST APIs are excellent for direct interactions, they introduce tight coupling and latency. To build resilient, scalable, and responsive applications, developers turn to asynchronous messaging and Event-Driven Architecture (EDA).

Spring Boot 4, building on Spring Framework 7, introduces significant enhancements to the messaging ecosystem. From the new fluent `JmsClient` API to native observability with OpenTelemetry and improved support for cloud-native brokers like Apache Pulsar and Kafka, Spring Boot 4 makes messaging a first-class citizen.

In this chapter, we will explore:

- **Spring Application Events**: Decoupling internal components.
- **JMS with `JmsClient`**: The new fluent API for Java Message Service.
- **Spring AMQP (RabbitMQ)**: Robust exchange-based routing and support for Streams.
- **Apache Kafka**: High-throughput event streaming.
- **Apache Pulsar**: Unified messaging and streaming.
- **RSocket**: Reactive, binary point-to-point communication.
- **WebSockets**: Real-time updates for the browser.
- **Spring Integration**: Implementing Enterprise Integration Patterns (EIP).

F. Gutierrez and D. Carter, *Pro Spring Boot 4*, https://doi.org/10.1007/979-8-8688-2640-5_12

We will distribute these technologies across our two sample applications:

1. **Customer Service (Maven)**: Acts primarily as an event producer (AMQP, Pulsar, JMS) and handles real-time UI updates (WebSockets).

2. **Management Service (Gradle)**: Acts as a consumer (Kafka, Pulsar) and leverages RSocket for high-performance internal communication.

Synchronous vs. Asynchronous Communication

Before diving into specific technologies, it is crucial to understand the architectural shift from synchronous to asynchronous communication.

- **Synchronous (REST/gRPC)**: The client waits for a response. This creates tight coupling; if Service B is down, Service A fails or hangs. Latency is additive (A + B + DB).

- **Asynchronous (Messaging)**: The client sends a message to a broker and immediately proceeds. The broker ensures delivery to Service B eventually. This decouples the services in both time and space, improving resilience and scalability.

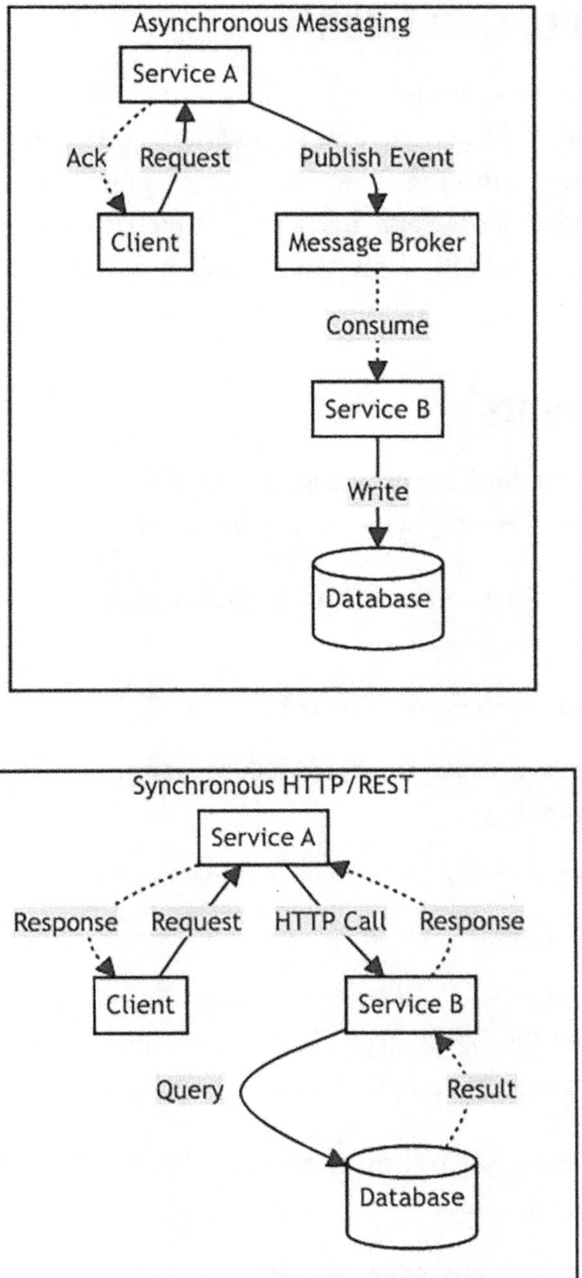

***Figure 12-1.** Synchronous vs. Asynchronous Communication*

Spring Application Events

Before reaching for external brokers, Spring provides a powerful in-process event mechanism. This allows you to decouple beans within the same application context.

Event-Driven Programming allows Service A to publish an event instead of directly calling a method on Service B. Service B (and C, D, etc.) listens for that event. This adheres to the Open/Closed Principle: you can add new listeners without modifying the publisher.

Publishing Events

In Spring Boot 4, you publish events using the `ApplicationEventPublisher`. Events can be any Java object (POJOs) or specific classes extending `ApplicationEvent`.

Listing 12-1. src/main/java/com/apress/crm/customer/event/CustomerCreatedEvent.java

```
package com.apress.crm.customer.event;

import com.apress.crm.customer.domain.Customer;
import java.time.Instant;

public record CustomerCreatedEvent(Customer customer, Instant timestamp) {}
```

What Is Happening?

- **POJO Events**: The event `CustomerCreatedEvent` is a simple Java Record. Spring 4+ no longer requires events to extend `ApplicationEvent`, making your domain model cleaner.

Listing 12-2. src/main/java/com/apress/crm/customer/service/CustomerService.java

```
package com.apress.crm.customer.service;

import com.apress.crm.customer.domain.Customer;
import com.apress.crm.customer.event.CustomerCreatedEvent;
import com.apress.crm.customer.repository.CustomerRepository;
import org.springframework.context.ApplicationEventPublisher;
```

```
import org.springframework.stereotype.Service;
import org.springframework.transaction.annotation.Transactional;

import java.time.Instant;

@Service
@Transactional
public class CustomerService {

    private final CustomerRepository customerRepository;
    private final ApplicationEventPublisher publisher;

    public CustomerService(CustomerRepository customerRepository,
    ApplicationEventPublisher publisher) {
        this.customerRepository = customerRepository;
        this.publisher = publisher;
    }

    public Customer createCustomer(Customer customer) {
        Customer saved = customerRepository.save(customer);
        // Publish event for internal listeners
        publisher.publishEvent(new CustomerCreatedEvent(saved, Instant.
        now()));
        return saved;
    }
}
```

Key Elements:

- **ApplicationEventPublisher**: This interface is automatically injected by Spring. It is the central hub for dispatching events within the application context.
- **publishEvent(...)**: This method broadcasts the event object to all registered listeners. By default, this is a synchronous call; the code execution blocks until all listeners have finished processing, unless the listeners are explicitly asynchronous.

Listening to Events

Listeners use the @EventListener annotation. Spring 6+ and Spring Boot 4 support asynchronous listeners and ordered execution.

Listing 12-3. src/main/java/com/apress/crm/customer/listener/CustomerAuditListener.java

```
package com.apress.crm.customer.listener;

import com.apress.crm.customer.event.CustomerCreatedEvent;
import org.slf4j.Logger;
import org.slf4j.LoggerFactory;
import org.springframework.context.event.EventListener;
import org.springframework.scheduling.annotation.Async;
import org.springframework.stereotype.Component;

@Component
public class CustomerAuditListener {

    private static final Logger log = LoggerFactory.
    getLogger(CustomerAuditListener.class);

    @Async // Requires @EnableAsync in configuration
    @EventListener
    public void onCustomerCreated(CustomerCreatedEvent event) {
        log.info("AUDIT: New customer created with ID: {}", event.
        customer().id());
        // Simulate complex processing
    }
}
```

What Is Happening?

- **@EventListener**: This annotation marks the method as a listener. Spring infers which event to listen to based on the method argument (CustomerCreatedEvent).

- **@Async**: This tells Spring to execute the listener in a separate thread. This is crucial for non-blocking operations. Without this, the `createCustomer` method in `CustomerService` would wait for this listener to finish, delaying the HTTP response to the user. Note that you must enable async support with `@EnableAsync` in a configuration class.

Transactional Events

Sometimes you only want to process an event if the surrounding transaction commits successfully. For example, you shouldn't send a "Welcome Email" if the database insert fails.

Use `@TransactionalEventListener`:

```
@TransactionalEventListener(phase = TransactionPhase.AFTER_COMMIT)
public void sendWelcomeEmail(CustomerCreatedEvent event) {
    // Only runs if the transaction commits
    emailService.send(event.customer().email(), "Welcome!");
}
```

Testing Application Events

Spring Boot provides the `@RecordApplicationEvents` annotation to simplify testing internal events without needing to mock the publisher.

Listing 12-4. src/test/java/com/apress/crm/customer/service/CustomerServiceEventTest.java

```
package com.apress.crm.customer.service;

import com.apress.crm.customer.domain.Customer;
import com.apress.crm.customer.event.CustomerCreatedEvent;
import com.apress.crm.customer.repository.CustomerRepository;
import org.junit.jupiter.api.Test;
import org.springframework.beans.factory.annotation.Autowired;
import org.springframework.boot.test.context.SpringBootTest;
import org.springframework.test.context.event.ApplicationEvents;
```

```
import org.springframework.test.context.event.RecordApplicationEvents;

import static org.assertj.core.api.Assertions.assertThat;

@SpringBootTest
@RecordApplicationEvents
class CustomerServiceEventTest {

    @Autowired
    private ApplicationEvents events;

    @Autowired
    private CustomerService customerService;

    @Test
    void testCustomerCreatedEventIsPublished() {
        customerService.createCustomer(new Customer("John Doe", "john@
        example.com"));

        long count = events.stream(CustomerCreatedEvent.class).count();
        assertThat(count).isEqualTo(1);
    }
}
```

This Code Shows:

- **`@RecordApplicationEvents`**: This test slice annotation records all events published in the `ApplicationContext` during the test.
- **`ApplicationEvents`**: A bean injected into the test that holds the history of recorded events.
- **`events.stream(...)`**: Allows you to query the history using Java Streams, filtering by event class type to verify expected behavior.

Working with JMS and the New JmsClient

The Java Message Service (JMS) is a standard API for messaging. Spring Boot 4 introduces the `JmsClient`, a modern, fluent API that replaces the imperative `JmsTemplate` for most use cases, aligning with the design of `JdbcClient` and `RestClient`.

JMS defines a common API for interacting with message brokers, supporting two main models: **Point-to-Point (Queue)**, where a message is consumed by only one consumer, and **Publish-Subscribe (Topic)**, where a message is broadcast to all active subscribers. It provides a **Standard API** that works with any JMS-compliant broker (ActiveMQ, IBM MQ, Solace) and supports **Transactions** (local and distributed/XA) and **Selectors** for filtering messages.

JMS is ideal for **Legacy Integration** (connecting to mainframes) and **Transactional Workflows** where you need strict ACID guarantees.

Best Practices:

- **Prefer JmsClient:** Use the new fluent API for cleaner code.
- **Connection Pooling:** Always use a connection pool (like pooled-jms) to avoid the overhead of creating connections.
- **Message Converters:** Use JSON serialization (`MappingJackson2MessageConverter`) instead of native Java serialization for interoperability.

Configuration (Customer Service)

We will use **ActiveMQ Artemis** as our JMS broker. Spring Boot auto-configures it if `spring-boot-starter-artemis` is present.

```
<!-- pom.xml -->
<dependency>
    <groupId>org.springframework.boot</groupId>
    <artifactId>spring-boot-starter-artemis</artifactId>
</dependency>
<dependency>
    <groupId>org.springframework.boot</groupId>
    <artifactId>spring-boot-starter-json</artifactId>
</dependency>
```

Using JmsClient

The `JmsClient` offers a chainable API for sending messages. It integrates seamlessly with Jackson for JSON serialization.

Listing 12-5. src/main/java/com/apress/crm/customer/messaging/jms/CustomerValidationProducer.java

```
package com.apress.crm.customer.messaging.jms;

import org.springframework.jms.core.JmsClient;
import org.springframework.stereotype.Component;

import java.util.Map;

@Component
public class CustomerValidationProducer {

    private final JmsClient jmsClient;

    public CustomerValidationProducer(JmsClient jmsClient) {
        this.jmsClient = jmsClient;
    }

    public void requestValidation(String customerId) {
        // Fluent API usage
        jmsClient.send()
                .destination("customer.validation")
                .property("priority", "high")
                .content(Map.of("customerId", customerId, "checkType",
                "FRAUD_DETECTION"))
                .send();
    }
}
```

What Is Happening?

- **`jmsClient.send()`**: Initiates the fluent message building chain.
- **`.destination("customer.validation")`**: Specifies the JMS queue name. ActiveMQ Artemis will automatically create this queue if configured to do so.
- **`.content(...)`**: Sets the payload. Since we included `spring-boot-starter-json`, `JmsClient` automatically serializes the `Map` to a JSON string before sending.

Consuming JMS Messages

For consumption, we still rely on the powerful `@JmsListener` annotation-driven model.

Listing 12-6. src/main/java/com/apress/crm/customer/messaging/jms/CustomerValidationListener.java

```
package com.apress.crm.customer.messaging.jms;

import org.slf4j.Logger;
import org.slf4j.LoggerFactory;
import org.springframework.jms.annotation.JmsListener;
import org.springframework.stereotype.Component;

import java.util.Map;

@Component
public class CustomerValidationListener {

    private static final Logger log = LoggerFactory.getLogger(CustomerValid
    ationListener.class);

    @JmsListener(destination = "customer.validation")
    public void validateCustomer(Map<String, String> payload) {
        log.info("Performing fraud check for customer: {}",
        payload.get("customerId"));
    }
}
```

Key Elements:

- **`@JmsListener`**: This annotation instructs Spring to create a message listener container behind the scenes. This container manages the connection to the broker, receives messages, and acknowledges them.
- **Automatic Deserialization**: The incoming JSON message is automatically deserialized back into a `Map<String, String>` before the method is invoked, matching the method signature.

Testing JMS

To test JMS interactions, we can use **Testcontainers** to spin up a real ActiveMQ Artemis instance, ensuring fidelity with production.

Listing 12-7. src/test/java/com/apress/crm/customer/messaging/jms/CustomerJmsTest.java

```
package com.apress.crm.customer.messaging.jms;

import org.junit.jupiter.api.Test;
import org.springframework.beans.factory.annotation.Autowired;
import org.springframework.boot.test.context.SpringBootTest;
import org.springframework.jms.core.JmsTemplate;
import org.springframework.test.context.DynamicPropertyRegistry;
import org.springframework.test.context.DynamicPropertySource;
import org.testcontainers.containers.GenericContainer;
import org.testcontainers.junit.jupiter.Container;
import org.testcontainers.junit.jupiter.Testcontainers;

import static org.assertj.core.api.Assertions.assertThat;

@SpringBootTest
@Testcontainers
class CustomerJmsTest {

    @Container
    static GenericContainer<?> artemis = new GenericContainer<>("apache/
activemq-artemis:latest-alpine")
            .withExposedPorts(61616);

    @DynamicPropertySource
    static void artemisProperties(DynamicPropertyRegistry registry) {
        registry.add("spring.artemis.broker-url",
            () -> "tcp://" + artemis.getHost() + ":" + artemis.
            getMappedPort(61616));
        registry.add("spring.artemis.user", () -> "artemis");
        registry.add("spring.artemis.password", () -> "artemis");
    }
```

```
    @Autowired
    private CustomerValidationProducer producer;

    @Autowired
    private JmsTemplate jmsTemplate;

    @Test
    void testValidationWorkflow() {
        producer.requestValidation("CUST-123");

        // Verify message landed on the queue using JmsTemplate to
           read it back
        Object payload = jmsTemplate.receiveAndConvert("customer.
        validation");
        assertThat(payload).asString().contains("CUST-123");
    }
}
```

This Code Shows:

- **`@Testcontainers`**: Manages the lifecycle of the Docker container.
- **`@DynamicPropertySource`**: Crucial for injecting the random ephemeral port assigned by Docker into the Spring Boot environment (`spring.artemis.broker-url`) before the ApplicationContext starts.
- **`JmsTemplate`**: We use the older template here to synchronously read the queue for verification, proving the `JmsClient` successfully sent the message.

RabbitMQ with Spring AMQP

RabbitMQ implements the Advanced Message Queuing Protocol (AMQP). Unlike JMS, which sends to queues or topics, AMQP sends to **Exchanges**, which then route to queues based on bindings.

RabbitMQ is a lightweight, easy-to-deploy message broker that supports multiple messaging protocols. Spring AMQP provides a high-level abstraction to work with RabbitMQ, focusing on the Exchange-Binding-Queue model.

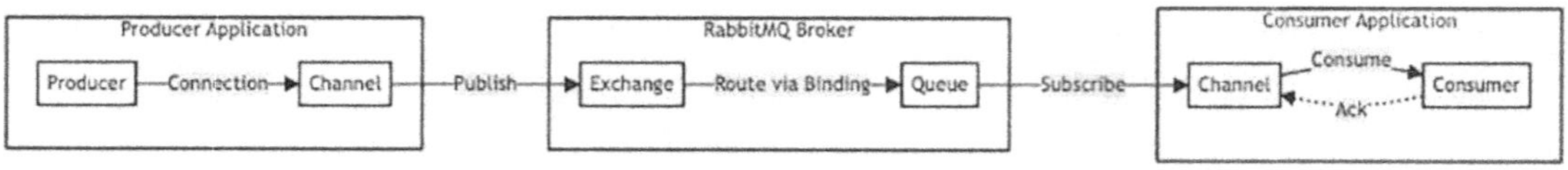

***Figure 12-2.** RabbitMQ Architecture Flow*

In RabbitMQ, producers **never** send messages directly to a queue. Instead, they send it to an **Exchange**. The exchange decides where to route the message based on the exchange type and binding rules.

Exchange Types: RabbitMQ offers several exchange types for different routing needs:

***Table 12-1.** RabbitMQ Exchange Types*

Exchange Type	Routing Logic
Direct	Routes to queues where the `binding key` exactly matches the message's `routing key`.
Topic	Routes based on wildcard matches (e.g., `audit.*` matches `audit.login`). # matches zero or more words * matches exactly one word.
Fanout	Broadcasts to **all** bound queues, ignoring the routing key. Ideal for "Pub-Sub."
Headers	Routes based on message header arguments instead of the routing key.
Consistent Hash	Distributes messages across queues based on the hash of the routing key, ensuring messages with the same key go to the same queue.

RabbitMQ excels at **Flexible Routing** via exchanges and bindings and provides **Reliability** through delivery acknowledgments and persistence. It is widely used for **Microservices Decoupling** and **Task Distribution**.

Best Practices:

- **Separate Connections:** Use separate connections for publishers and consumers.
- **Dead Letter Queues (DLQ):** Configure DLQs to capture failed messages.
- **Prefetch Count:** Control consumer load by configuring prefetch.

RabbitMQ Streams

RabbitMQ 3.9+ introduced **Streams**, a persistent and replicated data structure that models an append-only log, similar to Kafka. Unlike classic queues, streams are non-destructive (messages are not removed when consumed) and allow massive fan-out with high throughput.

To use Streams with Spring Boot, you need the `spring-rabbit-stream` dependency.

Listing 12-8. src/main/java/com/apress/crm/customer/messaging/rabbitmq/CustomerActivityStream.java

```java
package com.apress.crm.customer.messaging.rabbitmq;

import org.springframework.rabbit.stream.producer.RabbitStreamTemplate;
import org.springframework.stereotype.Component;

@Component
public class CustomerActivityStream {
    private final RabbitStreamTemplate streamTemplate;

    public CustomerActivityStream(RabbitStreamTemplate streamTemplate) {
        this.streamTemplate = streamTemplate;
    }

    public void logActivity(String customerId, String activity) {
        streamTemplate.convertAndSend("customer.activity.stream",
            new CustomerActivity(customerId, activity));
    }
}
```

Key Elements:

- **`RabbitStreamTemplate`**: A specialized template for the Streams protocol (which is binary and distinct from AMQP). It is optimized for high throughput and appending to the log.

Listing 12-9. src/main/java/com/apress/prospringboot4/management/messaging/rabbitmq/ActivityListener.java

```
package com.apress.prospringboot4.management.messaging.rabbitmq;

import org.springframework.amqp.rabbit.annotation.RabbitListener;
import org.springframework.stereotype.Component;

@Component
public class ActivityListener {

    @RabbitListener(queues = "customer.activity.stream",
                    containerFactory = "streamContainerFactory")
                    // Requires stream factory config
    public void listen(CustomerActivity activity) {
        System.out.println("Stream Activity: " + activity);
    }
}
```

What Is Happening?

- **`@RabbitListener`**: Used here just like for standard queues, but we specify a custom `containerFactory`.
- **Stream Consumption**: Unlike standard queues, consuming from a stream doesn't delete the message. The consumer maintains an `offset` to track its position in the stream.

Customer Service: Producer

The Customer Service will publish events to RabbitMQ.

Listing 12-10. src/main/java/com/apress/crm/customer/config/AmqpConfig.java

```
package com.apress.crm.customer.config;

import org.springframework.amqp.core.Binding;
import org.springframework.amqp.core.BindingBuilder;
import org.springframework.amqp.core.TopicExchange;
```

```
import org.springframework.amqp.core.Queue;
import
org.springframework.amqp.support.converter.Jackson2JsonMessageConverter;
import org.springframework.context.annotation.Bean;
import org.springframework.context.annotation.Configuration;

@Configuration
public class AmqpConfig {

    public static final String EXCHANGE_NAME = "crm.customer.exchange";
    public static final String QUEUE_NAME = "crm.customer.updates";

    @Bean
    public TopicExchange exchange() {
        return new TopicExchange(EXCHANGE_NAME);
    }

    @Bean
    public Queue queue() {
        return new Queue(QUEUE_NAME, true);
    }

    @Bean
    public Binding binding(Queue queue, TopicExchange exchange) {
        return BindingBuilder.bind(queue).to(exchange).with("customer.#");
    }

    @Bean
    public Jackson2JsonMessageConverter producerMessageConverter() {
        return new Jackson2JsonMessageConverter();
    }
}
```

What Is Happening?

- **Declarative Infrastructure**: By defining Exchange, Queue, and Binding beans, Spring AMQP automatically ensures these exist on the RabbitMQ broker at startup. This is known as "declarative configuration."

- **Topic Exchange**: We use a TopicExchange to allow consumers to filter based on routing keys (e.g., customer.created, customer.deleted).
- **Binding**: The binding customer.# means the queue crm.customer.updates will receive any message sent to the exchange with a routing key starting with customer.

Listing 12-11. src/main/java/com/apress/crm/customer/messaging/amqp/CustomerEventProducer.java

```
package com.apress.crm.customer.messaging.amqp;

import com.apress.crm.customer.event.CustomerCreatedEvent;
import org.springframework.amqp.rabbit.core.RabbitTemplate;
import org.springframework.stereotype.Component;

import static com.apress.crm.customer.config.AmqpConfig.EXCHANGE_NAME;

@Component
public class CustomerEventProducer {

    private final RabbitTemplate rabbitTemplate;

    public CustomerEventProducer(RabbitTemplate rabbitTemplate) {
        this.rabbitTemplate = rabbitTemplate;
    }

    public void sendCustomerCreated(CustomerCreatedEvent event) {
        rabbitTemplate.convertAndSend(EXCHANGE_NAME, "customer.
created", event);
    }
}
```

Key Elements:

- **RabbitTemplate**: The central helper class for RabbitMQ operations.
- **convertAndSend**: This method handles the conversion of the CustomerCreatedEvent object to JSON (thanks to the bean defined in Listing 12-10) and publishes it to the specified exchange with the routing key customer.created.

Testing RabbitMQ

We use the official `RabbitMQContainer` from Testcontainers.

Listing 12-12. src/test/java/com/apress/crm/customer/messaging/amqp/RabbitMqIntegrationTest.java

```
package com.apress.crm.customer.messaging.amqp;

import com.apress.crm.customer.config.AmqpConfig;
import com.apress.crm.customer.domain.Customer;
import com.apress.crm.customer.event.CustomerCreatedEvent;
import org.junit.jupiter.api.Test;
import org.springframework.amqp.rabbit.core.RabbitTemplate;
import org.springframework.beans.factory.annotation.Autowired;
import org.springframework.boot.test.context.SpringBootTest;
import org.springframework.boot.testcontainers.service.connection.ServiceC
onnection;
import org.testcontainers.containers.RabbitMQContainer;
import org.testcontainers.junit.jupiter.Container;
import org.testcontainers.junit.jupiter.Testcontainers;

import java.time.Instant;

import static org.assertj.core.api.Assertions.assertThat;

@SpringBootTest
@Testcontainers
class RabbitMqIntegrationTest {

    @Container
    @ServiceConnection
    static RabbitMQContainer rabbit = new RabbitMQContainer("rabbitmq:
    management-alpine");

    @Autowired
    private CustomerEventProducer producer;

    @Autowired
    private RabbitTemplate rabbitTemplate;
```

```
    @Test
    void testSendAndReceive() {
        CustomerCreatedEvent event = new CustomerCreatedEvent(new
        Customer("Rabbit", "rabbit@test.com"), Instant.now());

        producer.sendCustomerCreated(event);

        // Receive directly from the queue to verify delivery
        CustomerCreatedEvent received = (CustomerCreatedEvent)
        rabbitTemplate.receiveAndConvert(AmqpConfig.QUEUE_NAME);
        assertThat(received).isNotNull();
        assertThat(received.customer().name()).isEqualTo("Rabbit");
    }
}
```

This Code Shows:

- **`@ServiceConnection`**: A Spring Boot 3.1+ feature. It automatically configures the connection details (`spring.rabbitmq.host`, `port`, `username`, `password`) based on the running Testcontainer, removing the need for `@DynamicPropertySource`.
- **End-to-End Test**: The test verifies that the `producer` bean correctly integrates with the infrastructure, serializes the message, and that the message is actually routable to the expected queue.

Apache Kafka

Apache Kafka is a distributed event streaming platform. While RabbitMQ is great for complex routing, Kafka excels at high throughput and replayability.

Kafka is designed as a distributed, partitioned, replicated commit log service. It treats data as a stream of events rather than discrete messages. It offers **High Throughput** (millions of messages/sec), **Persistence** (configurable retention), and **Scalability** via partitioning.

Use Cases: Event Sourcing, **Log Aggregation**, and **Stream Processing**.

Best Practices:

- **Partitioning Key:** Choose a good key (e.g., `customerId`) to ensure ordering.
- **Consumer Groups:** Use groups for parallel processing.
- **Schema Registry:** Enforce contracts with Avro/JSON Schema.

Management Service: Consumer

The Management Service (built with Gradle) will consume messages from Kafka, perhaps originating from a legacy system or another microservice.

Listing 12-13. build.gradle.kts

```
dependencies {
    implementation("org.springframework.boot:spring-boot-starter-kafka")
    testImplementation("org.springframework.kafka:spring-kafka-test")
    testImplementation("org.testcontainers:kafka")
}
```

What Is Happening?

- **Dependencies**: We include `spring-boot-starter-kafka` for runtime support. For testing, we use `spring-kafka-test` (which provides embedded brokers, though Testcontainers is preferred) and the Testcontainers Kafka module.

Listing 12-14. src/main/java/com/apress/prospringboot4/management/messaging/kafka/LegacyEventConsumer.java

```
package com.apress.prospringboot4.management.messaging.kafka;

import org.apache.kafka.clients.consumer.ConsumerRecord;
import org.slf4j.Logger;
import org.slf4j.LoggerFactory;
import org.springframework.kafka.annotation.KafkaListener;
import org.springframework.stereotype.Component;

import java.util.concurrent.CountDownLatch;
```

```
@Component
public class LegacyEventConsumer {

    private static final Logger log = LoggerFactory.
    getLogger(LegacyEventConsumer.class);
    private final CountDownLatch latch = new CountDownLatch(1);

    @KafkaListener(topics = "legacy-system-events", groupId =
    "management-group")
    public void listen(ConsumerRecord<String, String> record) {
        log.info("Received Kafka Message: Key={}, Value={}", record.key(),
        record.value());
        latch.countDown();
    }

    public CountDownLatch getLatch() {
        return latch;
    }
}
```

Key Elements:

- **@KafkaListener**: Registers this method to subscribe to the legacy-system-events topic.
- **groupId**: Defines the consumer group. If multiple instances of this service run, Kafka will load-balance the partitions of the topic among them.
- **ConsumerRecord**: Provides access to metadata like the message key, partition, and offset, which are often critical in Kafka applications.

Testing Kafka

We use KafkaContainer to verify the listener correctly processes messages.

Listing 12-15. src/test/java/com/apress/prospringboot4/management/messaging/kafka/KafkaConsumerTest.java

```
package com.apress.prospringboot4.management.messaging.kafka;

import org.junit.jupiter.api.Test;
import org.springframework.beans.factory.annotation.Autowired;
import org.springframework.boot.test.context.SpringBootTest;
import org.springframework.boot.testcontainers.service.connection.Service
Connection;
import org.springframework.kafka.core.KafkaTemplate;
import org.testcontainers.containers.KafkaContainer;
import org.testcontainers.junit.jupiter.Container;
import org.testcontainers.junit.jupiter.Testcontainers;
import org.testcontainers.utility.DockerImageName;

import java.util.concurrent.TimeUnit;

import static org.assertj.core.api.Assertions.assertThat;

@SpringBootTest
@Testcontainers
class KafkaConsumerTest {

    @Container
    @ServiceConnection
    static KafkaContainer kafka = new KafkaContainer(DockerImageName.
    parse("confluentinc/cp-kafka:7.6.0"));

    @Autowired
    private KafkaTemplate<String, String> kafkaTemplate;

    @Autowired
    private LegacyEventConsumer consumer;
```

```
    @Test
    void testKafkaConsumption() throws InterruptedException {
        kafkaTemplate.send("legacy-system-events", "key-1", "Legacy Data
        Payload");

        boolean messageReceived = consumer.getLatch().await(10, TimeUnit.
        SECONDS);
        assertThat(messageReceived).isTrue();
    }
}
```

This Code Shows:

- **Asynchronous Verification**: Kafka is asynchronous. We cannot simply assert the result immediately after sending. We use a `CountDownLatch` (in the consumer bean defined in Listing 12-14) to wait for the message to be processed.
- **`@ServiceConnection`**: Again, this simplifies connecting the Spring context to the dynamic port of the Kafka Testcontainer.

Apache Pulsar

Apache Pulsar is a cloud-native, distributed messaging and streaming platform. Spring Boot 4 provides dedicated auto-configuration for Pulsar.

Pulsar unifies the best of both worlds: the queuing model of RabbitMQ and the streaming model of Kafka. It separates compute (brokers) from storage (BookKeeper), enabling seamless scaling. It features **Multi-Tenancy**, **Geo-Replication**, and **Tiered Storage**.

Use Cases: Unified Platform (queuing + streaming), **Multi-Region Apps**.

Best Practices:

- **Use Schemas:** Ensure type safety.
- **Batching:** Enable for high throughput.

Customer Service: Producer

We will use Pulsar to stream audit logs from Customer Service.

```
<!-- pom.xml -->
<dependency>
    <groupId>org.springframework.boot</groupId>
    <artifactId>spring-boot-starter-pulsar</artifactId>
</dependency>
```

Listing 12-16. src/main/java/com/apress/crm/customer/messaging/pulsar/AuditProducer.java

```
package com.apress.crm.customer.messaging.pulsar;

import org.springframework.pulsar.core.PulsarTemplate;
import org.springframework.stereotype.Component;

@Component
public class AuditProducer {

    private final PulsarTemplate<String> pulsarTemplate;

    public AuditProducer(PulsarTemplate<String> pulsarTemplate) {
        this.pulsarTemplate = pulsarTemplate;
    }

    public void logAction(String action, String user) {
        try {
            pulsarTemplate.send("crm-audit-topic", "User " + user + "
            performed " + action);
        } catch (Exception e) {
            throw new RuntimeException("Failed to send audit log", e);
        }
    }
}
```

What Is Happening?

- **PulsarTemplate**: Similar to JmsTemplate or KafkaTemplate, this is the high-level abstraction for publishing messages.
- **send(...)**: Sends the message synchronously. Pulsar also supports asynchronous sending via sendAsync(), which returns a CompletableFuture.

Management Service: Consumer

The Management Service consumes these audit logs.

Listing 12-17. src/main/java/com/apress/prospringboot4/management/messaging/pulsar/AuditConsumer.java

```
package com.apress.prospringboot4.management.messaging.pulsar;

import org.springframework.pulsar.annotation.PulsarListener;
import org.springframework.stereotype.Component;

import java.util.ArrayList;
import java.util.List;

@Component
public class AuditConsumer {

    private final List<String> messages = new ArrayList<>();

    @PulsarListener(subscriptionName = "management-audit-sub", topics =
"crm-audit-topic")
    public void listen(String message) {
        System.out.println("AUDIT LOG RECEIVED: " + message);
        messages.add(message);
    }

    public List<String> getMessages() { return messages; }
}
```

Key Elements:

- **@PulsarListener**: Configures a consumer.
- **subscriptionName**: Pulsar uses subscriptions to track cursor positions. Different subscriptions on the same topic allow for different consumption patterns (Exclusive, Shared, Failover).

Testing Pulsar

Spring Boot 4 integration with Pulsar is easily tested using `PulsarContainer`.

Listing 12-18. src/test/java/com/apress/prospringboot4/management/messaging/pulsar/PulsarTest.java

```
package com.apress.prospringboot4.management.messaging.pulsar;

import org.junit.jupiter.api.Test;
import org.springframework.beans.factory.annotation.Autowired;
import org.springframework.boot.test.context.SpringBootTest;
import org.springframework.boot.testcontainers.service.connection.ServiceC
onnection;
import org.springframework.pulsar.core.PulsarTemplate;
import org.testcontainers.containers.PulsarContainer;
import org.testcontainers.junit.jupiter.Container;
import org.testcontainers.junit.jupiter.Testcontainers;
import org.testcontainers.utility.DockerImageName;

import java.time.Duration;

import static org.assertj.core.api.Assertions.assertThat;
import static org.awaitility.Awaitility.await;

@SpringBootTest
@Testcontainers
class PulsarTest {

    @Container
    @ServiceConnection
```

```
    static PulsarContainer pulsar = new PulsarContainer(DockerImageName.
    parse("apachepulsar/pulsar:3.0.0"));

    @Autowired
    private PulsarTemplate<String> pulsarTemplate;

    @Autowired
    private AuditConsumer consumer;

    @Test
    void testPulsarFlow() {
        pulsarTemplate.send("crm-audit-topic", "Login Action");

        await().atMost(Duration.ofSeconds(5)).untilAsserted(() ->
            assertThat(consumer.getMessages()).contains("Login Action")
        );
    }
}
```

This Code Shows:

- **Awaitility**: A testing library (`await()...`) used here to poll the `consumer` bean until the message arrives. This is often cleaner than manually managing `CountDownLatch` for simple assertions.

RSocket

RSocket is an application protocol for Reactive Streams. It is binary and multiplexed and supports multiple interaction models: Request-Response, Fire-and-Forget, Request-Stream, and Channel.

Unlike HTTP, which is document-centric, RSocket is message-centric. It maintains a persistent connection and supports backpressure, preventing a fast producer from overwhelming a slow consumer.

Features: Four Interaction Models, Backpressure, Transport Agnostic (TCP, WebSocket, Aeron).

Use Cases: Service-to-Service, **Mobile Clients**, **Real-time Feeds**.

Best Practices:

- **Use TCP:** For internal service communication.
- **Use WebSocket:** For communicating with browsers or external clients through firewalls.
- **Resilience:** Configure retry and resume strategies for connection drops.

Management Service: RSocket Implementation

The Management Service will act as an RSocket Responder (server) that streams system metrics or status updates.

```
// build.gradle.kts
dependencies {
    implementation("org.springframework.boot:spring-boot-starter-rsocket")
}
```

Listing 12-19. src/main/java/com/apress/prospringboot4/management/messaging/rsocket/ManagementRSocketController.java

```
package com.apress.prospringboot4.management.messaging.rsocket;

import org.springframework.messaging.handler.annotation.MessageMapping;
import org.springframework.stereotype.Controller;
import reactor.core.publisher.Flux;

import java.time.Duration;

@Controller
public class ManagementRSocketController {

    @MessageMapping("system.status.stream")
    public Flux<String> streamStatus() {
        return Flux.interval(Duration.ofSeconds(1))
                .map(i -> "System OK - Tick " + i);
    }
}
```

What Is Happening?

- **@MessageMapping**: Similar to @RequestMapping in Spring MVC, but for RSocket routes.
- **Flux<String>**: Returns a reactive stream. RSocket handles the backpressure, sending items ("System OK...") to the client only when the client requests them.

Testing RSocket

We can test RSocket controllers using RSocketRequester.

Listing 12-20. src/test/java/com/apress/prospringboot4/management/messaging/rsocket/RSocketTest.java

```
package com.apress.prospringboot4.management.messaging.rsocket;

import org.junit.jupiter.api.Test;
import org.springframework.beans.factory.annotation.Autowired;
import org.springframework.boot.test.context.SpringBootTest;
import org.springframework.boot.test.rsocket.server.LocalRSocketServerPort;
import org.springframework.messaging.rsocket.RSocketRequester;
import reactor.core.publisher.Flux;
import reactor.test.StepVerifier;

@SpringBootTest
class RSocketTest {

    @Autowired
    private RSocketRequester.Builder builder;

    @LocalRSocketServerPort
    private Integer port;

    @Test
    void testStream() {
        RSocketRequester requester = builder.tcp("localhost", port);

        Flux<String> stream = requester
```

```
            .route("system.status.stream")
            .retrieveFlux(String.class)
            .take(3);

        StepVerifier.create(stream)
            .expectNext("System OK - Tick 0")
            .expectNext("System OK - Tick 1")
            .expectNext("System OK - Tick 2")
            .verifyComplete();
    }
}
```

Key Elements:

- **`RSocketRequester`**: The client-side abstraction for RSocket.
- **`StepVerifier`**: The standard testing tool for Project Reactor. It subscribes to the stream and asserts that the items arrive in the expected order.

WebSockets with STOMP

WebSockets allow full-duplex communication between a client (browser) and the server. We use the STOMP sub-protocol for message semantics.

Raw WebSockets are just a stream of bytes. STOMP (Simple Text Oriented Messaging Protocol) adds a frame-based structure (like HTTP), allowing us to define destinations (topics/queues) and message bodies.

Features: Full Duplex, **Fallback Options** (SockJS), **Broker Support**.

Use Cases: Chat Applications, **Dashboards**, **Notifications**.

Best Practices:

- **Security:** Always secure WebSocket endpoints (WSS).
- **Heartbeats:** Configure heartbeats to detect stale connections.
- **External Broker:** Use an external broker (RabbitMQ) for multi-instance deployments to ensure messages reach clients connected to different server nodes.

Customer Service: Real-Time Updates

The Customer Service will broadcast updates to a web dashboard.

Listing 12-21. src/main/java/com/apress/crm/customer/config/WebSocketConfig.java

```
package com.apress.crm.customer.config;

import org.springframework.context.annotation.Configuration;
import org.springframework.messaging.simp.config.MessageBrokerRegistry;
import org.springframework.web.socket.config.annotation.EnableWebSocket
MessageBroker;
import org.springframework.web.socket.config.annotation.StompEndpointRegistry;
import org.springframework.web.socket.config.annotation.WebSocketMessage
BrokerConfigurer;

@Configuration
@EnableWebSocketMessageBroker
public class WebSocketConfig implements WebSocketMessageBrokerConfigurer {

    @Override
    public void configureMessageBroker(MessageBrokerRegistry config) {
        config.enableSimpleBroker("/topic");
        config.setApplicationDestinationPrefixes("/app");
    }

    @Override
    public void registerStompEndpoints(StompEndpointRegistry registry) {
        registry.addEndpoint("/ws-crm").withSockJS();
    }
}
```

What Is Happening?

- **enableSimpleBroker("/topic")**: Configures a simple in-memory message broker. Clients subscribing to destinations starting with `/topic` will receive messages directly.
- **registerStompEndpoints**: Registers the HTTP endpoint (`/ws-crm`) that clients (browsers) use to initiate the WebSocket handshake.

Listing 12-22. src/main/java/com/apress/crm/customer/service/DashboardService.java

```
package com.apress.crm.customer.service;

import org.springframework.messaging.simp.SimpMessagingTemplate;
import org.springframework.stereotype.Service;

@Service
public class DashboardService {

    private final SimpMessagingTemplate messagingTemplate;

    public DashboardService(SimpMessagingTemplate messagingTemplate) {
        this.messagingTemplate = messagingTemplate;
    }

    public void notifyFrontend(String message) {
        messagingTemplate.convertAndSend("/topic/updates", message);
    }
}
```

Key Elements:

- **SimpMessagingTemplate**: A bean that allows any server-side component (Service, Controller, Scheduler) to push messages to WebSocket subscribers.

Testing WebSockets

Testing WebSockets involves setting up a `WebSocketStompClient` in an integration test.

Listing 12-23. src/test/java/com/apress/crm/customer/messaging/websocket/WebSocketTest.java

```
package com.apress.crm.customer.messaging.websocket;

import org.junit.jupiter.api.Test;
import org.springframework.boot.test.context.SpringBootTest;
import org.springframework.boot.test.web.server.LocalServerPort;
import org.springframework.messaging.converter.StringMessageConverter;
import org.springframework.messaging.simp.stomp.StompSession;
import org.springframework.messaging.simp.stomp.StompSessionHandlerAdapter;
import org.springframework.web.socket.client.standard.StandardWebSocketClient;
import org.springframework.web.socket.messaging.WebSocketStompClient;
import org.springframework.web.socket.sockjs.client.SockJsClient;
import org.springframework.web.socket.sockjs.client.WebSocketTransport;

import java.util.List;
import java.util.concurrent.CompletableFuture;
import java.util.concurrent.ExecutionException;
import java.util.concurrent.TimeUnit;
import java.util.concurrent.TimeoutException;

import static org.assertj.core.api.Assertions.assertThat;


@SpringBootTest(webEnvironment = SpringBootTest.WebEnvironment.RANDOM_PORT)
class WebSocketTest {

    @LocalServerPort
    private Integer port;

    @Test
    void verifyConnection() throws ExecutionException,
    InterruptedException, TimeoutException {
        WebSocketStompClient stompClient = new WebSocketStompClient(new
        SockJsClient(
```

```
                List.of(new WebSocketTransport(new
                StandardWebSocketClient())));
        stompClient.setMessageConverter(new StringMessageConverter());

        String url = "ws://localhost:" + port + "/ws-crm";
        CompletableFuture<StompSession> sessionFuture = stompClient.
        connectAsync(url, new StompSessionHandlerAdapter() {});

        StompSession session = sessionFuture.get(5, TimeUnit.SECONDS);
        assertThat(session.isConnected()).isTrue();
    }
}
```

This Code Shows:

- **`WebSocketStompClient`**: A programmatic STOMP client provided by Spring.
- **`connectAsync`**: Initiates the handshake. We verify that the session is established, confirming the server configuration is correct.

Introduction to Spring Integration

Spring Integration extends the Spring programming model to support the well-known Enterprise Integration Patterns (EIP). It provides a lightweight messaging framework within your application, often used as a foundation for Spring Cloud Stream.

Enterprise Integration Patterns (EIP) are a catalog of design patterns for integrating systems. Spring Integration implements these patterns (Filters, Transformers, Routers, Splitters, Aggregators) as first-class citizens.

Features: POJO-centric, **Loose Coupling**, **Wide Adapter Support**.

Use Cases: Legacy Integration, **Protocol Adaptation**, **Orchestration**.

Best Practices:

- **Use the DSL:** Prefer the Java DSL (IntegrationFlow) over XML configuration.
- **Keep It Simple:** Don't replace simple service calls with complex integration flows unless necessary.
- **Idempotency:** Ensure your flows can handle duplicate messages gracefully.

Spring Integration focuses on **Channels**, **Endpoints**, and **Adapters**.

Listing 12-24. src/main/java/com/apress/crm/customer/integration/FeedbackIntegrationConfig.java

```
package com.apress.crm.customer.integration;

import org.springframework.context.annotation.Bean;
import org.springframework.context.annotation.Configuration;
import org.springframework.integration.dsl.IntegrationFlow;
import org.springframework.messaging.MessageChannel;
import org.springframework.integration.channel.DirectChannel;

@Configuration
public class FeedbackIntegrationConfig {

    @Bean
    public MessageChannel feedbackInputChannel() {
        return new DirectChannel();
    }

    @Bean
    public IntegrationFlow processFeedbackFlow() {
        return IntegrationFlow.from("feedbackInputChannel")
                .filter(String.class, source -> !source.isEmpty())
                // Filter empty feedback
                .transform(String.class, String::trim)
                // Normalize: Trim whitespace
                .handle("feedbackProcessor", "process")
                // Service Activator
                .get();
    }

    @Bean
    public FeedbackProcessor feedbackProcessor() {
        return new FeedbackProcessor();
    }
```

```
    public static class FeedbackProcessor {
        public void process(String feedback) {
            System.out.println("Processing customer feedback: " +
            feedback);
        }
    }
}
```

What Is Happening?

- **IntegrationFlow**: Defines the pipeline.
- **from(...)**: The starting point (Input Channel).
- **filter(...)**: Discards messages that don't match the logic (empty strings).
- **transform(...)**: Modifies the payload (trims whitespace).
- **handle(...)**: The final endpoint, invoking a method on a managed bean (feedbackProcessor).

Testing Integration Flows

Spring Integration provides a dedicated test framework with MockIntegrationContext, allowing us to substitute endpoints (like external service calls) with mocks to verify flow logic without side effects.

Listing 12-25. src/test/java/com/apress/crm/customer/integration/FeedbackFlowTest.java

```
package com.apress.crm.customer.integration;

import org.junit.jupiter.api.Test;
import org.springframework.beans.factory.annotation.Autowired;
import org.springframework.beans.factory.annotation.Qualifier;
import org.springframework.boot.test.context.SpringBootTest;
import org.springframework.integration.test.context.MockIntegrationContext;
import org.springframework.integration.test.context.SpringIntegrationTest;
import org.springframework.messaging.MessageChannel;
import org.springframework.messaging.support.GenericMessage;
```

```
import java.util.concurrent.CountDownLatch;
import java.util.concurrent.TimeUnit;

import static org.assertj.core.api.Assertions.assertThat;
import static org.springframework.integration.test.mock.MockIntegration.
mockMessageHandler;

@SpringBootTest
@SpringIntegrationTest
class FeedbackFlowTest {

    @Autowired
    private MockIntegrationContext mockIntegrationContext;

    @Autowired
    @Qualifier("feedbackInputChannel")
    private MessageChannel inputChannel;

    @Test
    void verifyFeedbackProcessingFlow() throws InterruptedException {
        // 1. Setup a Latch to wait for the result
        CountDownLatch latch = new CountDownLatch(1);

        // 2. Substitute the final '.handle()' endpoint with a Mock
        mockIntegrationContext.substituteMessageHandlerFor("processFeedback
        Flow.handler",
                mockMessageHandler().handleNext(message -> {
                    // 3. Assert the transformation logic (Trim) happened
                    assertThat(message.getPayload()).isEqualTo("Great
                    Service!");
                    latch.countDown();
                }));

        // 4. Send a test message with whitespace
        inputChannel.send(new GenericMessage<>("   Great Service!   "));

        // 5. Verify the flow completed successfully
        assertThat(latch.await(5, TimeUnit.SECONDS)).isTrue();
    }
}
```

Key Elements:

- **`@SpringIntegrationTest`**: Enables the Spring Integration testing support.
- **`MockIntegrationContext`**: Allows replacing beans in the integration flow (like the final processor) with test-specific behavior, such as assertions or latches.

Summary

In this chapter, we covered the extensive messaging capabilities of Spring Boot 4.

- **Internal Decoupling:** Use `ApplicationEventPublisher`.
- **Enterprise Messaging:** Use **JMS** (via `JmsClient`) or **RabbitMQ**.
- **High Volume/Streaming:** Use **Kafka** or **Pulsar**.
- **High Performance IPC:** Use **RSocket**.
- **Real-Time Web:** Use **WebSockets**.

Table 12-2. *Messaging Technologies Summary*

Technology	Type	Key Use Case	Protocol
JMS	Queue/Topic	Enterprise Java legacy integration	TCP
RabbitMQ	Exchange/Queue/Stream	Complex routing, general microservices, Log Streaming	AMQP/Stream (Binary)
Kafka	Log/Stream	High throughput, event sourcing, replay	TCP (Binary)
Pulsar	Unified	Cloud-native streaming and queuing	TCP (Binary)
RSocket	Stream	Reactive service-to-service communication	TCP/WebSocket

Messaging is a vast topic, and Spring Boot 4 provides the abstractions to make it manageable, resilient, and observable. In the next chapter, we will explore **Spring Boot Actuator** to monitor these running systems.

CHAPTER 13

Spring Boot Actuator and OpenTelemetry

In the early days of microservices, knowing **if** an application was running (Health Checks) was often enough. Today, in complex distributed systems, we need to know **how** it is running, **where** requests are failing, and **why** performance is degrading. This is the domain of **Observability**.

Spring Boot 4 marks a paradigm shift in this area. Observability has been promoted from a sub-feature of the Actuator to a core framework capability, powered by the deep integration of **Micrometer 2** and **OpenTelemetry (OTel)**.

In this chapter, we will transform our CRM applications into fully observable systems. We will explore:

- **The New Architecture**: Understanding how Spring Boot 4 decouples Observability from Actuator.
- **Actuator Essentials**: Creating custom Health Indicators and Info endpoints for operations teams.
- **Business Metrics**: Implementing custom Counters and Timers using Micrometer 2.
- **Distributed Tracing**: Using the new `spring-boot-starter-opentelemetry` to trace requests across our microservices.
- **The Observation API**: A unified API to instrument custom business logic.
- **Infrastructure**: Setting up Prometheus, Grafana, and Jaeger to visualize our data.

F. Gutierrez and D. Carter, *Pro Spring Boot 4*, https://doi.org/10.1007/979-8-8688-2640-5_13

The New Observability Architecture

In previous versions, "Actuator" was synonymous with monitoring. In Spring Boot 4, these concerns are separated:

1. **Spring Boot Actuator**: Focuses on **Operational** concerns (Health, Shutdown, Thread Dumps, Log level changing). It provides the HTTP/JMX endpoints.

2. **Micrometer and OpenTelemetry**: Focuses on **Telemetry** data (Metrics, Traces, Logs). This is now deeply integrated into the core container, allowing you to export telemetry without even enabling Actuator endpoints.

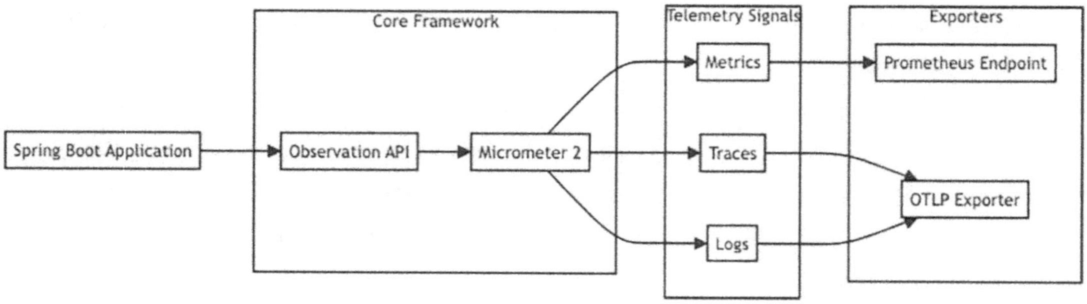

Figure 13-1. *Spring Boot 4 Observability Architecture*

We will implement this dual approach:

- **Customer Service (Maven)**: Will use the full **Actuator** suite for operational control and Prometheus metrics.
- **Management Service (Gradle)**: Will demonstrate the new **OpenTelemetry** focus, prioritizing tracing and OTLP export.

Project Setup and Dependencies

To start, we need to bring in the right starters. Spring Boot 4 introduces specific starters for OpenTelemetry to reduce bloat.

Customer Service (Maven)

For the Customer Service, we want the classic Actuator endpoints (for Health checks) and Prometheus support for metrics.

Listing 13-1. pom.xml

```
<dependencies>
    <!-- Core Operational Endpoints (Health, Info, etc.) -->
    <dependency>
        <groupId>org.springframework.boot</groupId>
        <artifactId>spring-boot-starter-actuator</artifactId>
    </dependency>

    <!-- Metrics export for Prometheus -->
    <dependency>
        <groupId>io.micrometer</groupId>
        <artifactId>micrometer-registry-prometheus</artifactId>
        <scope>runtime</scope>
    </dependency>
</dependencies>
```

What Is Happening?

- **spring-boot-starter-actuator**: Adds the @Endpoint infrastructure and exposes /actuator.
- **micrometer-registry-prometheus**: Configures Micrometer to collect metrics in a format Prometheus can scrape. It automatically adds the /actuator/prometheus endpoint.

Management Service (Gradle)

For the Management Service, we will use the new OpenTelemetry capabilities for distributed tracing.

Listing 13-2. build.gradle

```
dependencies {
    implementation 'org.springframework.boot:spring-boot-starter-webflux'

    // Core Actuator for Health checks
    implementation 'org.springframework.boot:spring-boot-starter-actuator'

    // NEW in Spring Boot 4: Native OTel Tracing support
    implementation 'org.springframework.boot:spring-boot-starter-
    opentelemetry'

    // Bridge OTel traces to Micrometer
    implementation 'io.micrometer:micrometer-tracing-bridge-otel'

    // Export traces via OTLP (to Jaeger)
    implementation 'io.opentelemetry:opentelemetry-exporter-otlp'
}
```

Key Elements:

- **`spring-boot-starter-opentelemetry`**: Provides auto-configuration for the OpenTelemetry SDK.
- **`micrometer-tracing-bridge-otel`**: Bridges the Spring `Observation` API to OpenTelemetry traces.
- **`opentelemetry-exporter-otlp`**: Allows the application to push traces directly to an OTel Collector or Jaeger using the OTLP protocol.

Operational Monitoring with Actuator

Actuator endpoints are the first line of defense for operations teams. They tell us if the application is alive and healthy.

Core Actuator Endpoints

Spring Boot 4 provides a rich set of built-in endpoints. By default, these are exposed under the base path `/actuator` (e.g., `http://localhost:8080/actuator/health`). While some are sensitive and disabled by default, others are safe for public exposure.

Table 13-1. *Common Actuator Endpoints*

ID	Description	Default Status
`health`	Application health information. Shows UP/DOWN status.	Exposed (Public)
`info`	Arbitrary application info (git commit, build version).	Exposed (Public)
`metrics`	Metrics collected by Micrometer (CPU, JVM, custom).	Hidden (Sensitive)
`loggers`	View and modify log levels at runtime.	Hidden (Sensitive)
`env`	Properties from `Environment` (Config, System Props).	Hidden (Sensitive)
`beans`	Complete list of all Spring beans in the context.	Hidden (Sensitive)
`mappings`	List of all `@RequestMapping` paths.	Hidden (Sensitive)
`prometheus`	Exposes metrics in Prometheus format (requires micrometer-registry-prometheus).	Hidden (Sensitive)

Exposing Endpoints over JMX

In addition to HTTP, all Actuator endpoints are also exposed over **JMX (Java Management Extensions)** by default. This allows you to monitor and manage your application using any JMX-compliant tool, such as JConsole or VisualVM. This is particularly useful for legacy monitoring systems or for performing deep JVM diagnostics.

By default, all endpoints are exposed. You can control this using properties similar to the web exposure.

Key Configuration Properties

Configuring Actuator in Spring Boot 4 involves enabling endpoints and fine-tuning their exposure. You can even move the management endpoints to a completely different network port for improved security.

Table 13-2. *Actuator Configuration Properties*

Property	Description
`management.server.port`	Specific HTTP port for management endpoints (e.g., `8081`). Defaults to application port.
`management.endpoints.web.base-path`	The base path for all endpoints. Defaults to `/actuator`.
`management.endpoints.web.exposure.include`	Comma-separated IDs of endpoints to expose over HTTP (e.g., `health,info,prometheus`). Use * for all.
`management.endpoints.web.exposure.exclude`	IDs to explicitly hide, even if included by wildcard.
`management.endpoints.jmx.exposure.include`	Comma-separated IDs of endpoints to expose over JMX. Defaults to *.
`management.endpoint.health.show-details`	Controls detail level: `never` (default), `when-authorized`, or `always`.
`management.endpoint.health.probes.enabled`	Enables Liveness and Readiness probes for Kubernetes (`/actuator/health/liveness`).
`management.otlp.tracing.endpoint`	URL of the OTel Collector for pushing traces (e.g., `http://localhost:4318/v1/traces`).
`management.tracing.sampling.probability`	Percentage of requests to trace (0.0 to 1.0). Default is 0.1 (10%).
`management.observations.key-values.allowed`	Filter which tags are attached to metrics/traces (for high-cardinality protection).

The Health Endpoint

The `/actuator/health` endpoint is arguably the most critical endpoint provided by Actuator. It aggregates the status of all registered `HealthIndicator` beans to provide a single, comprehensive view of the application's health. This is essential for automated monitoring, container orchestration (like Kubernetes probes), and load balancer integration.

Auto-Configured Health Indicators

One of Spring Boot's most powerful features is its auto-configuration of `HealthIndicator` beans. Whenever you add a specific Spring Boot starter to your classpath, Actuator automatically adds a health check for that component. This allows you to get a comprehensive view of your application's health with almost zero configuration.

The health endpoint aggregates the status of all these indicators. If any one of them reports a DOWN status, the overall application status will also be DOWN.

Table 13-3. *Common Auto-Configured Health Indicators*

Required Starter	Health Indicator ID	Description
`spring-boot-starter-actuator`	`diskSpace`	Checks for adequate free disk space.
	`ping`	A simple indicator that always returns UP.
	`livenessState/readinessState`	Support for Kubernetes Liveness and Readiness probes.
`spring-boot-starter-data-jpa` or `...-jdbc`	`db`	Checks that a connection can be established with the configured `DataSource`.
`spring-boot-starter-amqp`	`rabbit`	Checks the health of the RabbitMQ broker.
`spring-boot-starter-kafka`	`kafka`	Verifies connectivity to the Kafka cluster.
`spring-boot-starter-data-redis`	`redis`	Pings the Redis server.

You can disable a specific auto-configured health indicator via properties. For example, to disable the RabbitMQ health check, you would set `management.health.rabbit.enabled=false`.

Custom Health Indicators

While Spring Boot provides many built-in health indicators, you often need to check the health of application-specific components. For example, our **Customer Service** relies on an external currency API (from Chapter 3). If that API is down, our service is "degraded." Let's create a custom indicator.

Listing 13-3. src/main/java/com/apress/crm/customer/actuator/CurrencyServiceHealthIndicator.java

```
package com.apress.crm.customer.actuator;

import com.apress.crm.customer.client.CurrencyClient;
import org.springframework.boot.actuate.health.Health;
import org.springframework.boot.actuate.health.ReactiveHealthIndicator;
import org.springframework.stereotype.Component;
import reactor.core.publisher.Mono;

@Component
public class CurrencyServiceHealthIndicator implements
ReactiveHealthIndicator {

    private final CurrencyClient currencyClient;

    public CurrencyServiceHealthIndicator(CurrencyClient currencyClient) {
        this.currencyClient = currencyClient;
    }

    @Override
    public Mono<Health> health() {
        return currencyClient.checkHealth() // Assuming this returns a
        boolean or status
                .map(up -> up ? Health.up().build() : Health.down().
                withDetail("reason", "API Unreachable").build())
                .onErrorResume(ex -> Mono.just(Health.down(ex).build()));
    }
}
```

This Code Shows:

- **`ReactiveHealthIndicator`**: Since our Customer Service uses non-blocking clients (as set up in Chapter 3/12), we implement the reactive interface.
- **`Health.up() / down()`**: Fluent builders to construct the health status.
- **Details**: We attach specific details (like the exception) to help operators debug why the service is down.

How to Verify This:

1. Run the **Customer Service** application.
2. Open your browser or use `curl` to access the health endpoint: `http://localhost:8080/actuator/health`.
3. In the JSON response, you should see an entry similar to: `"currencyService": { "status": "UP" }` (or `DOWN` if the external API is unreachable).

Custom Info Contributors

The `/actuator/info` endpoint is useful for static metadata (Git commit, build version). We can also inject dynamic business info.

Listing 13-4. src/main/java/com/apress/crm/customer/actuator/CrmInfoContributor.java

```
package com.apress.crm.customer.actuator;

import com.apress.crm.customer.CustomerRepository;
import org.springframework.boot.actuate.info.Info;
import org.springframework.boot.actuate.info.InfoContributor;
import org.springframework.stereotype.Component;

import java.util.Map;

@Component
```

```java
public class CrmInfoContributor implements InfoContributor {

    private final CustomerRepository customerRepository;

    public CrmInfoContributor(CustomerRepository customerRepository) {
        this.customerRepository = customerRepository;
    }

    @Override
    public void contribute(Info.Builder builder) {
        // Warning: Don't do heavy queries here!
        long count = customerRepository.count();
        builder.withDetail("crm", Map.of(
            "customerCount", count,
            "region", "US-East"
        ));
    }
}
```

Key Elements:

- **`InfoContributor`**: Interface for adding custom sections to the info endpoint JSON output.
- **`builder.withDetail`**: Adds a nested JSON object under the "crm" key.

How to Verify This:

1. Run the **Customer Service** application.
2. Access the info endpoint: `http://localhost:8080/actuator/info`.
3. You should see a new section: `"crm": { "customerCount": ..., "region": "US-East" }`.

Best Practices: Securing Actuator

Actuator endpoints expose sensitive data. In Chapter 11, we learned how to secure applications. We must apply that to Actuator.

Listing 13-5. src/main/java/com/apress/crm/customer/ActuatorSecurityConfig.java

```
package com.apress.crm.customer;

import org.springframework.boot.actuate.autoconfigure.security.servlet.End
pointRequest;
import org.springframework.context.annotation.Bean;
import org.springframework.context.annotation.Configuration;
import org.springframework.security.config.annotation.web.builders.Http
Security;
import org.springframework.security.web.SecurityFilterChain;

@Configuration
public class ActuatorSecurityConfig {

    @Bean
    public SecurityFilterChain actuatorSecurity(HttpSecurity http) throws
    Exception {
        http
            .securityMatcher(EndpointRequest.toAnyEndpoint())
            .authorizeHttpRequests(auth -> auth
                .requestMatchers(EndpointRequest.to("health", "info")).
                permitAll()
                .anyRequest().hasRole("ADMIN")
            );
        return http.build();
    }
}
```

What is happening?

1. **`EndpointRequest.toAnyEndpoint()`**: A specialized matcher that targets all Actuator URLs, regardless of the configured base path (e.g., `/actuator` or `/monitor`).
2. **Public Access**: We allow `health` and `info` to be public so load balancers (like Kubernetes) can probe the app.
3. **Restricted Access**: All other endpoints (like `env`, `beans`, `metrics`) are restricted to users with the `ADMIN` role.

How to Verify This:

1. Run the **Customer Service** application.
2. Access `http://localhost:8080/actuator/health` (should return `200 OK` without authentication).
3. Access `http://localhost:8080/actuator/env` (should return `401 Unauthorized` or `403 Forbidden`).
4. If you configure basic authentication with an `ADMIN` user, you can then access `/actuator/env` with credentials.

Business Metrics with Micrometer 2

Metrics tell you **what** is happening over time (e.g., "Requests per second," "Error rate"). **Micrometer** is the instrumentation library integrated into Spring Boot that acts as a facade over various monitoring systems (like Prometheus, Datadog, or InfluxDB). It allows you to instrument your code once and then decide where to send the metrics via configuration.

Accessing and Interpreting Metrics

While monitoring systems like Prometheus scrape a dedicated endpoint (`/actuator/prometheus`), the `/actuator/metrics` endpoint provides a human-readable JSON API to explore available metrics.

1. **Discovering Available Metrics**

   First, make a GET request to /actuator/metrics. This provides a list of all registered meter names.

   Example GET /actuator/metrics Response

```
{
  "names": [
    "crm.customer.created",
    "crm.customer.onboarding",
    "executor.pool.size",
    "jvm.memory.used",
    "system.cpu.usage",
    "http.server.requests"
    // ... and many more
  ]
}
```

2. **Drilling Down into a Specific Metric**

   To get details about a specific metric, append its name to the URL. For example, a GET request to /actuator/metrics/jvm.memory.used will return detailed information about that meter.

   Example GET /actuator/metrics/jvm.memory.used Response

```
{
  "name": "jvm.memory.used",
  "description": "The amount of used memory",
  "baseUnit": "bytes",
  "measurements": [
    {
      "statistic": "VALUE",
      "value": 2.5165824E8
    }
  ],
  "availableTags": [
    {
      "tag": "area",
      "values": [ "heap", "nonheap" ]
```

```
      },
      {
        "tag": "id",
        "values": [ "G1 Eden Space", "G1 Old Gen", ... ]
      }
    ]
  }
```

How to Interpret the Response:

- **`name`**: The unique identifier for the metric.
- **`description`**: A human-readable explanation of what the metric tracks.
- **`baseUnit`**: The unit of measurement (e.g., bytes, seconds).
- **`measurements`**: The current values. For a `Gauge` like this one, it's a single `VALUE`. For a `Timer`, it would include `COUNT`, `TOTAL_TIME`, and `MAX`.
- **`availableTags`**: This is a crucial section. It shows the dimensions ("tags") you can use to filter the metric. For example, to see only the heap memory usage, you would query `/actuator/metrics/jvm.memory.used?tag=area:heap`.

Key Metric Types

Micrometer provides several core metric types, each suited for a different kind of measurement.

Table 13-4. *Core Micrometer Metric Types*

Metric Type	Description	Use Case
`Counter`	A cumulative metric that only goes up.	Counting total requests, number of customers created, exceptions thrown.
`Gauge`	A single numerical value that can go up and down.	Tracking the current number of active sessions, CPU temperature, or items in a queue.
`Timer`	Measures both the count of events and their duration.	Measuring request latency, batch job execution time.
`DistributionSummary`	Tracks the distribution of events.	Recording the size of payloads or the number of results returned from a query.

Best Practices for Metrics

- **Use Standardized Naming**: Follow a `.`-separated convention (e.g., `http.server.requests`).
- **Leverage Tags**: Use tags (or "dimensions") to add context (e.g., `status=200`, `region=us-east`). This is crucial for slicing and dicing data in your dashboards.
- **Avoid High Cardinality**: Be careful not to create tags with unbounded values (like `userId` or `orderId`), as this can overwhelm your monitoring system.
- **Publish Percentiles**: For Timers, always publish percentiles (e.g., 95th, 99th) to understand tail latency, which is often more important than the average.

Implementing Custom Metrics

In our Customer CRM, we want to track:

1. **Counter**: How many customers have been created?
2. **Timer**: How long does the onboarding process take?

Listing 13-6. src/main/java/com/apress/crm/customer/service/CustomerMetrics.java

```java
package com.apress.crm.customer.service;

import io.micrometer.core.instrument.Counter;
import io.micrometer.core.instrument.MeterRegistry;
import io.micrometer.core.instrument.Timer;
import org.springframework.stereotype.Component;

@Component
public class CustomerMetrics {

    private final Counter createdCounter;
    private final Timer onboardingTimer;

    public CustomerMetrics(MeterRegistry registry) {
        // 1. Define a Counter
        this.createdCounter = Counter.builder("crm.customer.created")
                .description("Total number of customers created")
                .tag("type", "standard") // Custom dimension
                .register(registry);

        // 2. Define a Timer
        this.onboardingTimer = Timer.builder("crm.customer.onboarding")
                .description("Time taken to onboard a customer")
                .publishPercentiles(0.95, 0.99)
                .register(registry);
    }

    public void incrementCreated() {
        createdCounter.increment();
    }

    public Timer.Sample startTimer() {
        return Timer.start();
    }
```

```
    public void stopTimer(Timer.Sample sample) {
        sample.stop(onboardingTimer);
    }
}
```

Key elements:

- **MeterRegistry**: The central registry where all metrics are held. Spring injects the appropriate implementation (Prometheus) based on our dependencies.
- **Tags**: Tags (or dimensions) are crucial. They allow you to slice and dice data in Grafana (e.g., "Show me creation counts by 'type'").
- **Percentiles**: Calculating 95th and 99th percentiles helps identify "tail latency"—the slow requests that frustrate users but get hidden in simple averages.

Using Metrics in Service

Listing 13-7. src/main/java/com/apress/crm/customer/service/CustomerService.java

```
// ... imports ...

@Service
@Transactional
public class CustomerService {

    private final CustomerRepository customerRepository;
    private final CustomerMetrics metrics;

    public CustomerService(CustomerRepository customerRepository,
CustomerMetrics metrics) {
        this.customerRepository = customerRepository;
        this.metrics = metrics;
    }
```

```
    public Customer createCustomer(Customer customer) {
        var sample = metrics.startTimer();
        try {
            Customer saved = customerRepository.save(customer);
            metrics.incrementCreated();
            return saved;
        } finally {
            metrics.stopTimer(sample);
        }
    }
}
```

What is happening?

1. **Injection**: We inject our custom `CustomerMetrics` bean.
2. **Start Timer**: We start the clock before the business logic.
3. **Increment**: If successful, we increment the counter.
4. **Stop Timer**: In the `finally` block, we stop the timer, recording the duration regardless of success or failure.

How to Verify This:

1. Run the **Customer Service** application.
2. Make several POST requests to create new customers (e.g., POST `http://localhost:8080/api/v1/customers`).
3. Access `http://localhost:8080/actuator/prometheus`.
4. Search for `crm_customer_created_total` and `crm_customer_onboarding_seconds` to see the metrics in Prometheus format.

Distributed Tracing with OpenTelemetry

Metrics show trends, but **Traces** tell the story of a single request as it hops between microservices. Spring Boot 4's integration with OpenTelemetry makes this nearly invisible to the developer.

Automatic Instrumentation

By adding `spring-boot-starter-opentelemetry` to our **Management Service**, Spring Boot automatically instruments:

- Incoming HTTP requests (WebFlux/MVC).
- Outgoing HTTP calls (`RestClient`, `WebClient`).
- Database queries (JDBC, R2DBC).

When the Management Service calls the Customer Service, OTel automatically injects headers (like `traceparent`) into the HTTP request. The Customer Service extracts these headers and continues the trace.

Custom Spans with Observation API

Sometimes you want to trace internal logic that isn't an I/O call. The **Observation API** (unified in Spring Framework 6+) bridges Micrometer Metrics and OTel Tracing.

Listing 13-8. src/main/java/com/apress/crm/management/service/ManagementService.java

```java
package com.apress.crm.management.service;

import io.micrometer.observation.Observation;
import io.micrometer.observation.ObservationRegistry;
import org.springframework.stereotype.Service;

import java.util.Map;
import java.util.concurrent.ConcurrentHashMap;

@Service
public class ManagementService {

    private final ObservationRegistry observationRegistry;
    private final Map<String, Object> internalCache = new
    ConcurrentHashMap<>();

    public ManagementService(ObservationRegistry observationRegistry) {
        this.observationRegistry = observationRegistry;
    }
```

```
    public void runComplexReport() {
        Observation.createNotStarted("management.report",
        observationRegistry)
                .lowCardinalityKeyValue("reportType", "full")
                .observe(() -> {
                    generateReport();
                });
    }

    private void generateReport() {
        // ... complex logic ...
        internalCache.put("lastReportTimestamp", System.
        currentTimeMillis());
    }

    public void clearCache() {
        internalCache.clear();
    }

    public int getCacheSize() {
        return internalCache.size();
    }
}
```

Key Elements:

- **`ObservationRegistry`**: The manager for observations.
- **`observe(Runnable)`**: This helper method handles starting the observation, putting it in scope (so logs get the trace ID), executing the logic, catching errors, and stopping the observation.
- **Dual Benefit**: This single API call creates **both** a Timer metric (`management.report` duration) **and** a Trace Span (visible in Jaeger).

How to Verify This:

1. Run the **Management Service** (with the OTel infrastructure running via `docker-compose up`).
2. Trigger the `runComplexReport()` method (e.g., via a test or a simple HTTP endpoint if exposed).
3. Open the Jaeger UI at `http://localhost:16686`. Search for traces, and you should find one named `management.report` showing the duration of your custom logic.

Global Telemetry Enrichment with ObservationHandler

A powerful feature of the Observation API is the ability to globally intercept all observations. By creating a custom `ObservationHandler` bean, you can add common contextual information—such as a region or environment tag—to every single metric and trace created by your application, whether auto-configured or custom.

Listing 13-9. src/main/java/com/apress/crm/management/actuator/RegionObservationHandler.java

```
package com.apress.crm.management.actuator;

import io.micrometer.observation.Observation;
import io.micrometer.observation.ObservationHandler;
import org.springframework.stereotype.Component;

@Component
public class RegionObservationHandler implements
ObservationHandler<Observation.Context> {

    @Override
    public void onStart(Observation.Context context) {
        context.addLowCardinalityKeyValue("region", "us-east-1");
    }

    @Override
    public boolean supportsContext(Observation.Context context) {
```

```
        // This handler will be applied to ALL observations
        return true;
    }
}
```

What Is Happening?

- **ObservationHandler<Context>**: We implement this generic handler to tap into the lifecycle of observations.
- **onStart(...)**: This method is called whenever an observation (a span or timer) begins. We use it to add a `region` tag.
- **supportsContext(...)**: By returning `true`, we ensure this logic applies to every observation created in the application context.

With this single bean, all metrics (`crm.customer.created`, `http.server.requests`, etc.) and all trace spans will automatically be enriched with the tag `region=us-east-1`, providing crucial context in your monitoring dashboards.

How to Verify This:

1. Run either **Customer Service** or **Management Service** (with the OTel infrastructure running).
2. Make a request to the application.
3. Check the Jaeger UI (`http://localhost:16686`) for any trace. You should see a `region=us-east-1` tag on all spans.
4. Check Prometheus metrics (`http://localhost:9090`). You should see `region="us-east-1"` as a tag on all exposed metrics.

Management Service: Custom Health and Endpoints

To provide deeper operational control over the Management Service, we will implement a custom Health Indicator and a management Endpoint.

Listing 13-10. src/main/java/com/apress/crm/management/actuator/CacheHealthIndicator.java

```
package com.apress.crm.actuator;

import com.apress.crm.management.service.ManagementService;
import org.springframework.boot.actuate.health.Health;
import org.springframework.boot.actuate.health.HealthIndicator;
import org.springframework.stereotype.Component;

@Component
public class CacheHealthIndicator implements HealthIndicator {

    private final ManagementService managementService;

    public CacheHealthIndicator(ManagementService managementService) {
        this.managementService = managementService;
    }

    @Override
    public Health health() {
        int size = managementService.getCacheSize();
        if (size == 0) {
            return Health.down().withDetail("cache", "Empty").build();
        }
        return Health.up().withDetail("items", size).build();
    }
}
```

What is happening here?

- **`HealthIndicator`**: The blocking counterpart to `ReactiveHealthIndicator`. It allows us to participate in the `/actuator/health` aggregate status.
- **`Health.down()`**: We mark the service as "DOWN" (or degraded) if the cache hasn't been warmed up yet, alerting operators to potential performance issues.

How to Verify This:

1. Run the **Management Service** application.
2. Access `http://localhost:8080/actuator/health`.
3. You should see `"cacheHealthIndicator": { "status": "UP", "items": ...}` in the JSON response.

Listing 13-11. src/main/java/com/apress/crm/management/actuator/ManagementControlEndpoint.java

```
package com.apress.crm.actuator;

import com.apress.crm.management.service.ManagementService;
import org.springframework.boot.actuate.endpoint.annotation.Delete
Operation;
import org.springframework.boot.actuate.endpoint.annotation.Endpoint;
import org.springframework.boot.actuate.endpoint.annotation.ReadOperation;
import org.springframework.stereotype.Component;

import java.util.Map;

@Component
@Endpoint(id = "managementControl")
public class ManagementControlEndpoint {

    private final ManagementService managementService;

    public ManagementControlEndpoint(ManagementService managementService) {
        this.managementService = managementService;
    }

    @ReadOperation
    public Map<String, Object> getCacheStats() {
        return Map.of("size", managementService.getCacheSize());
    }
```

```
    @DeleteOperation
    public void resetCache() {
        managementService.clearCache();
    }
}
```

Key elements:

1. **`@Endpoint`**: Marks the class as a web/JMX endpoint. The `id` determines the URL: `/actuator/managementControl`.
2. **`@ReadOperation`**: Maps to an HTTP `GET` request. Used to retrieve current state.
3. **`@DeleteOperation`**: Maps to an HTTP `DELETE` request. Used to perform destructive actions like clearing a cache.

How to Verify This:

1. Run the **Management Service** application.
2. Access `http://localhost:8080/actuator/managementControl` (GET) to see the cache size (e.g., `"size": 0`).
3. To reset the cache, send an HTTP `DELETE` request to the same URL (e.g., `curl -X DELETE http://localhost:8080/actuator/managementControl`).

Log Correlation

One of the most frustrating parts of debugging distributed systems is finding the logs for a specific failed request. Spring Boot 4 solves this with **Log Correlation**, a crucial feature for any distributed microservice architecture.

Because we included the OTel starter, Spring Boot automatically configures the logging system (Logback, Log4j2) to include the **Trace ID** and **Span ID** in the MDC (Mapped Diagnostic Context). This means every log line emitted within a request context automatically carries these identifiers, allowing you to easily filter and group logs from multiple services that belong to the same end-to-end transaction.

Let's see this in action by adding a simple log statement to our `ManagementService`.

Listing 13-12. src/main/java/com/apress/crm/management/service/ManagementService.java (Logging with Trace Context)

```
package com.apress.crm.management.service;

import io.micrometer.observation.Observation;
import io.micrometer.observation.ObservationRegistry;
import org.slf4j.Logger;
import org.slf4j.LoggerFactory;
import org.springframework.stereotype.Service;

import java.util.Map;
import java.util.concurrent.ConcurrentHashMap;

@Service
public class ManagementService {

    private static final Logger log = LoggerFactory.
    getLogger(ManagementService.class);

    private final ObservationRegistry observationRegistry;
    private final Map<String, Object> internalCache = new
ConcurrentHashMap<>();

    public ManagementService(ObservationRegistry observationRegistry) {
        this.observationRegistry = observationRegistry;
    }

    public void runComplexReport() {
        Observation.createNotStarted("management.report",
        observationRegistry)
                .lowCardinalityKeyValue("reportType", "full")
                .observe(() -> {
                    log.info("Generating a complex management report...");
                    generateReport();
                    log.info("Management report generated successfully.");
                });
    }
```

```
    private void generateReport() {
        // ... complex logic ...
        internalCache.put("lastReportTimestamp", System.currentTimeMillis());
    }

    public void clearCache() {
        internalCache.clear();
    }

    public int getCacheSize() {
        return internalCache.size();
    }
}
```

What is happening?

1. We define a standard SLF4J `Logger`.
2. Within the `observe` block (which creates an OpenTelemetry Span), we add a simple log statement.
3. Spring Boot automatically intercepts this log statement and enriches it with the current Trace ID and Span ID from the `Observation` context.

Expected Correlated Log Output:

When this service is called as part of a distributed trace, the logs will appear similar to this:

```
2025-11-15T10:00:00.123Z INFO [management-service, 65a8e...3b1, 123...456]
... : Generating a complex management report...
2025-11-15T10:00:00.125Z INFO [management-service, 65a8e...3b1, 123...456]
... : Management report generated successfully.
```

- The additional bracketed values [`management-service, <Trace ID>, <Span ID>`] are automatically injected into your log output.
- `65a8e...3b1`: The **Trace ID**. Unique for the entire request chain across all services.
- `123...456`: The **Span ID**. Unique for this specific operation within the service.

How to Verify This:

1. Run the **Management Service** (with the OTel infrastructure running).
2. Trigger a call to `ManagementService.runComplexReport()` (e.g., via a test or an exposed HTTP endpoint).
3. Observe the application's console output or log file. You should see the log lines from the service enriched with the `[<Trace ID>, <Span ID>]` context.

This "zero-config" log correlation significantly reduces the mean time to resolution (MTTR) by allowing you to instantly jump from a log error to the full distributed trace in Jaeger or other tracing systems.

Infrastructure: Docker Compose

To visualize this data, we need a backend. We will use a standard observability stack defined in `docker-compose.yml`.

Listing 13-13. docker-compose.yml

```
services:
  # 1. Prometheus: Collects Metrics
  prometheus:
    image: prom/prometheus:v2.45.0
    ports:
      - "9090:9090"
    volumes:
      - ./prometheus.yml:/etc/prometheus/prometheus.yml

  # 2. Jaeger: Collects Traces
  jaeger:
    image: jaegertracing/all-in-one:1.50
    environment:
      - COLLECTOR_OTLP_ENABLED=true
```

```
    ports:
      - "16686:16686" # UI
      - "4318:4318"   # OTLP HTTP Receiver

  # 3. Grafana: Visualizes Everything
  grafana:
    image: grafana/grafana:10.1.0
    ports:
      - "3000:3000"
    environment:
      - GF_SECURITY_ADMIN_PASSWORD=admin
```

How to start the Observability Stack:

Navigate to the directory containing this `docker-compose.yml` file and run:

```
docker compose up -d
```

This command will download the necessary Docker images and start Prometheus, Jaeger, and Grafana in detached mode.

How to shut down the Observability Stack:

To stop and remove all services defined in the `docker-compose.yml` file, run:

```
docker compose down
```

You will also need a simple `prometheus.yml` to tell Prometheus where to scrape our apps.

Listing 13-14. prometheus.yml

```
scrape_configs:
  - job_name: 'spring-boot-application'
    metrics_path: '/actuator/prometheus'
    scrape_interval: 5s
    static_configs:
      - targets: ['host.docker.internal:8080'] # Customer Service
```

Testing Observability

How do you verify that you didn't forget to add metrics? The `micrometer-observation-test` library provides tools to assert that observations happened.

Listing 13-15. src/test/java/com/apress/crm/customer/service/CustomerMetricsTest.java

```
package com.apress.crm.customer.service;

import com.apress.crm.customer.Customer;
import com.apress.crm.customer.CustomerRepository;
import io.micrometer.core.instrument.MeterRegistry;
import io.micrometer.core.instrument.simple.SimpleMeterRegistry;
import org.junit.jupiter.api.Test;
import static org.assertj.core.api.Assertions.assertThat;
import static org.mockito.Mockito.mock;

class CustomerMetricsTest {

    @Test
    void shouldIncrementCounter() {
        // Use SimpleMeterRegistry for in-memory testing
        MeterRegistry registry = new SimpleMeterRegistry();
        CustomerMetrics metrics = new CustomerMetrics(registry);
        CustomerRepository repo = mock(CustomerRepository.class);
        CustomerService service = new CustomerService(repo, metrics);

        service.createCustomer(new Customer("Test", "User", "test@email.
        com", "123"));

        // Assert the counter was incremented
        assertThat(registry.get("crm.customer.created").counter().count()).
        isEqualTo(1.0);
    }
}
```

This code shows:

- **`SimpleMeterRegistry`**: An in-memory implementation of the registry perfect for unit tests. It holds the metrics in a map so you can assert their values immediately.

Summary

In this chapter, we evolved our application from a "black box" to a fully observable system using Spring Boot 4's cutting-edge features.

- We decoupled **Operational Monitoring** (Actuator) from **Telemetry Data** (OpenTelemetry).
- We implemented **Custom Metrics** in the Customer Service using Micrometer 2.
- We enabled **Distributed Tracing** in the Management Service using the OTel starter.
- We unified these concepts using the **Observation API** for custom business logic tracing.
- We deployed a full infrastructure stack with **Prometheus**, **Jaeger**, and **Grafana**.

Table 13-5. *Actuator vs. OpenTelemetry*

Feature	Spring Boot Actuator	OpenTelemetry (OTel)
Primary Role	Operational Insight & Control	Data Generation & Export
Key Data	Health, Info, Thread Dumps, Heap	Traces, Metrics, Logs
Transport	HTTP (Pull/Scrape)	OTLP (Push)
Standard	Spring-specific	Vendor-neutral Industry Standard

With these tools in place, you are ready to detect, debug, and resolve issues in production before your customers even notice them.

Native Image Support: All observability features discussed in this chapter—including Actuator endpoints, Micrometer metrics, and OpenTelemetry tracing—are fully compatible with **GraalVM Native Images**. Spring Boot 4's AOT processing ensures that the telemetry infrastructure is pre-configured during the build, allowing your native binaries to start in milliseconds while still providing full observability.

In the next chapter, we will look at optimizing the runtime performance itself by exploring **GraalVM Native Images** and Ahead-of-Time (AOT) compilation.

CHAPTER 14

Going Native with Spring Boot and GraalVM

In the world of cloud computing, microservices, and serverless functions, startup time and memory consumption are critical metrics. Traditional Java applications, running on a Just-In-Time (JIT) compiled JVM, can be relatively slow to start and consume a significant amount of memory. This chapter explores a groundbreaking solution to this problem: compiling Spring Boot applications into self-contained native executables using GraalVM.

A native executable is a platform-specific machine code file that runs without needing a separate JVM. The benefits are dramatic:

- **Near-Instantaneous Startup Times**: Often measured in milliseconds instead of seconds.
- **Drastically Reduced Memory Footprint**: Consuming a fraction of the memory of its JVM counterpart.
- **Smaller Container Images**: Ideal for efficient cloud deployments.

We will explore how Spring's Ahead-of-Time (AOT) engine works in concert with GraalVM to make this possible and walk through the process of building and running our applications as native executables.

The "Why" of Native: JIT vs. AOT

For decades, the Java Virtual Machine's (JVM) greatest strength has been its Just-In-Time (JIT) compiler. The JIT compiler observes running code and performs "on-the-fly" optimizations, leading to excellent peak performance for long-running applications. However, this comes at the cost of a slow "warm-up" period and high memory usage.

F. Gutierrez and D. Carter, *Pro Spring Boot 4*, https://doi.org/10.1007/979-8-8688-2640-5_14

GraalVM Native Image flips this model on its head. It uses an **Ahead-of-Time (AOT)** compiler to perform all compilation and optimization at build time.

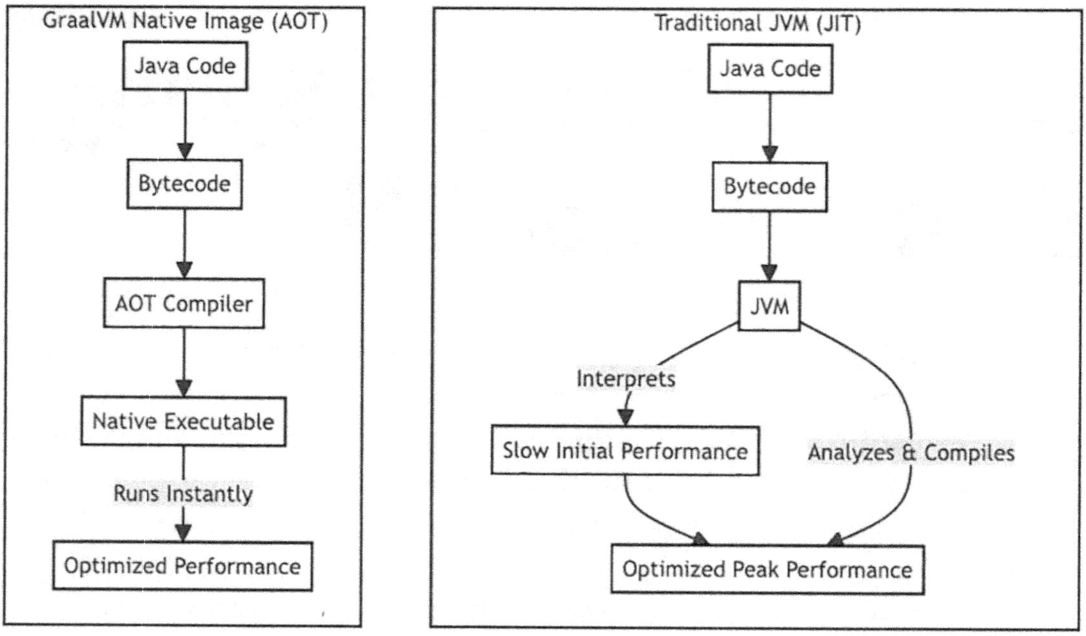

Figure 14-1. *JVM (JIT) vs. GraalVM Native Image (AOT)*

Table 14-1. *JIT vs. AOT Trade-Offs*

Feature	JVM (Just-In-Time)	GraalVM Native Image (Ahead-of-Time)
Startup Time	Slow (seconds)	Fast (milliseconds)
Memory Usage	High	Low
Build Time	Fast	Slow (minutes)
Peak Performance	Excellent (after warm-up)	Good (but may not reach JIT's absolute peak)
Flexibility	High (supports dynamic features like reflection)	Limited (requires static analysis and hints)

The AOT-First Paradigm in Spring Boot 4

GraalVM's AOT compiler requires a **closed-world assumption**: it must know every single piece of code that could possibly be executed at build time. This directly conflicts with Spring's dynamic nature (reflection, proxies, conditional configuration).

This is where the **Spring AOT engine** comes in. When you trigger a native build, the AOT engine runs an analysis of your application. It understands how Spring uses dependency injection, creates proxies, and evaluates conditions. It then generates Java source code and configuration "hints" that explicitly define all this dynamic behavior. This generated code is then fed to the GraalVM native compiler, giving it a complete, static picture of your application.

In Spring Boot 4, this is an **AOT-First** paradigm. The framework is designed with native compatibility as a primary goal, leveraging modular auto-configuration to create leaner executables.

Case Study 1: Building the Customer CRM (Maven) As a Native Image

Let's compile our simple **Customer Project** into a native executable.

Prerequisites

First, you need a GraalVM distribution installed. The easiest way is via SDKMAN!:

```
# Install Liberica NIK (Native Image Kit) for Java 21
sdk install java 23.1.2.r21-nik

# Set it as the default for your current shell
sdk use java 23.1.2.r21-nik
```

Project Configuration

To enable native compilation in a Maven project, you add the `native-maven-plugin` and a dedicated `native` profile to your `pom.xml`.

Listing 14-1. pom.xml

```
<profiles>
    <profile>
        <id>native</id>
        <build>
            <plugins>
                <plugin>
                    <groupId>org.graalvm.buildtools</groupId>
                    <artifactId>native-maven-plugin</artifactId>
                    <version>0.10.1</version>
                    <executions>
                        <execution>
                            <id>build-native</id>
                            <goals>
                                <goal>compile-no-fork</goal>
                            </goals>
                            <phase>package</phase>
                        </execution>
                    </executions>
                </plugin>
            </plugins>
        </build>
    </profile>
</profiles>
```

Compiling the Native Executable

With the profile added, you can now trigger a native build.

```
# This command activates the 'native' profile and runs the build
./mvnw package -Pnative
```

This command will take several minutes to complete. The final executable will be placed in the target/ directory.

Benchmarking the Application

Let's compare the performance.

1. **Startup Time**
   First, run the standard JAR:

   ```
   java -jar target/customer-0.0.1-SNAPSHOT.jar
   // Observe the startup time in the logs, e.g., "...in 4.875
   seconds"
   ```

   Now, run the native executable:

   ```
   ./target/customer
   // Observe the startup time, e.g., "...in 0.098 seconds"
   ```

2. **Memory Consumption**
   While the applications are running, open a separate terminal to inspect their memory usage (RSS—Resident Set Size).
   For the JVM process:

   ```
   ps -ef | grep "java -jar" | grep "customer"
   # Find the PID from the output and use it below
   ps -o rss= -p <JVM_PID>
   # Result might be around 450000 (which is ~450MB)
   ```

   Now, do the same for the native process:

   ```
   ps -ef | grep "target/customer"
   ps -o rss= -p <NATIVE_PID>
   # Result might be around 125000 (which is ~125MB)
   ```

   The difference is staggering. The native application starts orders of magnitude faster and uses significantly less memory.

Testing Native Applications

You can run your test suite within a native image to catch compatibility issues.

```
./mvnw test -Pnative
```

This command compiles your main code, your test code, and the testing framework into a native executable and then runs the tests.

Case Study 2: Native Observability with the Management CRM (Gradle)

Now, let's prove that even a complex, reactive application with OpenTelemetry tracing can be compiled natively.

Project Configuration

To enable native compilation in a Gradle project, you only need to add one plugin to your `build.gradle` file.

Listing 14-2. build.gradle

```
plugins {
    id 'java'
    id 'org.springframework.boot' version '4.0.0'
    id 'io.spring.dependency-management' version '1.1.7'
    id 'org.graalvm.buildtools.native' version '0.10.1' // Add this plugin
}
```

Build and Run

With the plugin applied, you can trigger a native build with a new Gradle task.

```
./gradlew nativeCompile
```

Before running, make sure your observability infrastructure (Jaeger, etc.) is running via Docker Compose (from Chapter 13).

```
# Run the native executable
./build/native/nativeCompile/management
```

Verification: Make a few requests to the Management Service API. Then, open the Jaeger UI at `http://localhost:16686`. You will see traces appearing, proving that your native executable is successfully exporting telemetry via OTLP. This seamless integration is a core strength of Spring Boot 4.

Advanced Native Concepts

While Spring Boot simplifies native compilation, "Pro" developers need to understand the advanced concepts for handling complex scenarios.

Runtime Hints

While the Spring AOT engine is incredibly powerful, it cannot predict every possible dynamic behavior in an application, especially when dealing with third-party libraries that were not designed with native compilation in mind. GraalVM's "closed-world" assumption means that any code not reachable through static analysis at build time will be eliminated. If your application later tries to access this code dynamically (e.g., via reflection), it will fail with an error at runtime.

Runtime Hints are the mechanism for solving this problem. They allow you to programmatically tell the AOT engine and the GraalVM compiler about the dynamic needs of your application.

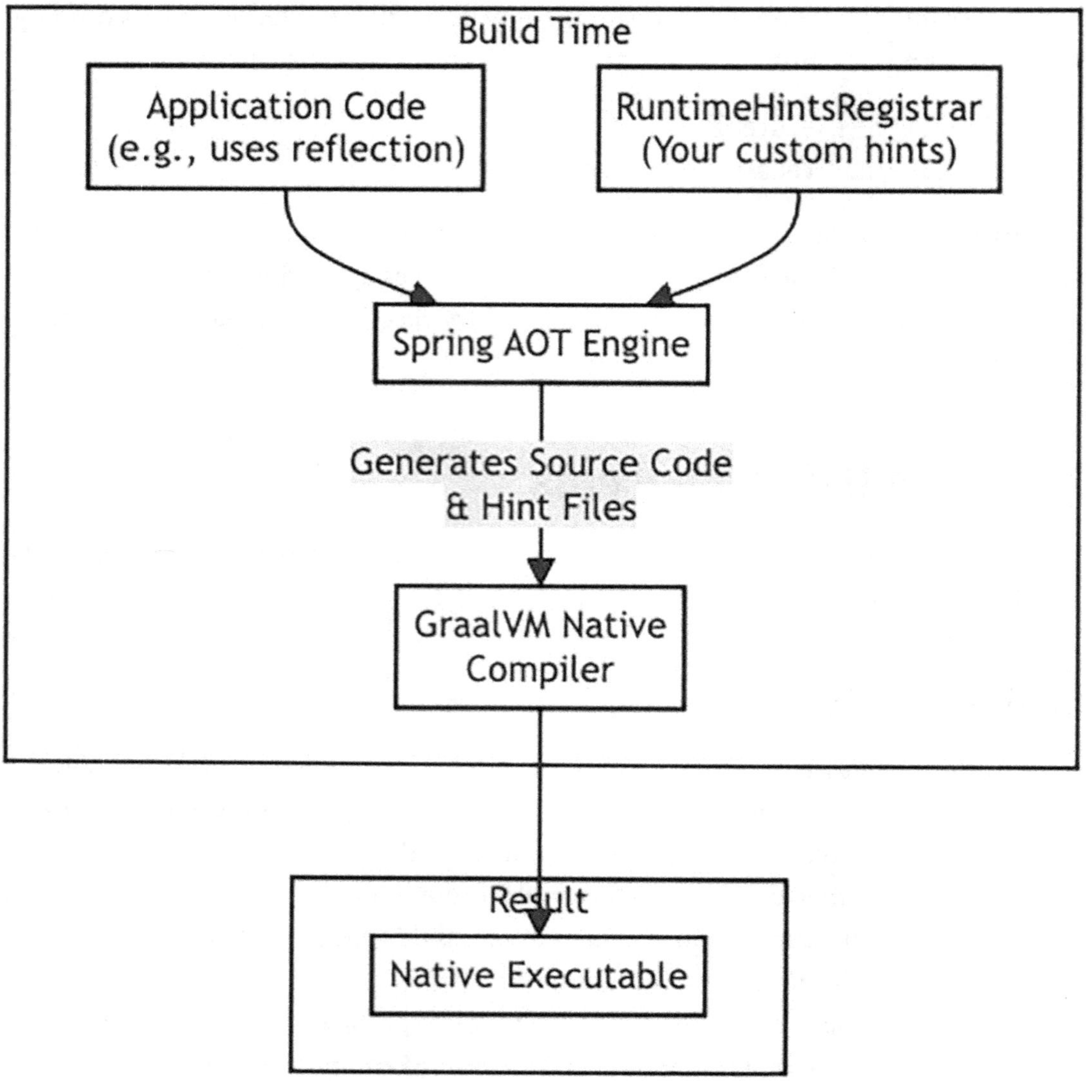

Figure 14-2. *The Role of Runtime Hints in a Native Build*

Types of Hints

The `RuntimeHints` API provides several categories of hints to address different dynamic features of the JVM.

Table 14-2. Common Runtime Hint Types

Hint Type	Description
`hints.reflection()`	Registers types, methods, or fields that are accessed via reflection (`Class.forName()`, `Method.invoke()`). This is the most common type of hint needed.
`hints.resources()`	Includes non-class files from the classpath (like `.properties`, `.json`, or `.xml` files) that are loaded dynamically.
`hints.serialization()`	Registers classes that are meant to be serialized using standard Java Serialization.
`hints.proxies()`	Registers JDK dynamic proxy definitions, typically for interfaces that are proxied at runtime (e.g., in some AOP scenarios).

Common Use Cases

You will typically need to provide hints when:

- Using a third-party library that uses reflection internally to inspect classes or annotations.
- Dynamically loading configuration or template files from the classpath.
- Serializing objects to be sent over the network or stored on disk using Java's built-in serialization.
- Creating dynamic proxies for interfaces at runtime.

Example 1: Basic Reflection and Resource Hints

You provide hints by creating a class that implements `RuntimeHintsRegistrar` and registering it in `META-INF/spring/aot.factories`.

Listing 14-3. src/main/java/com/apress/crm/management/CrmRuntimeHints.java

```
package com.apress.crm.management;

import org.springframework.aot.hint.RuntimeHints;
import org.springframework.aot.hint.RuntimeHintsRegistrar;
import org.springframework.aot.hint.TypeReference;

public class CrmRuntimeHints implements RuntimeHintsRegistrar {

    @Override
    public void registerHints(RuntimeHints hints, ClassLoader
    classLoader) {
        // Register reflection hints for a specific class
        hints.reflection().registerType(TypeReference.of("com.external.
        library.SomeClass"));

        // Register resource hints for a file needed at runtime
        hints.resources().registerPattern("config/external-rules.json");
    }
}
```

What Is Happening?

- **`RuntimeHintsRegistrar`**: The interface Spring's AOT engine scans for.
- **`hints.reflection().registerType(...)`**: This tells the GraalVM compiler not to discard `com.external.library.SomeClass` and to make its constructors and methods available for reflection at runtime. Using `TypeReference.of()` is safer as it allows build tools to verify the class name.
- **`hints.resources().registerPattern(...)`**: This ensures that the `config/external-rules.json` file from your classpath is included in the final native executable so it can be loaded at runtime.

Example 2: Advanced Hints for Serialization and Proxies

Let's imagine our **Management Service** needs to integrate with a legacy system that uses JDK proxies and Java serialization.

Listing 14-4. src/main/java/com/apress/crm/management/LegacyIntegrationHints.java

```
package com.apress.crm.management;

import com.apress.crm.management.service.LegacyTask;
import org.springframework.aot.hint.ProxyHints;
import org.springframework.aot.hint.RuntimeHints;
import org.springframework.aot.hint.RuntimeHintsRegistrar;
import org.springframework.aot.hint.SerializationHints;
import org.springframework.aot.hint.TypeReference;
import java.io.Serializable;

public class LegacyIntegrationHints implements RuntimeHintsRegistrar {

    @Override
    public void registerHints(RuntimeHints hints, ClassLoader
    classLoader) {
        // 1. Register a class for Java Serialization
        SerializationHints serialization = hints.serialization();
        serialization.registerType(TypeReference.of("com.legacy.Payload"));

        // 2. Register a JDK Proxy for a specific interface
        ProxyHints proxies = hints.proxies();
        proxies.registerJdkProxy(TypeReference.of(LegacyTask.class),
                                 TypeReference.of(Serializable.class));
    }
}
```

What Is Happening?

1. **hints.serialization().registerType(...)**: In a native image, only explicitly registered classes can be serialized. This hint tells the compiler to generate the necessary serialization metadata for the com.legacy.Payload class.

2. **`hints.proxies().registerJdkProxy(...)`**: This tells the compiler to generate a dynamic proxy class at build time that implements both our custom `LegacyTask` interface and `java.io.Serializable`. This is necessary if the application creates such a proxy at runtime using `Proxy.newProxyInstance()`.

Spring Boot's native test support (`./mvnw test -Pnative`) is your best friend for discovering missing hints. When a native test fails with an error related to reflection or missing resources, it's a strong indication that you need to add a custom hint.

Programmatic Bean Registration

In a standard Spring application, `@Bean` methods are the primary way to register beans. However, these methods are inherently dynamic; Spring must execute them at runtime, often using reflection, to discover the bean definitions. This model poses a challenge for GraalVM's static analysis.

The modern, native-friendly way to register beans based on dynamic conditions is to do so programmatically. This approach allows the AOT engine to understand exactly which beans will be created under which conditions, without relying on runtime execution of `@Configuration` classes.

Features of Programmatic Registration

- **Static and AOT-Friendly**: The logic is analyzed at build time, allowing GraalVM to create a complete picture of the application context.
- **Type-Safe**: You define beans using `BeanDefinitionBuilder`, which works directly with class types, reducing the risk of runtime errors.
- **Highly Flexible**: Allows for complex conditional logic that would be difficult or impossible to express with simple `@Conditional` annotations.
- **Decoupled**: The registration logic is decoupled from the bean's source code, adhering to the single-responsibility principle.

Key Interfaces: BeanRegistrar vs. ImportBeanRegistrar

Spring Boot 4 provides two primary interfaces for this pattern:

- **`BeanRegistrar`**: The most basic interface. You register implementations of this in `META-INF/spring/aot.factories`. It is used by the AOT engine at build time.
- **`ImportBeanRegistrar`**: This is a more common and flexible variant. It is used with the `@Import` annotation on a configuration class. This allows you to "import" a set of bean definitions based on custom logic.

Use Cases

- **Cloud-Specific Services**: Registering an `S3StorageService` only when the application detects it is running on AWS.
- **Feature Flagging**: Enabling or disabling an entire module of beans (e.g., an "auditing" feature) based on a single application property.
- **Dynamic Sub-Module Configuration**: Registering different implementations of an interface based on the available libraries on the classpath.

Example 1: Conditional Bean Registration

This example registers a cloud-specific storage service.

Listing 14-5. Example of a native-friendly BeanRegistrar

```
package com.apress.crm.management;

import org.springframework.beans.factory.support.BeanDefinitionBuilder;
import org.springframework.beans.factory.support.BeanDefinitionRegistry;
import org.springframework.boot.AotBeanRegistrar;
import org.springframework.boot.cloud.CloudPlatform;
import org.springframework.core.env.Environment;

public class CrmBeanRegistrar implements AotBeanRegistrar {
```

```
    @Override
    public void register(BeanDefinitionRegistry registry, Environment
    environment) {
        if (CloudPlatform.isKubernetes(environment)) {
            BeanDefinitionBuilder builder = BeanDefinitionBuilder.rootBeanD
            efinition(KubernetesHealthProbe.class);
            registry.registerBeanDefinition("k8sProbe", builder.
            getBeanDefinition());
        }
    }
}
```

What Is Happening?

- **`AotBeanRegistrar`**: A specialized registrar that provides access to the Spring `Environment`, allowing for property-based conditions.
- **`CloudPlatform.isKubernetes(...)`**: Spring Boot's utility for detecting the runtime environment.
- **`BeanDefinitionBuilder`**: A fluent API for creating a `BeanDefinition`, which is the core metadata Spring uses to manage a bean.
- **`registerBeanDefinition`**: This method programmatically adds the bean to the application context, equivalent to what a `@Bean` method does.

Example 2: Dynamic Sub-Module with `@Import`

A more powerful pattern is to use `@Import` with an `ImportBeanRegistrar`. Let's create a configurable auditing module for our **Management Service**.

First, we define an annotation to enable the feature:

Listing 14-6. src/main/java/com/apress/crm/management/audit/EnableCrmAuditing.java

```
package com.apress.crm.management.audit;

import org.springframework.context.annotation.Import;
import java.lang.annotation.*;
```

```
@Target(ElementType.TYPE)
@Retention(RetentionPolicy.RUNTIME)
@Import(CrmAuditingRegistrar.class)
public @interface EnableCrmAuditing {
}
```

Next, we create the registrar. This class will check for a property and register the AuditService only if it is enabled.

Listing 14-7. src/main/java/com/apress/crm/management/audit/CrmAuditingRegistrar.java

```
package com.apress.crm.management.audit;

import org.springframework.beans.factory.support.BeanDefinitionBuilder;
import org.springframework.beans.factory.support.BeanDefinitionRegistry;
import
org.springframework.context.annotation.ImportBeanDefinitionRegistrar;
import org.springframework.core.type.AnnotationMetadata;

public class CrmAuditingRegistrar implements
ImportBeanDefinitionRegistrar {

    @Override
    public void registerBeanDefinitions(AnnotationMetadata
    importingClassMetadata, BeanDefinitionRegistry registry) {
        // In a real app, you would check environment properties.
        boolean auditingEnabled = true; // Assume enabled for demo

        if (auditingEnabled) {
            BeanDefinitionBuilder builder = BeanDefinitionBuilder.
            rootBeanDefinition(AuditService.class);
            registry.registerBeanDefinition("auditService", builder.
            getBeanDefinition());
        }
    }
}
```

Finally, we apply the annotation to our main configuration.

Listing 14-8. src/main/java/com/apress/crm/management/ManagementApplication.java

```java
package com.apress.crm.management;

import com.apress.crm.management.audit.EnableCrmAuditing;
import org.springframework.boot.autoconfigure.SpringBootApplication;

@SpringBootApplication
@EnableCrmAuditing
public class ManagementApplication {
    // ...
}
```

This Code Shows:

1. **`@EnableCrmAuditing`**: A custom annotation that acts as a feature flag. When a developer adds this to their configuration, it triggers the import of our `CrmAuditingRegistrar`.
2. **`ImportBeanDefinitionRegistrar`**: This interface is the key. Its `registerBeanDefinitions` method is called during the application startup, giving us a hook to programmatically add our `AuditService` bean. This is fully compatible with GraalVM's static analysis.

This pattern is extremely powerful for building extensible libraries and starters that can be conditionally enabled by consumers of your code.

AOT Cache

To speed up local development, Spring Boot 4 provides an **AOT Cache**. When enabled, the AOT processing results from the first build are cached. Subsequent builds will only re-process changed files, significantly reducing compilation time.

Enable it in your `pom.xml` or `build.gradle`:

```xml
<!-- pom.xml plugin configuration -->
<configuration>
    <cacheAot>true</cacheAot>
</configuration>
```

Checkpoint and Restore (Project CRaC)

For even faster startup, Spring Boot 4 includes experimental support for **Coordinated Restore at Checkpoint (CRaC)**, an OpenJDK project. Where GraalVM achieves speed by compiling ahead-of-time, CRaC takes a different approach: it allows you to take a "snapshot" of a running, fully warmed-up JVM process and save it to disk. You can then restore this image almost instantly, complete with the JIT compiler's optimizations.

This is a powerful alternative to native compilation when you need the full dynamic capabilities of the JVM but still require sub-second startup times.

Key Features

- **Ultra-Fast Startup**: Restore times are often under 100ms, as you are loading a memory image directly, skipping class loading, configuration, and JIT compilation.
- **Preserved JIT Optimizations**: Unlike a native image, a restored CRaC image retains all the runtime optimizations made by the JIT compiler during the "warm-up" phase.
- **Full JVM Compatibility**: Because it runs on a standard (though specialized) JVM, it supports all dynamic Java features like reflection and proxies without the need for hints.

CRaC vs. Native Image

Table 14-3. *CRaC vs. GraalVM Native Image*

Feature	Checkpoint and Restore (CRaC)	GraalVM Native Image
Startup Time	Fastest (<100ms)	Fast (<200ms)
Memory Footprint	Medium (lower than standard JVM, higher than native)	Lowest
Peak Performance	Potentially highest (retains JIT optimizations)	Good (statically optimized)
Compatibility	High (full JVM)	Limited (requires AOT hints)
Requires	CRaC-enabled JDK, Linux kernel 5.9+	GraalVM JDK

Use Cases

- **Serverless Functions**: Drastically reduce “cold start” times for stateful functions.
- **Rapid Scaling**: Quickly add new application instances during a traffic spike.
- **Development Environments**: Instantly restart a development server in its fully warmed-up state.

Implementing CRaC with Spring Boot

1. **Prerequisites**: CRaC requires a specialized JDK. The most common is Azul’s Zulu build of OpenJDK.

   ```
   # Install a CRaC-enabled JDK
   sdk install java 21.0.1.crac-zulu
   sdk use java 21.0.1.crac-zulu
   ```

2. **Dependencies**: Add the CRaC starter to your project.

   ```
   <!-- pom.xml -->
   <dependency>
       <groupId>org.springframework.boot</groupId>
       <artifactId>spring-boot-starter-crac</artifactId>
   </dependency>
   ```

3. **Handling Resources**: The main challenge with CRaC is that open resources like file handles and network sockets cannot be saved in the checkpoint. Your application must implement the `org.crac.Resource` interface to close these resources before a checkpoint is taken and reopen them upon restore.

Listing 14-9. src/main/java/com/apress/crm/management/
CracManagedConnection.java

```
package com.apress.crm.management;

import org.crac.Context;
import org.crac.Core;
import org.crac.Resource;
import org.springframework.stereotype.Component;
import jakarta.annotation.PostConstruct;
import jakarta.annotation.PreDestroy;

@Component
public class CracManagedConnection implements Resource {

    private NetworkConnection connection;

    public CracManagedConnection() {
        Core.getGlobalContext().register(this);
    }

    @PostConstruct
    public void openConnection() {
        this.connection = new NetworkConnection(); // Simulate opening a
                                                      connection

        this.connection.open();
    }

    @PreDestroy
    public void closeConnection() {
        this.connection.close();
    }

    @Override
    public void beforeCheckpoint(Context<? extends Resource> context)
    throws Exception {
        System.out.println("CRaC: Closing network connection before
        checkpoint...");
        closeConnection();
    }
```

```
    @Override
    public void afterRestore(Context<? extends Resource> context) throws
    Exception {
        System.out.println("CRaC: Re-opening network connection after
        restore...");
        openConnection();
    }
}
```

What Is Happening?

1. **Core.getGlobalContext().register(this)**: We register our bean with the global CRaC context so it can be managed during the checkpoint/restore lifecycle.
2. **beforeCheckpoint**: This hook is called just before the JVM is frozen. We must close any open sockets or files here.
3. **afterRestore**: This hook is called immediately after the JVM is restored. We re-establish the resources we closed earlier.
4. **Creating and Restoring a Checkpoint:** To use CRaC, you run your application with a specific Java agent and then trigger a checkpoint.

```
# 1. Run the application with the CRaC agent
# The -XX:CRaCCheckpointTo=PATH argument specifies where to save the
image files
java -XX:CRaCCheckpointTo=./checkpoint -jar app.jar

# 2. In a separate terminal, trigger the checkpoint (e.g., via JMX)
# For this example, we'll assume a file trigger is configured
jcmd app.jar JDK.checkpoint

# 3. Restore the application almost instantly from the checkpoint files
java -XX:CRaCRestoreFrom=./checkpoint
```

Key Elements:

- **-XX:CRaCCheckpointTo**: A JVM flag that specifies the directory where the checkpoint image will be saved.
- **jcmd ... JDK.checkpoint**: A standard command to trigger the checkpoint on a running CRaC-enabled JVM.
- **-XX:CRaCRestoreFrom**: The JVM flag used to restore the application from the saved image files, resulting in near-instantaneous startup.

Optimizing Container Images

A major benefit of native executables is the ability to create highly optimized, secure container images.

Cloud Native Buildpacks

The easiest way to create a container image is with Spring Boot's built-in **Cloud Native Buildpacks**.

```
# For a native image
./gradlew bootBuildImage

# For a standard JVM image
./gradlew bootJar
```

Buildpacks automatically create an optimized, layered Docker image with a minimal base OS and the correct configuration for your application (JVM or native).

Efficient Dockerfiles

For maximum control, you can write a multi-stage `Dockerfile`. This allows you to compile the native executable in a "builder" image and then copy the final artifact to a minimal "distroless" image, resulting in the smallest possible footprint and attack surface.

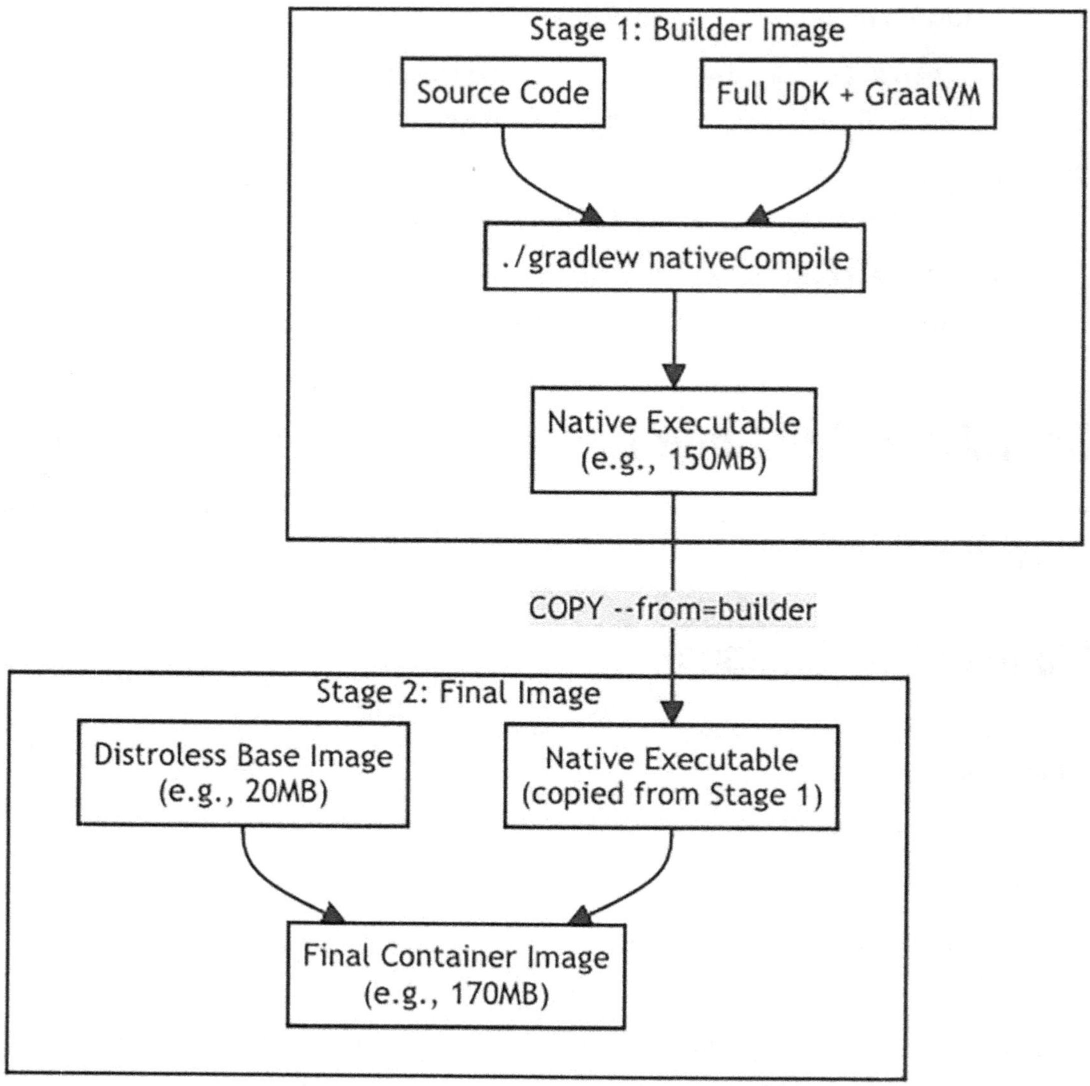

Figure 14-3. *Multi-Stage Docker Build*

Listing 14-10. Multi-Stage Dockerfile for a Native Image

```
# Stage 1: Builder
FROM liberica-nik:23.1-21 as builder
WORKDIR /workspace
COPY . .
RUN ./gradlew nativeCompile
```

```
# Stage 2: Final Image
FROM gcr.io/distroless/cc-static
COPY --from=builder /workspace/build/native/nativeCompile/management /app
ENTRYPOINT ["/app"]
```

What Is Happening?

- **Stage 1**: We use a full GraalVM/JDK image to build the native executable.
- **Stage 2**: We copy **only** the compiled binary into a `distroless` image, which contains nothing but the bare minimum libraries needed to run the application. The final image is often less than 100MB.

Table 14-4. *Buildpacks vs. Custom Dockerfile*

Feature	Cloud Native Buildpacks	Custom Dockerfile
Ease of Use	Very Easy (`bootBuildImage`)	More Complex (Requires Docker knowledge)
Optimization	Good (Automatic layering)	Best (Full control over base image and layers)
Security	Good (Minimal base OS)	Best (Can use distroless images)

Accessing the Source Code: The complete source code for all examples in this chapter, along with comprehensive README files and dedicated guides on AOT features, can be downloaded from the Apress website accompanying this book.

Summary

In this chapter, we unlocked a new level of performance for Spring Boot applications. We learned that **GraalVM** can compile Java applications into incredibly fast and memory-efficient **native executables**. We saw how the **Spring AOT engine** is the critical link that makes this possible by analyzing an application's dynamic behavior at build time.

Through practical benchmarks and case studies with both our CRM applications, we:

- Built and tested native images using both Maven and Gradle.
- Verified that even complex features like OpenTelemetry work seamlessly in native mode.
- Explored advanced concepts like **Runtime Hints**, **AOT Caching**, and **Project CRaC**.
- Learned how to create highly optimized and secure container images using both **Buildpacks** and multi-stage **Dockerfiles.**

While native compilation involves trade-offs like longer build times, it represents a powerful deployment option for cloud-native microservices and serverless functions where efficiency and speed are paramount. Spring Boot 4 makes choosing between a JIT-compiled JVM deployment and an AOT-compiled native executable a simple build-time decision, not a development-time one.

CHAPTER 15

Building Cloud-Native Microservices with Spring Cloud

In the previous chapters, we built the `customer` and `management` applications, focusing on their core functionalities, observability, and native compilation. While these applications are functionally independent, this chapter is about integrating them into a true **microservice architecture** capable of operating effectively in a cloud environment.

This is the domain of **Spring Cloud**.

Spring Cloud is not a single project, but an umbrella of projects that provide solutions to the common patterns of distributed systems. It builds on top of Spring Boot and provides a powerful, "batteries-included" experience for building cloud-native applications.

In this chapter, we will build a fully functional microservice ecosystem by implementing:

- **Docker Compose Support**: For a seamless local development experience.
- **Distributed Configuration**: Centralizing application properties with **Spring Cloud Config**.
- **Service Discovery**: Enabling services to find each other with **HashiCorp Consul**.
- **API Gateway**: Creating a unified entry point with **Spring Cloud Gateway**.

F. Gutierrez and D. Carter, *Pro Spring Boot 4*, https://doi.org/10.1007/979-8-8688-2640-5_15

- **Resilience**: Preventing cascading failures with **Circuit Breakers** (Resilience4j).
- **Event-Driven Architecture**: Decoupling services with **Spring Cloud Stream**.
- **Contract Testing**: Ensuring reliable integration with **Spring Cloud Contract**.
- **Short-Lived Tasks**: Running ephemeral jobs with **Spring Cloud Task**.

The Twelve-Factor App Revisited

Before we dive into the tools, it is essential to revisit the **Twelve-Factor App** methodology. These principles, originally conceived for Heroku, have become the de facto standard for building modern, scalable applications. Spring Cloud provides first-class solutions for nearly every factor.

Table 15-1. *Twelve-Factor App Principles and Spring Cloud Solutions*

Factor	Principle	Spring Cloud & Spring Boot Solution
I. Codebase	One codebase tracked in revision control, many deploys.	Standard practice (Git).
II. Dependencies	Explicitly declare and isolate dependencies.	Maven (`pom.xml`) and Gradle (`build.gradle`) dependency management.
III. Config	Store config in the environment.	**Spring Cloud Config**, Kubernetes ConfigMaps, environment variables.
IV. Backing Services	Treat backing services as attached resources.	**Spring Cloud's Service Discovery** allows services to be located and attached dynamically.
V. Build, release, run	Strictly separate build, release, and run stages.	CI/CD pipelines building Docker/OCI images. Native executables are the ultimate separation.

(continued)

Table 15-1. (continued)

Factor	Principle	Spring Cloud & Spring Boot Solution
VI. Processes	Execute the app as one or more stateless processes.	Standard deployment model for Spring Boot applications.
VII. Port Binding	Export services via port binding.	Embedded web servers (Tomcat, Netty) bind to a port specified by `server.port`.
VIII. Concurrency	Scale out via the process model.	Easily achieved by running multiple instances of the containerized application.
IX. Disposability	Maximize robustness with fast startup and graceful shutdown.	**Native Images** provide fast startup. **Actuator's/shutdown endpoint** enables graceful shutdown.
X. Dev/prod parity	Keep development, staging, and production as similar as possible.	**Spring Boot's Docker Compose support** and **Testcontainers** allow local development with the exact same backing services as production.
XI. Logs	Treat logs as event streams.	**Log Correlation** with OpenTelemetry streams structured logs to standard output for collection by platforms like Loki or Splunk.
XII. Admin processes	Run admin/management tasks as one-off processes.	**Spring Cloud Task** provides a framework for running short-lived microservices.

Local Development in the Cloud: Docker Compose Support

A common challenge in microservice development is the "it works on my machine" problem, where a developer's local environment differs from production. Spring Boot 4's native **Docker Compose support** solves this by managing all external services (databases, brokers) for local development automatically.

All you need is a `compose.yaml` (or `docker-compose.yml`) file in your project's root directory and the `spring-boot-docker-compose` dependency.

Listing 15-1. pom.xml (Customer Service)

```
<dependency>
    <groupId>org.springframework.boot</groupId>
    <artifactId>spring-boot-docker-compose</artifactId>
    <scope>runtime</scope>
</dependency>
```

What Is Happening?

When you run your application from your IDE or via the command line (`./mvnw spring-boot:run`), Spring Boot will automatically do the following: 1. Scan for a `compose.yaml` file in your project root. 2. Run `docker compose up` to start all defined services. 3. **Inspect the running containers** and automatically configure the connection properties (`spring.datasource.url`, `spring.rabbitmq.host`, etc.) to point to the correct dynamic ports. 4. When the application shuts down, it will automatically run `docker compose down`.

This feature provides the benefits of Testcontainers' dynamic configuration but for the application's main runtime, creating perfect dev/prod parity.

Centralized and Distributed Configuration

In microservice architecture, managing configuration across dozens of services is a major challenge. Hardcoding properties inside your application JAR (the `application.properties` file) is a violation of the Twelve-Factor App principles. It forces you to rebuild and redeploy your entire application just to change a database password or a feature flag.

Spring Cloud Config

Spring Cloud Config provides a robust solution for this problem. It introduces a centralized server that manages external properties for applications across all environments. Client applications connect to this server on startup to fetch their configuration, decoupling the configuration from the application code itself.

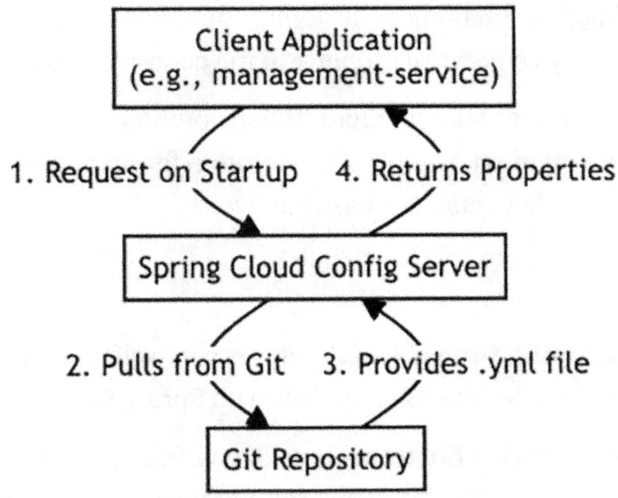

Figure 15-1. *Spring Cloud Config Architecture*

Features

- **Pluggable Backends**: Supports various backends to store configuration, with Git being the most popular. Other options include SVN, local filesystem, HashiCorp Vault, and JDBC.
- **Property Encryption**: Provides endpoints (`/encrypt` and `/decrypt`) to encrypt sensitive values (like passwords) so they can be safely stored in a Git repository.
- **Dynamic Refresh**: Allows applications to refresh their configuration at runtime without restarting, using the `/actuator/refresh` endpoint.
- **High Availability**: You can run multiple instances of the Config Server and register them with a service discovery tool (like Consul) for high availability.

Use Cases

- **Environment-Specific Properties**: Managing database URLs, credentials, and message broker addresses for `dev`, `qa`, and `prod` environments.

- **Feature Toggles**: Enabling or disabling application features dynamically by changing a property in the central repository.
- **Centralized Secret Management**: When combined with a Vault backend, it provides a highly secure solution for managing dynamic secrets like API keys and database passwords.

Best Practices

- **Secure the Config Server**: The Config Server itself is a critical piece of infrastructure. Secure its endpoints with Spring Security.
- **Use Git Branches for Environments**: A common pattern is to use a separate Git branch for each environment (e.g., `main` for prod, `develop` for dev) to manage configuration promotion.
- **Encrypt All Secrets**: Never store sensitive properties in plain text in your Git repository. Always use the Config Server's encryption features.
- **Bootstrap Configuration**: Remember that the location of the Config Server must be defined in `bootstrap.yml` (or `bootstrap.properties`), as it needs to be resolved before the main application context is created.

Setting Up the Config Server

First, we create a new Spring Boot project named `config-server`. It needs two dependencies: `spring-cloud-config-server` and `spring-cloud-starter-consul-discovery` (so it can register itself).

Next, we enable it in the main application class.

Listing 15-2. src/main/java/com/apress/crm/config/ConfigServerApplication.java

```
package com.apress.crm.config;

import org.springframework.boot.SpringApplication;
import org.springframework.boot.autoconfigure.SpringBootApplication;
import org.springframework.cloud.config.server.EnableConfigServer;
```

```
@SpringBootApplication
@EnableConfigServer
public class ConfigServerApplication {
    public static void main(String[] args) {
        SpringApplication.run(ConfigServerApplication.class, args);
    }
}
```

- `@EnableConfigServer` turns the application into a config server.

Finally, we configure it in `application.yml` to pull properties from a Git repository.

Listing 15-3. config-server/src/main/resources/application.yml

```
server:
  port: 8888
spring:
  application:
    name: config-server
  cloud:
    config:
      server:
        git:
          uri: https://github.com/pro-spring-boot/config-repo # A Git repo
          containing our config files
```

Configuring the Management Service

Our `management-service` will now become a client of the Config Server. We add the dependency to its `build.gradle`:

```
implementation 'org.springframework.cloud:spring-cloud-starter-config'
```

And create a new `bootstrap.yml` file.

Configuration for Spring Cloud Config must be loaded **before** the application context starts. Therefore, we place it in `src/main/resources/bootstrap.yml`, which is loaded during the bootstrap phase.

Listing 15-4. management-service/src/main/resources/bootstrap.yml

```
spring:
  application:
    name: management-service # Matches the file name in the git repo
    (management-service.yml)
  cloud:
    config:
      uri: http://localhost:8888 # Location of the Config Server
```

Now, when the `management-service` starts, it will first contact the Config Server at `http://localhost:8888`, ask for the configuration for `management-service`, and load the properties from Git.

Service Discovery and Communication

In a dynamic microservice environment where services are ephemeral—constantly being created, destroyed, or scaled—we cannot rely on hardcoded IP addresses. **Service Discovery** is the pattern that solves this. It provides a central, highly available registry where services can register their location upon startup and discover the locations of other services at runtime.

There are two primary patterns for service discovery:

- **Client-Side Discovery**: The client service is responsible for querying the service registry to get a list of available instances for a target service and then choosing one (often via a load balancer). This is the pattern used by Spring Cloud with libraries like Netflix Eureka and HashiCorp Consul.
- **Server-Side Discovery**: The client makes a request to a router or load balancer (like a Kubernetes service), which handles the discovery logic on behalf of the client.

For our example, we will implement client-side discovery using **HashiCorp Consul**, a popular and robust service mesh solution, integrated via **Spring Cloud Consul**.

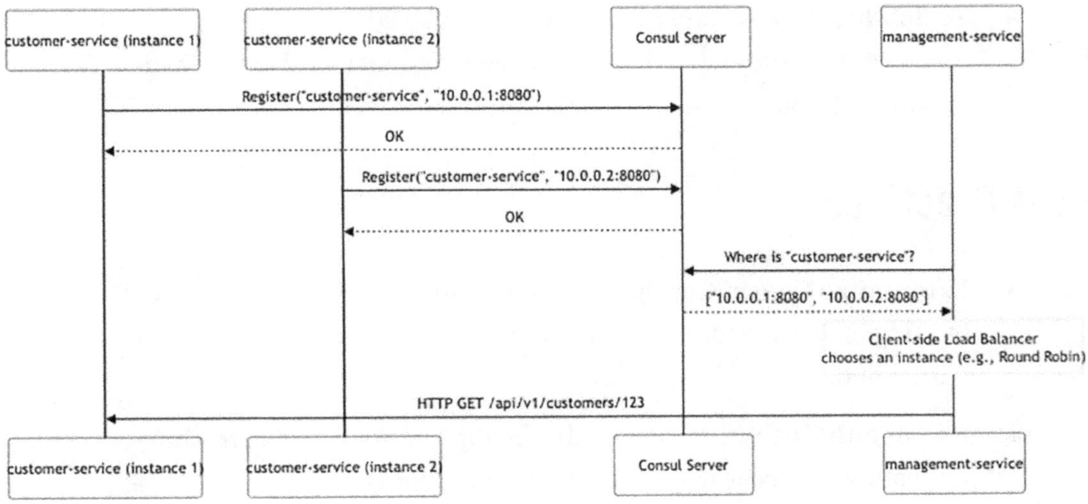

Figure 15-2. *Client-Side Service Discovery Flow*

Features of Spring Cloud Consul Discovery

- **Auto-Registration**: Spring Boot applications with the starter on the classpath automatically register themselves with the Consul agent.
- **Health Check Integration**: It integrates with Spring Boot Actuator. The service's health status in Consul is automatically updated based on the `/actuator/health` endpoint. If an instance becomes unhealthy, it is removed from the pool of available services.
- **Client-Side Load Balancing**: When used with `@LoadBalanced` `RestClient` or `WebClient`, requests are automatically distributed across all healthy instances of a target service.

Use Cases

- **Dynamic Microservice Communication**: The primary use case for enabling services to call each other without static configuration.
- **Resilience**: By integrating with health checks, the system can automatically route around failing service instances.

- **Scalability**: New instances of a service can be added to the cluster, and they will automatically be discovered and included in the load-balancing pool.

Best Practices

- **Externalize Consul Configuration**: The address of the Consul agent (`spring.cloud.consul.host` and `port`) should be externalized, not hardcoded.
- **Use Health Checks**: Always enable health checks. A registered but unhealthy service is worse than an unregistered one.
- **Prefer Kubernetes-Native (in Kubernetes)**: While Consul is an excellent tool, if your final deployment target is Kubernetes, prefer using Spring Cloud Kubernetes, which leverages the platform's built-in service discovery for a simpler architecture. We use Consul here to demonstrate the general client-side discovery pattern.

Setting Up Consul

We add Consul to our `docker-compose.yml`.

Listing 15-5. docker-compose.yml

```
services:
  consul:
    image: hashicorp/consul:1.18
    ports:
      - "8500:8500" # Consul UI and API
```

Registering Services

We add the `spring-cloud-starter-consul-discovery` dependency to both the `customer-service` and `management-service`. Spring Boot automatically detects Consul running on `localhost:8500`, and each service will register itself on startup. You can view the registered services in the Consul UI at `http://localhost:8500`.

Service-to-Service Calls

Now that services can find each other, let's make a call from the `management-service` to the `customer-service` using a load-balanced `RestClient`.

Listing 15-6. management-service/src/main/java/com/apress/crm/management/client/CustomerClient.java

```
package com.apress.crm.management.client;

import org.springframework.cloud.client.loadbalancer.LoadBalanced;
import org.springframework.context.annotation.Bean;
import org.springframework.stereotype.Component;
import org.springframework.web.client.RestClient;

@Component
public class CustomerClient {

    private final RestClient restClient;

    public CustomerClient(@LoadBalanced RestClient.Builder builder) {
        // The base URL uses the service ID, not a hostname
        this.restClient = builder.baseUrl("http://customer-service/api/
        v1").build();
    }

    public Mono<Customer> getCustomerById(UUID id) {
        return Mono.fromFuture(restClient.get()
                .uri("/customers/{id}", id)
                .retrieve()
                .toEntityAsync(Customer.class))
                .map(ResponseEntity::getBody);
    }
}
```

Key Elements:

1. **`@LoadBalanced`**: This annotation tells Spring Cloud to create a special `RestClient.Builder` that is integrated with the service discovery client (Consul).

2. **`http://customer-service`**: This is a "logical" hostname. When a request is made, the load balancer intercepts it, asks Consul for a healthy instance of `customer-service`, and replaces the logical name with a real IP address and port (e.g., `http://172.18.0.5:8080`).

A Unified Entry Point: Spring Cloud Gateway

The **API Gateway** pattern is a critical component in a microservice architecture. It provides a single, unified entry point for all external clients (e.g., web frontends, mobile apps), abstracting the complexity of the internal service landscape. Instead of clients having to know the address of every single microservice, they make all requests to the gateway, which then routes them to the appropriate downstream service.

Spring Cloud Gateway is the modern, recommended gateway solution for the Spring ecosystem. It is a non-blocking, reactive gateway built on Project Reactor, Netty, and Spring WebFlux, making it highly efficient and capable of handling massive concurrent traffic with a small memory footprint.

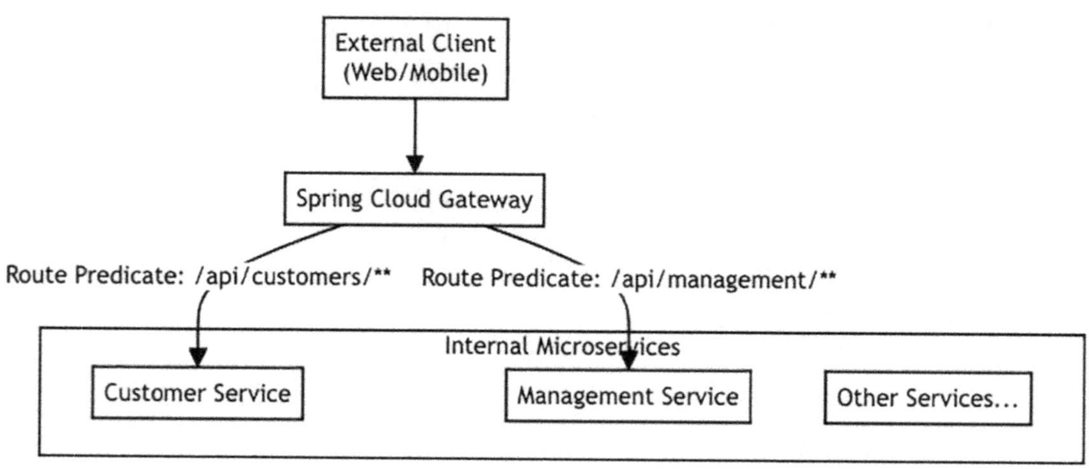

***Figure 15-3.** Spring Cloud Gateway Architecture*

Features

- **Reactive Core**: Built on Spring WebFlux, it is fully non-blocking and designed for high throughput.
- **Rich Predicate System**: Routes can be matched based on a wide range of attributes, including the path, host, HTTP method, headers, or query parameters.
- **Powerful Filter System**: Each route can have a chain of filters that modify the incoming request or outgoing response. Common filters include `AddRequestHeader`, `RewritePath`, and integrations for `CircuitBreaker` and `RateLimiter`.
- **Dynamic Routing**: Integrates seamlessly with service discovery (like Consul) to route requests to healthy service instances without static IP addresses.

Use Cases

- **Exposing Microservices**: The primary use case. It provides a stable, public-facing API while allowing the internal microservice architecture to evolve freely.
- **Centralized Cross-Cutting Concerns**: Offloading responsibilities like SSL termination, authentication/authorization, rate limiting, and caching from individual services to a central point.
- **API Aggregation**: Creating a new API endpoint at the gateway that aggregates data from multiple downstream services into a single response.

Best Practices

- **Keep It Lean**: The gateway should contain no business logic. Its only job is routing and applying crosscutting concerns.
- **Secure the Gateway**: The gateway is your front door; it must be robustly secured.

- **Use Discovery-Aware Routing**: Always use the `lb://` (load-balanced) URI scheme to leverage service discovery.
- **Configure Timeouts**: Set appropriate global and per-route timeouts to prevent the gateway from being blocked by slow downstream services.

Setting Up the Gateway

We create a new Spring Boot project named `api-gateway` and add the `spring-cloud-starter-gateway` and `spring-cloud-starter-consul-discovery` dependencies.

Configuration via `application.yml`

The most common way to define routes is declaratively in `application.yml`.

Listing 15-7. api-gateway/src/main/resources/application.yml

```
spring:
  application:
    name: api-gateway
  cloud:
    gateway:
      discovery:
        locator:
          enabled: true
      routes:
        - id: customer-service-route
          uri: lb://customer-service
          predicates:
            - Path=/api/customers/**
        - id: management-service-route
          uri: lb://management-service
          predicates:
            - Path=/api/management/**
```

What Is Happening?

1. **`discovery.locator.enabled: true`**: This tells the gateway to use the service discovery mechanism (Consul) to find services.
2. **`uri: lb://customer-service`**: The `lb` prefix indicates that this is a load-balanced route. The gateway will look up the location of `customer-service` in Consul before forwarding the request.

Now, a client can make a request to `http://api-gateway:8080/api/customers/123` and Spring Cloud Gateway will automatically route it to a healthy instance of the `customer-service`.

Programmatic Configuration with Java DSL

For more complex or dynamic routing logic, you can define routes programmatically using a `RouteLocator` bean.

Listing 15-8. api-gateway/src/main/java/com/apress/crm/gateway/GatewayConfig.java

```java
package com.apress.crm.gateway;

import org.springframework.cloud.gateway.route.RouteLocator;
import org.springframework.cloud.gateway.route.builder.RouteLocatorBuilder;
import org.springframework.context.annotation.Bean;
import org.springframework.context.annotation.Configuration;

@Configuration
public class GatewayConfig {

    @Bean
    public RouteLocator customRouteLocator(RouteLocatorBuilder builder) {
        return builder.routes()
                .route("customer_service_java_route", r -> r.path("/api/
                customers/**")
                        .uri("lb://customer-service"))
                .route("management_service_java_route", r -> r.path("/api/
                management/**")
```

```
                        .uri("lb://management-service"))
                .build();
    }
}
```

Key Elements:

1. **r.path(...)**: This is a route predicate that matches requests based on the URL path.
2. **uri("lb://...")**: This defines the target service. The Java DSL provides a fluent, type-safe way to construct the same routes defined in the YAML file. This approach is powerful when you need to build routing logic based on external configuration or feature flags.

Building Resilient Systems: Circuit Breakers

In a microservice architecture, a failure in one downstream service can cause a "cascading failure" that takes down the entire system. The **Circuit Breaker** pattern prevents this by "tripping" a circuit when a service becomes unresponsive, causing subsequent calls to fail fast instead of consuming resources.

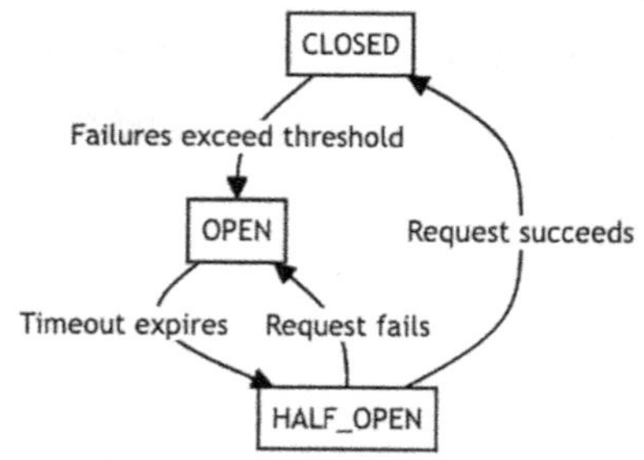

Figure 15-4. *Circuit Breaker State Diagram*

We will use **Resilience4j**, the recommended, lightweight fault tolerance library for Spring Boot, integrated via **Spring Cloud Circuit Breaker**.

Features

- **Multiple Backends**: While Resilience4j is the default, Spring Cloud Circuit Breaker also supports other libraries like Sentinel.
- **Time and Count-Based Monitoring**: Can trip based on failure rate over a period of time or a number of recent calls.
- **Declarative and Programmatic API**: Can be applied via annotations (`@CircuitBreaker`) or programmatically.
- **Actuator Integration**: Exposes the state of all circuit breakers via the `/actuator/health` and dedicated `/actuator/circuitbreakers` endpoints.

Use Cases

- **Protecting Against Slow Services**: Prevent a single slow service from exhausting all connection pools in upstream services.
- **Handling External API Failures**: Gracefully handle when a third-party API is down.
- **Graceful Degradation**: When combined with a fallback, you can provide a degraded but still functional experience to the user (e.g., showing cached data instead of live data).

Best Practices

- **Tune Thresholds Carefully**: Don't set your failure thresholds too low (trips too easily) or too high (doesn't trip soon enough).
- **Provide Sensible Fallbacks**: A fallback that returns a simple error message or cached data is better than an unhandled exception.
- **Monitor Your Circuits**: Actively monitor the state of your circuit breakers to detect instability in your system.

Implementing a Circuit Breaker in the Gateway

The API Gateway is a natural place to implement circuit breakers, as it can protect the entire system from a failing downstream service.

Listing 15-9. api-gateway/src/main/resources/application.yml (with Circuit Breaker)

```yaml
spring:
  cloud:
    gateway:
      routes:
        - id: customer-service-route
          uri: lb://customer-service
          predicates:
            - Path=/api/customers/**
          filters:
            - name: CircuitBreaker
              args:
                name: customer-service-cb
                fallbackUri: forward:/fallback/customers

resilience4j.circuitbreaker:
  instances:
    customer-service-cb:
      slidingWindowSize: 10
      failureRateThreshold: 50
      waitDurationInOpenState: 10s
```

Key Elements:

1. **`name: customer-service-cb`**: We apply a named circuit breaker filter to our route.
2. **`fallbackUri`**: This is crucial for graceful degradation. If the circuit is "open," instead of returning a generic error, the gateway will forward the request to an internal `/fallback/customers` endpoint. You would then create a simple `@RestController` within the gateway to handle this and return a cached or default response.

3. **`resilience4j.circuitbreaker.instances`**: Here we configure the circuit breaker's behavior. It will monitor the last 10 requests (`slidingWindowSize`), and if 50% of them fail (`failureRateThreshold`), it will "open" the circuit and stay open for 10 seconds (`waitDurationInOpenState`) before transitioning to half-open.

Event-Driven Architecture: Spring Cloud Stream

For asynchronous, decoupled communication between our services, we will use **Spring Cloud Stream**. This framework provides a powerful opinionated abstraction over message brokers like RabbitMQ and Kafka. It allows you to focus on your business logic (as simple functions) and then "bind" that logic to a message broker using external configuration.

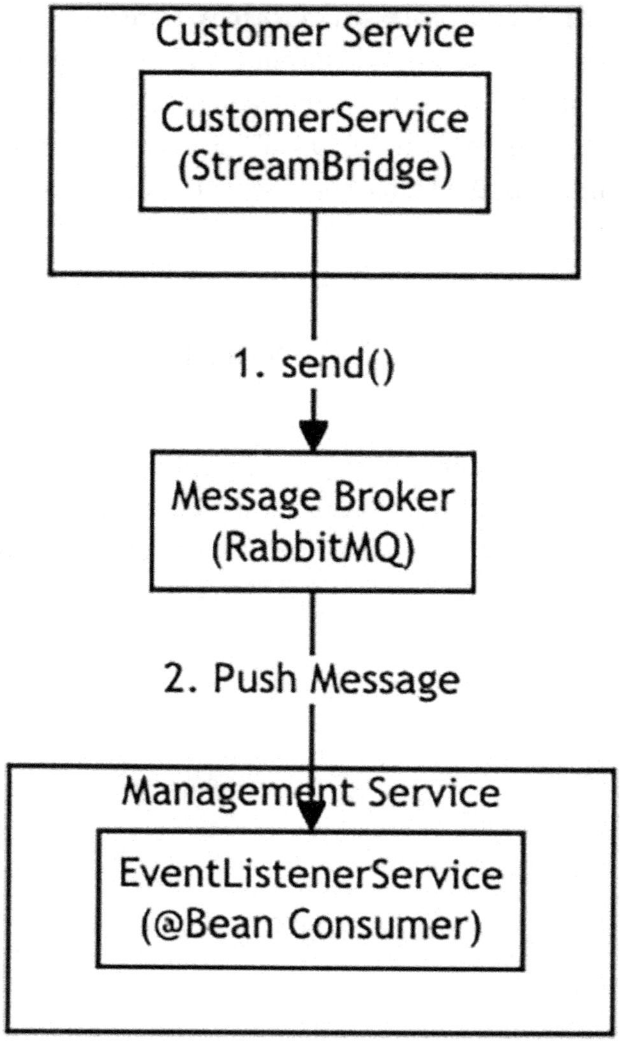

***Figure 15-5.** Spring Cloud Stream Event Flow*

Features

- **Binder Abstraction**: Provides interchangeable "binders" for different messaging systems (RabbitMQ, Kafka, etc.). You can switch brokers with only configuration changes.
- **Function-Based Programming Model**: Your business logic is a simple `java.util.function` (`Consumer`, `Function`, or `Supplier`), keeping it decoupled from the messaging infrastructure.

- **Content Type Conversion**: Automatically handles serialization and deserialization between Java objects and the message payload (e.g., JSON).
- **Durable Subscriptions**: Easily create consumer groups for shared, scalable consumption of messages.

Use Cases

- **Service Decoupling**: The most common use case. The `customer-service` can publish an event without knowing or caring which services (if any) are listening.
- **Asynchronous Workflows**: Triggering long-running, non-critical tasks (like sending a welcome email) in response to an event.
- **Resilience**: If the `management-service` is down, messages will queue up in RabbitMQ and be processed when it comes back online, preventing data loss.

Best Practices

- **Define a Clear Schema**: Use a consistent, versioned schema for your event payloads.
- **Use Consumer Groups**: For scalability and load balancing, always define a `group` for your consumers.
- **Handle Failures**: Configure a Dead-Letter Queue (DLQ) to capture and analyze messages that repeatedly fail processing.

Publishing an Event (Customer Service)

We use `StreamBridge`, a utility class provided by Spring Cloud Stream, to imperatively send a message to a named output "binding."

Listing 15-10. src/main/java/com/apress/crm/customer/service/CustomerService.java

```java
package com.apress.crm.customer.service;

import org.springframework.cloud.stream.function.StreamBridge;
import org.springframework.stereotype.Service;
// ...

@Service
public class CustomerService {
    private final StreamBridge streamBridge;
    // ...

    public Customer save(Customer customer) {
        Customer savedCustomer = customerRepository.save(customer);
        // Send event to the 'customer-events-out-0' binding
        streamBridge.send("customer-events-out-0", savedCustomer);
        return savedCustomer;
    }
}
```

- **`streamBridge.send(...)`**: We send the `savedCustomer` object to a logical destination named `customer-events-out-0`. We will map this logical name to a physical RabbitMQ topic in our configuration.

Consuming an Event (Management Service)

On the consumer side, we simply define a `java.util.function.Consumer` as a `@Bean`. Spring Cloud Stream automatically discovers this bean and binds it to an input channel.

Listing 15-11. src/main/java/com/apress/crm/management/service/EventListenerService.java

```java
package com.apress.crm.management.service;

import com.apress.crm.management.domain.Customer;
import org.springframework.context.annotation.Bean;
import org.springframework.stereotype.Service;
import java.util.function.Consumer;
```

```
@Service
public class EventListenerService {
    @Bean
    public Consumer<Customer> onCustomerChange() {
        return customer -> {
            System.out.println("Received event for customer: " + customer.
            getEmail());
            // Logic to update this service's state would go here.
        };
    }
}
```

- **onCustomerChange**: Spring Cloud Stream uses the bean name to derive the binding name, which will be `onCustomerChange-in-0`.

Finally, we configure the bindings in `application.yml` to connect the logical bindings to a physical topic.

Listing 15-12. management-service/src/main/resources/application.yml

```
spring:
  cloud:
    stream:
      bindings:
        onCustomerChange-in-0:
          destination: customer-events-topic
          group: management-group
```

What Is Happening?

1. **destination**: This maps our consumer to the `customer-events-topic` on RabbitMQ. The `customer-service` producer will also be configured to send to this same destination.
2. **group**: This is critical for scalability and durability. It creates a durable queue on RabbitMQ, ensuring that even if the `management-service` is offline, it will receive the events when it comes back up. If you run multiple instances of the `management-service` with the same group name, RabbitMQ will load-balance messages between them.

Consumer-Driven Contract Testing

In a microservice architecture, traditional integration tests are fragile and slow. If the `customer-service` (the provider) changes its API, it can break the `management-service` (the consumer) without warning. **Consumer-Driven Contract Testing** inverts this relationship. The consumer defines a "contract" of its expectations, and the provider is continuously tested to ensure it upholds that contract.

Spring Cloud Contract is a framework that implements this pattern.

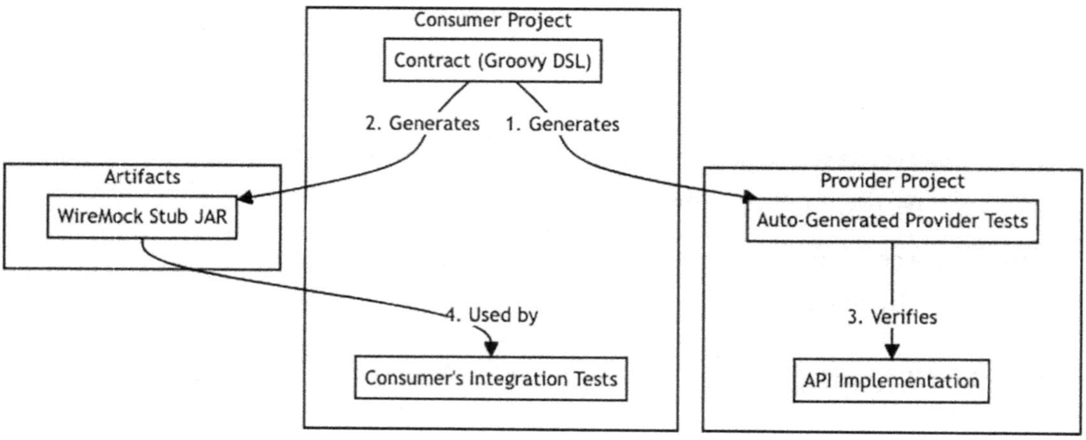

***Figure 15-6.** Spring Cloud Contract Workflow*

Features

- **Contract As Code**: Contracts are defined in a clear Groovy or YAML DSL and live alongside the consumer's code.
- **Auto-Generated Provider Tests**: Automatically creates JUnit tests for the provider to ensure it complies with the contract.
- **Auto-Generated Stubs**: Automatically creates WireMock stubs that the consumer can use to test its client code in complete isolation.

Use Cases

- **Ensuring API Compatibility**: The primary use case. Guarantees that providers and consumers can evolve independently without breaking each other.
- **Enabling Independent Deployments**: Gives teams the confidence to deploy their services without needing to run slow, full end-to-end test suites.

Best Practices

- **Contracts Live with the Consumer**: The team consuming the API is the one that knows its requirements best.
- **Share Stubs via a Repository**: The generated stubs (JAR files) should be published to an artifact repository like Nexus or Artifactory so other teams can consume them.
- **Keep Contracts Focused**: Each contract should test a single interaction, not the entire API.

Defining the Contract (Provider: Customer Service)

First, in the `customer-service` project, we define a contract using a Groovy DSL. This specifies a request and the expected response.

Listing 15-13. src/test/resources/contracts/customers/shouldReturnCustomer.groovy

```
package contracts.customers

import org.springframework.cloud.contract.spec.Contract

Contract.make {
    request {
        method 'GET'
        url '/api/v1/customers/123e4567-e89b-12d3-a456-426614174000'
    }
```

```
    response {
        status 200
        headers {
            contentType('application/json')
        }
        body(
            id: '123e4567-e89b-12d3-a456-426614174000',
            name: 'John Doe',
            email: 'john.doe@example.com'
        )
    }
}
```

When we build the customer-service, the Spring Cloud Contract plugin reads this file and **auto-generates a JUnit test** that makes a real request to our CustomerController and asserts that the response matches the contract. If the test fails, the build fails, preventing a breaking change from being published.

Verifying the Contract (Consumer: Management Service)

On the consumer side (management-service), we use @AutoConfigureStubRunner to fetch the "stub" (a mock server JAR) generated from the provider's contract.

Listing 15-14. src/test/java/com/apress/crm/management/client/CustomerClientTest.java

```
package com.apress.crm.management.client;

import org.junit.jupiter.api.Test;
import org.springframework.beans.factory.annotation.Autowired;
import org.springframework.boot.test.context.SpringBootTest;
import org.springframework.cloud.contract.stubrunner.spring.AutoConfigure
StubRunner;
import org.springframework.cloud.contract.stubrunner.spring.StubRunner
Properties;
import static org.assertj.core.api.Assertions.assertThat;
```

```
@SpringBootTest
@AutoConfigureStubRunner(ids = "com.apress.crm:customer-
service:+:stubs:8081",
                         stubsMode = StubRunnerProperties.StubsMode.LOCAL)
class CustomerClientTest {

    @Autowired
    private CustomerClient customerClient;

    @Test
    void shouldGetCustomerFromStub() {
        // This test makes a real HTTP call to localhost:8081
        Customer customer = customerClient.getCustomerById(UUID.
        fromString("123e4567-e89b-12d3-a456-426614174000")).block();

        assertThat(customer.name()).isEqualTo("John Doe");
    }
}
```

Key Elements:

1. **`@AutoConfigureStubRunner(ids = ...)`**: This annotation tells Spring Cloud Contract to download the stub JAR for `customer-service` and run it on port 8081.
2. **`stubsMode = LOCAL`**: Tells the runner to look in the local Maven (`.m2`) repository for the stub. In a CI environment, this would point to a remote repository like Nexus or Artifactory.

This allows the `management-service` to test its `CustomerClient` integration against a reliable mock server that is guaranteed to be in sync with the provider's actual API.

Short-Lived Microservices: Spring Cloud Task

Not all processes in a distributed system are long-running services. Many are **short-lived tasks** that need to run to completion, such as database migrations, batch jobs, or nightly reports. **Spring Cloud Task** provides a simple framework for developing and managing these ephemeral applications.

Features

- **Execution Auditing**: Automatically records the execution of each task (start time, end time, parameters, exit code) in a database.
- **Lifecycle Callbacks**: Provides listeners (`@BeforeTask`, `@AfterTask`, `@FailedTask`) to hook into the task's lifecycle.
- **Integration with Spring Batch**: Provides seamless integration for running Spring Batch jobs as tasks.

Use Cases

- **Database Schema Migrations**: A task can be run as part of a deployment pipeline to apply database changes.
- **Data Import/Export**: Triggering a one-off task to import a large dataset.
- **Scheduled Jobs**: When combined with a scheduler, tasks can be used for running nightly or hourly jobs.

Best Practices

- **Make Tasks Idempotent**: Design your tasks so that running them multiple times has the same effect as running them once.
- **Externalize Configuration**: Just like any other microservice, tasks should pull their configuration (e.g., database credentials) from an external source.
- **Use `ApplicationRunner`**: The `ApplicationRunner` interface is the simplest way to define the logic for your task.

Implementing a Simple Task

We create a new Spring Boot project and add the `spring-cloud-starter-task` dependency.

Listing 15-15. src/main/java/com/apress/crm/task/MigrationTask.java

```java
package com.apress.crm.task;

import org.springframework.boot.ApplicationRunner;
import org.springframework.boot.SpringApplication;
import org.springframework.boot.autoconfigure.SpringBootApplication;
import org.springframework.cloud.task.configuration.EnableTask;
import org.springframework.context.annotation.Bean;

@SpringBootApplication
@EnableTask
public class MigrationTask {

    @Bean
    public ApplicationRunner run() {
        return args -> {
            System.out.println("Running database migration...");
            // ... migration logic would go here ...
            System.out.println("Migration complete.");
        };
    }

    public static void main(String[] args) {
        SpringApplication.run(MigrationTask.class, args);
    }
}
```

What Is Happening?

1. **`@EnableTask`**: This annotation enables the Spring Cloud Task infrastructure. When the application starts, it will automatically create a `TaskExecution` record in the database.

2. **ApplicationRunner**: This is a functional interface from Spring Boot. The code inside its run method is executed after the application context is loaded. For a task, this is the main business logic. Once the run method completes, the application exits.

When you run this application as a standard JAR, Spring Cloud Task will connect to the configured database, log the start of the task, execute the ApplicationRunner, log the completion (or failure), and then shut down.

Summary

In this chapter, we built a complete cloud-native architecture using the Spring Cloud ecosystem. We started by using **Docker Compose Support** for a seamless local development experience. We externalized our configuration with **Spring Cloud Config** and enabled services to find each other with **Spring Cloud Consul**. We unified access through **Spring Cloud Gateway** and made our system resilient with **Resilience4j Circuit Breakers**. We built a decoupled, event-driven flow with **Spring Cloud Stream** and ensured reliable integration with **Spring Cloud Contract**. Finally, we saw how to manage one-off jobs with **Spring Cloud Task**.

These powerful, battle-tested patterns provide the foundation you need to build and deploy robust, scalable, and maintainable microservice systems with Spring Boot 4.

CHAPTER 16

Building Intelligent Applications with Spring AI

The landscape of software development is undergoing a profound transformation driven by **Artificial Intelligence**, particularly **Large Language Models (LLMs)**. These powerful models, capable of understanding and generating human-like text, are moving beyond niche applications to become integrated components of mainstream business systems. Spring AI is at the forefront of this evolution, offering a robust and idiomatic way for Spring developers to leverage AI in their applications.

In this chapter, our goal is to build a single, cohesive, and powerful **AI-powered CRM Assistant**. We will start with a simple Q&A service and progressively layer on advanced capabilities, transforming it into an intelligent agent that can:

- Answer knowledge-based questions using **Retrieval-Augmented Generation (RAG)**.
- Interact with our other microservices by using **Function Calling** and **Tools**.
- Discover and use external, standardized AI "skills" via the **Model Context Protocol (MCP)**.
- Query a database using natural language.
- Leverage both powerful cloud LLMs and private, local models via **Ollama**.

By the end, we will have a fully functional intelligent assistant, built with a modular design that anticipates its packaging as a reusable Spring Boot starter in the next chapter.

F. Gutierrez and D. Carter, *Pro Spring Boot 4*, https://doi.org/10.1007/979-8-8688-2640-5_16

The AI Revolution in Spring: Core Concepts

To build our assistant, we need to understand the key patterns of modern AI applications, all of which are supported by Spring AI.

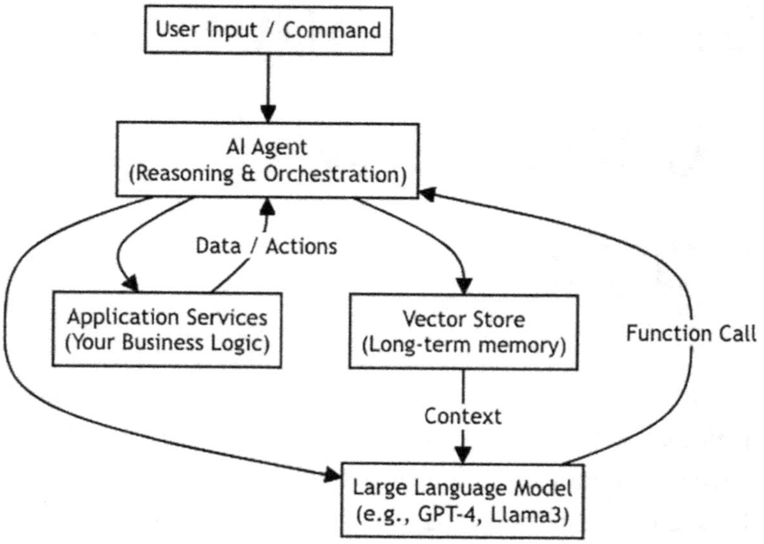

Figure 16-1. *Key AI Application Patterns*

Large Language Models (LLMs)

LLMs like GPT-4, Llama 3, and Claude are the "reasoning engines" of modern AI. They are trained on vast amounts of data to predict the next token in a sequence, allowing them to understand context, generate code, and simulate conversation.

Why We Need Them:

- **Natural Language Understanding**: They allow users to interact with our systems using plain English instead of rigid UIs or query languages.
- **Reasoning and Planning**: They can break down complex tasks (e.g., "Analyze our sales in NY and compare them to last year") into smaller steps.
- **Code Generation**: They can translate natural language into structured formats like SQL or JSON.

Embeddings and Vector Databases

A **Vector Database** is a specialized store for "Embeddings"—numerical representations of meaning. When we "embed" a sentence, we turn it into a list of numbers (a vector) that maps its semantic meaning in a high-dimensional space.

Why We Need Them:

- **Semantic Search**: Unlike keyword search, semantic search finds data based on meaning. "How do I reset my password?" and "I forgot my login credentials" will be recognized as semantically similar.
- **Long-Term Memory**: They allow us to store and retrieve massive amounts of private data that the LLM wasn't originally trained on.

Retrieval-Augmented Generation (RAG)

RAG is the most powerful pattern for grounding an LLM in reality. It combines the reasoning power of an LLM with the retrieval power of a Vector Database.

Why We Need It:

- **Accuracy**: It significantly reduces "hallucinations" by providing the model with factual context from your own documents.
- **Up-to-Date Information**: While LLMs have a training cutoff, your RAG system can have data from five minutes ago.
- **Privacy**: You can give the model access to private enterprise data without sending that data to the model provider for training.

AI Agents and Function Calling

An **Agent** is an LLM that has been given "tools" (functions it can call).

Why We Need Them:

- **Autonomy**: Agents can decide **which** tool to use and **when**.
- **Interactivity**: They can interact with live systems—querying a database, sending an email, or calling a microservice.
- **Multi-Step Tasks**: They can perform complex workflows, checking the result of one step before proceeding to the next.

Local LLMs with Ollama

At the heart of our **CRM Assistant** is a large language model (LLM), which acts as its "brain" or reasoning engine. We need an LLM to perform several critical tasks:

- Understand the user's intent from a natural language prompt.
- Decide which tool to use (e.g., query the vector store for product info, or query the database for customer data).
- Generate code, such as a SQL query, based on the user's request and the provided context.
- Synthesize the results from a tool into a final, human-readable response.

While powerful cloud-based models exist, for professional development and many enterprise scenarios, it is invaluable to be able to run these models locally. This is where **Ollama** comes in. It is a revolutionary tool that allows you to download and run powerful open-source LLMs directly on your local machine with incredible ease.

By choosing Ollama for our development process, we gain several key advantages:

- **Rapid, Cost-Free Development**: We can build and test our RAG, Tools, and Agent logic without incurring any API costs or network latency.
- **Data Privacy**: It enables us to build features that can run in a completely private environment where sensitive customer data never leaves the network.
- **Flexibility**: Spring AI's abstractions mean that we can develop and test against a local model like `Llama3` and then switch to a more powerful cloud model like `GPT-4o` in production by changing a single configuration property.

You can download Ollama from its official website: ollama.com

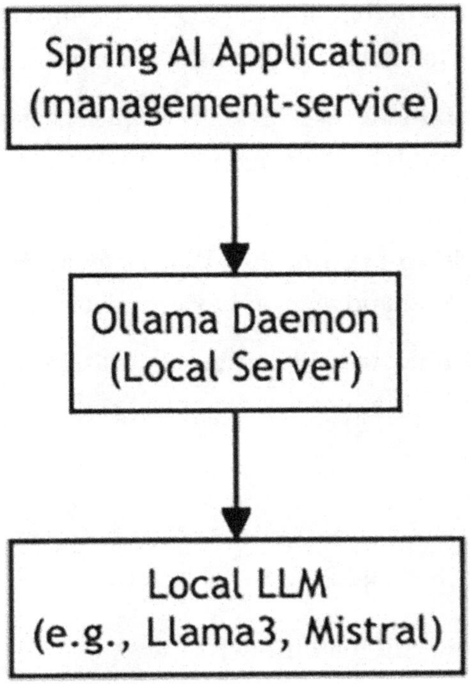

Figure 16-2. *Ollama Architecture (Simplified)*

Before using a model, you must download it via the command line: `ollama pull llama3`.

Building the CRM Assistant: Project Setup

Before we begin the technical setup, it is crucial to understand the business case for our **AI-powered CRM Assistant**. The `management` project is used by internal teams like business analysts and support staff who need quick access to a wide range of information. Currently, getting this information requires them to manually query databases, search through product documentation, or look up customer records in different systems. This is slow and requires specialized skills.

Our goal is to build an assistant that provides a unified, natural language interface to all this data. By the end of this chapter, our assistant will provide tangible business value by:

- **Increasing Productivity**: Allowing staff to get answers instantly without needing to know SQL or how to use complex dashboards.
- **Democratizing Data Access**: Making complex customer and product data accessible to non-technical users through plain English questions.
- **Improving Decision-Making**: Providing faster access to information, which leads to better and quicker business decisions.

With this clear goal in mind, we will now build the assistant inside the `management` project (the Gradle project).

Dependencies

First, we add the necessary Spring AI starters to `build.gradle`.

Listing 16-1. build.gradle (management)

```
dependencies {
    // ... existing dependencies ...
    implementation 'org.springframework.ai:spring-ai-core'
    implementation 'org.springframework.ai:spring-ai-openai-spring-
    boot-starter'
    implementation 'org.springframework.ai:spring-ai-ollama-spring-
    boot-starter'
    implementation 'org.springframework.ai:spring-ai-pgvector-store-spring-
    boot-starter'
    runtimeOnly 'org.postgresql:postgresql'
    implementation 'io.r2dbc:r2dbc-postgresql'
    implementation 'org.springframework.boot:spring-boot-starter-web'
}
```

Configuration

Next, we configure our AI providers and vector store in `application.yml`.

Listing 16-2. management/src/main/resources/application.yml

```
spring:
  application:
    name: management-service
  ai:
    ollama:
      chat:
        options:
          model: llama3
      embedding:
        options:
          model: mxbai-embed-large
    openai:
      api-key: ${OPENAI_API_KEY}
      chat:
        options:
          model: gpt-4o
    vectorstore:
      postgresql:
        embedding-dimension: 1024
        initialize-schema: true
        table-name: crm_vectors
  r2dbc:
    url: r2dbc:postgresql://root@localhost:26257/defaultdb
  datasource:
    url: jdbc:postgresql://localhost:26257/defaultdb?sslmode=disable
    username: root
```

Key Elements:

- **`spring.application.name: management-service`**: This defines the unique ID for our application when it registers with a service discovery mechanism.
- **`spring.ai.ollama.chat.options.model`**: Specifies the default LLM to use with Ollama.

- **spring.ai.vectorstore.postgresql.embedding-dimension**: Critical! This must match the output dimension of the embedding model you use.

Creating the Assistant Controller

To provide a single entry point for our assistant, we create a central controller. We will add endpoints to this controller as we build new capabilities.

Listing 16-3. src/main/java/com/apress/crm/management/ai/AssistantController.java

```java
package com.apress.crm.management.ai;

import org.springframework.ai.chat.ChatClient;
import org.springframework.web.bind.annotation.PostMapping;
import org.springframework.web.bind.annotation.RequestBody;
import org.springframework.web.bind.annotation.RequestMapping;
import org.springframework.web.bind.annotation.RestController;

@RestController
@RequestMapping("/api/assistant")
public class AssistantController {

    private final ChatClient chatClient;

    public AssistantController(ChatClient chatClient) {
        this.chatClient = chatClient;
    }

    @PostMapping("/chat")
    public String chat(@RequestBody String message) {
        return chatClient.call(message);
    }
}
```

This Code Shows:

- A simple `/api/assistant/chat` endpoint that takes a user's message and passes it directly to the configured `ChatClient`. This is our baseline functionality.

Step 1: Providing Knowledge with RAG

Retrieval-Augmented Generation (RAG) is the pattern for giving LLMs access to private, up-to-date knowledge.

What Is a Vector Database?

A **Vector Database** (or Vector Store) is a specialized database designed to store, manage, and query high-dimensional vectors. In the context of AI, these vectors are the "embeddings" generated from our text, images, or other data.

The key purpose of a vector database is to perform **semantic search.** Unlike a traditional keyword search, which looks for exact matches, a semantic search finds data based on meaning and contextual similarity. When you ask a question, it's converted into a vector, and the database finds the vectors (and their associated documents) that are "closest" in the high-dimensional space, effectively finding the most relevant information even if the wording is completely different. This capability is the engine that powers RAG.

Setting Up and Using the Vector Store

We will use **CockroachDB** as our vector store. We create a `ProductDocumentInitializer` to load product documents into it on startup and an `RAGService` to perform semantic searches. Now, we expose this capability through our controller.

Listing 16-4. src/main/java/com/apress/crm/management/ai/AssistantController.java (Updated)

```
// ... imports ...
@RestController
@RequestMapping("/api/assistant")
```

```
public class AssistantController {
    // ... other fields and constructor ...
    private final RAGService ragService;

    // ... updated constructor ...

    @PostMapping("/products")
    public String productChat(@RequestBody String message) {
        return ragService.askAboutProducts(message);
    }
}
```

What Is Happening?

- **RAGService**: We inject the RAG service that encapsulates the logic for querying our vector store and augmenting the LLM prompt.
- **/products Endpoint**: We create a new endpoint dedicated to product questions. When a user sends a message here, it will be answered using the RAG pattern.

Step 2: Enabling Actions with Tools

Function Calling allows an LLM to request the execution of your application's Java code (a "Tool") to get information or perform actions.

Local Tools

A "local" tool is a Spring bean within the same application. We first define a reactive RestClient to communicate with our customer-service.

Listing 16-5. src/main/java/com/apress/crm/management/client/CustomerClient.java

```
package com.apress.crm.management.client;

import com.apress.crm.management.domain.Customer;
import org.springframework.web.bind.annotation.PathVariable;
import org.springframework.web.service.annotation.GetExchange;
```

```
import org.springframework.web.service.annotation.HttpExchange;
import reactor.core.publisher.Mono;

@HttpExchange(url = "http://customer-service/api/v1")
public interface CustomerClient {
    @GetExchange("/customers/email/{email}")
    Mono<Customer> getCustomerByEmail(@PathVariable String email);
}
```

This Code Shows:

- **`@HttpExchange`**: This declarative annotation marks the interface as an HTTP client, with a base URL that uses the service ID (`customer-service`) for discovery.
- **`@GetExchange`**: Maps the Java method to an HTTP GET request on the specified path.
- **`Mono<Customer>`**: The return type is reactive, ensuring the call remains non-blocking.

We then create a tool bean that uses this client.

Listing 16-6. src/main/java/com/apress/crm/management/ai/CustomerTools.java

```
package com.apress.crm.management.ai;

import com.apress.crm.management.client.CustomerClient;
import org.springframework.context.annotation.Bean;
import org.springframework.context.annotation.Description;
import org.springframework.stereotype.Component;
import java.util.function.Function;

@Component
public class CustomerTools {
    private final CustomerClient customerClient;

    public CustomerTools(CustomerClient customerClient) {
        this.customerClient = customerClient;
    }
```

```
    @Bean
    @Description("Get customer details by their email address.")
    public Function<CustomerByEmailRequest, String> getCustomerByEmail() {
        return request -> customerClient.getCustomerByEmail(request.
        email())
                .map(customer -> String.format("Customer: %s, Email: %s",
                customer.name(), customer.email()))
                .defaultIfEmpty("Customer not found.")
                .block(); // Addressed later
    }

    public record CustomerByEmailRequest(String email) {}
}
```

What Is Happening?

- **`@Bean` and `@Description`**: We define a Spring bean of type `Function`. The `@Description` is critical, as it provides the natural language text the LLM uses to understand what the tool does.
- **`Function<...>`**: The signature defines the input (`CustomerByEmailRequest` record) and output (`String`) for the tool.

External Tools with the Model Context Protocol (MCP)

The **Model Context Protocol (MCP)** is an emerging standard for external, discoverable AI "skills."

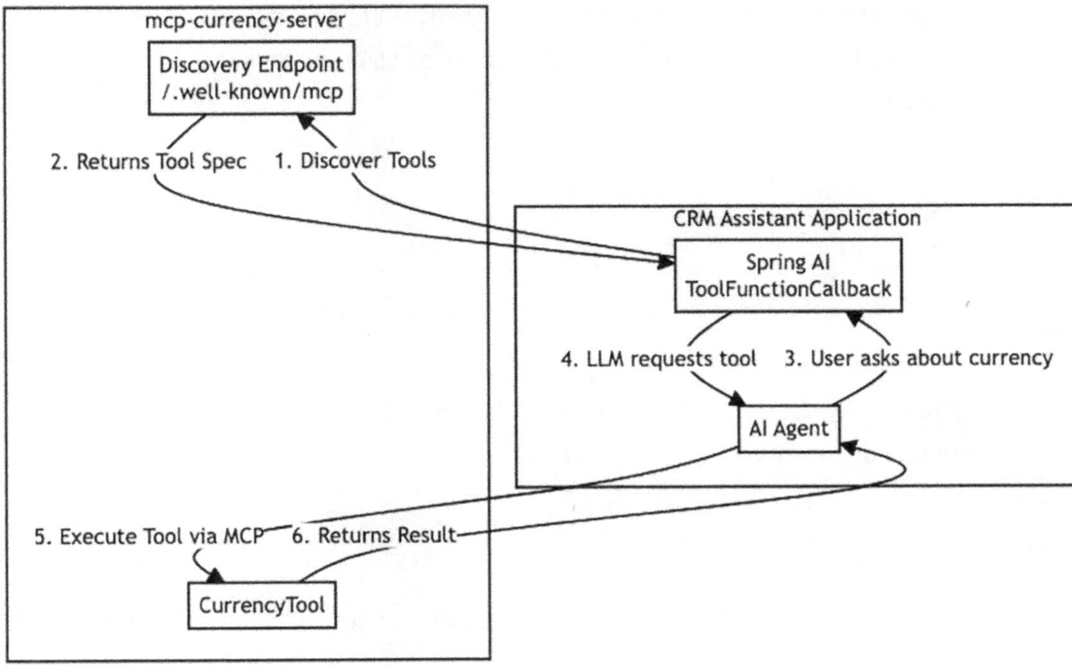

Figure 16-3. *MCP Discovery and Execution Flow*

Building an MCP Server

We will create a new project, `mcp-currency-server`, with a hypothetical `@McpTool` annotation.

Listing 16-7. mcp-currency-server/src/main/java/com/apress/crm/mcp/CurrencyTool.java

```
package com.apress.crm.mcp;

import org.springframework.context.annotation.Description;
import org.springframework.stereotype.Component;

@Component
public class CurrencyTool {
    @Description("Get the exchange rate between two currencies.")
```

```
    public double getExchangeRate(String from, String to) {
        if ("USD".equals(from) && "EUR".equals(to)) return 0.92;
        return 1.0;
    }
}
```

This Code Shows:

- A simple tool implementation meant to be exposed via an MCP server.
- The use of `@Description` to allow an AI Agent to understand when to invoke this exchange rate capability.

Integrating the MCP Tool

In our `management` application's `application.yml`, we tell Spring AI where to find this server.

Listing 16-8. management/src/main/resources/application.yml (MCP config)

```
spring:
  ai:
    mcp:
      servers:
        currency:
          base-url: http://localhost:8081
```

What Is Happening?

- By adding the `base-url` of an external MCP server, we enable Spring AI to automatically discover its tools at startup.
- The `currency` tool will now be available to our `ChatClient` automatically, just like our local tools.

Step 3: Agentic Database Queries

The most advanced capability of our assistant is translating natural language into database queries. As our `management` project is reactive, we must use a non-blocking approach.

The R2DBC Tool

We use **R2DBC** to create a non-blocking database query tool.

Listing 16-9. src/main/java/com/apress/crm/management/ai/R2dbcQueryTool.java

```
package com.apress.crm.management.ai;

import org.springframework.context.annotation.Bean;
import org.springframework.context.annotation.Description;
import org.springframework.data.r2dbc.core.R2dbcEntityTemplate;
import org.springframework.stereotype.Component;
import java.util.List;
import java.util.Map;
import java.util.function.Function;

@Component
public class R2dbcQueryTool {
    private final R2dbcEntityTemplate r2dbcEntityTemplate;
    public R2dbcQueryTool(R2dbcEntityTemplate r2dbcEntityTemplate) {
        this.r2dbcEntityTemplate = r2dbcEntityTemplate;
    }

    @Bean
    @Description("Execute a fully non-blocking SQL query against the CRM
    database.")
    public Function<SqlQueryRequest, List<Map<String, Object>>>
    executeR2dbcQuery() {
        return request -> r2dbcEntityTemplate.databaseClient().sql(request.
        sqlQuery())
```

```
                .fetch().all().collectList().block();
    }

    public record SqlQueryRequest(String sqlQuery) {}
}
```

What Is Happening?

- **R2dbcEntityTemplate**: The reactive client for performing database operations using R2DBC.
- **.block()**: While the management project is reactive, the Spring AI tool framework expects a direct, synchronous return value from the tool function. Because the underlying R2DBC operations are non-blocking, this block() call is acceptable in this context.

A Two-Step Agentic Chain

To demonstrate a true agent, we'll implement a two-step query.

Listing 16-10. src/main/java/com/apress/crm/management/ai/DatabaseAgentService.java

```
package com.apress.crm.management.ai;

import org.springframework.ai.chat.ChatClient;
import org.springframework.ai.chat.messages.SystemMessage;
import org.springframework.ai.chat.messages.UserMessage;
import org.springframework.ai.chat.prompt.Prompt;
import org.springframework.stereotype.Service;
import java.util.List;
import java.util.Map;

@Service
public class DatabaseAgentService {
    private final ChatClient chatClient;

    public DatabaseAgentService(ChatClient chatClient) { this.chatClient =
    chatClient; }
```

```
    public String generateSql(String userQuery) {
        String systemPrompt = """
            You are a SQL expert. Given the user's question, generate a
            single, valid SQL query for a table named 'customer' with
            columns: id, name, email, state.
            """;
        Prompt prompt = new Prompt(List.of(new SystemMessage(systemPrompt),
        new UserMessage(userQuery)));
        return chatClient.call(prompt).getResult().getOutput().
        getContent();
    }

    public String formatResults(String originalQuery, List<Map<String,
    Object>> results) {
        String systemPrompt = "Given the user's original question and the
        following SQL query results, formulate a clear, natural language
        answer.";
        String content = String.format("Original Question: %s\nSQL Results:
        %s", originalQuery, results);
        Prompt prompt = new Prompt(List.of(new SystemMessage(systemPrompt),
        new UserMessage(content)));
        return chatClient.call(prompt).getResult().getOutput().
        getContent();
    }
}
```

What Is Happening?

- **generateSql Method**: This method takes a user's natural language query and uses the ChatClient with a specialized system prompt (containing the DB schema) to generate a SQL query string.
- **formatResults Method**: This method takes the raw results from the database and the user's original question and again uses the ChatClient to synthesize a final, human-readable answer.

We then expose this two-step process in our AssistantController.

Listing 16-11. src/main/java/com/apress/crm/management/ai/AssistantController.java (Final)

```java
// ... imports and constructor ...
@RestController
@RequestMapping("/api/assistant")
public class AssistantController {
    // ... other fields ...
    private final DatabaseAgentService databaseAgentService;
    private final R2dbcQueryTool r2dbcQueryTool;

    // ... updated constructor ...

    @PostMapping("/db-query")
    public String dbQuery(@RequestBody String question) {
        String sql = databaseAgentService.generateSql(question);
        var results = r2dbcQueryTool.executeR2dbcQuery().apply
        (new R2dbcQueryTool.SqlQueryRequest(sql));
        return databaseAgentService.formatResults(question, results);
    }
}
```

This Code Shows:

- The orchestration of the two-step agentic chain. First, it calls `databaseAgentService.generateSql()`, then uses the `r2dbcQueryTool` to execute the SQL, and finally passes the results to `databaseAgentService.formatResults()` to get the natural language response.

Preparing for Abstraction and Testing

Knowing our goal is to create a starter, we structure our code for reusability.

The `CrmAssistant` Interface

This is the public contract of our AI agent.

Listing 16-12. src/main/java/com/apress/crm/management/ai/CrmAssistant.java

```java
package com.apress.crm.management.ai;

public interface CrmAssistant {
    String chat(String message);
    String askProductQuestion(String question);
    String queryDatabase(String naturalLanguageQuery);
}
```

This Code Shows:

- A clean, public-facing interface that defines the high-level capabilities of our AI agent. An end-user of our starter will only ever need to interact with this interface.

Auto-Configuration

This class contains all the bean definitions for our agent.

Listing 16-13. src/main/java/com/apress/crm/management/ai/CrmAssistantAutoConfiguration.java

```java
package com.apress.crm.management.ai;

import com.apress.crm.management.client.CustomerClient;
import org.springframework.ai.chat.ChatClient;
import org.springframework.ai.vectorstore.VectorStore;
import org.springframework.boot.autoconfigure.AutoConfiguration;
import org.springframework.context.annotation.Bean;
import org.springframework.data.r2dbc.core.R2dbcEntityTemplate;

@AutoConfiguration
public class CrmAssistantAutoConfiguration {

    @Bean
    public RAGService ragService(ChatClient chatClient, VectorStore
    vectorStore) {
```

```
        return new RAGService(chatClient, vectorStore);
    }

    @Bean
    public CustomerTools customerTools(CustomerClient customerClient) {
        return new CustomerTools(customerClient);
    }

    @Bean
    public R2dbcQueryTool r2dbcQueryTool(R2dbcEntityTemplate template) {
        return new R2dbcQueryTool(template);
    }

    @Bean
    public DatabaseAgentService databaseAgentService(ChatClient
    chatClient) {
        return new DatabaseAgentService(chatClient);
    }

    @Bean
    public CrmAssistant crmAssistant(RAGService ragService,
    DatabaseAgentService databaseAgentService, R2dbcQueryTool queryTool) {
        return new DefaultCrmAssistant(ragService, databaseAgentService,
        queryTool);
    }
}
```

What Is Happening?

- **`@AutoConfiguration`**: Marks this as a class that provides beans to the application context. This is the key to creating a starter.
- **`CrmAssistant` Bean**: This central bean wires together all the underlying AI services, providing a single, clean entry point.

Putting It All Together with Spring Shell

To provide an interactive experience, we build a CLI client using **Spring Shell**.

Figure 16-4 shows you the high-level component calls and their relationships.

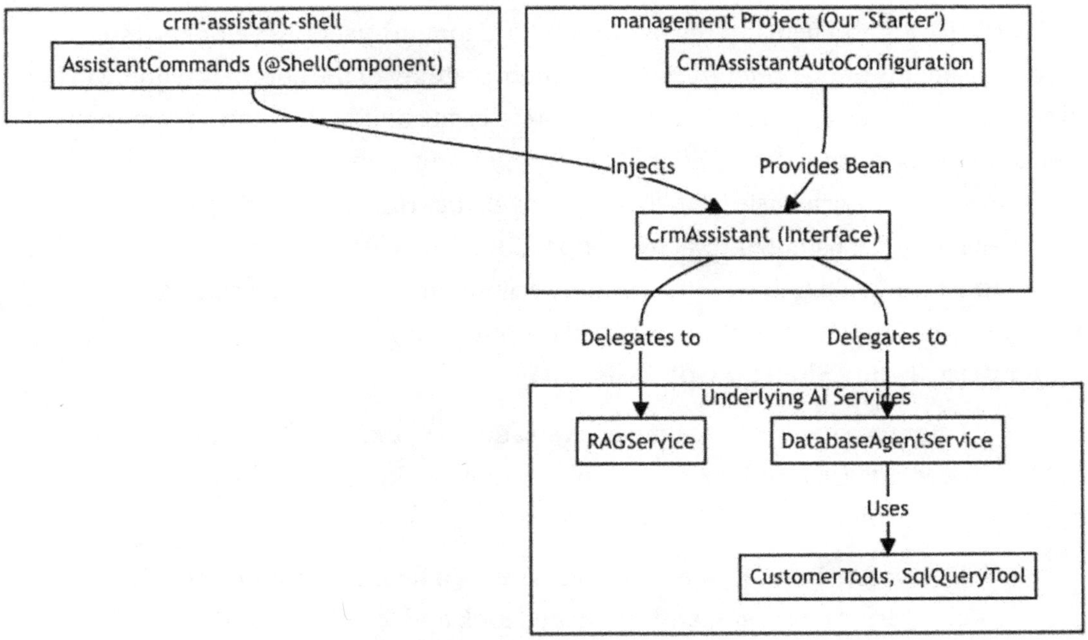

Figure 16-4. *High-Level Assistant Architecture*

Figure 16-5 shows you the more detailed steps that are happening in our app when a user asks a natural language question to the database.

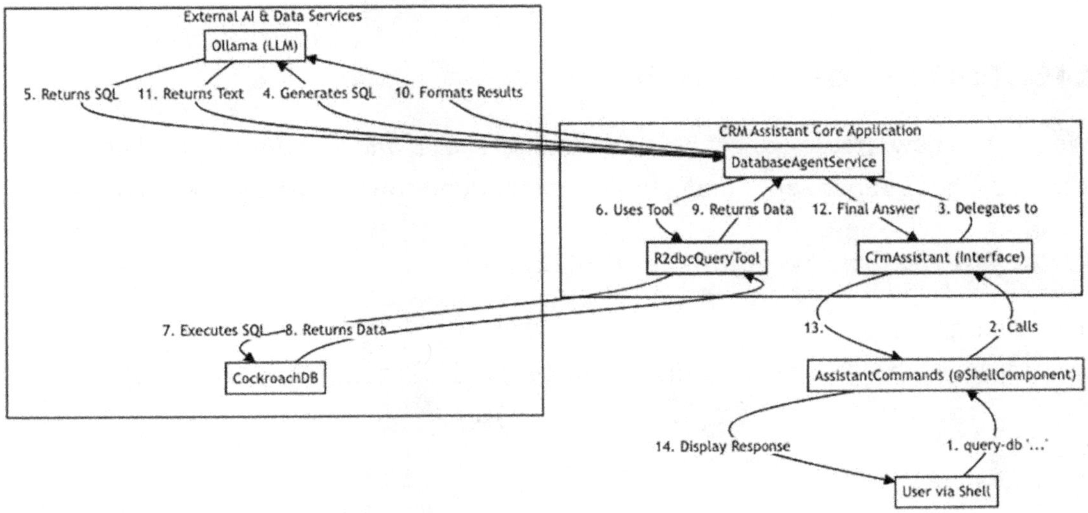

Figure 16-5. *Detailed Agentic Workflow*

Introducing Spring Shell

While REST APIs and web interfaces are standard for end-users, developers and operations teams often prefer the speed and scriptability of the command line. **Spring Shell** is a powerful framework that allows you to easily build full-featured, interactive shell applications using the familiar Spring programming model.

Instead of writing a basic `CommandLineRunner` that runs once and exits, Spring Shell provides a persistent, interactive loop (REPL—Read-Eval-Print Loop). It handles the complex work of parsing command-line arguments, validating inputs, and even providing tab completion and color-coded output.

Why Use Spring Shell for Our Assistant?

- **Interactivity**: It allows for a conversational workflow where the user can ask multiple follow-up questions without restarting the application.
- **Developer Experience**: It provides built-in help commands (`help`), clear error messages, and a polished look and feel that mimics professional CLI tools like the AWS CLI or `kubectl`.
- **Ease of Integration**: Because it's a Spring Boot starter, we can inject our `CrmAssistant` bean directly into our shell commands, bridging the gap between our complex AI logic and a simple user interface.

Creating the Shell Client

We create a new Gradle project, `crm-assistant-shell`, and add the `spring-boot-starter-shell` dependency and a project dependency on our `management` module.

Listing 16-14. crm-assistant-shell/build.gradle

```
dependencies {
    implementation 'org.springframework.shell:spring-shell-starter'
    implementation project(':management')
}
```

What Is Happening?

- **`implementation project(':management')`**: This is the key. By including our `management` project as a dependency, we make all its components, including our `CrmAssistantAutoConfiguration`, available to this new CLI application.

We then create a component with `@ShellMethod`-annotated methods that inject and use our clean `CrmAssistant` interface.

Listing 16-15. src/main/java/com/apress/crm/shell/AssistantCommands.java

```java
package com.apress.crm.shell;

import com.apress.crm.management.ai.CrmAssistant;
import org.springframework.shell.standard.ShellComponent;
import org.springframework.shell.standard.ShellMethod;

@ShellComponent
public class AssistantCommands {

    private final CrmAssistant crmAssistant;

    public AssistantCommands(CrmAssistant crmAssistant) {
        this.crmAssistant = crmAssistant;
    }

    @ShellMethod(key = "ask", value = "Ask a question about products.")
    public String ask(String question) {
        return crmAssistant.askProductQuestion(question);
    }

    @ShellMethod(key = "query-db", value = "Ask a question of the customer
    database.")
    public String queryDatabase(String query) {
        return crmAssistant.queryDatabase(query);
    }
}
```

What Is Happening?

- **`@ShellComponent`**: Marks this class as a container for shell commands.
- **`@ShellMethod`**: Exposes a method as a command in the interactive shell (e.g., `ask "..."`).
- **`CrmAssistant` Injection**: The shell component knows nothing about AI. It simply injects our clean interface, demonstrating the power of our abstraction.

Testing the AI Agent

Testing AI components requires a focus on the inputs and outputs of the `ChatClient`. We use mocks to verify that our service sends the correct prompts without making real (and costly) API calls.

Listing 16-16. src/test/java/com/apress/crm/management/ai/DatabaseAgentServiceTest.java

```java
package com.apress.crm.management.ai;

import org.junit.jupiter.api.Test;
import org.mockito.ArgumentCaptor;
import org.springframework.ai.chat.ChatClient;
import org.springframework.ai.chat.ChatResponse;
import org.springframework.ai.chat.prompt.Prompt;
import static org.assertj.core.api.Assertions.assertThat;
import static org.mockito.Mockito.*;

class DatabaseAgentServiceTest {

    @Test
    void shouldIncludeSchemaInSystemPrompt() {
        // Arrange
        ChatClient chatClient = mock(ChatClient.class);
        when(chatClient.call(any(Prompt.class))).
        thenReturn(mock(ChatResponse.class));
```

```
        DatabaseAgentService agentService = new DatabaseAgentService(
        chatClient);

        // Act
        agentService.generateSql("show me customers from NY");

        // Assert
        ArgumentCaptor<Prompt> promptCaptor = ArgumentCaptor.
        forClass(Prompt.class);
        verify(chatClient).call(promptCaptor.capture());
        String systemPrompt = promptCaptor.getValue().getInstructions().
        get(0).getContent();
        assertThat(systemPrompt).contains("The database has a table named
        'customer'");
    }
}
```

This Code Shows:

- **Mocking `ChatClient`**: We provide a mock `ChatClient` to isolate our service from the external AI model.
- **`ArgumentCaptor`**: We use a captor to inspect the `Prompt` object that was actually sent to the `chatClient`.
- **Assertion**: We verify that our service correctly included the database schema in the system prompt.

Summary

In this chapter, we built a sophisticated, multi-faceted **AI-powered CRM Assistant**. We constructed a cohesive application, starting with basic chat and layering on RAG for product knowledge, inter-service communication via local tools, and a standardized external skill via **MCP**, culminating in a two-step, agentic database query using R2DBC. We validated our design by building an interactive **Spring Shell** client.

The world of AI is rapidly evolving, and Spring AI provides the powerful, flexible abstractions needed to integrate these cutting-edge capabilities into your enterprise applications. In the next chapter, we will take this `CrmAssistant` and package it as a custom Spring Boot Starter.

CHAPTER 17

Extending Spring Boot with Custom Starters

Throughout this book, we have leveraged numerous Spring Boot starters like `spring-boot-starter-web` and `spring-boot-starter-data-jpa`. These starters are the cornerstone of Spring Boot's convention-over-configuration philosophy, abstracting away complex setup and configuration. But what if you have common components, configurations, or intelligent agents like our **AI-powered CRM Assistant** that you want to share across multiple microservices or applications in your own organization?

This is where creating a custom starter becomes incredibly powerful. A custom starter allows you to encapsulate complex functionality, define intelligent auto-configurations, and provide a seamless "just add the dependency" experience for other developers, ensuring consistency and dramatically reducing boilerplate code.

In this technical chapter, we will build a professional-grade custom starter: **`crm-assistant-spring-boot-starter`**. We will package the sophisticated AI agent logic from Chapter 16 into a reusable module and leverage advanced Spring Boot features like `@Conditional` annotations, custom `@Enable` patterns, and AOP (Aspect-Oriented Programming) for cross-cutting concerns. Finally, we will publish this starter to **GitHub Packages** and demonstrate its consumption in a brand-new application.

From Application to Platform

In Chapter 16, we developed a highly capable AI agent within our `management` application. While powerful, its code is currently "locked" inside that project. To truly unlock its value for other teams (e.g., a `sales-dashboard` application, a `customer-support-portal`), we need to abstract away its complexity and make it trivially easy to integrate.

F. Gutierrez and D. Carter, *Pro Spring Boot 4*, https://doi.org/10.1007/979-8-8688-2640-5_17

The goal of this chapter is to elevate our `management` project's AI capabilities into a reusable platform component. Remember how `spring-boot-starter-web` just "knew" to configure an embedded Tomcat server, JSON converters, and dispatcher servlets? We are going to build that same level of intelligence and "magic" for our AI Assistant.

Architecture of a Professional Starter

A well-designed Spring Boot starter typically follows a multi-module design to separate concerns.

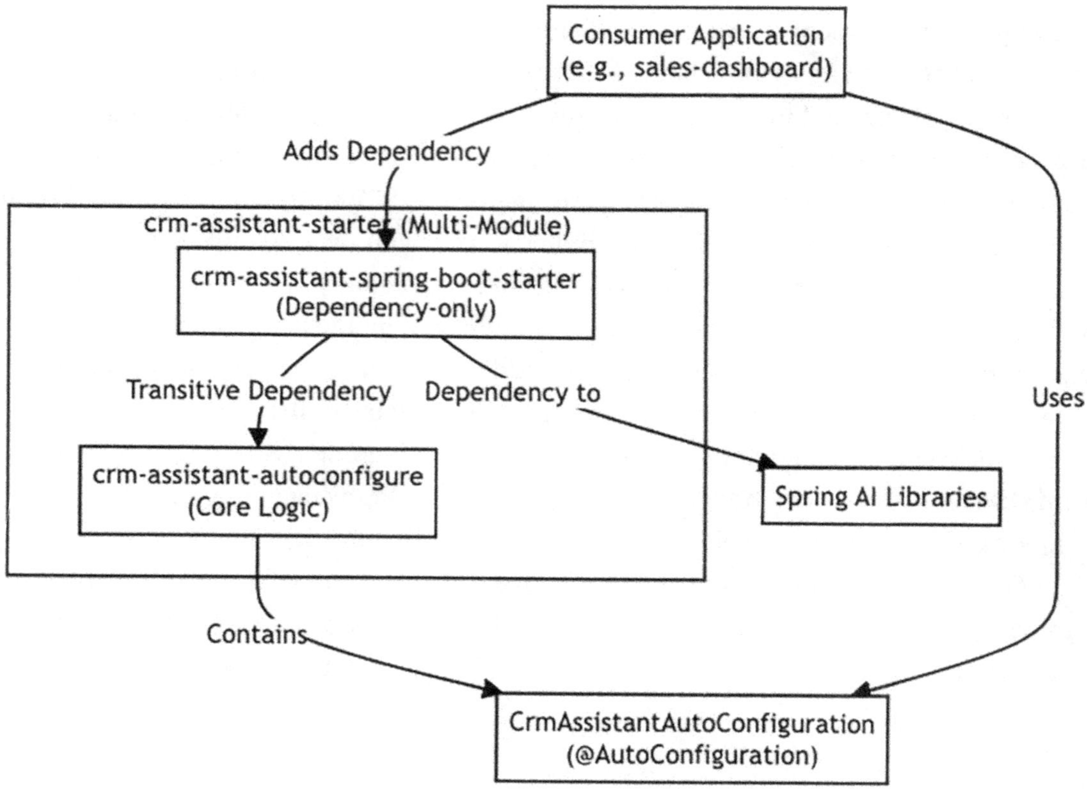

***Figure 17-1.** Custom Starter Multi-Module Architecture*

- **`crm-assistant-autoconfigure` Module**: This is the core. It contains all the auto-configuration logic, properties, and beans (like `CrmAssistant`, `RAGService`, `CustomerTools`) that our starter provides. This module defines **how** the feature is set up.

- **crm-assistant-spring-boot-starter Module**: This is the lightweight wrapper. It primarily contains the necessary transitive dependencies (including our autoconfigure module and any other libraries required for the feature, like Spring AI). End-users will only add this module as a dependency.

Benefits of This Structure:

- **Decoupling**: The autoconfiguration logic is separate from the dependency management.
- **Clarity**: It's clear what the user needs to add as a dependency.

Step 1: The Foundation (Migrating Core Logic)

We will start by setting up our multi-module project and migrating the core AI agent logic from the management project into the crm-assistant-autoconfigure module.

Project Structure and Dependencies

First, create a new multi-module Gradle project. The crm-assistant-autoconfigure module will contain our Spring AI components, and the crm-assistant-spring-boot-starter will be our dependency-only wrapper.

Listing 17-1. crm-assistant-starter/build.gradle

```
plugins {
    id 'java-library'
    id 'maven-publish'
    id 'org.springframework.boot' version '4.0.1' // Corrected to 4.0.1
    id 'io.spring.dependency-management' version '1.1.5'
}

group = 'com.apress'
version = '0.0.1-SNAPSHOT'

repositories {
    mavenCentral()
}
```

```
// Subproject configuration
subprojects {
    apply plugin: 'java-library'
    apply plugin: 'maven-publish'
    apply plugin: 'io.spring.dependency-management'

    group = rootProject.group
    version = rootProject.version

    repositories {
        mavenCentral()
    }

    dependencyManagement {
        imports {
            mavenBom org.springframework.boot.gradle.plugin.
            SpringBootPlugin.BOM_COORDINATES
        }
    }
}
```

Listing 17-2. crm-assistant-starter/crm-assistant-autoconfigure/build.gradle

```
dependencies {
    // Spring Boot AutoConfigure support
    compileOnly 'org.springframework.boot:spring-boot-autoconfigure'
    annotationProcessor 'org.springframework.boot:spring-boot-
    configuration-processor'

    // Spring AI core
    api 'org.springframework.ai:spring-ai-core'
    api 'org.springframework.ai:spring-ai-openai-spring-boot-starter'
    api 'org.springframework.ai:spring-ai-ollama-spring-boot-starter'
    api 'org.springframework.ai:spring-ai-pgvector-store-spring-
    boot-starter'
    runtimeOnly 'org.postgresql:postgresql'
    api 'io.r2dbc:r2dbc-postgresql'
```

```
    api 'org.springframework.boot:spring-boot-starter-web'
    // For HttpExchange, etc.

    // AOP for logging
    api 'org.springframework.boot:spring-boot-starter-aop'

    // Testing
    testImplementation 'org.springframework.boot:spring-boot-starter-test'
}
```

What Is Happening?

- **`java-library` Plugin**: Provides API and implementation configurations.
- **`compileOnly 'org.springframework.boot:spring-boot-autoconfigure'`**: Ensures auto-configuration classes are compiled but not bundled.
- **`api 'org.springframework.ai:...'`**: All Spring AI dependencies are declared as `api`. This makes them transitive dependencies, meaning any project consuming our starter will automatically get these without explicitly declaring them.

Listing 17-3. crm-assistant-starter/crm-assistant-spring-boot-starter/build.gradle

```
dependencies {
    // Pull in our autoconfigure module
    implementation project(':crm-assistant-autoconfigure')
}
```

What Is Happening?

- This module is deliberately simple. It only has one `implementation` dependency on our `autoconfigure` module. This is the module users will add to their `build.gradle`.

Migrating the AI Agent Code and Properties

Now, we move all the CrmAssistant related classes (interfaces, implementations, services, tools) from management/src/main/java/... to crm-assistant-autoconfigure/src/main/java/....

We also need to define configuration properties that allow users to customize the AI agent.

Listing 17-4. crm-assistant-autoconfigure/src/main/java/com/apress/crm/assistant/config/CrmAssistantProperties.java

```java
package com.apress.crm.assistant.config;

import org.springframework.boot.context.properties.ConfigurationProperties;

@ConfigurationProperties("crm.assistant")
public class CrmAssistantProperties {
    private boolean enabled = true;
    private String chatModel = "gpt-4o";
    private String vectorTableName = "crm_vectors";
    private boolean auditEnabled = false;

    // Getters and Setters
}
```

Step 2: Intelligent Configuration with @Conditional

This is where Spring Boot's "magic" comes from. @Conditional annotations allow us to define when our auto-configuration should apply, preventing unwanted side effects and enabling user overrides.

Listing 17-5. crm-assistant-autoconfigure/src/main/java/com/apress/crm/assistant/config/CrmAssistantAutoConfiguration.java

```
package com.apress.crm.assistant.config;

import com.apress.crm.assistant.CrmAssistant;
import com.apress.crm.assistant.impl.DefaultCrmAssistant;
import com.apress.crm.assistant.service.DatabaseAgentService;
import com.apress.crm.assistant.service.RAGService;
import com.apress.crm.assistant.tool.CustomerTools;
import com.apress.crm.assistant.tool.R2dbcQueryTool;
import com.apress.crm.management.client.CustomerClient; // Assuming this is
needed by CustomerTools
import org.springframework.ai.chat.ChatClient;
import org.springframework.ai.vectorstore.VectorStore;
import org.springframework.boot.autoconfigure.AutoConfiguration;
import org.springframework.boot.autoconfigure.condition.ConditionalOnClass;
import org.springframework.boot.autoconfigure.condition.Conditional
OnMissingBean;
import org.springframework.boot.autoconfigure.condition.Conditional
OnProperty;
import org.springframework.boot.context.properties.EnableConfiguration
Properties;
import org.springframework.context.annotation.Bean;
import org.springframework.data.r2dbc.core.R2dbcEntityTemplate;

@AutoConfiguration
@ConditionalOnClass(ChatClient.class)
@EnableConfigurationProperties(CrmAssistantProperties.class)
@ConditionalOnProperty(prefix = "crm.assistant", name = "enabled",
havingValue = "true", matchIfMissing = true)
public class CrmAssistantAutoConfiguration {

    // ... Bean definitions for RAGService, CustomerTools, R2dbcQueryTool,
    DatabaseAgentService ...

    @Bean
    @ConditionalOnMissingBean
```

```
    public CrmAssistant crmAssistant(RAGService ragService,
    DatabaseAgentService databaseAgentService, R2dbcQueryTool queryTool) {
        return new DefaultCrmAssistant(ragService, databaseAgentService,
        queryTool);
    }
}
```

What Is Happening?

- **`@AutoConfiguration`**: This annotation marks the class as a Spring Boot auto-configuration.
- **`@ConditionalOnClass(ChatClient.class)`**: This **condition** ensures that our auto-configuration is only processed if `ChatClient` (a core Spring AI class) is present on the classpath. If a user doesn't add Spring AI dependencies, our starter won't load, preventing errors.
- **`@EnableConfigurationProperties(CrmAssistantProperties.class)`**: This registers our custom properties class, allowing users to configure the agent via `application.yml`.
- **`@ConditionalOnProperty(...)`**: This condition allows users to entirely disable our auto-configuration by setting `crm.assistant.enabled=false`. `matchIfMissing = true` means it's enabled by default if the property isn't set.
- **`@ConditionalOnMissingBean`**: This condition is applied to our `CrmAssistant` bean definition. It tells Spring: "Only create this `CrmAssistant` bean if the user hasn't already defined their own `CrmAssistant` bean." This is crucial for extensibility, allowing users to provide custom implementations.

Step 3: The @Enable Annotation Pattern

While `AutoConfiguration.imports` is how Spring Boot **automatically** discovers and applies auto-configurations, the `@EnableXxx` annotation pattern provides users with **explicit opt-in** control. It's a clear signal in their code: "Yes, I want to enable this specific feature."

Listing 17-6. crm-assistant-autoconfigure/src/main/java/com/apress/crm/assistant/config/EnableCrmAssistant.java

```
package com.apress.crm.assistant.config;

import org.springframework.context.annotation.Import;
import java.lang.annotation.*;

@Target(ElementType.TYPE)
@Retention(RetentionPolicy.RUNTIME)
@Documented
@Import(CrmAssistantAutoConfiguration.class)
public @interface EnableCrmAssistant {
}
```

What Is Happening?

- **`@Import(CrmAssistantAutoConfiguration.class)`**: This is the core of the `@Enable` pattern. When a user adds `@EnableCrmAssistant` to one of their `@Configuration` classes (or their main `@SpringBootApplication`), Spring will process our `CrmAssistantAutoConfiguration`. This provides an alternative, explicit way to enable our starter's features, allowing users to choose between automatic or explicit enablement.

Step 4: Adding Cross-Cutting Concerns with AOP

Aspect-Oriented Programming (AOP) is a powerful paradigm for cleanly separating cross-cutting concerns (like logging, security, or transaction management) from business logic. For a starter, AOP is invaluable because it allows us to add behavior to **user code** without them writing a single line. We will use AOP to implement an audit log for every interaction with our `CrmAssistant`.

Dependencies for AOP

First, add the `spring-boot-starter-aop` dependency to our `crm-assistant-autoconfigure` module (already done in Listing 17-2).

Implementing the Audit Aspect

We create a simple aspect that logs calls to the CrmAssistant methods.

Listing 17-7. crm-assistant-autoconfigure/src/main/java/com/apress/crm/assistant/aop/AssistantAuditAspect.java

```
package com.apress.crm.assistant.aop;

import org.aspectj.lang.ProceedingJoinPoint;
import org.aspectj.lang.annotation.Around;
import org.aspectj.lang.annotation.Aspect;
import org.slf4j.Logger;
import org.slf4j.LoggerFactory;
import org.springframework.boot.autoconfigure.condition.ConditionalOn
Property;
import org.springframework.stereotype.Component;

@Aspect
@Component
@ConditionalOnProperty(prefix = "crm.assistant", name = "audit.enabled",
havingValue = "true")
public class AssistantAuditAspect {

    private static final Logger log = LoggerFactory.
    getLogger(AssistantAuditAspect.class);

    @Around("execution(* com.apress.crm.assistant.CrmAssistant.*(..))")
    public Object auditAssistantCall(ProceedingJoinPoint joinPoint) throws
    Throwable {
        long startTime = System.currentTimeMillis();
        String methodName = joinPoint.getSignature().getName();
        Object[] args = joinPoint.getArgs();

        log.info("CRM Assistant - Call started: {} with args: {}",
        methodName, args);

        Object result = joinPoint.proceed();
```

```
        long endTime = System.currentTimeMillis();
        log.info("CRM Assistant - Call finished: {} in {}ms. Result: {}",
        methodName, (endTime - startTime), result);

        return result;
    }
}
```

What Is Happening?

- **`@Aspect`**: Declares this class as an Aspect.
- **`@ConditionalOnProperty(...)`**: This aspect will only be enabled if `crm.assistant.audit.enabled=true` in the user's configuration, giving them control.
- `@Around("execution(* com.apress.crm.assistant.CrmAssistant.*(..))")`: This is the **pointcut expression**. It tells Spring AOP to intercept **any** method call (`*(..)`) within **any** class that implements `CrmAssistant` (`CrmAssistant.*`) in the `com.apress.crm.assistant` package. `@Around` means the advice executes before, during, and after the method call.
- **`joinPoint.proceed()`**: This calls the actual method being intercepted (e.g., `crmAssistant.queryDatabase(...)`).

Step 5: Packaging and Publishing to GitHub Packages

Now that our autoconfigure module is complete, we need to package it and make it available for others.

Registering the Auto-Configuration (Spring Boot 3+)

For Spring Boot to discover our `CrmAssistantAutoConfiguration`, we need to register it in a specific file.

Listing 17-8. crm-assistant-autoconfigure/src/main/resources/META-INF/spring/org.springframework.boot.autoconfigure.AutoConfiguration.imports

```
com.apress.crm.assistant.config.CrmAssistantAutoConfiguration
```

What Is Happening?

- This file lists the fully qualified class names of our auto-configuration classes. Spring Boot scans for these files in `META-INF/spring/` within our starter JAR and automatically imports the listed configurations. This is the modern, preferred mechanism for auto-configuration discovery since Spring Boot 2.7 (replacing `spring.factories`).

Publishing to GitHub Packages

GitHub Packages provides a convenient way to host private Maven and Gradle packages directly within your GitHub repositories.

Listing 17-9. crm-assistant-starter/build.gradle (Publishing Configuration)

```
// ... (root build.gradle) ...

allprojects {
    // ...
    publishing {
        publications {
            mavenJava(MavenPublication) {
                from components.java
            }
        }
        repositories {
            maven {
                name = "GitHubPackages"
                url = uri("https://maven.pkg.github.com/YOUR_GITHUB_
                 USERNAME/YOUR_GITHUB_REPOSITORY_NAME")
                credentials {
                    username = System.getenv("GITHUB_ACTOR") ?: project.
                    properties["gpr.user"]
```

```
                password = System.getenv("GITHUB_TOKEN") ?: project.
                properties["gpr.key"]
            }
        }
    }
  }
}
```

What Is Happening?

- **`maven-publish` Plugin**: Enabled on all subprojects to create Maven publications.
- **`publications.mavenJava`**: Defines our main artifact (JAR).
- **`repositories.maven`**: Configures a Maven repository named `GitHubPackages`.
- **`url`**: Points to your GitHub Packages Maven repository. Replace `YOUR_GITHUB_USERNAME` and `YOUR_GITHUB_REPOSITORY_NAME`.
- **`credentials`**: Retrieves credentials from environment variables (`GITHUB_ACTOR`, `GITHUB_TOKEN`). `GITHUB_ACTOR` is your GitHub username, and `GITHUB_TOKEN` is a **Personal Access Token (PAT)** with at least `write:packages` scope.
- **Creating a PAT**: Go to GitHub ➤ Settings ➤ Developer settings ➤ Personal access tokens. Generate a new token with `write:packages` scope.

To publish, simply run:

```
./gradlew publish
```

Step 6: The "Sales Dashboard" Demo (Consuming the Starter)

Now for the payoff! Let's create a brand-new Spring Boot application, `sales-dashboard`, and give it AI capabilities with our custom starter.

Project Setup

Create a new Spring Boot application.

Listing 17-10. sales-dashboard/build.gradle

```
plugins {
    id 'org.springframework.boot' version '4.0.1'
    id 'io.spring.dependency-management' version '1.1.5'
    id 'java'
}

repositories {
    mavenCentral()
    maven {
        name = "GitHubPackages"
        url = uri("https://maven.pkg.github.com/YOUR_GITHUB_USERNAME/YOUR_
        GITHUB_REPOSITORY_NAME")
        credentials {
            username = System.getenv("GITHUB_ACTOR") ?: project.
            properties["gpr.user"]
            password = System.getenv("GITHUB_TOKEN") ?: project.
            properties["gpr.key"]
        }
    }
}

dependencies {
    implementation 'org.springframework.boot:spring-boot-starter-web'
    implementation 'org.springframework.boot:spring-boot-starter-actuator'

    // Spring AI core dependencies needed by our starter
    implementation 'org.springframework.ai:spring-ai-openai-spring-
    boot-starter'
    implementation 'org.springframework.ai:spring-ai-ollama-spring-
    boot-starter'
    implementation 'org.springframework.ai:spring-ai-pgvector-store-spring-
    boot-starter'
```

```
    runtimeOnly 'org.postgresql:postgresql'
    implementation 'io.r2dbc:r2dbc-postgresql'

    // Our custom starter!
    implementation 'com.apress:crm-assistant-spring-boot-starter:0.0.1-
    SNAPSHOT'
}
```

What Is Happening?

- **`repositories` Block**: We explicitly configure the GitHub Packages repository to allow Gradle to find and download our custom starter artifact.
- **Spring AI Dependencies**: While our starter technically pulls in `spring-ai-core`, users still need to explicitly include the **provider-specific** Spring AI starters (e.g., `spring-ai-openai-spring-boot-starter`) and any backing service dependencies (like `postgresql` for CockroachDB). This is a common pattern for custom starters to avoid pulling in every possible provider.
- **`crm-assistant-spring-boot-starter`**: This is the single dependency that brings in all the AI agent's auto-configuration and components.

Enabling and Using the Starter

Now, we enable the starter and use the `CrmAssistant` in our `sales-dashboard` application.

Listing 17-11. sales-dashboard/src/main/java/com/apress/sales/dashboard/SalesDashboardApplication.java

```
package com.apress.sales.dashboard;

import com.apress.crm.assistant.CrmAssistant;
import com.apress.crm.assistant.config.EnableCrmAssistant;
import org.springframework.boot.CommandLineRunner;
import org.springframework.boot.SpringApplication;
```

```
import org.springframework.boot.autoconfigure.SpringBootApplication;
import org.springframework.context.annotation.Bean;

@SpringBootApplication
@EnableCrmAssistant
public class SalesDashboardApplication {

    public static void main(String[] args) {
        SpringApplication.run(SalesDashboardApplication.class, args);
    }

    @Bean
    public CommandLineRunner runAssistant(CrmAssistant crmAssistant) {
        return args -> {
            System.out.println("Sales Dashboard AI Assistant Ready!");
            System.out.println("Product Question: " + crmAssistant.
            askProductQuestion("Tell me about the CRM Pro plan."));
            System.out.println("DB Query: " + crmAssistant.
            queryDatabase("How many customers in California?"));
        };
    }
}
```

What Is Happening?

- **`@EnableCrmAssistant`**: This annotation explicitly enables our custom starter's auto-configuration, bringing all the AI agent's features into this application.
- **`CrmAssistant` Injection**: The `SalesDashboardApplication` simply injects the `CrmAssistant` interface, demonstrating that all the complex AI logic is now available through a simple, high-level API.

To enable the AOP audit logging, simply add `crm.assistant.audit.enabled=true` to `sales-dashboard/src/main/resources/application.yml`. When you run the application, you will see the audit logs in the console for each call to the `CrmAssistant`.

Summary

This chapter demonstrated the ultimate power of the Spring Boot programming model: extensibility. We learned how to transform our sophisticated AI agent from Chapter 16 into a reusable **Spring Boot starter**. We explored:

- The **multi-module architecture** for professional starters.
- Intelligent auto-configuration using advanced **`@Conditional` annotations** to control when our components load.
- The **`@EnableXxx` annotation pattern** for explicit feature enablement.
- How **AOP** (Aspect-Oriented Programming) can be leveraged within a starter to transparently add cross-cutting concerns like audit logging to a consuming application.
- The process of **publishing our starter to GitHub Packages** and seamlessly consuming it in a new application.

We have truly completed a journey in this book: from basic REST APIs to building resilient, cloud-native, AI-powered systems, and finally, extending the Spring Boot framework itself. This pattern of building intelligent, reusable components is key to creating scalable, maintainable, and consistent microservice ecosystems.

CHAPTER 18

What's New in Spring Boot 4

Welcome to the future of Spring. Spring Boot 4, built on the foundation of Spring Framework 7 and requiring Java 17, is a major evolution of the platform. It brings significant improvements in performance, developer experience, and a strong, opinionated push towards modern cloud-native patterns.

This chapter provides a comprehensive overview of the most impactful changes and new features you should leverage as you start building with Spring Boot 4. We will use a "before and after" format to clearly illustrate the benefits and simplifications these new features bring.

We will explore:

- Core improvements in the underlying Spring Framework 7.
- First-class observability with a dedicated OpenTelemetry starter.
- Modern HTTP clients: `RestClient` and `@HttpExchange`.
- A new unified client for testing REST APIs.
- Built-in support for Project CRaC for ultra-fast startup.
- Seamless Docker Compose integration for local development.
- Compile-time null-safety to build more robust applications.
- Advanced AOT processing and testing capabilities.
- Enhancements to configuration properties and error handling.
- Simplified and enhanced security patterns in Spring Security 7.

F. Gutierrez and D. Carter, *Pro Spring Boot 4*, https://doi.org/10.1007/979-8-8688-2640-5_18

Core Improvements in Spring Framework 7

Many of Spring Boot 4's most powerful features are built upon the significant advancements in its foundation, **Spring Framework 7**. This major release fully embraces the modern Java landscape by continuing with a **Java 17 baseline**, while supporting the newer capabilities in Java 21 and Java 25.

Virtual Threads (Project Loom)

Perhaps the most anticipated feature, Spring Framework 7 is designed to work seamlessly with **Virtual Threads**. This allows imperative, thread-per-request applications to scale to massive levels of concurrency with minimal code changes. In Spring Boot 4, enabling virtual threads is as simple as a single property.

Enabling Virtual Threads

```
spring.threads.virtual.enabled=true
```

When this is enabled, Spring Boot automatically configures the embedded Tomcat server to use a virtual thread for each incoming request.

Enhanced AOT Engine

Spring Framework 7 deepens its commitment to Ahead-of-Time (AOT) processing. The AOT engine is now more sophisticated, performing deeper analysis of your application at build time. This allows it to generate more efficient code and reduce the amount of reflection needed at runtime.

Modern, Declarative HTTP Clients

The new `RestClient` and `@HttpExchange` features are born from improvements in Spring Framework 7.

Listing 18-1. Declarative Client with `@HttpExchange`

```
@HttpExchange("/data")
public interface NewApiClient {
    @GetExchange
    Mono<Data> fetchData();
}
```

This pattern, now a core part of the framework, makes inter-service communication more robust and type-safe.

Observability: Embracing OpenTelemetry

The industry is standardizing around **OpenTelemetry (OTLP)**. Spring Boot 4 embraces this with a new, dedicated starter that greatly simplifies setup.

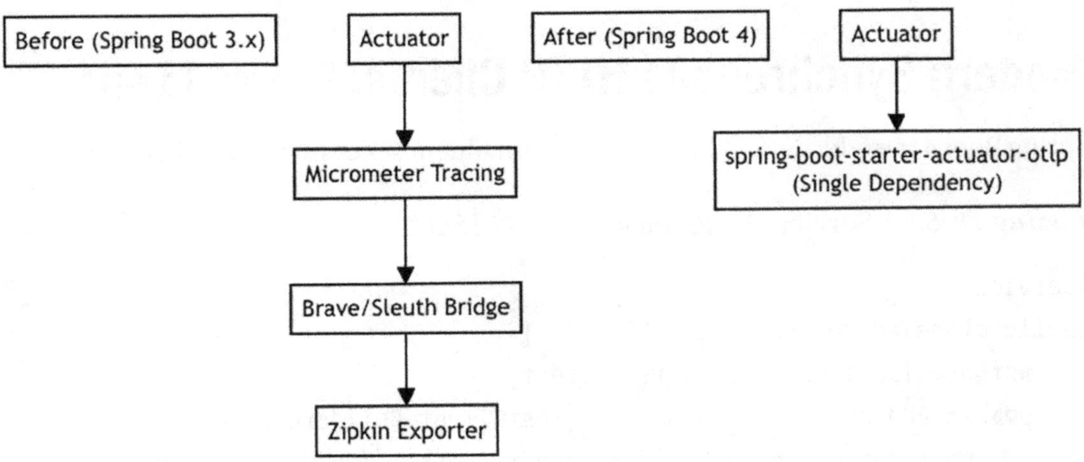

Figure 18-1. *Simplified observability dependencies*

Before (Spring Boot 3.x): Setting up tracing required multiple dependencies.

Listing 18-2. build.gradle (Old Way)

```
dependencies {
    implementation 'org.springframework.boot:spring-boot-starter-actuator'
    implementation 'io.micrometer:micrometer-tracing-bridge-brave'
    implementation 'io.zipkin.reporter2:zipkin-reporter-brave'
}
```

After (Spring Boot 4): This is simplified to a single dependency.

Listing 18-3. build.gradle (New Way)

```
dependencies {
    implementation 'org.springframework.boot:spring-boot-starter-actuator'
    implementation 'org.springframework.boot:spring-boot-starter-
    actuator-otlp'
}
```

Configuration also uses the standard OTLP properties.

Listing 18-4. application.properties (OTLP Configuration)

```
management.otlp.tracing.endpoint=http://localhost:4318/v1/traces
management.otlp.tracing.sampling.probability=0.1
```

Modern Synchronous HTTP Clients: RestClient

Spring Boot 4 introduces RestClient, a modern, fluent successor to RestTemplate.

Listing 18-5. A Service Using the New RestClient

```
@Service
public class AddressValidationService {
    private final RestClient restClient;
    public AddressValidationService(RestClient.Builder builder) {
        this.restClient = builder.baseUrl("http://api.example.com").
        build();
    }
    public boolean isAddressValid(String address) {
        return this.restClient.get()
            .uri("/validate?address={addr}", address)
            .retrieve()
            .body(Boolean.class);
    }
}
```

Simplified Testing with RestTestClient

Spring Boot 4 introduces RestTestClient to unify the testing of web layers.

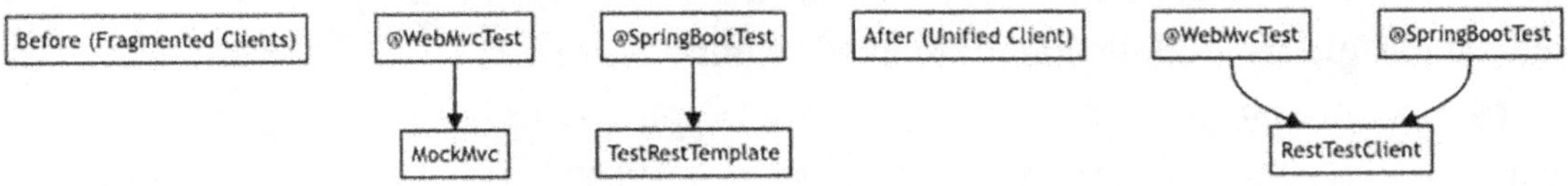

Figure 18-2. *Unified web testing client*

Listing 18-6. Integration Test with RestTestClient

```
@SpringBootTest(webEnvironment = SpringBootTest.WebEnvironment.RANDOM_PORT)
class CustomerControllerIntegrationTest {
    @Autowired
    private RestTestClient restTestClient;

    @Test
    void shouldReturnCustomer() {
        restTestClient.get().uri("/api/customers/{id}", 1L)
            .exchange()
            .expectStatus().isOk()
            .expectBody().jsonPath("$.name").isEqualTo("John Doe");
    }
}
```

Modern Security with Spring Security 7

Spring Security 7, the version aligned with Spring Boot 4, continues the path of simplification and modernization, focusing on securing modern application architectures.

Simplified Two-Factor Authentication (2FA)

Implementing Two-Factor Authentication (2FA) with TOTP (e.g., Google Authenticator) was a complex, manual process in previous versions. Spring Security 7 introduces a new, dedicated support module that dramatically simplifies this.

Before: You had to manually create several components: a service to generate secrets, another to validate codes, and a custom `AuthenticationSuccessHandler` to trigger the 2FA flow.

After: Configuration is now streamlined. You provide a `TwoFactorAuthenticationManager` and a `TwoFactorAuthenticationSuccessHandler`, and Spring Security handles the rest of the flow.

Listing 18-7. Simplified 2FA Configuration

```
@Configuration
@EnableTwoFactorAuthentication
public class TwoFactorAuthConfig {
    @Bean
    public TwoFactorAuthenticationManager twoFactorAuthenticationManager(
            TotpService totpService, UserDetailsService
            userDetailsService) {
        return new TwoFactorAuthenticationManager(totpService,
        userDetailsService);
    }
}
```

This new, focused support makes implementing 2FA a matter of configuration rather than complex coding.

Declarative mTLS with SSL Bundles

Mutual TLS (mTLS), a cornerstone of Zero Trust security, was previously complex to configure. Spring Boot 4 introduces **SSL Bundles**, a declarative way to manage Keystores and Truststores directly from `application.properties`.

Before: You would need to write complex Java configuration to programmatically load keystores and create an `SslContext`.

After: You now declare your SSL bundles directly in your properties file.

Listing 18-8. Declarative mTLS Configuration

```
server.ssl.bundle=server-bundle
spring.ssl.bundle.jks.server-bundle.keystore.location=classpath:server.p12
spring.ssl.bundle.jks.server-bundle.keystore.password=password
spring.ssl.bundle.jks.server-bundle.truststore.location=classpath:ca.p12
spring.ssl.bundle.jks.server-bundle.truststore.password=password
```

This makes configuring complex mTLS setups for service-to-service communication trivial and consistent.

Instant Startup with Project CRaC

While GraalVM is for stateless apps, **Project CRaC (Coordinated Restore at Checkpoint)** is a game-changer for stateful applications needing instant startup. Spring Boot 4 provides first-class support via the `spring-boot-starter-crac` and the `org.crac.Resource` interface.

Listing 18-9. A CRaC-Aware Database Connection Pool

```
@Component
public class CracManagedConnectionPool implements Resource {
    // ...
    @Override
    public void beforeCheckpoint(Context<? extends Resource> context) {
        this.connectionPool.close(); // Close connections before checkpoint
    }
    @Override
    public void afterRestore(Context<? extends Resource> context) {
        this.connectionPool.reopen(); // Re-open connections after restore
    }
}
```

Seamless Docker Compose Integration

Spring Boot 4's new **Docker Compose support** dramatically improves the local development experience. By adding the `spring-boot-docker-compose` dependency, you can remove hardcoded URLs from your properties file. Spring Boot will automatically start your `docker-compose.yml` and configure the connections for you.

Listing 18-10. build.gradle (Docker Compose Support)

```
dependencies {
    developmentOnly 'org.springframework.boot:spring-boot-docker-compose'
}
```

Advanced AOT Testing with ApplicationContextRunner

Spring Boot 4 enhances the `ApplicationContextRunner` to be fully AOT-aware, allowing for precise unit tests of your auto-configuration logic.

Listing 18-11. Testing Conditional Bean Creation

```
class CrmAssistantAutoConfigurationTest {
    private final ApplicationContextRunner contextRunner = new
    ApplicationContextRunner()
        .withConfiguration(AutoConfigurations.of(CrmAssistantAuto
        Configuration.class));
    @Test
    void assistantIsNotCreatedWhenDisabled() {
        this.contextRunner.withPropertyValues("crm.assistant.
        enabled=false")
            .run(context -> {
                assertThat(context).doesNotHaveBean(CrmAssistant.class);
            });
    }
}
```

Enhanced Configuration Properties

Spring Boot 4 improves how structured configuration is handled, with better support for Java Records as value objects.

Listing 18-12. Modern Properties with Records

```
@ConfigurationProperties("acme")
public record AcmeProperties(List<ServerRecord> servers) {
    public record ServerRecord(String ip, int port) {}
}
```

First-Class Problem Details Support

RFC 7807, "Problem Details for HTTP APIs," is the standard for returning error responses. Spring Boot 4 makes this a first-class citizen.

Listing 18-13. Modern Exception Handler

```
@ExceptionHandler(OrderNotFoundException.class)
public ErrorResponse handleOrderNotFound(OrderNotFoundException ex) {
    return ErrorResponse.builder(ex, HttpStatus.NOT_FOUND,
    ex.getMessage()).build();
}
```

Compile-Time Null-Safety

Spring Framework 7 embraces JSpecify's `@NullMarked` annotation to provide compile-time null-safety, helping catch potential `NullPointerExceptions` before your code runs.

Listing 18-14. Enabling Null-Safety at the Package Level

```
@org.jspecify.annotations.NullMarked
package com.apress.crm.customer;
```

Summary

Spring Boot 4 is a significant leap forward, designed for the next generation of cloud-native Java development. Its foundation on **Spring Framework 7** brings core improvements like **virtual threads** and an enhanced **AOT engine**. On top of this, Spring Boot adds a superb developer experience with **modern security patterns**, the new **`RestClient`**, **unified `RestTestClient`**, and seamless **Docker Compose integration**. Finally, the dedicated **OpenTelemetry starter** and first-class **Problem Details** support align Spring Boot with the future of cloud-native development, making it easier than ever to build high-performance, robust, and observable applications.

APPENDIX A

Spring for GraphQL with Spring Boot

Spring for GraphQL provides a comprehensive programming model for building GraphQL applications with Spring Boot. In Spring Boot 4, this integration reaches a new level of maturity with **Spring for GraphQL 2.0+**, built on **Spring Framework 7** and **GraphQL Java 25**. This appendix explores how to leverage these new capabilities to build efficient, null-safe, and highly concurrent APIs.

Introduction and Key Features

GraphQL is a query language for APIs that allows clients to request exactly the data they need, nothing more and nothing less. Unlike REST, which is resource-centric (URLs), GraphQL is graph-centric (Schema).

Spring for GraphQL 2.0 introduces significant enhancements aligned with the Spring Boot 4 ecosystem:

- **Virtual Thread Integration**: The `webmvc` and `webflux` transports now seamlessly leverage Java 21+ Virtual Threads for high-throughput concurrent data fetching without blocking platform threads.
- **Null-Safety with JSpecify**: The API is fully annotated with JSpecify, providing compile-time null-safety checks in modern IDEs, aligning with Spring Framework 7's null-safety initiatives.
- **ArgumentValue API**: A new wrapper type to distinguish between an argument that was explicitly set to `null` versus one that was omitted entirely, enabling true "partial updates" (PATCH-like behavior) in mutations.

F. Gutierrez and D. Carter, *Pro Spring Boot 4*, https://doi.org/10.1007/979-8-8688-2640-5

- **Schema Inspection**: Enhanced validation at startup that detects mismatches between your Schema (`.graphqls`) and your Data Fetchers (`@Controller`), preventing runtime failures.
- **Client Improvements**: The `HttpGraphQlClient` now supports improved request cancellation propagation.

Architecture

In Spring for GraphQL, the runtime engine (GraphQL Java) is wrapped by Spring's familiar programming model.

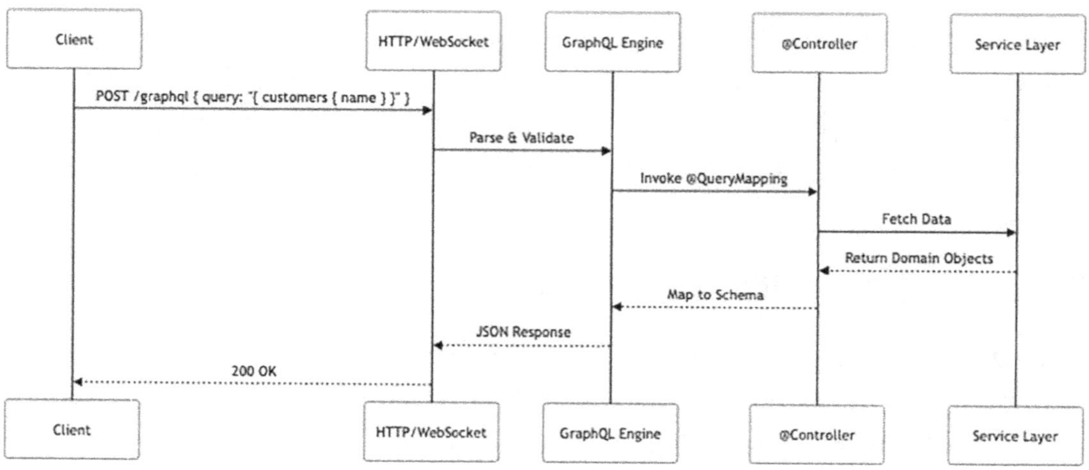

***Figure A-1.** Spring for GraphQL Request Processing Architecture*

Use Cases for GraphQL

GraphQL is not a replacement for REST in all scenarios, but it excels in specific use cases:

- **Mobile and Low-Bandwidth Clients**: Where minimizing network overhead (over-fetching) is critical.
- **Aggregation Layers (BFF)**: When a frontend needs to combine data from multiple microservices (e.g., Customer + Orders + Shipments) in a single request.
- **Complex Domain Graphs**: When data is highly interconnected, and clients need to traverse deep relationships dynamically.

Case Study 1: The Customer Project (Queries and Optimization)

We will implement the "Read" side of our API in the **Customer Project** (Maven). We focus on efficient data fetching and solving the "N+1 Select" problem.

Defining the Schema

First, we define our schema in `src/main/resources/graphql`.

Listing A-1. src/main/resources/graphql/customer.graphqls

```
type Query {
    customers: [Customer]!
    customerById(id: ID!): Customer
}

type Customer {
    id: ID!
    firstName: String!
    lastName: String!
    email: String!
    # A computed or expensive field
    auditStatus: String
}
```

Implementing the Controller

We use `@Controller` with `@QueryMapping` to fetch data.

Listing A-2. src/main/java/com/apress/crm/customer/graphql/CustomerGraphController.java

```
package com.apress.crm.customer.graphql;

import com.apress.crm.customer.domain.Customer;
import com.apress.crm.customer.service.CustomerService;
import org.springframework.graphql.data.method.annotation.Argument;
```

```
import org.springframework.graphql.data.method.annotation.QueryMapping;
import org.springframework.graphql.data.method.annotation.SchemaMapping;
import org.springframework.stereotype.Controller;

import java.util.List;
import java.util.Optional;

@Controller
public class CustomerGraphController {

    private final CustomerService customerService;

    public CustomerGraphController(CustomerService customerService) {
        this.customerService = customerService;
    }

    @QueryMapping
    public List<Customer> customers() {
        return customerService.findAll();
    }

    @QueryMapping
    public Optional<Customer> customerById(@Argument Long id) {
        return customerService.findById(id);
    }

    @SchemaMapping(typeName = "Customer", field = "auditStatus")
    public String getAuditStatus(Customer customer) {
        // Simulating an expensive computation or separate service call
        return "VERIFIED_" + customer.email().hashCode();
    }
}
```

Key Elements:

- **`@QueryMapping`**: Maps the `customers` query field to this method. The name matches automatically.
- **`@Argument`**: Binds the GraphQL argument `id` to the method parameter.

- **@SchemaMapping**: Solves the N+1 problem partially by allowing a specific field (auditStatus) to be resolved only when requested. **Note: For true batch loading, use @BatchMapping.**

Solving the N+1 Problem

If we query 100 customers, and each needs an address, naive GraphQL implementations execute 1 query for customers + 100 queries for addresses. Spring for GraphQL provides @BatchMapping to solve this efficiently using the DataLoader pattern transparently.

Listing A-3. src/main/java/com/apress/crm/customer/graphql/AddressGraphController.java

```
package com.apress.crm.customer.graphql;

import com.apress.crm.customer.domain.Address;
import com.apress.crm.customer.domain.Customer;
import org.springframework.graphql.data.method.annotation.BatchMapping;
import org.springframework.stereotype.Controller;

import java.util.List;
import java.util.Map;
import java.util.UUID;
import java.util.function.Function;
import java.util.stream.Collectors;

@Controller
public class AddressGraphController {

    // In a real app, inject AddressRepository

    @BatchMapping
    public Map<Customer, Address> address(List<Customer> customers) {
        // Select * from addresses where customer_id IN (...)
        // This executes ONE query for the entire batch
        return customers.stream()
                .collect(Collectors.toMap(
                    Function.identity(),
```

```
                    c -> new Address("123 Main St", "City", "NY")
                    // Mock lookup
                ));
    }
}
```

What Is Happening Here?

- **`@BatchMapping`**: Spring collects all `Customer` objects from the parent query and passes them as a `List`. You perform a single database lookup and return a Map. This reduces 101 queries down to 2.

Case Study 2: The Management Project (Mutations and Nullability)

In the **Management Project** (Gradle), we focus on changing data. Spring for GraphQL 2.0 introduces powerful tools for handling partial updates.

Defining the Mutation Schema

Listing A-4. src/main/resources/graphql/management.graphqls

```
type Mutation {
    createCompany(input: CompanyInput!): Company!
    updateCompany(id: ID!, input: CompanyUpdateInput!): Company!
}

type Company {
    id: ID!
    name: String!
    industry: String
    status: String
}
```

```
input CompanyInput {
    name: String!
    industry: String
}

input CompanyUpdateInput {
    name: String
    industry: String # Can be null, or omitted
}
```

Partial Updates with ArgumentValue

The CompanyUpdateInput has nullable fields. In Java, a null value is ambiguous: did the client send null (to delete the value), or did they omit the field (to keep it unchanged)?

Spring for GraphQL 2.0 solves this with ArgumentValue.

Listing A-5. src/main/java/com/apress/crm/management/graphql/CompanyGraphController.java

```
package com.apress.crm.management.graphql;

import com.apress.crm.management.domain.Company;
import com.apress.crm.management.service.CompanyService;
import org.springframework.graphql.data.ArgumentValue;
import org.springframework.graphql.data.method.annotation.Argument;
import org.springframework.graphql.data.method.annotation.MutationMapping;
import org.springframework.stereotype.Controller;

@Controller
public class CompanyGraphController {

    private final CompanyService companyService;

    public CompanyGraphController(CompanyService companyService) {
        this.companyService = companyService;
    }
```

```
    @MutationMapping
    public Company createCompany(@Argument CompanyInput input) {
        return companyService.create(input.toEntity());
    }

    @MutationMapping
    public Company updateCompany(@Argument Long id,
                                 @Argument ArgumentValue<String> name,
                                 @Argument ArgumentValue<String>
                                 industry) {

        Company company = companyService.findById(id);

        if (name.isPresent()) {
            company.setName(name.value()); // Can be null if client
            sent null
        }

        if (industry.isPresent()) {
            company.setIndustry(industry.value());
        }

        return companyService.save(company);
    }

    // DTO Record
    record CompanyInput(String name, String industry) {
        Company toEntity() { return new Company(null, name, industry); }
    }
}
```

Key Elements:

- **`ArgumentValue<T>`**: Wraps the input argument.
- **`isPresent()` vs `value()`**: `isPresent()` returns true if the field was in the JSON request (even if null). `value()` returns the actual value. If `isPresent()` is false, the field was omitted, so we skip the update.

Exception Handling

GraphQL handles errors differently than REST. A 200 OK can contain a partial data response and an errors array.

Listing A-6. src/main/java/com/apress/crm/management/graphql/GraphQLExceptionHandler.java

```
package com.apress.crm.management.graphql;

import graphql.GraphQLError;
import graphql.schema.DataFetchingEnvironment;
import
org.springframework.graphql.execution.DataFetcherExceptionResolverAdapter;
import org.springframework.stereotype.Component;
import org.springframework.graphql.execution.ErrorType;

@Component
public class GraphQLExceptionHandler extends
DataFetcherExceptionResolverAdapter {

    @Override
    protected GraphQLError resolveToSingleError(Throwable ex,
    DataFetchingEnvironment env) {
        if (ex instanceof IllegalArgumentException) {
            return GraphQLError.newError()
                    .errorType(ErrorType.BAD_REQUEST)
                    .message(ex.getMessage())
                    .path(env.getExecutionStepInfo().getPath())
                    .location(env.getField().getSourceLocation())
                    .build();
        }
        return null; // Let other resolvers handle it
    }
}
```

Testing with HttpGraphQlTester

Spring Boot 4 provides the HttpGraphQlTester for unified, high-level testing of GraphQL endpoints.

Listing A-7. src/test/java/com/apress/crm/customer/graphql/CustomerGraphControllerTests.java

```
package com.apress.crm.customer.graphql;

import org.junit.jupiter.api.Test;
import org.springframework.beans.factory.annotation.Autowired;
import org.springframework.boot.test.autoconfigure.graphql.tester.AutoConfi
gureHttpGraphQlTester;
import org.springframework.boot.test.context.SpringBootTest;
import org.springframework.graphql.test.tester.HttpGraphQlTester;

@SpringBootTest
@AutoConfigureHttpGraphQlTester
class CustomerGraphControllerTests {

    @Autowired
    private HttpGraphQlTester graphQlTester;

    @Test
    void shouldFetchCustomers() {
        // language=graphql
        String query = """
            query {
                customers {
                    firstName
                    email
                }
            }
        """;

        graphQlTester.document(query)
                .execute()
                .path("customers")
```

```
                .entityList(Object.class)
                .hasSizeGreaterThan(0);
    }

    @Test
    void shouldFindCustomerById() {
        graphQlTester.documentName("customerById") // Loads from src/test/
        resources/graphql-test/customerById.graphql
                .variable("id", 1)
                .execute()
                .path("customerById.firstName")
                .entity(String.class)
                .isEqualTo("John");
    }
}
```

REST vs. GraphQL Comparison

Choosing between REST and GraphQL depends on your specific constraints.

Table A-1. *Spring MVC (REST) vs. Spring for GraphQL*

Feature	Spring MVC (REST)	Spring for GraphQL
Data Fetching	Server defines the structure (Resource). Client gets everything.	Client defines the structure (Query). Client gets exactly what it asks for.
Versioning	Explicit versioning (URL v1/v2 or Headers) is common.	"Evolutionary" design. Fields are deprecated (`@deprecated`) but rarely removed.
Caching	Native HTTP Caching (ETags, Cache-Control) works out of the box.	Harder to cache at HTTP level (POST requests). Requires application-level caching (e.g., Redis).
Error Handling	HTTP Status Codes (404, 500, 400).	Always 200 OK (usually). Errors are in the response body payload.
Performance	Risk of N+1 calls (Over-fetching).	Risk of N+1 queries (backend). Solved with `@BatchMapping`.

Best Practices

1. **Schema First**: Always design your schema (`.graphqls`) before implementing the Java code. It serves as the contract.
2. **Avoid N+1**: Aggressively use `@BatchMapping` for any relationship traversal.
3. **Security**: Limit query depth and complexity to prevent Denial of Service (DoS) attacks from deeply nested recursive queries.
4. **Nullability**: Be precise with `!` in your schema. If a field can fail (e.g., external service), make it nullable so the rest of the query can succeed.

Summary

Spring for GraphQL seamlessly integrates the power of GraphQL into the Spring Boot 4 ecosystem. By leveraging **JSpecify** for null safety, **Virtual Threads** for concurrency, and **ArgumentValue** for precise mutations, you can build APIs that are both flexible for clients and robust for servers. While it introduces complexity in areas like caching and complexity management, it offers unmatched flexibility for data-rich applications.

APPENDIX B

gRPC with Spring Boot

In the modern landscape of microservices, efficient communication between distributed components is paramount. While REST (Representational State Transfer) remains the standard for public-facing APIs, internal service-to-service communication often demands higher performance, stricter contracts, and better developer productivity. This is where **gRPC (Google Remote Procedure Call)** shines.

In 2025, the **Spring gRPC** project reached its **1.0.0 General Availability (GA)** milestone, becoming the official standard for integrating gRPC into the Spring ecosystem. This appendix explores how to leverage Spring gRPC 1.0.0 with **Spring Boot 4** and **Spring Framework 7**, focusing on high-performance features like Virtual Threads and native observability.

What Is gRPC?

gRPC is a high-performance, open-source universal RPC framework. It is based on three core pillars:

1. **Protocol Buffers (Protobuf)**: A language-neutral, platform-neutral mechanism for serializing structured data. It serves as the Interface Definition Language (IDL) to define service contracts.
2. **HTTP/2**: The underlying transport protocol, providing features like multiplexing, bidirectional streaming, and header compression.
3. **Code Generation**: Client and server stubs are automatically generated from `.proto` files, providing a strongly typed development experience.

F. Gutierrez and D. Carter, *Pro Spring Boot 4*, https://doi.org/10.1007/979-8-8688-2640-5

Core Architecture

Spring gRPC 1.0.0 integrates seamlessly with the Spring application lifecycle, allowing you to define gRPC services as standard Spring beans.

As shown in the diagram, the gRPC architecture abstracts away the complexity of network communication and serialization, allowing developers to call remote methods as if they were local.

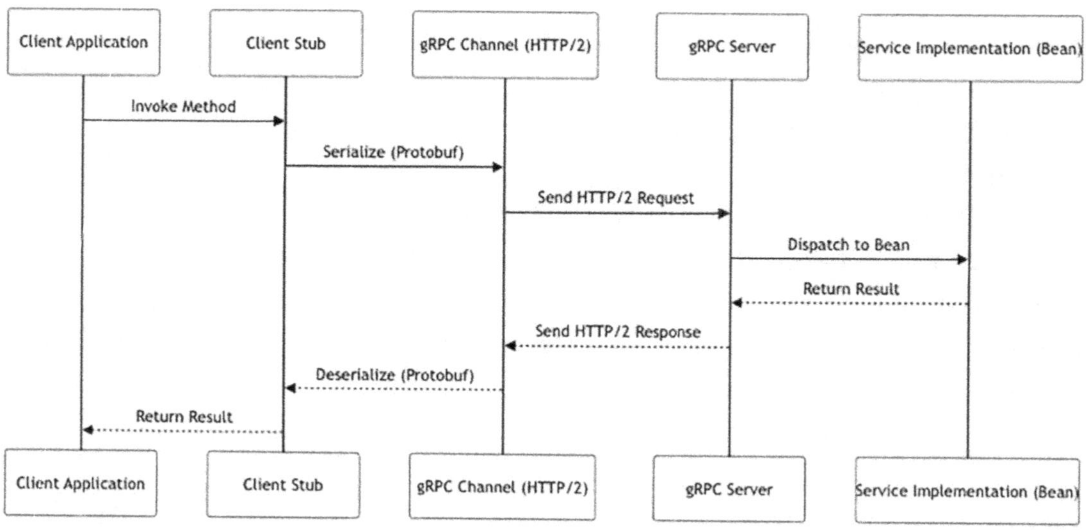

Figure B-1. *gRPC Request Processing Architecture*

Key Features, Use Cases, and Best Practices

Spring gRPC 1.0.0 transforms gRPC from a niche high-performance tool into a standard component of the Spring developer's toolkit.

Key Features in Spring gRPC 1.0.0

- **Virtual Threads Integration**: Fully embraces Java 21's Project Loom. By enabling `spring.threads.virtual.enabled=true`, gRPC servers can handle thousands of concurrent requests with a blocking paradigm, eliminating the complexity of reactive chains while maintaining high throughput.

- **JSpecify Null Safety**: The entire API surface is annotated with JSpecify annotations, providing comprehensive compile-time null-safety checks in modern IDEs, aligning with Spring Framework 7's null-safety initiatives.
- **Native Observability**: Built-in interceptors automatically contribute metrics (Micrometer) and distributed traces (OpenTelemetry/Zipkin) to Spring Boot Actuator, removing the need for manual instrumentation.
- **Simplified Configuration**: The new `@ImportGrpcClients` and `@GrpcService` annotations significantly reduce boilerplate compared to earlier community starters.

When to Use gRPC?

While REST is ubiquitous, gRPC is superior in specific scenarios:

- **Internal Microservices**: For east-west traffic between backend services where low latency and high throughput are critical.
- **Polyglot Environments**: When services are written in different languages (e.g., a Spring Boot service calling a Go or Python service), Protobuf provides a strict, language-agnostic contract.
- **Mobile Clients**: The compact binary format saves battery and bandwidth on mobile devices compared to verbose JSON.
- **Real-Time Streaming**: Applications requiring bi-directional data flow (e.g., chat apps, stock tickers) benefit from HTTP/2 streaming native to gRPC.

Best Practices

- **Contract First**: Always start by designing your `.proto` files. Treat them as the immutable API contract.
- **Error Handling**: Do not throw Java exceptions directly. Map them to standard `io.grpc.Status` codes (e.g., `NOT_FOUND`, `INVALID_ARGUMENT`) to ensure clients can handle errors gracefully.

- **Deadlines**: Always set deadlines (timeouts) on clients to prevent cascading failures in distributed systems.
- **Share Protobufs**: Create a separate "API" module or repository that contains only the `.proto` files and generated code, shared between server and client projects.

Setting Up Spring gRPC

Spring gRPC 1.0.0 is fully optimized for Spring Boot 4. Depending on your build tool, you need to add the official starter and the Protobuf plugin.

Spring gRPC handles the **runtime** integration (server startup, client injection), but it does **not** generate the Java code from your `.proto` files. You must configure the standard Google Protobuf compilers in your build tool (Maven or Gradle) to generate the stubs during the build process.

Maven Setup (customer)

In our Maven-based **customer** project, we add the `spring-grpc-spring-boot-starter` and configure the `protobuf-maven-plugin`.

Listing B-1. src/main/resources/../pom.xml (Snippet)

```
<dependencies>
    <dependency>
        <groupId>org.springframework.grpc</groupId>
        <artifactId>spring-grpc-spring-boot-starter</artifactId>
    </dependency>
</dependencies>

<build>
    <plugins>
        <plugin>
            <groupId>org.xolstice.maven.plugins</groupId>
            <artifactId>protobuf-maven-plugin</artifactId>
            <version>0.6.1</version>
```

```
            <configuration>
                <protocArtifact>com.google.protobuf:protoc:3.25.5:exe:
                ${os.detected.classifier}</protocArtifact>
                <pluginId>grpc-java</pluginId>
                <pluginArtifact>io.grpc:protoc-gen-grpc-
                java:1.69.0:exe:${os.detected.classifier}</pluginArtifact>
            </configuration>
            <executions>
                <execution>
                    <goals>
                        <goal>compile</goal>
                        <goal>compile-custom</goal>
                    </goals>
                </execution>
            </executions>
        </plugin>
    </plugins>
</build>
```

Gradle Setup (management)

For our Gradle-based **management** project, we use the `com.google.protobuf` plugin and the official starter.

Listing B-2. src/main/resources/../build.gradle.kts (Snippet)

```
plugins {
    id("com.google.protobuf") version "0.9.4"
}

dependencies {
    implementation("org.springframework.grpc:spring-grpc-spring-boot-
    starter")
}
```

```
protobuf {
    protoc {
        artifact = "com.google.protobuf:protoc:3.25.5"
    }
    plugins {
        id("grpc") {
            artifact = "io.grpc:protoc-gen-grpc-java:1.69.0"
        }
    }
    generateProtoTasks {
        all().forEach {
            it.plugins {
                id("grpc")
            }
        }
    }
}
```

Generating the Stubs

While the build tools will automatically generate the Java code from your `.proto` files during the standard compilation lifecycle, you can also trigger this step manually. This is useful when you want to inspect the generated code or when your IDE needs a refresh.

For Maven (customer):

```
./mvnw compile
# or more specifically
./mvnw protobuf:compile protobuf:compile-custom
```

The generated files will be located in `target/generated-sources/protobuf`.

For Gradle (management):

```
./gradlew generateProto
```

The generated files will be located in `build/generated/source/proto`.

Implementing a gRPC Server (Customer)

Let's implement a high-performance gRPC service in the **customer** project to expose customer risk profiles.

Defining the Contract

We start by defining the interface in a `.proto` file. This file is the "source of truth" for both server and client.

Listing B-3. src/main/proto/customer-service.proto

```
syntax = "proto3";

option java_multiple_files = true;
option java_package = "com.apress.prospringboot4.customer.grpc";

service CustomerRiskService {
  rpc GetRiskProfile (RiskRequest) returns (RiskResponse);
}

message RiskRequest {
  string customer_id = 1;
}

message RiskResponse {
  string customer_id = 1;
  string risk_level = 2; // e.g., LOW, MEDIUM, HIGH
  double score = 3;
}
```

Server Implementation

After compiling the proto file, we implement the generated base class. Spring gRPC provides the `@GrpcService` annotation to automatically register our implementation as a gRPC service.

Listing B-4. src/main/java/com/apress/prospringboot4/customer/grpc/CustomerRiskGrpcService.java

```
package com.apress.prospringboot4.customer.grpc;

import io.grpc.stub.StreamObserver;
import org.springframework.grpc.server.service.GrpcService;

@GrpcService
public class CustomerRiskGrpcService extends CustomerRiskServiceGrpc.
CustomerRiskServiceImplBase {

    @Override
    public void getRiskProfile(RiskRequest request,
    StreamObserver<RiskResponse> responseObserver) {
        // Business logic to determine risk
        RiskResponse response = RiskResponse.newBuilder()
                .setCustomerId(request.getCustomerId())
                .setRiskLevel("LOW")
                .setScore(0.95)
                .build();

        responseObserver.onNext(response);
        responseObserver.onCompleted();
    }
}
```

- `@GrpcService` marks this class as a Spring-managed gRPC service.
- `onNext` sends the response back to the client.
- `onCompleted` signals the end of the RPC call.

Key Elements:

- **Generated Base Class**: We extend `CustomerRiskServiceImplBase`, which was generated from our `.proto` file.
- **StreamObserver**: gRPC uses the observer pattern to handle asynchronous streaming. Even for simple unary calls (one request, one response), we use `onNext` and `onCompleted`.

Consuming gRPC Services (management)

The **management** project needs to consume the risk profile from **customer** service.

Client Configuration

Spring gRPC 1.0.0 introduced `@ImportGrpcClients` to scan and register gRPC stubs as Spring beans.

Listing B-5. src/main/java/com/apress/prospringboot4/management/config/GrpcClientConfig.java

```
package com.apress.prospringboot4.management.config;

import com.apress.prospringboot4.customer.grpc.CustomerRiskServiceGrpc;
import org.springframework.context.annotation.Configuration;
import org.springframework.grpc.client.ImportGrpcClients;

@Configuration
@ImportGrpcClients(CustomerRiskServiceGrpc.class)
public class GrpcClientConfig {
}
```

- `@ImportGrpcClients` tells Spring to create and manage the gRPC stub for the specified service.

We also need to configure the connection details in `application.yml`.

Listing B-6. src/main/resources/application.yml

```
spring:
  grpc:
    client:
      channels:
        customer-service:
          address: 'static://localhost:9090'
          negotiation-type: plaintext
```

- The address of the gRPC server. In production, this would likely be a Kubernetes service DNS or a Load Balancer address.

Injecting and Using the Stub

Now we can inject the generated stub directly into our business services.

Listing B-7. src/main/java/com/apress/prospringboot4/management/service/RiskAssessmentService.java

```
package com.apress.prospringboot4.management.service;

import com.apress.prospringboot4.customer.grpc.CustomerRiskServiceGrpc;
import com.apress.prospringboot4.customer.grpc.RiskRequest;
import com.apress.prospringboot4.customer.grpc.RiskResponse;
import org.springframework.stereotype.Service;

@Service
public class RiskAssessmentService {

    private final CustomerRiskServiceGrpc.CustomerRiskServiceBlocking
    Stub riskStub;

    public RiskAssessmentService(CustomerRiskServiceGrpc.
    CustomerRiskServiceBlockingStub riskStub) {
        this.riskStub = riskStub;
    }

    public void assessCustomer(String customerId) {
        RiskRequest request = RiskRequest.newBuilder()
                .setCustomerId(customerId)
                .build();
        RiskResponse response = riskStub.getRiskProfile(request);
        System.out.println("Risk Level: " + response.getRiskLevel());
    }
}
```

- We inject the **BlockingStub**, which provides a simple synchronous API.
- Calling the remote gRPC method feels like calling a local function.

Advanced Features in Spring gRPC 1.0.0

Spring gRPC 1.0.0 brings several modern Java and Spring features to the gRPC world.

Virtual Threads Support

With Spring Boot 4 and Java 21+, you can enable Virtual Threads to handle gRPC requests. This allows the server to handle a massive number of concurrent connections with minimal memory overhead.

```
spring:
  threads:
    virtual:
      enabled: true
```

When enabled, Spring gRPC automatically uses a Virtual Thread executor for processing incoming gRPC calls, making your services extremely scalable without the complexity of traditional reactive programming.

Observability

Spring gRPC includes built-in interceptors that integrate with **Micrometer Tracing** and **Actuator**. It automatically captures metrics like:

- **`grpc.server.calls`**: Number of calls to the server.
- **`grpc.client.calls`**: Number of calls from the client.
- Response times, error rates, and message sizes.

To see these metrics, simply ensure the Actuator dependency is present and the metrics endpoint is exposed.

REST vs. gRPC: A Comparison

Choosing between REST and gRPC depends on your specific requirements. The following table summarizes the key differences.

Table B-1. Comparison between REST and gRPC

Feature	REST	gRPC
Protocol	HTTP 1.1 / HTTP 2	HTTP/2 (Required)
Payload	JSON (Textual)	Protobuf (Binary)
Contract	Optional (OpenAPI/Swagger)	Mandatory (.proto files)
Streaming	Limited (SSE/WebSockets)	Bidirectional Streaming
Performance	High overhead (Headers/Text)	Low overhead (Binary/Multiplexing)
Browser Support	Excellent	Limited (requires gRPC-Web)

Summary

Spring gRPC 1.0.0 is a game-changer for building high-performance microservices in the Spring ecosystem. By providing first-class support for Spring Boot 4, native observability, and Virtual Threads, it simplifies the adoption of gRPC for enterprise applications. Whether you are building a high-frequency trading system or a simple internal service mesh, Spring gRPC provides the tools you need to succeed with speed and safety.

Index

A

F. Gutierrez and D. Carter, *Pro Spring Boot 4*, https://doi.org/10.1007/979-8-8688-2640-5

D

K

L

M

N

O

T

U

V

W, X, Y

Z

www.ingramcontent.com/pod-product-compliance
Lightning Source LLC
Chambersburg PA
CBHW081433100826
49614CB00018B/478
* 9 7 9 8 8 6 8 8 2 6 3 9 9 *